The Architecture of

H. H. RICHARDSON

and His Times

HENRY-RUSSELL HITCHCOCK

The Architecture of
H. H. RICHARDSON
and His Times

THE M.I.T. PRESS

Massachusetts Institute of Technology
Cambridge, Massachusetts, and London, England

To the Memory of A. Kingsley Porter

PREFACE TO THE 1966 EDITION

THE PRESENT NEW EDITION, bibliographically more a re-issue than a true third edition, is all but identical with the revised edition published five years ago by Archon Books. The page size has been slightly reduced, and certain minor typographical errors have been corrected, but no material has been added.

Since 1961 a new generation of scholars in American architectural history has begun to study Richardson's work with fresh mid-20th-century eyes. They are already making a more thorough investigation than was previously feasible of the innumerable drawings in the Houghton Library at Harvard University by Richardson and his associates of executed buildings and projects as well as archival sources in the cities and towns where Richardson built.

My Katharine Asher Engel Lecture, "H. H. Richardson as a Victorian Architect," given at Smith College on October 14, 1965, made some use of this unpublished material. The printed version of this lecture, to be brought out by the College in the spring of 1966, will give specific citations, with acknowledgements to individual students. Even so I would like here, as well as there, to express my pleasure in the enthusiasm and the assiduity which the members of a graduate seminar held at Harvard through the spring months of 1965 brought to their study of Richardson's work, and also my gratitude to Miss C. E. Jakeman of the Houghton Library, who made the drawings available to them. Such renewed interest, precisely a century after Richardson's architectural career began, on the part of young scholars makes appropriate the appearance of a paperback version of the book at this time.

H. R. HITCHCOCK

Northampton, Massachusetts
December 1965

PREFACE TO THE NEW EDITION

JUST TWENTY-FIVE years ago the original edition of this book appeared. To reissue without change or to rewrite completely: these are the two extreme possibilities when a new edition is to be offered after so long a time. My *Architecture: 19th and 20th Centuries* of 1958 might be considered a rewriting, a generation later, of my *Modern Architecture: Romanticism and Reintegration* of 1929, which had likewise covered the period from the late 18th century to the then present. Several years ago Bernard Berenson, deeming certain of his early writings already "classics", reissued them without modification. Practical considerations, based on current book-production methods by offset lithography, favor the latter method, even though I can hardly claim that my text is a "classic".

Fortunately in the present instance, despite the fact that the original text from the Preface through the Bibliography is repeated unchanged, it has been possible both to remake the greater part of the illustrations from new copy—only three or four plans and other drawings are reproduced directly from the original edition—and to provide an extensive secondary system of new Notes, referenced from the margins of the text, which are intended to bring various aspects of the subject up to date.

Among the new illustrations are views of three executed buildings and of three projects not included in the first edition (Figures 2, 9, 10, 11, 12, 25, and 29) ; and the most interesting of the Notes—at least to those who know the original edition—will presumably be those that discuss these designs, as well as a few others that provide data on lost works (IV-1, V-11, VI-1, VIII-1, VIII-6, VIII-7 and XIII-8). I give these references here since they will not be found in the Index, which is still that of the 1936 edition.

In the Notes will also be found many new references to articles and to books dealing in whole or in part with Richardson's work or with significant matters that are broadly relevant to the period in which he worked. In this connection the writings of Vincent Scully and of Winston Weisman are especially important. I hope they and the others to whose articles reference is made, or who have communicated to me various sorts of information, will accept the mere acknowledgement, given in each case in the Notes, as an inadequate expression of my gratitude for their aid. So also in the List of Illustrations the names of photographers and of institutions who have supplied copy are given as individual credits except where the copy was an old photograph or some other document in my own possession and of uncertain provenience. "Houghton Library" stands for the main collection of Richardson drawings, still belonging to Henry R. Shepley, Richardson's grandson, but now for many years deposited at Harvard. I must thank Mr. Shepley for permitting the use of much material at Harvard as well as for additional information and documents that he has generously provided. Copy for Figures 36 and 41 was supplied by the Avery Library of Columbia University.

Since exact references to the most relevant later articles and passages in books, as well as a great deal of more accurate bibliographical data than appeared in the 1936 edition on the books in Richardson's own library, are given at the appropriate points in the Notes to the various chapters, no attempt has been made to repeat these in the Notes to the Bibliography at the end. Nor has it seemed worthwhile to attempt to include in such Notes references to the many general works on American architecture and on 19th-century architecture published since 1936 in which more or less attention has been given to Richardson's work. Some dozen of these, from Montgomery Schuyler's *American Architecture* of 1892, now at last appearing in a new edition, to Lewis Mumford's *Brown Decades* of 1931, also now available in a later edition, are given in the original Bibliography (pp. 337-8); at least as many could have been listed for the last thirty years.

However, as not uncharacteristic examples of the increasing interest in Richardson in the mid-20th century, one early and one late example may be cited here. In 1941 the Swiss critic Sigfried Giedion in *Space Time and Architecture*—a book that recurrent new editions have kept in print ever since—made some dozen references to Richardson, as well as illustrating the Marshall Field Wholesale Store and Sever Hall. This was in contrast to no more than one reference each to Norman Shaw and Philip Webb, two of the architects of the period outside America who were perhaps most comparable in stature to Richardson. (There are, however, eleven references to the great French engineer Eiffel). In 1961 John Burchard and Albert Bush-Brown in *The Architecture of America* have referred twice as often as Giedion to Richardson, offering moreover a seven-page general account of his work at one point and also providing six illustrations. Like Giedion, they refer once to Shaw and once to Webb, though only three times to Eiffel.

Already by 1936, alas, a number of Richardson's buildings had been destroyed, including his late masterpiece the Field Store in Chicago. It is perhaps a testimony to the growing consciousness of the intrinsic value of fine 19th-century buildings that not very many more have been demolished since; I have mentioned in the Notes those of whose fate I was sure. One at least, the Pittsburgh Jail, has been the subject of a so-far successful campaign of preservation. Fortunately several that were once in serious danger, such as the Sherman house in Newport and the Glessner house in Chicago, are now in hands that may be trusted to maintain and to use them. Of the railroad stations, some minor examples have been demolished and others have been remodelled almost beyond recognition, while that at New London is recurrently threatened. Yet, on the whole, a wide range of his most notable works, from large masonry monuments like Trinity Church, the Allegheny Courthouse or Austin Hall to modest houses like Trinity Rectory, the Ames gate lodge, and the Stoughton and Brown houses, may now be expected to survive as long as will any buildings of their period. Considering the tragic fate of the greater part of the work of America's first great architect Latrobe, Richardson has certainly been lucky. Even the canons of

Sullivan's and of Wright's work are not much more completely intact.

In concluding this Preface, I would like to note that much still remains to be found out about Richardson, his work, and his projects. The collection of drawings at the Houghton Library demands detailed study over a considerable period of time by well-prepared scholars if it is to yield all that it undoubtedly contains. In a rather casual visit last winter, primarily to set aside for photographing the same drawings that had already been used for illustrations in the 1936 edition, I came on four or five unpublished projects only two of which could even be referred to in this new edition. Old photographs, moreover, keep turning up in various collections that give more visual information on both destroyed and remodelled buildings.

There is, furthermore, the question of Richardson's influence outside this country to which scholars are only now turning their attention. The results of Robert Koch's and Dimitri Tselos's investigations presented at the meeting of the Society of Architectural Historians in Cleveland in 1959 have not yet been fully published (see Note Bibl. 2). I am the more grateful to Arnold Lewis for permitting me to extract from his University of Wisconsin doctoral dissertation, "Evaluations of American Architecture by European Critics, 1875-1900," the references to English and German articles and books given in Note Bibl. 1. Among the new illustrations, Figure 25 presents a project by Richardson that appeared in England in 1872, a year earlier than any of his work was published in America so far as I know.

H. R. Hitchcock

Northampton, Mass.
April, 1961

PREFACE TO FIRST EDITION

THE PREPARATION of the exhibition of Richardson's architecture at the Museum of Modern Art on the fiftieth anniversary of his death and the gathering of the material for this book were carried on together. Many of the photographs and the drawings in the exhibition also appear as illustrations in the book. Yet the two are by no means merely alternative methods of presenting Richardson's work. They are intended to complement one another. In an exhibition it is possible to have a few photographs enlarged to a great scale and to display many original drawings. For there exist a considerable number of drawings in Richardson's own hand, and many more of the plans and elevations prepared in his office. In this book the illustrations are necessarily much smaller and they can hardly do justice to such drawings. But it is possible to round out the story of Richardson's development and background with more graphic material than can be shown in an exhibition.

This book is not a biography of Richardson. An excellent biography by Mrs. Schuyler Van Rensselaer exists. Although out of print this is by no means unobtainable. Monographs on several of Richardson's buildings, illustrated with magnificent plates, were published in the eighties and most of his buildings were presented at one time or another in fair illustrations in the architectural press of the day.

This is a study of Richardson's architecture in the light of the setting in which he worked. The setting could be taken for granted by Mrs. Van Rensselaer when she wrote in 1888. But the setting and Richardson's architecture itself were denigrated and forgotten by the next generation. Current references to Richardson make it plain that a general rehabilitation of his reputation has occurred in the last decade. For this Lewis Mumford is chiefly responsible. Mrs. Van Rensselaer observed this rehabilitation with pleasure in the last years of her life, after a generation had passed during which her book was little appreciated. Yet despite Lewis Mumford's able and suggestive chapter in the *Brown Decades,* the lack of a more detailed study by modern critics of the architectural world in which Richardson was educated, and of the world of the seventies and eighties in which his work was done, has permitted certain misapprehensions to continue. Such misapprehensions it is one of the purposes of this book to dispel.

Mrs. Van Rensselaer was an admirable architectural critic, intelligent, sensitive, and discriminating. Her comments on Richardson's buildings are almost always extremely sound. But, as a biographer should be, she was somewhat carried away by the personality of her subject. Richardson's personality is now a datum like any other. We can now assess better its advantages and disadvantages in his own career and in the general course of architectural history. We can also, perhaps, see Richardson's work more clearly in relation to the period which followed and even to the period which preceded, than could any critic in the eighties, no matter how intelligent and sensitive. But in concluding this Preface I can do no better than recommend to everyone interested in American architecture Mrs. Van Rensselaer's book. Her name should not be forgotten nor her work. For she was one of America's few distinguished architectural critics.

Henry-Russell Hitchcock

Wesleyan University
May 1935

ACKNOWLEDGEMENTS

THE FOUNDATION of all study of Richardson is Mrs. Van Rensselaer's monograph.[1] The list of Richardson's work she published is
here modified chiefly in minor particulars: the dates of several buildings are altered; one remodelling is added which she does not mention;
one building which she lists as executed was never more than a project;
finally two buildings for which the commissions entered the office in
the spring of 1886 have been added, since there was evidence in the
office time-book that they were considerably studied before Richardson left the office forever. These, like many of the other works completed by Shepley, Rutan and Coolidge, were at least semi-posthumous.
The most important addition to the factual matter in Mrs. Van Rensselaer's book is the discussion of all the projects of which important
traces remain, either as published in the magazines of the time, or in
the more or less complete studies in the office sketch books. These
projects throw light upon some questions of which the executed works
only give hints. In most cases they are also of intrinsic interest.

With Mrs. Van Rensselaer's book as a foundation it was possible
to lay out the field for research and to visit almost all the buildings
not destroyed, except those in St. Louis; Sherman, Wyoming; and
Burlington, Vermont; Emmanuel Church in Pittsburgh and the Armory in Detroit were also not studied except from documents. The
next step was the examination of the material in the offices of Coolidge,
Shepley, Bulfinch and Abbott, the present firm of Richardson's successors. Here Mr. Charles A. Coolidge, whose architectural career
began in Richardson's office, and Mr. Henry Richardson Shepley, Rich-

[1] No specific references to pages in this book are given in the text, as they
would need to be almost continuous.

ardson's grandson, both very generously provided every assistance. From the rolls of drawings left from Richardson's day and the sketch books, the material was selected which Mr. Coolidge and Mr. Shepley are kindly lending to the exhibition and permitting to be reproduced in this book.

Not only Mr. Coolidge and Mr. Shepley, but others of the office force, particularly Miss Marian Coffin, who had been with Richardson before his death, aided in many ways. Although the fullest advantage was taken of their memories, they are of course not responsible for the statements in this book; with the treatment of some questions they may very well disagree. But I hope that they will not feel that their piety in the preservation of so much of Richardson's material and their generosity in lending it have been betrayed by the way that material has been used. The freedom with which they permitted me to delve in the sketch books, in which so many preparatory studies were mounted, made it possible to fill out the list of Richardson's work with many interesting projects, and to study Richardson's methods of design from early sketches to finished working drawings.

The important correlative work of examining nineteenth century architectural magazines was begun in the winter of 1933 by Mrs. Russell Lynes (then Miss Mildred Akin) and continued by Miss Natalie Hoyt of Smith College. Much additional research at the Boston Public Library and in the Coolidge, Shepley, Bulfinch and Abbott offices was carried on through the summer and fall by Miss Hoyt.

The new photographs for the exhibition and this book were mostly taken by Miss Berenice Abbott and Mr. Beaumont Newhall. The old photographs and plates from magazines were loaned by many different persons: some by Mr. Coolidge, some by Mr. Charles Rutan Strickland, the grandson of Mr. Rutan, some by Mr. Karl S. Putnam of Smith College. Some old photographs as well as much information was provided by past and present owners of Richardson's buildings. I trust they may pardon the omission of a complete list of their names here.

It is equally difficult to name all the individuals and institutions who gave assistance in gathering correlative material. Besides the officials of the Connecticut Valley Historical Society in Springfield and Mr. Ernest Newton Bagg, many others helped in the search for photographs there. Mr. John Howard Benson and Mr. W. King Covell aided in Newport; Mr. George Dudley Seymour, and Professor Theodore Sizer in New Haven; Mr. Clarence Brigham in Worcester. Some of the earlier research was done in company with Mr. Philip Johnson, then Chairman of the Department of Architecture of the Museum of Modern Art.

Mr. James T. Soby, Miss Elizabeth Mongan and Mr. John P. Coolidge were most helpful in reading and criticizing the text. Suggestions also came from Dean Hudnut of the Columbia School of Architecture and Hugh Morrison of Dartmouth College.

The book was seen through the press by Miss Ernestine M. Fantl and Mrs. Loyd A. Collins, Jr., of the Publications Department of the Museum.

The Lord Duveen of Millbank, Mr. Philip L. Goodwin, Mr. John Hay Whitney and other friends of the Museum of Modern Art graciously assisted in financing this first full-length book published by that institution.

CONTENTS

PART FOUR: Achievement. 1877-1883

PART FIVE: Late Works. 1882-1886

in 1885. Harrison Avenue Ames Building. Debatable work and projects. Office conditions in the spring of 1886. Shepley, Rutan and Coolidge.

ILLUSTRATIONS

42. Project for James Cheney house. Perspective and plan, 1878. From *American Architect and Building News,* May 23, 1878.

43. Cheney Block, Hartford. Exterior, 1875-76. Photo. Berenice Abbott.

44. New York State Capitol, Albany. South elevation study, 1877. Houghton Library.

45. Project for Cheney Block Annex. Perspective, 1877. From *American Architect and Building News,* Oct. 27, 1877.

46. Ames Memorial Library, North Easton. Fireplace, 1878. From *Monographs of American Architecture,* III.

47. Winn Memorial Library, Woburn. Exterior, 1877-78. Houghton Library.

48. Winn Memorial Library, Woburn. Plan, 1877-78. Houghton Library.

49. Ames Memorial Library, North Easton. Exterior, 1877-79. From *Monographs of American Architecture,* III.

50. Ames Memorial Library, North Easton. Interior of stack wing, 1877-79. From *Monographs of American Architecture,* III.

51. Sever Hall, Cambridge. Front, 1878-80. From Van Rensselaer.

52. Sever Hall, Cambridge. Rear, 1878-80. Photo. Beaumont Newhall.

53. Ames Memorial Town Hall, North Easton. Exterior, 1879-81. From *Monographs of American Architecture,* III.

54. New York State Capitol, Albany. Senate Chamber, 1878-81. From Van Rensselaer.

55. New York State Capitol. Court of Appeals, fireplace, 1881. From Van Rensselaer.

56. Ames Monument, Sherman, Wyoming, 1879. Photo. Wayne Andrews.

57. Rectory of Trinity Church, Boston. Exterior, 1879-80. Houghton Library.

58. F. L. Ames gate lodge, North Easton. Exterior from North, 1880-81.

59. F. L. Ames gate lodge, North Easton. Exterior from South West, 1880-81. From *Monographs of American Architecture,* III.

60. Bryant house, Cohasset. Elevation, 1880. Houghton Library.

61. Bryant house, Cohasset. Plan, 1880. From 1936 edition.

62. Bryant house, Cohasset. Exterior from South West, 1880. Houghton Library.

63. Bryant house, Cohasset. Exterior from South East, 1880. Houghton Library.

64. Crane Memorial Library, Quincy. Perspective sketch of rear, 1880. Houghton Library.

65. Crane Memorial Library, Quincy. Exterior, 1880-83.

66. Metal bridge in the Fenway, Boston, 1880-81. Photo. Beaumont Newhall.

67. Stone bridge in the Fenway, Boston, 1880-81. Photo. Berenice Abbott.

68. City Hall, Albany. Exterior, 1880-82. Photo. Berenice Abbott.

69. Higginson house, Boston. Exterior, with Whittier house by McKim, Mead & White to the right, both 1881-83. From *American Architect and Building News,* Nov. 24, 1883.

70. Project for Ames house, Boston. Plan study, 1880. Houghton Library.

71. Anderson house, Washington. Plan, 1881. From 1936 edition.

72. Anderson house, Washington. Perspective, 1881. From Van Rensselaer.

73. Anderson house, Washington. Entrance, 1881.

74. Brown house, Marion. Exterior, 1881-82, with later changes. Photo. Wayne Andrews.

75. Brown house, Marion. Plan, 1881-82. From 1936 edition.

76. Brown house, Marion. Elevation, 1881-82. From 1936 edition.

77. Boston & Albany Station, Chestnut Hill. Exterior, 1883-84. From Van Rensselaer.

78. Boston & Albany Station, Auburndale. Exterior, 1881. From Van Rensselaer.

79. Austin Hall, Cambridge. Exterior, 1881-83. From *Monographs of American Architecture,* I.

80. Austin Hall, Cambridge. Plans, 1881-83. From *Monographs of American Architecture,* I.

81. Ames Building, Kingston and Bedford Streets, Boston. Exterior, 1882-83. From Van Rensselaer.

82. Stoughton house, Cambridge. Exterior, 1882-83. Boston Athenaeum.

83. Stoughton house, Cambridge. Plan, 1882-83. From 1936 edition.

84. Channing house, Brookline. Exterior, 1882-83. Photo. Berenice Abbott.

85. Sard house, Albany. Exterior, 1882-83. From *American Architect and Building News,* June 1, 1889.

86. Project for Episcopal Cathedral in Albany. Perspective, 1883. From *American Architect and Building News,* Sept. 1, 1883.

87. Emmanuel Church, Pittsburgh. Exterior, 1885-86. Photo. A. Church.

88. Billings Library, Burlington. Exterior, 1883-86. Photo. Wayne Andrews.

89. Converse Memorial Library, Malden. Exterior, 1883-85. Photo. Berenice Abbott.

90. Allegheny County Courthouse, Pittsburgh. Perspective, 1884-88. From Van Rensselaer.

91. Allegheny County Courthouse, Pittsburgh. Plan, 1884-88. From Van Rensselaer.

92. Allegheny County Jail, Pittsburgh. Exterior, 1884-86.

93. Allegheny County Courthouse, Pittsburgh. Court, 1884-88.

94. Allegheny County Courthouse, Pittsburgh. Court, 1884-88.

95. Marshall Field Wholesale Store. Exterior, 1885-87. Photo. Chicago Architectural Photographing Company.

96. Project for private railroad car. Plan and section, 1884. Houghton Library.

97. Marshall Field Wholesale Store. Perspective project, 1885. From Van Rensselaer.

98. Marshall Field Wholesale Store. Plan, 1885. Houghton Library.

99. Paine house, Waltham. Exterior, 1884-86, with later bay windows. Photo. Berenice Abbott.

100. Paine house, Waltham. Stairway, 1884-86. Photo. Berenice Abbott.

101. Adams and Hay houses, Washington. Elevation study, 1884. Houghton Library.

102. Hay house, Washington. Entrance, 1884-86. Boston Athenaeum.

103. Hay house, Washington. Hall, 1884-86. From Van Rensselaer.

104. Gurney house, Pride's Crossing. Early perspective sketch, 1884. Houghton Library.

105. Glessner house, Chicago. Exterior, 1885-87. Henry R. Shepley.

106. Glessner house, Chicago. Plan, 1885. From Van Rensselaer.

107. Lululund, Bushy, Middlesex. Exterior, 1886-94.

108. MacVeagh house, Chicago. Exterior, 1885-87. From Van Rensselaer.

109. Warder house, Washington. Exterior, 1885-87. From Van Rensselaer.

110. Gratwick house, Buffalo. Exterior, 1886-89. Houghton Library.

111. Potter house, St. Louis. Exterior, 1886-87. From *Missouri's Contribution to American Architecture*.

PART I

BACKGROUND AND PREPARATION

1838–1865

CHAPTER ONE

1838-1860

RICHARDSON was born at the Priestley Plantation in the Parish of St. James, Louisiana, on September 29th, 1838. His father was a prosperous business man who died when Richardson was sixteen. At this time his mother, who was a granddaughter of Dr. Joseph Priestley, married Mr. John D. Bein, a partner in her brother's large hardware business. In his childhood Richardson's summers were spent on the family plantation; his winters in New Orleans. Except for a few months in a public school, he was educated until he was sixteen in a private school kept by Mr. George Blackman. When an impediment in his speech made it impossible for him to go to West Point, to which he had been nominated by Judah P. Benjamin, he spent a year at the University of Louisiana, and then went to Cambridge where a tutor prepared him to enter Harvard.

These are the bare facts of his earliest years as given by Mrs. Schuyler Van Rensselaer, his biographer.[1] More interesting than any attempt to fill out the details of his life and education, and more necessary to understand what American architecture was like when he became its leader around 1870, is an appreciation of the course of architectural development in America in the years before Richardson went to Paris in 1859 to obtain his professional training.

---

[1] *Henry Hobson Richardson and His Works*, Boston and New York, 1888. This is, of course, the book from which most of our knowledge of Richardson comes.

The specific architectural predispositions he may have received on the plantation and in New Orleans cannot be known, but the general history of the decades before the Civil War, complex though it is, can be clearer to us today than it could be to Richardson or anyone else who grew up in the midst of it. The confused architectural situation which he left behind when he went to Europe in 1859 and the chaos to which he returned in 1865 after the Civil War were the natural consequence of the series of self-conscious stylistic movements which followed the ultimate death of the Colonial vernacular in the decades just before his birth.

Richardson would perhaps never have been particularly interested in an account of the architectural development in the thirty years before his return in 1865; to himself he may very justly have appeared not merely the first American architect in quality but also in time. What preceded him must have seemed in his maturity hardly architecture at all. After the very provincial imitation of English styles in the eighteenth century, it must have represented an increasingly meaningless confusion, into the very deepest whirlpool of which he was cast on his return from Paris.

If we are properly to understand and evaluate his work, we must see it against its real background. The real background is neither the generic and charming one of the quaint early Victorian decades nor yet the specific and sinister one of the brazen first administration of Grant. All the currents in the whirlpool of the late sixties had earlier beginnings: the true complexity of the picture can be made clear only if those beginnings are at least enumerated and the rate of multiplication of alternative manners made visible. For, although Richardson's training in Paris would have been little different had he gone there a decade or more earlier, or even later, the particular disadvantages and advantages with which he began his work in America in the late sixties would have been decisively different had he returned earlier or later.

At the time of Richardson's birth in the late thirties the Greek Revival had become without any question the national style in architecture and building. For the last time in this country architects and

4

carpenters, engineers and farmers of the East, the South and the West, all built in a single homogeneous way, as consistently, if less instinctively, as the colonies had done before the introduction of English pattern books in the early eighteenth century and the gradual establishment of a Late Baroque hierarchy of design.

The Greek vernacular, once established, lived on as the basic style of the nation almost down to the Civil War. There was little internal development within the style except the substitution of square pilasters for proper columns, or the use of skeleton supports of wood or metal, made light and transparent in order that porches and piazzas should not complicate the plain solid cube of the house. It was against a very real regimentation of architecture that the generation active just before Richardson reacted, out of boredom perhaps as much as anything else, beginning to destroy the Greek Revival just as soon as it was firmly established.

The criteria of judgement within the Greek Revival were too pedantic and too subtle to be widely appreciated. Between one building and another the differences in the materials used might be generally appreciated; matchboarding was obviously more suitable than shingles or even clapboards, granite than brick or even ordinary stone; but the fine points of quality of proportions, execution of detail (not mere accuracy of imitation of the orders), distribution of rectangular planes, can hardly have interested more people than they do today.

The Greek Revival presented the paradox of a popular style without popular visual appeal. Its popularity was in part ideological, lying in the prestige of Greece. But more important was its simplicity, which made it possible for anyone with a copy of the frequent new editions of Benjamin's and Lafever's architectural handbooks to build houses which might by the untravelled be considered comparable to the greatest monuments of the Classical past.

The attack against the Greek Revival was led by the intellectuals, who, as men of a Romantic generation, desired something with more scope for the imagination. This attack was not from a single angle nor was it often bold-fronted. Those who began to come forward in the thirties and forties to offer alternatives were usually ready to offer several; and they were content to pay lip-service to the absolute superiority of Greek design, if not to admit its suitability for all uses. Indeed, long after the Greek Revival had passed out of existence, in the later sixties and seventies, the term Grecian was most inaccurately used as a term of vague praise for types of design in almost every way unrelated to Classical antiquity except for the continued and increasingly corrupt use of the orders.

Although the most serious and the earliest opposition arose from the proponents of the Gothic, there was no drawn battle in which the Greeks were routed and the country delivered over to the Goths. The country was never delivered over to the Goths any more than was England, where the Gothic Revival was much more successful. But it was, as a matter of fact, delivered over to architectural advisers who were barbarians in the literal sense, in that they spoke all manner of strange tongues and spoke them very ill. Richardson, or any other architect of foreign training who set out to practice in the decades after the disappearance of the Greek Revival tradition, could have an immense advantage merely from the superior linguistic knowledge of the styles which were obtainable in Europe.

The Gothic Revival in this country as in Europe had its origins well before the Greek Revival rose to dominance. In 1805, for example, Latrobe offered an alternative Gothic design together with his accepted Classical but hardly Grecian design for the Baltimore Cathedral. By the thirties, the Gothic, in rudimentary form distinguished chiefly by pointed arches and finials, was already an acceptable alternative to the latest post-Colonial and to the rising Greek Revival in the design of churches. From the forties, the architectural handbooks usually provided the barely necessary "Pointed" details as a supplement to the Greek orders.

In addition to the churches, educational institutions also made current use of Gothic, emulating the eighteenth and early nineteenth century Gothic buildings of Oxford. Finally, the Tudor Cottage mode was launched in residential architecture, under the effective auspices

6

of Washington Irving, by the rebuilding of Sunnyside in 1835.[2] But the Tudor Cottage, like the Pointed Church, continued for several decades as merely a minor although generally accepted variant of the dominant vernacular. At best, it was one of several alternatives to the Grecian offered in the extremely popular books of Downing which first appeared in the early forties and continued to come out in new editions through the sixties. By the fifties, however, the genre had been widened and subdivided to include all the various classifications by that time currently imitated in England, the Castellated, the Elizabethan, etc. The symmetry, and even to some extent the bare, thin, papery quality of the earlier models were, moreover, now more frequently avoided.

I-2

In 1839, the year after Richardson's birth, Richard Upjohn began the building of Trinity Church in New York. This well proportioned and rather correct Perpendicular design, more than comparable in quality to the best Gothic ecclesiastical work in England, established on its completion in 1846 a new standard of revived mediaeval design and really initiated the serious Gothic Revival in America. Henceforth, in addition to the vernacular Pointed, there was a body of work produced by architects, usually, like Vaux and Withers, trained in England, which followed with a delay of some five or ten years the various stages of the Gothic Revival as it developed after the opening of Queen Victoria's reign and the design by Barry and Pugin of the Houses of Parliament.

By the Civil War, these men and the men of the oncoming generation, such as Upjohn's son, Richard M., and Ware and Van Brunt, were practicing currently and not unsuccessfully in the Victorian Fourteenth Century Gothic of Pugin and Scott. They were as yet, however, hardly touched by the Italianate and eclectic embellishments initiated by Butterfield in 1848 at All Saints Margaret Street in London, and popularized by Ruskin's writings. In America, in spite of the interest in Ruskin's ideas evidenced in the fifties by early local editions, so-

I-3

I-4

---

[2] Gothic forms had appeared on occasional houses from shortly after 1800, but there had been no general vogue.

7

called "Ruskinian Gothic"—more properly the Italianate High Victorian Gothic—made no real appearance until after the Civil War. Wight's National Academy of Design in New York, which imitated the Doges' Palace, dates from 1865 and is therefore exactly coincident with the opening of Richardson's career.

But if the Gothic in the forties and fifties more and more established its claim on American architects and on the American popular mind as the most suitable ecclesiastical and even educational style, in the field of residential architecture not even all the new variants of Gothic design together succeeded alone in displacing the Grecian mode.

The pattern books and guides of the forties and particularly the fifties frequently offered succinct histories of all the styles; and, emulating the similar English books of the previous decades, provided Italian Villas, Swiss Chalets, Indian Pavilions, Norman Castles (at much reduced scale) and even Byzantine Cottages. Compared with the Greek detail in the books of the thirties, even beside the Gothic of the forties, these designs were incredible masterpieces of inaccuracy, but they must have seemed immensely beguiling in reaction to the increasing dullness and the evident sterility of the Greek Revival. Builders and even architects fell on them with avidity.

But there was also a popular conviction that the Greek was somehow national and not imported; while these other types of design, although certainly entertaining, were evidently foreign and more than possibly immoral. Thus, while farmers and men in small towns might embellish their Greek pediments with Gothic or Italian windows, and a little barely recognizable Tudor or Swiss gingerbread, they rarely used the gables of the Tudor cottages or the towers of the Italian villas. Only parvenu magnates like Barnum at Bridgeport, or Moses Beach at Wallingford, were likely to indulge in houses that completely resembled the drawings in the books in being wholly Indian (*sic*) or provided with all the newest and most elaborate Italian (*sic*) features.

While all this modification was taking place in the vernacular, at first in the East and gradually spreading just before the Civil War to the already conservative West, individual architects were more and

8

more ready to throw off the irksome rules of the Greek Revival and adventure into the rich bazaar of historic and exotic styles as their European colleagues had been doing for several decades.

Ammi Young, as Supervising Architect to the Treasury from 1852, forsook the Greek style in which he built the Boston Custom House, 1837-47, for an equally severe style based on that version of the High Renaissance first developed by Barry in England in his Traveller's Club in 1829. This astylar type of design, usually executed in brownstone or in stucco painted to imitate it, also became the fashionable manner for private city residences, clubs and banks. Richer than the Greek Revival, with elaborate modillion cornices, heavy mouldings and pedimented windows, it satisfied a more ornate taste. In increasingly crude form, it lasted into the sixties and even beyond. But it had little influence on the rural vernacular and was hence never ubiquitous nor felt to be particularly national.

The Italian Villa style, which was in a sense a more informal variant of the Barry style, was more interesting. The best architects were building fine mansions throughout the East in the late forties and fifties with loggia topped towers asymmetrically placed, arched windows often coupled, and heavy but not crude Renaissance detail. Some architects succeeded, as Schinkel and Persius had done at Potsdam in the previous decade, in preserving in the Italian Villa style the refinement of the best Greek work and in achieving a real mastery of occult balance in mass composition. Sikes' Stebbins villa of 1849 in Springfield is perhaps the best example. But as this genre sunk into the vernacular it soon grew awkward in proportions and confused in detail.

The Italian Villa style was not restricted to houses. In the very years when Upjohn was completing Trinity Church in New York in the Perpendicular, he carried out the Church of the Pilgrims in Brooklyn, 1844-46, in a manner hard to define otherwise than as Italian Villa. Such buildings, usually executed in random ashlar, or painted brick or stucco, or even siding in the smooth manner of the Greek Revival, tended to induce a monolithic, sculptural treatment

9

of mass peculiarly suited to tower and spire design. The tower of the Church of the Pilgrims, with its chamfered corners and its spire of scalloped outline rising from a calyx of stone, is, although relatively small in execution, one of the finest in conception in the world.[3]

Besides these two Italian manners, the Barryesque and the Villa style, which rose to something of the importance of the better known Gothic Revival, few others deserve particular mention except the Romanesque, and this not merely because of its later association with Richardson's developed style. For the Romanesque in the fifties was undoubtedly well thought of in intellectual circles if not very widely popular. Robert Dale Owen had caused Renwick, primarily a Gothicist, to build the Smithsonian Institution in Washington, 1846-52, in the form of a rather ecclesiastical Norman castle of red sandstone. He also wrote a whole book, 1849, elaborately illustrated, to justify the proceeding. Henry Austin and others also adapted the Romanesque to the vernacular in a cardboard version executed in siding like the cardboard Pointed, and it had some success in churches in the fifties and even after the Civil War. Eidlitz in New York and Schulze at Harvard introduced a different version of the Romanesque based on the style of von Gärtner and Hübsch in South Germany, which hardly influenced building in general.

But, by the time of the Civil War, the Romanesque, with the Italian manners and the Gothic manners, had taken its place among the barbarian styles which had quite driven out the Grecian. The round-arched mediaeval styles were therefore no novelty when Richardson turned to them for inspiration in 1870, although they were less fashionable than they had been in the fifties.

Nor was academic classicism unknown, of somewhat the type in which Richardson was to be particularly trained at the Ecole des Beaux Arts. When Walter in 1851-59 was adding the white marble wings to the Washington Capitol, which so swamp the early Classical Revival design of Thornton, Hallet, Bulfinch and Latrobe, he neither tried to

I-7

I-8

---

[3] The spire in the last year has had to be removed on account of the vibration of the subway. This is a very serious loss to American architecture.

imitate the original style nor did he make his additions Italian or Gothic or Romanesque. Instead he turned to the more splendid French academic tradition of the mid-eighteenth century, quite as Hittorf and Labrouste were then doing in France. But nothing could make clearer the fact that the true Greek Revival was now quite dead than a comparison between this important classical work of the fifties and the Treasury, built in the thirties by Robert Mills. Gone was all the old precision: the carefully studied proportions, the smooth masses, the sharply cut detail which even the farmers of the Western Reserve had grasped (and as a matter of fact could still grasp). Instead there were false monumentality and a pompous dullness, carefully emulated in most of the state capitols begun after the Civil War.

Yet Walter's Girard College in Philadelphia, built in the heyday of the Greek Revival, 1833-47, had not been inferior to other comparable monuments of its day. The fault, in other words, lay not in Walter but in the times. A mixed architectural diet had already played havoc with American taste; the search for new stylistic stimulation had jaded both architects and public. Although in looking back over the fifties and forties we can pick out more exceptional buildings that were individually fine than in the previous decade, the general level had dropped, in the excitement of frenzied competition, far below the naive vernacular level of excellence of the thirties.

A democratic architectural order like the Greek Revival had not been conducive to the attainment of much individual distinction. On the other hand, a chaotic architectural laissez-faire raised the achievement of the few only by reducing the quality of general production well below mediocrity.

Except for the general loss of symmetry, the most conspicuous innovations of the quarter century before the Civil War were merely new types of surface design. The net effect of their acceptance was to destroy the Greek Revival without providing any authoritative substitute. In destroying the Grecian discipline of design, and hence the last repository of Baroque vernacular traditions, something else was destroyed as well: a certain integrity of construction, whether in wood or in masonry, inherited from the days when building materials were plentiful. In the seventeenth and eighteenth century men built well and commodiously first, and then embellished if money and time and talent were available. For this, in the nineteenth century, was substituted, in Europe as well, a programme of designing as elaborately as possible on paper and then executing the design shoddily in whatever materials were cheapest, using paint and stucco and cheap plastic ornament to cover poverty and even deficiency in construction. New building materials and devices were for the most part mere slipshod substitutes for what had been used earlier. No one gave much thought to how their buildings would look as they weathered or even how they would stand up under the action of time.

It is in relation to this almost complete loss of the sense of architecture as sound building that Richardson's achievement after the Civil War is most remarkable. Yet, of course, all the serious mediaeval revivalists, under English leadership, realized the decline in building craftsmanship even if they were able to do little to stop it. Richardson was, in this respect, destined not to be an innovator. He merely carried out a reform of which all the more intelligent architects and critics felt the need. In his use of materials he was a sound reactionary, not a radical. But for this very reason he was able to overthrow completely the immediate tradition of mere surface design which had grown up during his youth.

Since Richardson was never much interested in the use of new materials, he did not profit by the most interesting development of the period preceding his own. For there was in the mid-century one innovation of great importance: the use of castiron, from which the structure of modern architecture was eventually to be developed. Metal had been used for bridges and in buildings in Europe and, to a lesser extent, in America from the end of the eighteenth century. But it was Paxton's Crystal Palace, built for the Great Exposition in Hyde Park, London, in 1851, which turned the eyes of the world to the immense possibilities of the new material in combination with glass. This building was no more than a giant example of the conservatories

I-9

which were already in general use as adjuncts to large houses. But it was on a scale and of a prominence which made it necessary for architects and amateurs to consider a mode of setting up whole buildings basically different from masonry. It was even very unlike anything that had been done with wood since the half-timber houses of the late Middle Ages. At first the chief progeny of the Crystal Palace were the direct imitations erected for expositions in the great cities of the world —New York's was built in 1853. For several decades after the original had been taken down in Hyde Park and reerected at Sydenham in 1854 in rather more elaborate form, it remained one of the great I-10 modern wonders of the world.

Even before the Crystal Palaces began to be built, however, James Bogardus in New York had begun to make very considerable use of iron in the construction of commercial buildings. In his own factory in New York, built in 1848, he used not only castiron supports within but facades of castiron as well. Thenceforth city buildings with party I-11 walls of masonry were more and more frequently supplied not only with metal interior supports but with such facades. Even those buildings which continued to be faced with masonry generally had piers of iron instead of stone on the ground floor in order to make possible wide shopwindows.

Castiron construction, however, did not reach its apogee until the period after the Civil War, and because of fires and rebuilding, castiron facades of the fifties are difficult to find in American cities. The early type of design was still quite Greek, with slender Doric columns and narrow spandrels at the floor levels, and, for ornament, only a little scroll work in flat bosses bolted on here and there.

The use of metal developed further with the substitution of wrought iron, which was less brittle than castiron, for beams in the Harper's Building in New York, 1853, and the backing of the facades with brickwork as vain protection against fire. Soon the new facades were sanded and painted until they were almost indistinguishable from stone. Indeed, they were a great deal fussier in design than the best vernacular granite facades that continued the earlier utilitarian tradition. In the typical castiron type of design established in the late fifties, the bays on each floor were arched and the columns were provided with Corinthian capitals of acanthus leaves bolted to the top of the support. The piers tended to grow wider and were often complicated by subsidiary orders. In the sixties the ornament grew larger in scale and more lush. It is understandable that Richardson on his return from Europe should have found this type of construction barbarous and commercial. Even technically, the great fires of the early seventies were to prove that it was inferior to traditional masonry.[4]

The elevator, which, together with metal construction fireproofed with masonry, was in time to make the skyscraper technically possible, was first publicly demonstrated in America at the New York Crystal Palace in 1853. It was not used in a permanent building, however, until the construction of the Fifth Avenue Hotel in 1858.

I-12

The French or mansard or curb roof was in the mid-century the characteristic feature from which a new national type of design drew its name. It became in the sixties, together with the castiron front, the symbol of modernity, but its first appearance was in the fifties. Of course, the broken-pitched or gambrel roof had been extremely popular in the seventeenth and eighteenth century vernacular, and roofs with central flat decks were frequently used where the great area of a building and the lack of a gable or a pediment made them convenient and possible. Indeed, as soon as the successful revolt against the Greek Revival no longer made the pediment and the low-pitched roof obligatory, rather flat gambrels came into use to cover city buildings which now began to extend increasingly far back from the street. The urban sin of excessive ground coverage preceded that of excessive height.

But the newly imported French roof was distinguished from any of the preceding types in use in this country by the shortness and

---

[4] The dome of the Capitol in Washington built through the sixties was the most prominent example of the use of castiron in monumental architecture. It was rarely imitated.

steepness of the first slope above the cornice and the comparative invisibility of the flatter upper slope. Such a mansard had been used once just after the Revolution by l'Enfant on Robert Morris' palace in Philadelphia, but this was unique. The real introduction of the type was in the fifties, partly as a stylistic feature, partly as a technical innovation. Its modest claim to being a technical device lies in the fact that it provides an attic storey hardly inferior to the main storeys of the building. With the demand for larger buildings in the boom period of 1865-73, the mansard sometimes was extended upward to provide two storeys above the cornice. With the French roof, quite tall buildings could be designed with facades of the conventional two or three storeys below the cornice. Thus the difficult problem of designing vertically instead of horizontally was postponed a few years. But the frequent use of the mansard roof on one storey houses indicates that its popularity was more due to a desire for prestige than to semi-practical, semi-aesthetic reasons.

An obscure architect named Lemoulnier is credited by Fiske Kimball with having brought the curb roof to Boston from France at the beginning of the decade. In spite of the Classical Revival it had lasted on in France as a current vernacular device through the late eighteenth and even into the early nineteenth century. Then, well before the Revolution of 1848, there had been occasional revivals of the style of Louis XIV, of which it was a constituent part. In the fifties, the setting of the brilliant Imperial court in the Renaissance Palace of the Tuileries, and the construction of the new Louvre further focussed attention on the high although not specifically mansard roofs of the French sixteenth century style. On private Parisian mansions, which rivalled the Imperial palaces in splendour, the later type of curb roof used under Louis XIII, Louis XIV and Louis XV became equally prominent. Moreover, whatever the surface style imitated on the apartment houses which lined the new avenues of Paris, they were rarely without one mansarded storey or more above the main cornices, the height of which was fixed by the building laws. In buildings not isolated and monumental, few advanced French architects of the day

I-13

would have omitted some form of high roof.

Richard M. Hunt returned from Paris in 1855. He was apparently the first American architect to study at the Ecole des Beaux Arts. He had later worked under Lefuel on the new Louvre as supervisor in the construction of the Pavillon des Bibliothèques. Naturally he brought with him all the features of Second Empire architecture, of which the revived mansard was undoubtedly the most prominent in the design of individual houses. But he soon went to work with Walter on the Capitol in Washington, after building very little on his own in New York and only one house in Boston.

By the end of the fifties the French roof was only beginning to be familiar in the East. No real integrated Second Empire manner had arrived by this time. The French roof, if used at all, was merely applied indiscriminately to all the types of design then in current use. It was not until after the Civil War that it became the dominant characteristic of a special type of non-ecclesiastical design which soon drove out or submerged all the others except the Victorian Gothic. Indeed, even the Victorian Gothic donned its own type of high two-pitched roof.

The later popularity of the mansard roof is not to be attributed solely to the prestige of Paris. It is fairly clear from a study of the English magazines of the fifties and sixties that the developed Second Empire manner came to America for the most part via England. Much of its character, which can hardly be explained on the basis of French prototypes, is to be explained by its passage through Victorian England. Needless to say, it was not the later classicists like Elmes and Cockerell nor the leaders of the Gothic Revival who were responsible for the English version, but obscure architects whose work consisted largely of hotels and commercial buildings. But like the Italianate Victorian Gothic, this English Second Empire was seldom imitated here until after the Civil War. While Richardson was at Harvard from 1854 to 1859, the French roof and the Second Empire manner of design were not conspicuous in the general architectural scene of Cambridge and Boston. It was only on his return from Europe that they were definitely enthroned.

CHAPTER TWO

1854-1865

RICHARDSON had come North with the intention of becoming a Civil Engineer after he had failed to qualify for West Point. He might have been expected, therefore, to pay some attention to the first cast-iron buildings which were in course of construction in downtown Boston during the years he was at Harvard.[1]

But the structural innovations which were being made during his student days in Boston, if he observed them at all, certainly did not in the least affect the direction of his later development. For he never made important use of metal in his buildings. Indeed, despite his early choice of engineering as a vocation, he never in his mature life took a direct interest in the technical side of architecture. He left problems of construction to his builders, Norcross Bros., or to Rutan, who trained himself as the engineer of the office.

Richardson was rather brilliant in mathematics. This doubtless determined at this period his choice of engineering as a profession (if, indeed, the choice was his and not his parents') far more than any real interest in problems of construction. His mathematical ability and training stood him in good stead when he came to take the examinations for the Ecole des Beaux Arts, as did also the fact that he had spoken French since childhood.

---

[1] The first castiron front in New England was built by Elbridge Boyden for Calvin Foster, on the S.W. corner of Main and Pearl Streets, Worcester, in 1854. Bogardus built a building in Boston within the next few years.

His inferior preparation in the Classics held him back a class on entering Harvard, but once there he kept a fair standing in his work. He also continued outside his college courses the study of drawing, which he had begun in New Orleans as a child of ten. This would have been of some assistance to him in Paris, although the drawing taught in New England in the late fifties was a conventional exercise hardly related to the active practice of the arts.

The picture of Harvard in these years which Henry Adams gives in his *Education* is not an inspiring one. He does, however, suggest that a man like Richardson, who was not a New Englander, could profit from the atmosphere of Cambridge and Boston. Adams also remarks, referring to Richardson among others, that the potentialities of his classmates who later achieved distinction were already so clear to him that their later success never surprised him. One question is of interest: what caused Richardson while at Harvard to give over his intention of becoming a Civil Engineer and to decide to become an architect? It is unanswerable. We can only assume that the atmosphere of the fifties at Harvard, which was at its best strongly marked by the influence of German philosophy, encouraged the selection of the more humane profession. Until the time of Eliot, there was in Cambridge a certain prejudice against the exact sciences which has never altogether lost its force. Whatever the ultimate motivation, well before Richardson finished his four years in Cambridge, he had determined to become an architect and he knew sometime before his graduation that his step-father was ready to send him to Europe to study.

While it would be absurd to suggest that Richardson, any more than any other undergraduate, was particularly familiar with the developments in American architecture during the two decades of his life, it is justifiable to assume that he observed rather carefully most of the buildings about him in Cambridge and Boston, and even to believe that his impression of them played an important part in his decision to study abroad. Thus it is desirable to examine in detail what the architecture of Harvard and Cambridge and Boston was like in the late fifties—his specific environment during the important years when he decided to occupy himself with architecture—although we can only guess rather wildly the favorable or unfavorable impression he may have had of particular buildings.

It is clear that he had little if any theoretical instruction in the fine arts. The teaching of drawing trains the eye to see but not the mind to judge. In college courses in the Classics the conventional beauties of Greek and Roman art were undoubtedly mentioned with respect. But any impression such a classroom acquaintance with ancient temples may have made on Richardson must have been as dim as that of the temple houses of the plantations and the vernacular building of New Orleans in his childhood. He left the South with its Athenian reflections in architecture when he was sixteen and never saw it again. The ancient Italy and, above all, the Athens, which he so yearned to see before he returned from Paris, were not the cold monochrome prototypes of the American Greek Revival but the sumptuous and highly colored images created by the restorations of Romantic archaeologists like Labrouste and Hittorf.

As to Colonial Cambridge, with the Tory mansions along Brattle Street, or the Boston of the eighteenth century, which was still at least half intact, Richardson must have taken them for granted. They were already too much a part of the setting, too neutral and indistinguishable a background to attract or fix the attention of an undergraduate. The Greek Revival, moreover, had taught Americans to see only faults of Classical grammar and syntax in eighteenth century detail. At this time Americans apologized for the barbarisms of their ancestors as Europeans after the Renaissance had apologized for the art of the Middle Ages.

At Harvard, however, Richardson must have liked the plain solid late Baroque vernacular of the old buildings, Massachusetts and Hollis and Stoughton, or he could not have rediscovered their essential qualities so effectively when he later built Sever. This his successors, Coolidge, Shepley, Bulfinch and Abbott, have hardly been able to do in the present century when imitating the old buildings directly. Sever was the work of one who had known and loved the old buildings almost unconsciously, in the instinctive way impossible to the avowed revivalist who sees the monuments of the past merely as documents to copy. In this same way the shingle-covered New England farm houses, seen on country excursions, also made their quiet impression.

As regards his attitude toward the newer architecture, we may guess that the formal Greek buildings would have received only the lip-service due things which echoed so obviously the classic idols. The simpler vernacular would have seemed for the most part so dull as to escape notice—as for the most part it does still. At best it may have served as the general basis for some plaint of native prosiness such as has ever been a prime excuse to justify post-graduate study of the arts in Europe.

Yet here also a qualification is necessary. The bare sturdy buildings of smooth or rock-faced granite which, at this period, made of Boston's waterfront and commercial district one of the most impressive in the world, surely made their impression on Richardson. Where could he have developed that feeling for masses of granite in great rough blocks except along lower State Street and Commercial Street or on the wharf where the Customs House Block still stands?

In the fifties the Gothic was the accepted style for churches. But surely the cardboard wooden Gothic of Isaiah Rogers' First Unitarian Church of 1833, across from the Yard, already appeared trivial and silly. Even Richard Bond's Gore Hall, the college library, like a rather heavy Tudor wedding cake, built in granite the year of Richardson's birth, was old-fashioned and primitive according to the new Mediaeval standards of the Eastern seaboard. But St. John's Chapel, which was II-1 building for the Episcopal Theological Seminary on Brattle Street the last year Richardson was in Cambridge, was much more advanced. There Ware and Van Brunt were following the asymmetrical Victorian ecclesiastical pattern based on fourteenth century parish churches quite as well as any of their American—or even most of their English—contemporaries. The random ashlar walls were of Roxbury Pudding-stone with buff sandstone trim, simply and not incorrectly moulded, and occasional voussoirs of brownstone in the arches: exactly the materials Richardson was to use so successfully for the Brattle Square Church in Boston a decade later.

The wooden Gothic houses, of which Cambridge had several fair specimens near the Yard, would hardly interest very much a young man whose heart seems to have been set on monumental architecture. His few Gothic house projects of the late sixties were rather half-hearted; even so, they showed little connection with the naive Tudor of the fifties. The other, more exotic, Romantic types—chalets, Indian villas and the like—with their many different varieties of gingerbread, can hardly have made a more consistent impression then than they do today. They indicated only that the Greek Revival was definitely over and that American taste was capricious and fussy when pampered. Doubtless such things were considered pretty or not pretty in conversation, much as today we find their rehabilitation amusing or not amusing. But for a young man with a serious architectural vocation they can have had little reality.

The Barryesque High Renaissance in buff or brown sandstone—or, in the case of houses, buff or brown painted siding—came as near as any to being accepted as the most solid non-ecclesiastical style. There were plenty of good examples in Boston and Cambridge, but none of them was likely to seem to a young man of the fifties anything but a slightly more modern and less dull alternative to the dying Greek Revival.

It is unlikely but not impossible that Richardson saw Upjohn's admirable unexecuted project for Appleton Chapel with its basilican plan, isolated campanile and simple Italian Villa detail. If he did, it could have reenforced the testimony of the newer Gothic churches, such as St. John's, that church towers need not be placed symmetrically as they had been in the forties. It might also perhaps have offered the suggestion, generally in the air in America at this time, that other more or less Mediaeval styles were quite as Christian and quite as suitable for modern use as the fourteenth century Gothic of England.

But it was not necessary to see Upjohn's project to appreciate this. Buildings actually built at Harvard in these years indicated as much and more. While N. J. Bradlee's new Grays Hall, begun in 1858, was distinguished only by its French roof from the dullest and most nondescript works of the current vernacular, the Appleton Chapel commission had gone neither to Upjohn nor to the leading Boston firm, Cabot and Gilman (to whom $200 had been paid for unused plans in 1855), but to the Romanesque project of an obscure German named Paul Schulze. As Henry Adams makes clear, the cultural prestige of Germany was very high at Harvard in these years. Lowell and others who had studied in Germany would have encouraged the selection of a German architect.

This chapel, finished in 1857 and destroyed a few years ago to make way for the gargantuan War Memorial Chapel by Richardson's successors, Coolidge, Shepley, Bulfinch and Abbott, was of buff sandstone throughout and had a corner spire which was a reduced version of one of those on von Gärtner's Ludwigskirche in Munich, begun in 1829. The design of the chapel with its deep triple-arched loggia on the facade, and with the windows on the sides set under very flat blind arches, was a creditable version of the South German Romanesque style of von Gärtner in Bavaria, and of Hübsch in Baden and the Rhineland. This, of course, Eidlitz had already introduced in the forties in New York. Richardson was never directly influenced by this building. But its prominence as the chief new construction at Harvard while he was an undergraduate may well have prepared him for the popularity of the Romanesque as an ecclesiastical style in Paris when he went there to study in the sixties.

Perhaps, also, Richardson may have preferred Schulze's rather less Romanesque Boylston Hall built in the same year. Certainly, without its mansard, which was added later, it was an admirable building. Its simple, solid mass, round-arched windows, and rough-cut granite masonry sound in a description—more than they appear in actuality— unexpectedly proto-Richardsonian to anyone who knows Richardson's later work. Of course, these two buildings, built while Richardson was at Harvard, are not to be considered the direct inspiration of his later use of the Romanesque and of rock-faced granite. Had they been

II-2

a direct and uniquely motivating influence he would have gone not to Paris but to Munich, and he would have used rock-faced granite much earlier than he actually did.

Yet, like all the other elements in his architectural environment, these buildings bear a real relation to his development. Their existence is not a mere coincidence. In the absence of documents we can only say that that relation apparently lay beneath the articulate surface on which life is lived and work done. In the subconscious or semiconscious reservoir of the universal memory into which the historian and critic may often claim to see more clearly than the artist or the statesmen he studies, such an influence, like that of other Cambridge and Boston buildings, may be held true, although not ascertainable.

Two events of his years in Cambridge were indirectly important to his later career: his engagement to Miss Hayden of Boston, which influenced him against settling in Paris or in the South, and his election to the Porcellian Club, which meant that his intimate friends were among the richest and most prominent men of his day. This provided him with those influential associations which Henry Adams evidently thought were what Harvard had chiefly to offer at this time. At least three fellow members of the Porcellian Club employed him or aided him to obtain commissions at the opening of his career: J. A. Rumrill, B. W. Crowninshield, and Richard Codman.

Neither the preceding analysis of the architectural scene in the late fifties in Cambridge and Boston nor any written document makes clear why Richardson went to Paris to study and not to England, where most of his compatriots were still drawn, or to Germany, which was then the rising fashion. Paris has been ever since Richardson's day so much the obvious goal of the aspiring student of art that it is easily forgotten that he was only the second American architect to study there, and that in the fifties and sixties more students of art still went elsewhere. It is doubtful if the fact that Hunt had gone to Paris a few years earlier influenced Richardson. Yet, of course, he may have been struck by Hunt's house for Dr. Williamson built in Boston in 1857, or impressed by the position Hunt held as Walter's assistant on the Capitol in Washington. It seems more probable that being an American college graduate and hence believing in formal rather than informal education, Richardson chose Paris because the Ecole des Beaux Arts offered a systematic course, while in other countries there were still only opportunities for apprenticeship, or rather feeble academies. With his knowledge of French and his command of mathematics, he would not have been deterred by fear of the entrance difficulties.

But the primary reason, the essential motivation, was, it is arguable, more logical still. We know from his later career that Richardson was not much interested in building churches, even though he easily made his reputation with them when they offered the best opening on his return to America. Nor was he, according to Mrs. Van Rensselaer, much interested in houses; although in his maturity he came to find them welcome and artistically fruitful commissions. Churches and houses were the stock in trade of the English Victorian Gothic, and had he wished to design them he might well have gone to England. But he was chiefly interested in monumental architecture, as are many young men when they first decide to become architects. This was obviously the field in which France was most active under the Second Empire and for which the education offered by the Ecole des Beaux Arts was the best preparation. Nearer to an answer to this question, as to many others, we can hardly come in the absence of Richardson's letters home in the fifties, in which the matter was presumably discussed. These were, unfortunately, burned during the Civil War.

When Richardson left Cambridge in the June of 1859 after his examinations were over, he spent the summer before he settled in Paris travelling with college friends in the British Isles. It is unlikely that he spent much time examining modern architecture. He must have seen the Crystal Palace and the Houses of Parliament. Perhaps he was impressed by neither. For the most part he and his companions spent their time like other cultured tourists visiting respectfully the cathedrals, the abbeys and the castles. Probably he received from these monuments no particular impression except of their bulk and of the variety of real Mediaeval work which was so completely lacking in America.

Probably, also, the early books on English Mediaeval architecture in his library were bought at this time, when he was still well off. As he was on vacation, it is unlikely that he studied them very carefully. Many more hours surely were spent experiencing at first hand the delights of being tailored by Poole's, to which he ever afterward remained addicted. He knew more of England and its architecture than the new colleagues he was going to join at the Ecole des Beaux Arts, and he would have been more ready than they to look out for English books and magazines, if only for the archaeological documents they contained. But in his education he owed very little to England altogether, and nothing, apparently, to new buildings he may have seen at this time. The English influence on his developing style came in the late sixties through the magazines which he began to see regularly on his return to America.

The Cambridge and Boston which Richardson left on his graduation from Harvard have all but disappeared with later expansion and rebuilding. But the Paris in which he spent the next five years was II-4 already more like the Paris of today than like the Paris of the eighteenth century. The main web of boulevards and great broad streets, the focal architectural monuments of the city as we now know it, the very social distribution of the quarters which still exists in the twentieth century, were established under the Second Empire. Napoleon III was the last and the most ambitious of the French building monarchs. Beside his architectural programme for Paris even that of Louis XV appears haphazard and incidental. Thus Richardson saw not only the construction of an extraordinary number of major public monuments, but also the widest application of a standardized formula of urban design which the western world had even known.

Garnier's Opéra, of which the design was selected in a competition in 1860, was to provide the very hub and center of Napoleon III's II-5 city. The preparation of the setting for it began even earlier. The Avenue de l'Opéra leading from the Louvre had been begun at the Place du Théatre Français in 1854.[2] The Place de l'Opéra itself was laid out in 1858. The Opéra today is considered the great achievement of the Second Empire in architecture, the symbol of the official style of the Ecole des Beaux Arts, and even of Paris itself. But it did not so appear in the early sixties while Richardson was in Paris. The florid High Renaissance design of Garnier's project, recalling Sansovino and even the Venetian Baroque of Longhena, was exceptional and novel. It was the bold bid for fame of a talented young man, admirably suited to the taste of a somewhat parvenu court anxious to rival the splendours of Versailles. But it was by no means acceptable to the conservative taste of the Academy and the bureaucracy in general.

II-6

The established architects and the more conventional young men were content to repeat on a larger scale in their projects the theatres built in Paris and in the provinces under the Restoration and the July Monarchy. They had every reason to believe that was what was wanted. Thus, rather cold, classical designs predominated. These were of a type consecrated by an earlier generation of classicists under the First Empire. Alternatively there were several schemes in the dry, thin Palladian which had been the established vernacular of the second quarter of the century. Garnier's project was therefore very exceptional.

Moreover, although the Opéra was in construction all through the sixties and substantially complete on the exterior before 1870, it was by no means then the universally accepted masterpiece and source of inspiration that it became after its ultimate completion in 1874. This prime monument, in other words, is more accurately to be considered not the symbol of the Second Empire official style at all, but rather of the later development and elaboration of French academic architectural traditions under the Third Republic. The setting is a

[2] It was further extended from that end in 1864; but not until 1878 was it finally carried through to meet the spur extending from in front of the Opéra.

typical achievement of the sixties, but not the jewel for which the setting was prepared.

II-7

The new Louvre also is an exceptional monument. It was begun by Visconti in 1852 in a style based on the French High Renaissance of the contiguous Louvre and the Tuileries. The original scheme was pompous enough, but the style grew richer still as it was executed by Lefuel, who succeeded Visconti as architect on the latter's death in 1853. The north side was completed in 1857. The southern Galerie du Bord de l'Eau was reconstructed by Lefuel in even more florid taste between 1862 and 1868.

II-8

But the new Louvre and the old Tuileries, the actual residence of the Emperor and the scene of the splendours of the Imperial Court, did not exercise the influence in France that they did in England and America. The particular derivative from the style of the Imperial residences which Bryant & Gilman introduced in Boston in the City Hall, 1861-65, and which Mullet made the official style of General Grant's first administration, was not, except for its high roofs, in general use in France under the Second Empire. Indeed its stigmata, the mansarded dome and tower, were hardly known there except on the new Louvre even in the seventies. As has been stated earlier, the manner came to America from England exactly as had its rival, the Victorian Gothic. There, as we can still see in the very magazine illustrations which bore the influence to America, it was particularly popular for banks and hotels.[3]

II-9

II-10

Quite as prominent as the new Louvre and the Opéra were other public monuments, which to the contemporary student must have seemed more characteristic of the official design of the times. The new building of the Ecole des Beaux Arts itself (Fig. 1), with the facade on the Quai Malaquais, was carried out by Duban in 1860-62, while Richardson was a student there.[4] This was cold, reserved and rather

[3] A typical example is the Cavendish Hotel, Eastbourne, Sussex, by Knightley. The *Builder*, Vol. XXIV, 1866, p. 597.

[4] The most prominent earlier building at the Ecole, the museum, was also by Duban. It was a characteristic cold Renaissance design of the thirties. Duban, of course, had had contact with a more Baroque style in his restoration of the

rationalistic in design, with very large segmental arched windows, dry Neo-Grec ornament and a general avoidance of strong relief quite opposed in character to the exuberance of Garnier or even Lefuel. The roof was high but not of the characteristic mansard type.

The two state theatres in the Place du Châtelet, built in the same years by Davioud, were slightly richer and less classical in ornamentation, but they preserved in the main the flatness and rationalism of design of the previous generation. Their roofs were not mansarded any more than those of the majority of nearby buildings with which they were carefully harmonized in proportion. Hittorf's Mairie du Louvre side of St.-Germain l'Auxerrois, 1857-61, was not dissimilar in character. It had, however, a low mansard. There was also a high pointed gable in the center, with an early Renaissance rose window to balance the gable of the church the other side of the tower. This was an ingenious scheme for a particular location, which might easily have been evolved under the July Monarchy. Bailly's Tribunal de Commerce, 1860-65, resembles Hittorf's Marie more than Lefuel's new Louvre, except for its dome, of which the bold Baroque outline conflicts in character with the metallic Neo-Grec detail. The ornament on the lower storeys is, however, of a delicate early Renaissance character.

The great complex of reconstruction and new building by Duc at the Palais de Justice was begun as early as 1841. The cold, thin Neo-Grec style established in the facade toward the Rue de la Barillerie was continued through the fifties and sixties with elegant variety and an increasing structural rationalism. The facade toward the Quai des Orfèvres was rebuilt in an equally cold Gothic style between the two old towers of the Conciergerie.

The western facade, finished in 1868, was, however, bolder and more original. The large windows under segmental arches recall those at the Ecole des Beaux Arts, but the half columns and the ornament generally give an effect of higher relief, although the detail is sparse

Louvre in the forties, notably the Galerie d'Apollon, but this had hardly influenced his style in modern work.

and dry in outline like the work of the forties and fifties. The construction details of the earlier wings around the Cour de la Sainte Chapelle show a consistent use of metal trusses of ingenious and carefully studied design.

For the Second Empire, like the July Monarchy, made bold use of metal in public buildings; not only in markets—Baltard's great Halles Centrales were begun in 1853—which were more utilitarian than monumental in character, but also in the interior of railroad stations, exposition halls and even libraries. Yet the facade of Hittorf's Gare du Nord, 1861-65, was even more classical than Duc's Palais de Justice, and the admirable stations built by Cendrier for the P. L. M. might easily have been designed a generation earlier, so bare and well proportioned and rational were they. The Palais de l'Industrie projected by Cendrier and built by Viel, 1853-55, for the exposition of the latter year, was very similar and more conspicuously located.

Henri Labrouste's magnificent Bibliothèque Ste.-Geneviève with its metal-supported vaulting was built from 1843 to 1850. But throughout the years of the Second Empire he was at work restoring and enlarging the Bibliothèque Nationale. As regards the exterior, this consisted largely of imitating the brick and stone Louis XIII design of the original Hôtel Mazarin toward the Rue Vivienne and extending the Louis XVI design of the court facade along the Rue de Richelieu and the Rue des Petits Champs. But in both cases he did this in a characteristically stiff, flat, Neo-Grec manner. The Salle de Travail, however, with its elegant metal pillars and terra cotta domes above arches of metal lattice, opened in 1868, was an even more ingenious and brilliant example of the use of new materials than the Bibliothèque Ste.-Geneviève.

In industrial building there was even more extensive use of metal, as in the Docks de St.-Ouen by Prefontaine of 1865. Here, on the rear and sides, there was a visible metal framework for the exterior walls, filled with thin panels of brick.

Iron was even introduced into prominent new churches in these

II-11

II-12

II-13 years: at St.-Augustin, 1860-68, by Baltard, the architect of the Halles Centrales; and at St.-Eugène, 1854-55, by Boileau, who in the next decade built at le Vésinet, outside Paris, another Church of II-14 St.-Eugène entirely of iron and concrete.

The last two churches were both of a tinny Late Gothic style, somewhat like those of the pre-Pugin Gothic Revival in England. By the fifties the Classical and Renaissance Basilican types of the Restoration, initiated originally before the Revolution by Chalgrin's St.-Philippe-du-Roule, 1769-84, were rarely followed any longer, and the most prominent new churches were Gothic. The most conspicuous example was Ste.-Clothilde. This was begun by Gau in 1846 and completed by Ballu in 1859 in the very dead, underscaled High Gothic which succeeded the prettier, fussier Late Gothic of the generation of 1830.

The archaeologists and restorers, Viollet-le-Duc and Lassus, although primarily busy with the Sainte-Chapelle and Notre Dame, each built, in the suburbs, a church of substantial thirteenth century (sic) design; Lassus, St.-Jean Baptiste, Belleville, finished in 1858; Viollet-le-Duc, the parish church of St.-Denis, finished in 1867. In Paris, and in the provinces also, many more new Gothic churches were built, and even more old churches were so far restored that they were to all intents and purposes reconstructed. Except for the practically new nave of the Collégiale of Eu by Viollet-le-Duc, almost none of them is equal in quality to comparable English or American churches of the Gothic Revival.

Already in the fifties as many churches were built in some version of the Romanesque style as in the Gothic, varying from a sort of II-15 Syrian proto-Byzantine to Norman. In Paris not only Baltard's St.-Augustin, 1860-68, which is anything but correct or archaeological, but almost all the great new churches fronting on the new boulevards and avenues are more Romanesque than anything else. The most elaborate and plausible was St.-Ambroise, completed in 1868 by Ballu. The best was St.-Pierre de Montrouge, built at the same time by II-16 Vaudremer with a basilican exterior, plain solid exterior walls, flat rather Syrian detail, and excellent massing at the east end resembling that of the fourth century Church of the Nativity at Bethlehem. The front tower was less successful and followed rather the Perigordine Romanesque (Fig. 2). Three or four others in Paris are no more remarkable than the many distributed through the provinces. Of these, perhaps only that at La Ferté-Macé, with its walls all brilliantly diapered in stones of three colours, merits particular attention.

Of the two other large and prominent churches built in Paris during the sixties, one, Ballu's La Trinité, 1861-67, at the foot of Montmartre, was a very elaborate adaptation of the François I style; the other, St.-François-Xavier, begun by Lusson in 1861 and completed after his death by Uchard in 1875, was a flat, cold basilica with Early Renaissance detail of the Louis Philippe type. These were exceptional.

None of the new churches, except, perhaps, La Trinité, resembled in the slightest the new Opéra or the new Louvre. But the Romanesque style so popular for churches was frequently echoed in convents and even in hospitals and asylums whose barrenly utilitarian design almost defies stylistic description. The Asile at Roucy by Destors, built in 1861-62, is typical enough, but the finest and most important example is Vaudremer's Prison de la Santé, begun in 1865. This enormous institution is perhaps hardly Romanesque. But for a certain crudeness in the sparse detail, it might well have been built two generations earlier by one of the pupils of Durand.

Before leaving the question of the Second Empire use of the Romanesque, two projects must be mentioned. One is Guadet's design for a hospital in the Alps with which he won the Premier Grand Prix de Rome in 1864, Richardson's last year in Paris. (Fig. 3). Of this he gave signed photographs to Richardson. Of course, it was never executed. The other is Abadie's winning design in the competition for the Sacre Coeur in 1874, the first great church planned after the Franco-Prussian War, for which, indeed, all the submitted designs but one were Romanesque or Byzantine. This was not completed for another generation, but it belongs more in spirit to the Second Empire than does Garnier's equally familiar Opéra.

31

In any other country but France, private construction rather than public would be more significant of the architectural current. A student such as Richardson, visiting England or America at this time, would probably have been far less interested in contemporary theatres or hospitals than in country and city houses or commercial buildings. Yet with the exception of the Saint-Ouen Docks and the Sacre Coeur—begun under the anti-clerical regime of the Third Republic and hence not a government commission—all the buildings thus far mentioned, undoubtedly the most important of the period, were official or semi-official commissions.

Indeed, the design of still another class of buildings serving various commercial and residential purposes and particularly prominent in the Paris of the Second Empire was under semi-official control. In the tradition of the Place des Vosges, the Place Vendôme and the Rue de Rivoli, such open areas as the Place de l'Etoile, now for the first time built up, and the new Place de l'Opéra, with the streets and boulevards opening into it, were treated as public monuments. In both cases they were provided in the fifties and sixties with continuous facades erected under government auspices, behind which were set shops and cafés, mansions, apartments, hotels and even theatres. The buildings around the Place de l'Etoile, built by Hittorf and Charles Rohaut de Fleury in 1857-58, were paired between the radiating avenues under single low mansards. They were decorated with corner pilasters above a basement storey and had pedimented windows with mouldings of slight projection.

II-17   Even more dignified and standardized were the buildings about the Place de l'Opéra with their completely continuous design of a sort of modernized monumental Louis XVI. Here the ground storey and mezzanine intended for shops or cafés, such as the Café de la Paix, had wide bays with light metal supports between alternate heavier rusticated piers of stone. Above this base, giant pilasters, with lightly framed windows between, extended for two storeys to a cornice. Above this main cornice was an attic and above that a mansard broken by simple stone dormers. Except for the substitution of coupled pilasters or of rustication at the corners for the single pilasters of the standard bay, this treatment was carried without variation all around the square and for some distance into the seven important streets which joined there.

Only at the acute angles on the corners of the Rue de la Paix and the Rue du 4 Septembre were there real changes in the continuous design: rounded pavilions with low domed roofs instead of the mansard, and coupled engaged columns instead of pilasters. Eventually the same scheme of design was carried along the streets that flanked the Opéra on the sides. Even where the urban constructions along the newly opened streets were not the work of architects commissioned by the government, the cornice heights and the profile of the mansards were determined by the state, so that a continuous effect was imposed all along the avenues and boulevards. Although the splendour and absolute standardization of the Place de l'Opéra were rarely achieved elsewhere, architects seldom strayed far from a simplified repetition of its pattern except in a few palatial private houses.

Thus the state established a definite level of amenity for the solid rows of five, six, and occasionally seven, storey buildings which were erected in such quantities under the stimulus of real estate speculation. Against this controlled background the public monuments of more or less marked individuality were seen to admirable advantage. The florid exuberance of the Opéra has its foil in the severity of the Place de l'Opéra and the streets around it. Neither St.-Pierre de Montrouge nor La Trinité is exactly harmonious with its setting, but these settings are so consistent and recessive as to throw the churches into justifiable prominence.

No foreign architect, and, above all, no American student of architecture in the mid-nineteenth century, could expect to apply this important lesson of urbanism. For elsewhere, and particularly in America, standards of vernacular amenity had just been thrown to the winds. The English and the Americans in the fifties and sixties attempted rather to make of hotels, banks, and even office buildings, isolated monuments like Parisian palaces or major state theatres. Thus, the even more highly characterized churches and public buildings of the Anglo-Saxons were set perforce in the most heterogeneous and aggressive surroundings. The importance of placing individualized public monuments in standardized urban settings has hardly been appreciated yet in America.

Richardson in a way conformed to this rule by building chiefly public monuments or isolated houses. What he would have done with a whole street it is impossible to say. For neither he nor any other American of his time, in the face of a chaotic political and economic situation, could succeed, as did French architects as late as the Second Empire, in providing dignified urban facade design that could be unrolled by the mile to take care of the ever-growing cities of the second half of the century. The reasons for this lie partly in the relatively weak control of the law over building in America and partly in the absence of a consistent accepted tradition and a center of training. Well down into the fifties, as long as the discipline of the Greek Revival lasted, the American urban vernacular was of a very high standard of excellence. But by the end of the Civil War this fine tradition had been forgotten and the post-war mood demanded assertive competition in architectural design as in everything else. Insurance companies had far more power to enforce their technical standards of structure than municipalities had to compel even a modicum of aesthetic amenity.

In the construction of large private houses, *hôtels particuliers*, French architects of the sixties showed more originality than in the type of building just discussed, although usually less than the men of the Romantic generation before them. There are no more semi-suburban Gothic *castels* like Bridaut's at Passy, built in 1835; no such exquisite if dull Renaissance palaces as Duban's Hôtel de Pourtalès of 1850. Instead, the architects provided semi-archaeological imitations of the styles of Louis XIII, Louis XIV, Louis XV and Louis XVI for clients who wished to imitate the splendours of Eugénie's Louis-Seize-Imperatrice apartments at the Tuileries and Saint-Cloud. Visconti before his death in 1853 had built, for example, the Hôtel de Pontalba (now Edmond de Rothschild) in the Rue du Faubourg St.-Honoré, with interiors copied from Versailles. This set a new standard of splendour. In the same street, in 1858, Henri Labrouste built the Hôtel Fould in the brick and stone Louis XIII style he was using on the Rue Vivienne facade of the Bibliothèque Nationale. The nearby Hôtel Péreire by Armand was also Louis XIII in style. This general French use of the mansarded styles of the seventeenth and eighteenth centuries for private houses, even by mediaevalists like Viollet-le-Duc, best explains the ambitions of so many American builders and even architects between 1865 and 1875. Of course they had no acquaintance with the originals. Inspiration came to them at second or third hand through the woodcuts in English architectural magazines of English buildings, already much corrupted in crossing the channel, and in the designs published in Godey's *Lady's Book* and such handbooks as the later editions of Woodward's *Homes*. II-18

Occasionally in the newer quarters around the Parc Monceaux and the Place Péreire and in provincial cities, the level both of mere competence and stylistic correctness fell to a level not far above the English and American. For the quality of this type of design continued to decline in France from its first introduction under Louis Philippe until long after the Second Empire was over. Perhaps, indeed, it was the backwash of American "taste" and "refinement" in revivalism, making itself felt in France in the late nineties, which finally reestablished a higher standard of accuracy in such imitations.

Bourgeois country houses, other than *villas coquettes et pimpantes* —which certainly no French architect seriously considered to be architecture, and probably few foreigners—were much less frequently built in France than in England or America in the mid-century. Those that were built are rather solid and sober and quite uninspiring. Châteaux, like churches, were freely restored and enlarged, usually in some approximation of a presumed sixteenth or seventeenth century original style. Similar ones were constructed *de novo*. But French contemporary architecture was centered in Paris quite as it had been for a hundred years. Provincial architects for the most part lost the important local commissions to men from Paris. They were forced to occupy themselves with dubious restoration and archaeological research that was often little sounder. Foreigners rarely suspected that the work of such men was contemporary, although they saw plenty of it when they visited supposedly authentic ancient monuments.

CHAPTER THREE

1859-1865

THE FRENCH architectural scene, at the time when Richardson reached Paris and during the five years he remained there, may be briefly summarized thus: activity was concentrated in Paris and under the central government. The official classical tradition had been inherited through two intermediate regimes from the First Empire. It was cold, hard, dry, and usually dull, priding itself on its utility and on the elegance of its sparse Neo-Grec detail. It remained basically rationalistic in the expression of masonry construction, yet bold in using new materials. The Romanesque was favored as against the Gothic. III-1 Once the first heat of the Troubadour Romanticism of the thirties was over, the Romanesque appeared to offer a kind of mediaeval Revivalism more consistent with the dominant Classicism. There was a sufficient outlet for the energies of the avowed Gothicists in restoration and reconstruction, yet even they were less faithful to the styles of the Middle Ages in civil construction than their English contemporaries.

The older men still designed much as their fathers and even their grandfathers had done. They and those they approved received most of the public commissions. Only a very few younger men who sought the bolder relief and richer ornamentation of the later Renaissance and Baroque styles, as against the official Neo-Grec or an alternative Palladianism, were rewarded with direct imperial favor. The revival of sixteenth, seventeenth and eighteenth century design was barely acceptable except in private work.[1]

If Richardson had gone to Europe merely to study modern architecture in contemporary buildings, as so many Americans have done in the last decade, this is the material of which his education would have been made. He might have brought back to America, as Hunt had after his work under Lefuel, the solider, more utilitarian tradition, with strong overtones of the newer, more lush manner of Lefuel and Garnier. Or he might have returned ready and avid to revive in America the High Gothic as the great French Mediaeval archaeologists were doing; or perhaps the Louis XIII, XIV, XV styles of the *hôtels particuliers* in the elegant faubourgs. Had he been more of an engineer he might rather have continued in America the development of the use of metal by Henri Labrouste, Baltard and Hittorf, reaching the skyscraper by a rather different route from that taken by Jenney in the early eighties.

III-2

But Richardson had come to Paris for formal and not informal education in architecture. He came to follow the regular courses in the Ecole des Beaux Arts and to work in an associated atelier. Later, because of economic necessity, he worked for a prominent and rather conservative official architect. What he drew from his years in Paris was none of the things suggested by the alternatives in the previous paragraph; not even the first, by which Hunt, his predecessor at the Ecole, achieved a position equalling his own in America in the seventies and eighties. The reasons lie partly, of course, in his particular associations in Paris, but more in his own character and tastes, and, above all, in the necessity of cutting short his formal education and working at architecture for his living in Paris.

For a Frenchman the Ecole des Beaux Arts was something like the Ecole de Droit, as the official preparation for a career in which the

---

[1] This is the Paris that can be recreated from the plates of *Paris dans sa Splendeur*, 1858; or Calliat's *Parallèle des Maisons de Paris depuis 1850*, 1864. It is, moreover, in large part still intact.

best commissions were official. The basic *Code Napoléon* of the art of architecture, established after the Revolution, was, perforce, continuously modified in practice by what amounted to contemporary judicial decisions: that is, although the Ecole formally offered instruction in the principles of the art, the particular applications of theory which were currently winning official commissions from the administration had the most prestige for students. Indeed, they had as much prestige for professors, whose positions were essentially bureaucratic commissions of an honorific order, perhaps as desirable to the French bourgeois mind as those which entailed the construction of buildings.

But a foreigner like Richardson, who intended to practice architecture in another land where there was no bureaucratic hierarchy in the art, could afford to approach the instruction offered by the Ecole in a freer spirit. Such a student could, if his own mind were developed at all, distinguish between general principles and particular applications. The principles deduced by several generations of academicians might be expected to have a certain continuing validity when properly adapted to a later time and the needs of a different country; but the applications of such principles in contemporary French practice deserved to be considered as special and local. Hunt, who apparently failed to make this distinction, might have been a better, although hardly a more successful architect, had he stayed on in France. Certainly his best works were those which could have been equally well built by his colleagues in France, like the Lenox Library. Richardson, with a stronger character and the courage of more individual tastes, never once built anything which would have been accepted in Paris as the conventional and expected product of a Frenchman thoroughly trained at the Ecole. But, perhaps, since he had to cut short his work at the Ecole and find paid employment, the French would not have considered that his training was really thorough at the time he left Paris.

III-3

When Richardson first attempted his entrance examinations for the Ecole in the fall of 1859, he failed in all but algebra and plane geometry. This was not surprising, as few foreigners are able to pass these examinations without special preparation. His first year he spent in a pension in the Rue de Vaugirard working hard at the subjects in which he now knew he was weak, and in mid-November of 1860 he entered very well, eighteenth in a field of one hundred and twenty, of whom only sixty were accepted.

Architectural students at the Ecole des Beaux Arts owe the greater part of their detailed instruction and criticism not to the Ecole itself but to their atelier. It is in one of a group of ateliers, each directed by a single architect, and associated with the Ecole, that they spend the greater part of their time. The atelier Richardson entered was that of Jules-Louis André. André had won the Premier Grand Prix de Rome in 1847.[2] On his return from Italy, André accepted the position of architect to the Jardin des Plantes, where during the rest of his life he occasionally built new pavilions of no particular intrinsic interest. He also supervised for Henri Labrouste his extensive work at the Bibliothèque Imperiale and was for a time diocesan architect in Corsica. In 1867 he became a professor at the Ecole des Beaux Arts and in 1884 a member of the Institut. He was already a Chevalier of the Légion d'Honneur. His career was, in other words, quite typical of that of many professionally successful French architects of the nineteenth century, full of honors and well supported by retaining fees, yet quite without important opportunities for actual construction.

André's distinction is of a type almost impossible for a foreigner to understand. As in the case of so many winners of the Prix de Rome, his activity went essentially into preserving and continuing the system of which the Premier Grand Prix was the first great goal and the In-

[2] His project was for a legislative chamber in the most characteristic official style of the period. The main feature was an enormous Corinthian temple portico at the rear of a court, as at Rousseau's Hôtel de Salm or Gondoin's Ecole de Médecine two generations earlier. But in the treatment of the side wings he used the broad cold wall surfaces and the sparse High Renaissance detail of the First Empire. This project was unexceptional even among the predominantly dull prize winning designs of the forties. It was much less interesting, for example, than the more French Renaissance project with which Charles Garnier won the Grand Prix the following year.

stitut the last. In his work at the Jardin des Plantes he continued, as was natural, the rationalistic manner of Molinos and the elder Rohaut de Fleury, who had preceded him there. His most ambitious project was that entered in the competition for the new Opéra in 1860. This had a giant colonnade above a basement with low, broad, almost Richardsonian arches, and might easily have been prepared in Durand's courses at the Ecole Polytechnique around 1800.

Richardson liked André and respected his professional taste; but he can hardly have found in his work—despite those broad, low arches —any very direct inspiration. Because of his contact with Henri Labrouste, however, André was a sort of channel through which the best and most active side of the rationalistic classical tradition of the First Empire came down into the Second Empire and to Richardson, untinged with the meretricious novelties of Lefuel and Garnier. Hence he was an admirable atelier *patron* to supplement and explain and prepare for the more formal instruction at the Ecole itself.

After the Civil War brought an end to Richardson's remittances from his family in New Orleans and he was forced to find professional work to earn his living, it was to the atelier he clung when he no longer had time for the regular work at the Ecole. He continued to follow this work vicariously, through helping his fellows at the atelier. Thus, although Richardson did not have the advantage of studying with a great architect like Henri Labrouste or Hittorf, or even of pursuing to the end the formal course of instruction on which he set out, he did learn through André the architectural *Code Napoléon,* very little distorted and specialized by the actualities of government apportionment of commissions under the Second Empire.

His friend, Adolphe Gerhardt, with whom he shared rooms in the Rue de Bac after giving up more luxurious quarters in the Rue Cambon, was more open to the influence of Garnier. This can be clearly seen in his project for a banker's mansion, which failed to win the Prix de Rome, but of which he gave Richardson a set of photographs in 1865. But, when the tide of florid design was rising in the mid-sixties, Richardson, thanks to his poverty, was already engaged in practical work under an architect even more sober in taste than André. Furthermore, the public charitable institution on which he worked was far more typical of really important contemporary French commissions than the *hôtel particulier* of a banker.

It is possible to believe that Richardson was fortunate in the loss of his revenues at the end of his first two years in Paris. It was certainly fortunate that his unwillingness to take the oath of allegiance to the Northern States created an impasse when he returned to Boston in 1862 and obliged him to go back to Paris to earn his living. His French education was thus completed in the best possible way. Three more years at the Ecole, where the eyes of the students as they advance are increasingly focussed on winning the Prix de Rome, would hardly have failed to involve him rather deeply in the mere game of winning prizes with the greatest prize, by arbitrary definition, out of his reach. For Richardson would not have been eligible to obtain the Prix de Rome without becoming a French subject.

In July of 1862, when Richardson went to work for Théodore Labrouste, the older but less well known brother of Henri Labrouste, he was set to work not on the imaginary assembly chambers and imperial palaces which were the current problems at the Ecole, but on a hospital for the incurable: an actual government commission. Labrouste gave him entire charge of the preliminary studies, handing him the whole official correspondence, and expecting him to develop plans to satisfy the dictated programme.

The programme of the Ivry hospital, for which the Administration de l'Assistance Publique already possessed the land, is rather precise in its specifications.[3] The problem was far more the technical one of translating these specifications into a satisfactory plan than of creating an impressive public monument. Indeed, except insofar as there existed an aesthetic of plan in which the French tradition firmly believed and which was barely differentiated consciously from pure functionalism, there was hardly any aesthetic problem of creation at all: once the

[3] Published in Husson, Armand, *Etude sur les Hôpitaux*, Paris, 1862, pp. 305-7.

plans were sufficiently studied the exterior appearance of the buildings would follow inevitably in terms of the official vernacular. There would have been almost no opportunity for applied or developed design except on the central chapel.

A young man could hardly have had at any period a more instructive problem to work out. Romantic ideas of Art had to be forgotten; at best aesthetic achievement could only consist of a certain amenity in superficial matters; but in fundamentals of the practical art of building, as opposed to capitalized Architecture, here was the training no school could ever give. Dignity and fine proportions and soundness in the use of materials were attainable, if not the pompous splendour of porticos and vaults.

The Hospice des Incurables at Ivry was not actually begun until 1864. As it stands, it is certainly to be considered a work of Théodore Labrouste and not of Richardson. There is no way of finding out how much was retained of the scheme worked out by Richardson two years earlier. It is not even definitely known whether Richardson continued to work with Labrouste and on this commission until he left Paris in the fall of 1865. If, as Mrs. Van Rensselaer states, he later worked with Hittorf, the supposition must be that he did not stay with Labrouste more than a year or two at the most. About all this no first-hand information exists. The only letters remaining from the latter part of his stay in Paris stop in August, 1862, when he was, of course, still with Labrouste.

The Hospice certainly represents the form in which Richardson absorbed most completely the French official tradition. No matter how carefully Richardson tried to do only what Labrouste would be ready to put his name to, the Ivry project must have been more real to him than those projects in the atelier and at the Ecole which he and everyone else knew would never be built. What he drew with his own hands, in the knowledge that it was actually to rise in solid masonry, must have impressed him more even than his work under Hittorf on the Gare du Nord. That monument had been first designed in 1861, and Richardson can hardly have done more than supervise, sometime after

43

1862 and before its completion in 1864-65, a work already complete in all essentials.

The Hospice d'Ivry (Fig. 1) is in no way remarkable nor like anything Richardson ever designed by himself later. It is simple to the point of barrenness, but impressive in size and excellent in distribution. The administration building, a long mansarded block with a very slightly projecting pavilion in the center, faces the main road from Ivry to Vitry as do also the end pavilions of two much longer side buildings. These side buildings, which face each other across a rather large court, are not mansarded except on their rather strongly projecting pavilions. The roofs, indeed, are of the same very low pitch as the upper slope of the mansards. The chapel is at the further end of the court, which is now agreeably landscaped with alleys of trimmed trees at the sides and a fountain and flower-edged grass plots in the center. The chapel has the only elaborate architectural embellishment in the group. Behind the chapel are grouped three low service buildings. The main buildings are tied together at the front by an arcade on square piers which is carried under the administration building on the court side. More delicate arcades on columns join the front of the chapel to the side buildings, while the service buildings are connected with simple but elegant galleries of metal and glass.

The buildings around the court are three storeys tall with rather large, evenly spaced windows of conventional shape. The walls are stucco-covered, with limestone cornices and string courses as well as simple mouldings outlining the windows. The corners are marked by plain chains of rustication. The dormers repeat the rhythm of the windows below. They have very simple segmental arched metal casings. The mansards are low and obviously of practical rather than decorative significance.

These buildings are cold and dull but dignified. The stone trim is simple and conventional but well cut and well placed. Only a certain hardness and lack of subtlety in the proportions, together with the use of a rather dead stucco instead of good brick or stone for the walls, really differentiates this hospice from many of the finest châteaux of

44

the period of 1650 to 1750. As it is, these buildings are hardly colder than those of the Salpètrière, *c.* 1660.

The chapel, which is the most elaborate member of the group, is almost the least happy part of it. ~~(Fig. 5)~~ . The tower with its pointed domed spire of slate is inadequate and inharmonious as the focus of the general plan. The flat Renaissance detail, of the type of Lequeux's or Godde's basilicas of the July Monarchy, is equally out of scale; the very relation between the parts of the design, moreover, is inferior to Lusson's contemporary church of St.-François-Xavier. One would surmise the intervention of an architect other than the one responsible for the large buildings. More probably, the truth is that in the chapel Labrouste tried to put his best, if somewhat reactionary, foot forward; while in the other buildings the design, whoever was responsible for it, represented a natural expression of the plan in the terms of a vernacular two hundred years old. Little more was thought of it as architecture, probably, than was thought of factories in the early twentieth century in America. To fresh American eyes of the sixties such buildings might have appeared monumental and consequential in design; to Richardson and his generation at the Ecole this would have seemed merely the most obvious way to do the job.

Whether or not the executed buildings are exactly like Richardson's designs of 1862, they cannot be very different. Study of the virtues and vices of the Hospice makes plain the essential virtues and vices of Richardson's French training. He could never have done this work but for his previous training at the Ecole and in the atelier. He doubtless owed the opportunity of working with Théodore Labrouste to the association of André with Henri Labrouste, and to André's own standing in the bureaucracy. But, as Richardson was a foreigner, André would certainly never have recommended him if he had not considered that Richardson had attained full command of the technical and aesthetic rudiments of the French tradition in architecture.

The chief virtue of the French tradition lay in large-scale planning and composition. Richardson's command of institutional planning and

45

complicated general composition stood him in good stead in the Buffalo State Hospital, designed in 1870 at the opening of his American career. But the power to think precisely in plan and to compose in the resultant fixed units of space and mass was quite as important to him in all types of design. Once he had this command in principle he could apply it to the most disparate problems. Thanks to the practical experience he gained on the Ivry hospital, it was no longer chiefly adapted to the symbolic requirements of throne rooms and the lobbies of senates, as it might have been had he never left the Ecole. It was useful, as well, in meeting economically practical needs.

It was at least partly a vice and also partly a virtue that the expression and execution of complicated plans in the elaborate general composition were worked out so completely in terms of traditional masonry construction. The light metal and glass service galleries apparently left little impression on Richardson. Americans who stayed at home and whose first experience was with frame construction in wood were to be bolder than he in using iron. Even his association with Hittorf's Gare du Nord did not arouse his interest in the use of metal.

This was certainly more due to his personal taste for the heavy and the solid than to the environment in which he was trained. Paris in the sixties might have set any young man on fire with the possibilities of new materials. Yet it did so neither in the case of Richardson nor of anyone else. Metal construction took longer to come into its own in France than in America, where the tradition of wooden construction prepared the way. After the day of Labrouste and Hittorf, it was not until the late nineties that French architects were ready to vie with engineers like Eiffel in the use of metal.

A definite vice of French architecture of the sixties was the attitude toward elaboration of design represented by the chapel at the Hospice d'Ivry. Sound buildings were designed from the inside out, but decorative embellishment was too frequently thought out flat on paper without much relation to plan or structure. It was many years before Richardson altogether threw off this attitude in his most mature buildings.

It must be admitted that this attitude was possibly less general in France than elsewhere in the early sixties. Yet, the difference between Henri Labrouste's Bibliothèque Ste.-Geneviève, completed in 1850, and his later work under the Second Empire at the Bibliothèque Imperiale, where the surface treatment is so arbitrarily archaeological, makes it plain that even the conservatives of the day were already almost as tainted in this respect as those who sought more frankly to satisfy the gaudy tastes of the imperial court.

In addition to his work in architecture Richardson attended some courses in drawing in Paris. Either there or in the atelier he learned an expressive draftsmanship at once free and precise. In his later work the ability to develop his ideas graphically in minute sketches of plan and composition was a very important asset to him. This was based on the French *esquisse-esquisse* and was almost completely lacking among his American contemporaries. In his maturity his own primary studies were made almost entirely in this way and then worked up by draftsmen under his careful supervision. At the first, however, he had to do all his drawings himself, and his sure, free style of rendering must have been impressive to clients beside the cold, mathematical hardness or the vague fuzziness which marked the finished drawings of his American contemporaries.[4]

In Paris he must also have developed his taste in painting, at least sufficiently to call later on the equally French-trained La Farge to do the decoration in Trinity Church. This is rather exceptional. Later generations of American architects at the Ecole have rarely had any taste except for the academic style of their confrères there. And whatever may have been the virtues of French academic training in architecture in the nineteenth century, there were certainly none in painting.

Richardson was not, while in Paris, a mediaevalist or a rebel or even a bohemian. He was, as a matter of fact, involved in the student

[4] Improvements in American rendering came in the mid-seventies quite generally as the plates in the *Architectural Sketch Book* show. *V.* Chapter IX, *infra*.

demonstration against Viollet-le-Duc when the imperial administration attempted to force him upon the conservative Ecole. But he was let out of jail by the Minister of Fine Arts, de Nieuwerkerke, in person, since he was so fortunate as to be incarcerated in the same cell as Théophile Gautier. He admired Viollet-le-Duc as an archaeologist and already owned his *Dictionnaire,* but he believed, perhaps rightly, that the tradition of the Ecole would not be strengthened by an attempt to combine its own inherited discipline of rationalism of plan with the Gothic archaeologists' mediaeval rationalism of structure. To judge from the comparative merits of the original work of Viollet-le-Duc and of those who stayed closer to the official doctrine of the Ecole under the Second Empire, he was certainly right. Nor did the value of the training of the Ecole increase when its doctrine later grew more eclectic.

Yet the styles of the Middle Ages were not completely disregarded by the French official world. As we have seen earlier, Guadet, who was one of Richardson's friends and was destined to be the great theorist of the next generation at the Ecole, won his Prix de Rome in 1864 with a project for a hospital in the Alps which was Romanesque. Of this, the chapel at least was manifestly a better design than the more conventional scheme of Labrouste for the Hospice d'Ivry. Other Prix de Rome designs in the next few years by men whom Richardson must have known were also Romanesque. Even within the Ecole and the economic world generally, the Romanesque was clearly an acceptable alternative to Classical or Renaissance design, and considered less extreme than François I. It was certainly more amenable to the first principles of the architectural *Code Napoléon.*

Richardson's life was not all work, although perhaps he enjoyed nothing more than the hard communal drudgery in the atelier at all hours of the night helping his confrères finish their competition drawings for the Ecole on time. He went to such American houses as there were in Paris, notably Miss Edith Mason's, whose Newport house he later remodelled. But there was no such colony of expatriates in the sixties of the last century as in the twenties of this. Without ceasing to be an American, Richardson lived largely as a Parisian among Parisians. This immersion in the actual life of the city, which was in his case eventually economic as well as educational and social, meant that his years abroad gave him a breadth of experience that it was far harder for Americans to obtain later, when the Ecole and Paris as a whole were full of their compatriots. It is a paradox of expatriation that its psychological dangers are increased by mutual association among expatriates. The American abroad who lives as an individual in a foreign land and not as a member of an American colony remains far more American and less expatriated. When he finally returns to his own land he is also able to see it the more clearly for having really seen a foreign land and not merely a group of exiles.

Richardson never felt later, or at least never expressed, any excessive nostalgia for the life of Paris. He knew its advantages and he knew its disadvantages. He knew above all that his French friends who had remained immersed in the official architectural world had never profited as much from their training as he had by going far away.

He enjoyed Paris and he developed there his taste for good food and good wine. As to those aspects of Paris to which he referred as "life" in a letter to his fiancée on his return in the spring of 1862, the testimony about his experience is far from clear. He is anxious to emphasize in those letters his preference for "our old fashioned ideas and ways"—that the new world already thought of itself as old-fashioned compared to the old we know equally well from the novels of Henry James. When he says, "Had I remained longer in France, I fear I should have been prejudiced," we may catch the most delicate possible allusion to wild oats previously sown. But in his later life it is clear that he was instinctively monogamous, with that feeling toward wife and family which Anglo-Saxons so persistently believe to be their tradition when it is really that of the French. Therefore, we may believe in the essential sincerity of the protestations of virtue sent back to Boston.

Amid all the turgid emotions of which English artistic life was so full during Richardson's lifetime, the healthy figure of William Morris stands out, apparently always happy with his wife and children,   III-5

49

but sensual in matters of food and drink and the material stuff of his art. Richardson, about whose private life almost no information exists, must have been a similar type, well adjusted and "old-fashioned," in an age when among artists the life of sex was often even more of a torture than a sin.

Richardson's gusto was simple and objective. In Paris as in his later life, he enjoyed his work and his friends and the simple pleasures of the table. His tastes were never for the delicate nor even usually for the subtle, and his spirit found natural and easy expression in what was material. Paris, despite all tradition to the contrary, has much to offer a man of such character.

PART II

FIRST WORKS IN AMERICA

1865–1870

CHAPTER FOUR

1865-1867

RICHARDSON returned to America in October, 1865, after the Civil War was well over. Although his family had naturally urged his settling in New Orleans and his fiancée and his Harvard friends had urged his settling in Boston, it was to New York that he came. Apparently this choice of New York was deliberate, for he continued to live there until the spring of 1874, although he never had more than a single commission in that city.   IV-1

How conscious he was that to return to the South would have meant a serious handicap, a handicap that would have restricted his career to the end, no one can say. But certainly he was not alone among Southerners in the years after the Civil War in seeking his own future in the section that had reestablished the national unity.

For the architect the practical consideration of working where the biggest and most varied commissions are to be had is not merely a matter of earning the most money: it is the necessary basis for any adequate practice of the art at all. The architect, unlike the painter or the poet, cannot die in a garret in his twenties and leave behind on paper or canvas the rich fruit of a talent for which everything else has been justifiably sacrificed. The architect has not produced at all unless his work exists in solid materials joined permanently together under the conditions of production dictated by the existing economic system.

Richardson, because of his education, and particularly, perhaps, because of those years of his education passed in Europe when his own country was divided, was an American and not a Southerner. Richardson never did any work of consequence in New York. Yet he was justified in feeling that New York, rather than Boston or Philadelphia, Charleston or New Orleans, was the center of material gravity in the new America that came out of the Civil War. If he was, in the end, to do the most work in New England, with which he had the strongest relations on account of his education, his marriage and his later residence and friendships, the work he did there was hardly more significant than his work in Buffalo and Pittsburgh and Chicago.

The centrifugal and disintegrating forces in American architecture, which reached a climax of effectiveness in the late fifties, had been suspended during the years of the Civil War. The architectural design books published just at the end of the War, and, even more, the few buildings built during the course of the War, indicate a suspension of that process of borrowing and modifying and inventing new stylistic types which had gone on for a generation. All the manners of the fifties continued to be practiced down to the end of the decade without important modifications. But the popular Italian Villa and the Swiss Chalet manners of the fifties, for example, although still acceptable in the rural vernacular, were deader in the cities and in the practice of professional architects than the national Greek Revival of the thirties. The Barryesque High Renaissance style and the more academic Classicism initiated by Walter's additions to the Capitol were donning French roofs. Thus they were merging imperceptibly with the newer manner derived from the Tuileries and the new Louvre for use in public buildings and houses. The simpler, more cardboard-like Gothic of the thirties and forties had advanced under English inspiration to extraordinary freedom and complexity, both in ecclesiastical and civil design. It made use of motifs predominantly of Italian origin, grafted on to the underlying English fourteenth century types in the fashion which we have called High Victorian.

The tendency to subdivide and multiply the acceptable manners of design with new borrowings from the past and meaningless differen-

54

tiations and combinations was now definitely counterbalanced by a tendency to gather together the elements of "modern" design under two headings, the English Victorian Gothic and the French Second Empire. There was not a French School separate and distinct from an English School. Indeed, as has been pointed out, the manner that is identified as Second Empire in this country was hardly in as current use in Paris in the fifties and sixties as it was in England.

The same architects, moreover, used both manners: Elbridge Boyden, for example, in 1866 at the Worcester Polytechnic Institute built the Gothic Boynton Hall and the mansarded Washburn Machine Shop side by side. The fields suited to the two dominant manners of design were barely differentiated and the confusion in educational architecture was typical of all sorts of building.

No mansarded churches were built, probably, before the seventies when the French roof became a part of the rural vernacular. Most of the churches were Gothic; the rest were in some late vernacular corruption of the Greek tradition. Only a few represented a rough approximation of the style of Wren, like Bryant and Gilman's Arlington Street Church of 1861 in Boston. City houses, on the other hand, were rarely Gothic before the seventies. Suburban houses might be either Gothic or mansarded, but almost all the country houses of real pretensions must be called Gothic for want of a vaguer name.

IV-2

The French style was urban and parvenu, the expression of a pathetic will to rival the splendours of the world capitals on the part of a rising class of "new men." The connection of this class with traditions of any kind had been quite broken by the years of the War. Their attitude toward aesthetic and intellectual traditions, moreover, seemed to them justified by the enormous opportunities for gain that existed for men who concentrated on the business of the moment and neglected all the supposedly nobler interests of culture. The expression of their patronage of architecture is the official style of Mullet, used for Federal buildings during the first administration of their figurehead, Grant.

The English style, however, was supported by those classes whose attitude and interests remained Colonial, by the church and by the educational establishments insofar as they were not at the mercy of "tasteless" benefactors. Predominantly it was the choice of Eastern gentlemen who still believed in their own gentility, however much their economic interests were associated with the rise of the new North after the Civil War. Such men preferred an illusionary tradition sanctioned by similar British gentlemen to the gilded pomps associated with an upstart Latin emperor. These patrons of architecture were still dominant socially and even, perhaps, economically. They were accustomed to follow English writers, such as Ruskin, and English magazines in general at least as closely and possibly as intelligently as the subjects of Queen Victoria. Their tastes, however, were somewhat less romantic than their fathers had been. They were less well educated than their fathers, if perhaps better informed, and they were cut off by several decades from any sound local tradition of design or construction.

Richardson, by his Parisian training, was in theory better prepared to serve the rising "new men" of the business world. In actuality, because of his temperament and his Harvard associations, his personal friends were rather among the gentlemen of culture. But until he found his personal style at the end of the decade, his relation to the two dominant architectural currents of the day really did not differ from that of his contemporaries: like most of them, he selected a manner from the wide range of either the Victorian Gothic or the Second Empire—whichever the context seemed to demand. As soon as he felt himself established, however, he showed an increasing boldness in attempting to merge the two. So, indeed, did many other American architects of the time.

In retrospect, the modern student has great difficulty in distinguishing Richardson's earliest work from the work around it. His work of the sixties, like that of most of his compatriots, is full of things which may be described either as original or corrupt in terms of the architecture of the past or of his European contemporaries. What is interesting is to see how the quirks of style in his early buildings, each in itself apparently negligible, led gradually to an originality, positive and not negative, which could never be described as corruption. In other words, he turned the tide of stylistic disintegration, at that time only a little less sweeping than in the fifties, and began the process of reclaiming the solid architectural land which had been so largely frittered away by the wavelets of Late Romantic exoticism and pure vagary.

There was never a time, perhaps, in which an architect was freer to create a personal style. Anything, essentially, was permitted, except a return to the Greek Revival. Criticism, whether lay or professional, having given up the criterion of archaeological correctness, which had hardly been applied in America except to Greek forms, was ready to defend or attack any sort of architecture on the basis of metaphysical sophistries without force or widely accepted authority. To return from abroad to such an environment, to be by one's age and one's economic situation a growing part of it, was a stimulus in any field of material and intellectual activity.

Richardson had ambition. He had also the assurance that his training was unsurpassed by that of any American rival. Thus his naturally sanguine character, his strongly personal taste, and his sympathetic acceptance of the commissions which he was able almost at once to obtain were never tempered by a sense of inferiority or of doubt. Such a sense was (and still is) as much an essential weakness in the more cultivated American as a compensatory brashness is a kind of strength in the American who is lacking in formal education and knowledge of the European world.

Richardson undoubtedly felt within himself the strength of genius, a feeling which is often enough the guarantee of nothing more than a psychopathic condition. But Richardson was not in the least neurotic. His genius, to call it that quite simply, was not a cross he had to bear, or a light hidden under a bushel: it was quite recognizable to his contemporaries.

Although Richardson was no mediaevalist and not particularly interested in problems of construction, he had a matter-of-fact and craftsmanlike attitude toward his architectural work. He knew he could do such work better than anyone else—later he was even to charge accordingly. But he knew it with the same simple and unromantic instinct as Poole, the English tailor he patronized even when he was poorest.

Thus, when he began to work, he did not force any greater novelties on his clients than his most conventional rivals would have done. While he was feeling his way, often very awkwardly and with results which must have distressed him very soon afterward, he felt no shame or inadequacy. He had the justifiable conviction that at least he was offering as much as anyone else in America. He knew also that he could only find out in stone and brick what the lines he drew on paper meant.

The first work he did on his return to America was with a Brooklyn builder named Roberts, in accordance with some sort of partnership agreement. There are in the sketch books [1] certain drawings in perspective and in elevation of a French roof with cornices and dormers above a typical three-window city house. These are probably studies for the work in Brooklyn, since neither the character of the draftsmanship nor the type of work can be assigned to any later point in his career.

In Boston the new houses in the Back Bay were by this time predominantly French-roofed, although they rarely showed any other conspicuous marks of the Second Empire manner. In New York the contemporary formula for the brownstone-fronted house was still usually of the Barryesque type. The academic detail was rather heavier and clumsier than that of the fifties, sometimes with a little incised Neo-Grec ornament. These city houses of the sixties, wherever they were

IV-3   [1] Preserved today in the offices of Coolidge, Shepley, Bulfinch and Abbott in Boston. The original drawings from the sketch books are in many cases shown in the Exhibition.

built, had a narrow frontage on the street, generally with three windows. The only embellishment was provided by some sort of clumsy modillion cornice, often continued the length of a block, the heavy window mouldings, and a pediment over the entrance door supported on heavy brackets or conventional columns.

The Richardson drawings (with which may perhaps be associated a quite conventional plan, also in the sketch books, for a city house three rooms deep with hall at the side) show nothing but the plain moulding-surrounded windows of the top storey below a rather clearly articulated cornice with brackets. ~~(Fig. 6)~~ . Above there are three decorated dormers set against a French roof which is crowned with a band of ornament and a decorative metal cresting. The details vary somewhat in the different studies. In all cases the houses on either side are indicated as of slightly different cornice level, although also with French roofs. This suggests that the studies were for a single house rather than for a typical row-house of the sort usually built in large groups on the side streets of New York in that decade and the next. It may be that these were merely designs for enlarging and remodelling older houses. Indeed, a cursory study of the Brooklyn Heights district shows many examples of such remodelling. The house is certainly by no means a mansion and is of a purely American type bearing no relation in conception either to the *maisons de rapport* or to the *hôtels particuliers* of Paris.

The drawing is vigorous and sharply accented, freely done with soft pencil, and yet with all the lines except the curves outlined and shaded with the T-square and triangle. It is doubtful if any other American at the time, except possibly Hunt, could have used so professional and accomplished a manner of rapid sketching. This manner is very similar to that of the lithographs in the French magazine, *Croquis d'Architecture*, which began to appear two years later. The type of detail and the general feeling of form are neither those of the older and still dominant Parisian school, which continued the Neo-Grec of the July Monarchy (with which Richardson, as we have seen, was most closely associated) , nor are they in the more floridly moulded and spiky manner of Garnier, which is found in the projects of Richardson's close friend, Adolphe Gerhardt. The outlines are still the Neo-Grec as it had been modified by the general revival in Parisian residence architecture of the Louis XIV and Louis XV styles; but there is indicated, also, a robustness of modelling which suggests Duc or Bailly more than the Labroustes.

These drawings, of course, are only hypothetically identifiable with Richardson's work for Roberts, nor is it possible, among the mass of Brooklyn houses of this date and type, to attribute any definitely to Richardson. But the drawings are of interest as representing, presumably, his earliest work in America. We may judge from them that he would then have been quite capable of working in the conventional Second Empire style with such distinction as it allowed, had he cared to do so or had suitable commissions been offered him.

After leaving Roberts, Richardson sought work designing gas fixtures for Tiffany's and did some drawing on unidentified projects in office space which he took in New York. He was without resources, but apparently he never sold, as Mrs. Van Rensselaer believed, his entire architectural library. Several books in the library, which has come down in the offices of his successors, Coolidge, Shepley, Bulfinch and Abbott, have "Paris" and occasionally a date in the early sixties written on the flyleaf after his name. It is extremely unlikely that if he ever sold such books he would have been able to buy back later the identical copies. Peter B. Wight, moreover, in the obituary he wrote in the *Inland Architect* in 1886, says that Richardson told him that he sold at this time not his architectural books but only the general library he had brought together at Harvard when he was well off.

In developing such designs as the Brooklyn house sketches, Richardson obviously had no need either of Letarouilly's *Edifices de Rome Moderne* and Viollet-le-Duc's *Dictionnaire,* both of which he certainly brought with him from Paris, nor of the early English and French

60

works on mediaeval architecture which he had probably bought before this time.[2] Such books were an important part of his stock-in-trade which few American architects of his age could have rivalled. He would have been very foolish to part with them; the suits from Poole's might well have been sacrificed first.

Richardson's first real opportunity came in 1866, after some months of inactivity, through a college classmate and fellow member of the Porcellian Club, James A. Rumrill of Springfield. Rumrill had married the daughter of Chester W. Chapin, the president of the Western (later Boston and Albany) Railroad and a leading member of the Unitarian congregation of Springfield. He was able, thus, to obtain permission for Richardson to enter the competition for the Church of the Unity in Springfield, along with several established architects.

At this time Richardson had space in the offices of Emlen T. Penchard Littell, an architect about two years his senior, in the Trinity Building on Broadway. The relation with Littell was in no sense a partnership, but, of course, Richardson must have consulted with Littell to some extent in working on the competition plans for the Unity Church, especially since his Parisian training left him singularly unprepared to design a very Protestant church in a Massachusetts town. But there was certainly nothing that could be described as an influence upon Richardson by Littell, whose own ecclesiastical work is of a colorless Victorian Gothic character not even significantly bad. Littell could have told him that an English parish church type would be wanted, with a corner tower and, since the congregation was Unitarian, without a chancel, if Richardson did not already know this from professional gossip or a hint from Rumrill. If Richardson lacked documents on the English Gothic, as there is no reason to believe he did, Littell must either have had them or been able to borrow them. Doubtless he provided graphic documents showing contemporary

IV-4

---

[2] He would have been little likely to acquire such archaeological productions of the first half of the nineteenth century, all primarily devoted to the Gothic, after he turned to the Romanesque for inspiration in the seventies.

English and American churches of the appropriate size and type. These Richardson himself would hardly have had.

Richardson certainly lacked experience in using documents of mediaeval design. But the almost complete absence of detail, the curiously varied proportions of the openings, and the other features of the Unity Church which have no recognizable English mediaeval precedent, are certainly the result not of ignorance but of conscious intention. Accepting as predetermined the convention of the English parish church type, Richardson modified it—as indeed all his contemporaries were doing, however great their archaeological pretensions—to suit the functions of the proposed building. For this functional adaptation his training prepared him at least in a general way. But his modifications of detail certainly express a definite personal taste also, already quite dissociated from the taste of those with whom he had worked most closely in Paris.

IV-5

The low aisles of the Unity Church are useless, but they are required by an ecclesiastical convention so universal and so strong that even twentieth century architects like Perret and Moser, working in ferro-concrete, have usually retained them. The narthex, on the other hand, is not conventional; it had appeared, however, in the competition for the First Church of Boston the previous year, on several projects which may well have been familiar to Richardson. The placing of the Sunday School room with its axis at right angles to that of the church was probably determined more by Richardson's desire to finish off the mass composition at the east end in the absence of a chancel or an apse than by practical considerations. The arrangement by which the organ is heard directly in the Sunday School room as well as in the church is ingenious and may possibly increase the resonance in an interior without apse or transepts. The south porch and the tower are perfectly conventional. Thus the plan and general distribution of the parts is in no way extraordinary. (Fig. 3).

The general silhouette is also quite ordinary and, like the plan, is less modified from type than that of Upjohn's Memorial Church begun in Springfield the previous year. Of course, the corner tower becomes detached from the composition unless seen against the mass of the church. This is almost inevitable with such a plan. The little gable at the other end of the narthex, with the higher gable at right angles, is inadequate and awkward. The exterior was undoubtedly designed in perspective, as the above considerations suggest. This represents a vital break with the formal French tradition. It is also worth remarking as further proof of this, that the narthex and its buttresses bear no axial relationship to the main facade when seen in elevation.

The general proportions of the interior, with its low aisles, are better than those of the exterior and the whole is better coördinated. (Fig. 5). The focusing of attention on the east end of a congregational and non-ritualistic auditorium has perhaps never been more brilliantly handled. The pulpit in the center is conspicuous without being absurdly high; the two side balconies for the organist and the choir fill up space without distracting attention from the preacher. Finally, the simple, balanced but asymmetrical arrangement of the organ pipes, held by diagonal bands at different angles decorated with lettering and music, forms an abstract pattern in relief of great interest and splendid scale against the great eastern arch.

The interior is much darker than the photograph indicates, but that is not necessarily a fault in a church. The simple wooden detail of the railings at the east end and of the structural beams of the roof is crude but inconspicuous. At least it is very well scaled to the whole, as is rarely the case in more modern Gothic churches. The broad fields of painted plaster, with stencilled borders worked out by Richardson, lack subtlety in scale and color, but are effective enough in the dim light, warm and now mellowed by time. The stone capitals are not badly carved and more French than English in type. The interior has a quality of coherence in proportion, in scale of detail and in tone which even Richardson rarely achieved.

Yet there are several very awkward features, particularly in the photograph, which reveals more than the eye sees easily in actuality. The colonnettes above the aisle columns serve no purpose and are quite out of scale. These, however, are relatively unimportant. The worst feature of the interior, as of the exterior, is the extraordinary shape of the clerestorey windows and their rudimentary tracery. These broad, low openings are certainly the ugliest form of pointed arch, and they are almost without mediaeval precedent even in England. The obvious alternative, grouped lancets, would have changed the scale. Possibly a wooden clerestorey wall with square-headed windows forming practically the entire bay, or even round windows in the existing masonry, would have been more satisfactory. The clerestorey windows are echoed outside in the narthex windows, in slightly less peculiar form. The doors, the aisle windows, and the bell chamber windows are also rather short in proportion. On the other hand, as if to make up for one excess by the opposite, the lower tower windows and the windows flanking the eastern rose are the narrowest of slot-like lancets.

Thus the design of the exterior in which the openings play such an important part seriously lacks that coherence and that balance of parts which makes the interior so fine. The absence of detail on the exterior, and, for the most part, even of mouldings, merely emphasizes this clumsy disposition of the openings. On the exterior as on the interior, the most effective and almost the only ornament is an inscription. This is carved at the top of the narthex wall. The slightly splayed section of the openings with the heavy, flat watertable above, is suited to the rugged character of Longmeadow stone and perhaps derived from the flat archivolts of the French Neo-Grec tradition. But such detail appears ignorant and primitive, not so much because it has no archaeological sanction as because it calls attention by its unconventionality to the worst features of the design.

There are similar minor faults, such as the awkward caps, like children's building blocks, on the front buttresses and at the base of the gables. Iron fretwork accents unnecessarily the peak of the roof. More important, the slopes of roofs and buttresses throughout are so steep that the tower buttresses, in particular, look as if they were slipping. The very high placing of the little windows above the rose is gratuitous and unduly stylized.

Not many of these criticisms would have been appreciated by contemporaries; indeed, it is probable that the contrasted shapes of the openings, which would have been criticized on archaeological grounds and not on those advanced here, had then a definite piquancy. They certainly do enhance the characteristic look of the church and are not unknown in Richardson's more mature work.[3]

To later eyes, the only markedly Richardsonian feature of this church is the rock-faced Longmeadow stone, in the eighties the favorite material of the master's imitators. Yet this was not, in the circumstances, a particularly original thing for him to use. Longmeadow stone and Monson granite (which Richardson used on his next Springfield commission) were the two building stones most available in the vicinity. Upjohn's Memorial Church, then in construction, used both materials in the combination which Richardson was to use so frequently later: light granite walling and dark red-brown trimming. The Memorial Church was, moreover, rock- or quarry-faced, as were most of the Gothic churches built in America since the thirties. Even in France, many buildings were currently built, like Vaudremer's Santé Prison, of rough rubble; or, like the chapel of the Hospice des Incurables, with small scale rock-faced walling and only the trim of fine dressed freestone.

Longmeadow stone lends itself naturally to rough-cut random ashlar and indeed wears badly when it is smooth-surfaced. It would have been strange, therefore, if Richardson had not used his material as he did. We need not recall in this connection the hypothetical impression made on Richardson in his youth by Schulze's Boylston Hall at Harvard, or by the commercial buildings along the Boston waterfront to which reference was made in an earlier chapter.

It is necessary to discuss this church chiefly as an executed building, although Richardson worked on it for several years and there must have been several stages in its design. It would be interesting to study the competition drawings and observe the changes made as the work progressed: such changes were always of great importance in Richardson's later career and often largely responsible for the ultimate appear-

[3] The present tracery in the western rose window came from St. Paul's Universalist Church and replaces more appropriate original wheel tracery.

ance of his finest buildings. Unfortunately, there remain only an undated sketch of the tower and the west end in his own draftsmanship, and, in addition, one very complete study in perspective, also undated. The latter was probably engraved on wood after a drawing by Richardson and is published in Mrs. Van Rensselaer's book. It differs from the executed design only in very minor points. But the tower sketch shows a rather more original type of the fourteenth century Northampton-shire broached spire than was executed.

IV-7

Was the study for the tower, which is perhaps superior to the executed design, made in the summer of 1866? And was the perspective, or rather the drawing on which the presumed wood engraving was based, submitted in the competition in November of that year? Probably not. It is more likely that the tower sketch is one of several alternative schemes prepared after the construction of the church was under weigh.[4] For the draftsmanship appears much more advanced in personal expression than that of the Brooklyn house sketches. The perspective was probably prepared from elevations when the church was practically complete.

Although the interior of this church has real excellence and the exterior is not without quality in the general massing, the whole does not constitute a very remarkable monument. It is superior to Upjohn's Memorial Church built in Springfield at the same time, but not to other churches which Upjohn built earlier, nor to the best contemporary work by Vaux and Withers or Ware and Van Brunt. The important difference is that the Gothic work of other Eastern architects conformed much more closely to English Victorian standards and stood or fell aesthetically by its success in imitating the achievements of the best contemporary English architects. Whereas the Unity Church, if one studies it carefully enough in its context, can even today be considered of interest for its potentialities, or, as the phrase has it, as the work of a young man full of "promise"—an impression as clearly to be derived from its particular faults as from its particular virtues.

[4] The absence of the narthex and the very low proportions of the elevation make it possible that this is a very early study, however.

This "promise," as contemporaries understood it, can be seen all naked and meaningless in the rather poor brick copy of the Unity Church built in West Springfield in 1870 by Eugene C. Gardner. Inferior though this is, it appears even more out of the common run of Victorian Gothic than its original.

Another important consideration with regard to the Unity Church is that anywhere but in America Richardson would hardly have been permitted to design and build it as he did. In France, the picturesque mass composition in perspective, and the avoidance of archaeological detail were used even less in the ecclesiastical work of Gothicists like Viollet-le-Duc or Lassus than in the buildings of more conventional architects like Vaudremer. Moreover, with the light freestone or the crumbly mottled rubble of the region around Paris, the particular sturdiness and rich sober color of random rock-faced ashlar in Longmeadow stone could not possibly have been paralleled. Vaudremer's St.-Pierre de Montrouge is undoubtedly a finer and more mature work, but it should be compared not to this work of Richardson's, finished at the same time, but rather to his work in the seventies to which it is definitely inferior.

In England the rigid imitation of fourteenth century national forms had been completely broken up by the sixties. But very articulate standards of criticism and taste demanded Continental if not English IV-8 mediaeval precedent for all features of design, as well as a high degree of ornamental elaboration and mechanical finish. Less emphasis was placed upon primary considerations of planning and composition and simple expressive quality in masonry. While, therefore, the qualities of Unity Church would have appeared subversive in France, in England they would have seemed to indicate merely inadequate knowledge and invention in the development of a completely conventional theme. Only in America was such a monument actually "promising" both for the creation of a national sense of style and for the career of its architect.

American architecture was so far decadent, that a sophisticated foreign-trained architect could begin almost as a primitive and, by sloughing off the accumulated baggage of the Gothic Revival, take the first step toward new creation. Fortunately, contemporaries seem to have sensed this. Difficult as it is for us to believe, those who saw the Unity Church when it was new, correctly prophesied that great things would be done by its young architect.

Richardson must have sensed as well that his career had opened. For even before a second commission came to him, he married Miss Hayden in January, 1867. They settled at Clifton on Staten Island, a curiously inconvenient spot for an architect whose work for several years was to be entirely in Massachusetts.

Richardson's second church, Grace Episcopal in West Medford, Massachusetts, has many of the virtues of the Unity Church. (Fig. 6). Grace Church was begun in 1867, the commission having been obtained in competition, and the construction of the two must have been almost parallel in time. It is smaller and simpler, with fewer positive faults in design, and yet perhaps of less quality as a whole. The plan follows an alternative convention of the English parish church, very like that used by Ware and Van Brunt for St. John's Chapel in Cambridge. Aisles are omitted, but there is a low polygonal chancel, and the tower is placed nearer the center of gravity of the mass at the north side of the crossing. The interior is low, dark and rather constricted.[5] The exterior, however, is more tightly composed and better scaled than that

IV-9

of the church in Springfield. There is no ornamental detail except for the crude wooden tracery in the western rose window. Almost all that has been said of the Unity Church applies to this equally.

The most characteristic thing is the walling of glacial boulders, suggested by Mrs. Brooks, one of the donors, who had used them for her barn. But Richardson would hardly have accepted the suggestion and profited from it had he not had a personal taste for the strong, the simple and the rough. The trim is of quarry-surfaced cut granite,

[5] The wall decoration is not of the original period, but the Morris patterns in gold, stencilled on the choir ceilings, are very rich and effective. Some of the glass, which is large in scale and raw in colour, is perhaps of Richardson's choice. It has a certain perverse distinction in contrast to the slick later windows.

heavy and massive enough to preserve the scale of the boulder walls and to frame solidly their rather shapeless patterns.

Several times in later life Richardson turned again to glacial boulders as walling materials: in the Ames Gate Lodge, the Gurney house, and the Paine house, all of the eighties. By that time his assurance had enormously increased as well as his command of scale, so that he used the glacial boulders with titanic boldness, almost as if he commanded the forces of nature. Yet, of these later examples, only the Ames Gate Lodge is more successful than this first use of the theme. Like the random ashlar Longmeadow walling of the Unity Church, he did not invent the use of glacial boulders but, finding them ready to his hand, to his taste, and to the purse of his clients, he made the most of them. His clients, fortunately, preferred to have money spent on solidity rather than on fine finish and elaborate detail.

CHAPTER FIVE

1867-1869

BEFORE Richardson was commissioned to do the West Medford Church, his Springfield connections had brought an important piece of work in a field perhaps more sympathetic to him than church design. For he was not a man of strong religious feeling, and the tradition of his distinguished grandfather, Dr. Joseph Priestley, was not one to encourage in him the aesthetic passion for ritual and ecclesiastical symbolism which many very Protestant Americans acquire in the old world.

Moreover, although church building was an activity of the French state, under the Second Empire, his particular training, and Parisian architectural training generally, were in the field of civil construction. There was in France none of that alliance between the leaders of architectural and religious thought that there had been in England, particularly in the previous generation. Almost all the leaders of taste in England were converted to the Gothic Revival. Yet, whereas the movement could never produce whole Gothic streets in London, but only isolated monuments set down in a heterogeneous muddle, in France there was a definite relationship between the official and the commercial branches of civil architecture. This led to sounder urban design as long as the state retained the upper hand of commerce in patronage.

It has been said that the father-in-law of Richardson's Springfield friend, Rumrill, was Chester W. Chapin, the president of the Western Railroad, then largely controlled by Springfield capitalists. Chapin, who must have found the young man's work satisfactory on the Church of the Unity, was undoubtedly responsible for his selection without competition as architect of the new Western Railroad offices on the Main Street side of the old railroad station.

Commissions of this type were not unknown in the practice of the best French contemporary architects. In 1862, Henri Labrouste had built in Paris a similar building for the P. L. M. Railroad. But Richardson could hardly have adapted the standardized sort of building appropriate in the central quarters of Paris to the still rather open Main Street of Springfield. The nondescript character of the surrounding buildings—some of the simplest Greek vernacular in brick and stone, two storeys high, others a storey taller in rusticated wood or brownstone with Barryesque detail; the corner site by the station; all made it easy and justifiable for him to give an individual and monumental character to a relatively small private building. This would have been almost *lèse majesté* for railroad offices in a similar location in Paris.

Two features gave the building importance in the Springfield of the sixties. One was the French roof, used not so much because it was common in Paris as because it was the symbol of modernity in the American commercial world; the other was the high basement with a double flight of steps leading up to the entrance in the principal storey. This, of course, was also a metropolitan symbol, as the contemporary brownstone houses of New York indicate, but it was of Dutch rather than French origin. These two devices made it possible to keep the cornice line low and to design a five-storey building with a three-storey facade, thus providing the needful height without raising the problem of composing vertically in a more or less classical style. (Fig. 7).

The stylistic treatment of this design is, in its way, as unexpected as that of the two churches in the work of an architect just returning from Second Empire Paris. The general feeling is closer to the design of French apartment houses under Louis Phillipe and the Restoration than it is to anything done in Paris during the Second Empire. But the relief of the detail is high and vigorous, unlike the flat quality usual in France in the second quarter of the nineteenth century, while the forms follow quite as closely the palace architecture of Rome and Florence in the early sixteenth century. The total effect is curious. Except for its French roof, the building superficially resembles, more than anything else here or abroad, American work of the eighties and nineties produced by the men who reacted away from Richardson's mature mediaeval style toward the Renaissance.

The design of this building can be explained in terms of the particular group with which Richardson had been associated in Paris and the particular documents he had to work with on his return to America. There was no reason why Richardson in Springfield should vie with Lefuel or Garnier, or even with Richard M. Hunt. Hence, his design, if not colder than that of the utilitarian buildings of the Hospice d'Ivry, is quite naturally colder than the one suggested by the earlier Brooklyn house sketches.

We cannot know to which Romantic English documents of mediaeval archaeology Richardson turned in working out his two churches. It is clear only that he drew little from them. In this case, however, we can place his sources rather precisely. We know that he had brought back from Paris Letarouilly's *Edifices de Rome Moderne.* He probably also had bought in Paris Grandjean de Montigny's *Architecture Toscane,* for it is not a book which he would have needed at any later period in his career. The *Architecture Toscane,* which included monuments of the sixteenth as well as the fifteenth century, is a magnificent First Empire production with brilliant engravings in the best eighteenth century tradition successfully presenting Renaissance precision of form and the actual relief of fifteenth and sixteenth century profiling. The Letarouilly, which was the particular stock-in-trade of Richardson's successors in the eighties and nineties, is, nonetheless, a production of the second quarter of the nineteenth century. Its line-engraved plates have the characteristic dryness and deadness of Restoration and Louis Phillipe vision.

The features of the design of the Western Railroad offices may therefore be described, in terms of their highly presumable sources, as Roman High Renaissance from Letarouilly seen in terms of the stronger relief and better texture of Grandjean de Montigny. Thus, the main storey is indeed a rather fair piece of archaeology in the style of Raphael or Baccio d'Agnolo. The top storey windows represent a sort of corruption of those of the Cancelleria Palace. Yet the way they are tied to the windows of the intermediate storey parallels very closely the treatment to be seen on the Foreign Office-India Office buildings in London by G. G. Scott and M. D. Wyatt.* This design, surely ac- V-1 cepted in Springfield as the last word from the Paris of the later Second Empire, owes almost nothing to advanced contemporary work in France. On the other hand, the chances are very great that it owes something to the work of a leading English Gothic Revivalist forced by a Liberal prime minister to design Palladian government buildings!

The cornice, the basement storey, and the dormers are all of an unusually simple type of High Renaissance design. Their effectiveness is due more to the fine granite of which the building is built than to their particular forms. For in this building Richardson used neither the smooth-faced brownstone of the Barryesque High Renaissance tradition of the fifties in America, nor yet the random rock-faced ashlar of the ecclesiastical tradition as he had done at the Unity Church. Instead he chose the local grey granite from nearby Monson which Upjohn was using for the Memorial Church. However, where Upjohn kept the granite rock-faced for a church, Richardson, with his Parisian habit of thinking in freestone and his French documents of Italian Renaissance design, sought a higher degree of finish. The detail is smooth-cut although rather simplified to facilitate execution in a hard material; the corners and most of the basement wall are heavily rusticated. But the general wall surface is of a quarry-face only slightly rough, not unlike that of the walling of the Ivry chapel. The effect is, therefore,

* This was illustrated in a woodcut in the English *Builder* for July 14, 1866. The *Builder* is not today in Richardson's library, nor, for that matter, are any French magazines containing contemporary designs of the least relevance here; but he must have been able to see the *Builder* currently at Littell's or elsewhere.

73

quite unlike any comparable American work in all smooth- or all rock-faced granite.

The minor vices of the design largely derive from the fact that it was in a sense thought out in soft French limestone and then executed in hard granite. The awkwardness of the third storey window detail, at best too small in scale for the rest of the composition, and the crudity of the diagonal brackets beneath the window balconies, although frequently paralleled elsewhere in work of the sixties done in soft stone, must in this otherwise suave work be due to difficulties of granite cutting rather than to stylistic intention.

But the main fault of the design is the lack of a compositional skeleton underlying the separate features. The two lower floors are markedly horizontal except for the somewhat inadequate steps piling up to the main entrance. The two upper storeys are markedly vertical and almost unrelated to those below, except in the spacing of the openings. The cornice is again very horizontal. Even the characteristic Second Empire brackets or modillions are omitted as not of High Renaissance character. But the dormers are again vertical in feeling, like the roof with its rather mediaeval iron cresting.

Something of the relative purity and coldness of the design may perhaps be attributed to the taste of Mr. Chapin. For his own house, built in 1844, was a magnificent example of the square-piered, wide-eaved symmetrical Italian Villa type. He, moreover, as an older man of Puritan stock and a New England Unitarian, may well have distrusted the parvenu taste for the more florid Second Empire style.

On the whole, the Western Railroad offices are chiefly interesting as showing a rather different type of accomplishment and promise from the churches, and a promise of qualities equally important in Richardson's developed style. The study of the simple outline is good, even if the building is not very well handled as solid mass. There is a certain balance of horizontal and vertical elements, however awkwardly they are combined. The relief is bold, although merely stuck on the outside, except for the rusticated basement. Above all, there is a calm sense of order and of the aesthetic worth of fine materials intelligently if not very personally used.

Most later American buildings in the Roman Renaissance tradition appear flurried and unstable beside this very early and untypical work of Richardson's. Unlike the churches, however, this could have been built equally well in almost any country, particularly, perhaps, in Germany. There, the rationalist tradition of Schinkel and the later High Renaissance manner of Semper combined with the borrowed splendour of the Second Empire to produce, in the sixties and seventies, many similar if slightly more ornate productions. V-2

It is interesting to compare, in old photographs, the Western Railroad offices, unfortunately demolished several years ago, with another Springfield building of the same year which still stands, much modified, on the corner of Main and State Streets. (Fig. 11) . The Springfield Institution for Savings is by George Hathorne, a New York architect, who, like Richardson, did much work in Springfield in the late sixties and early seventies. The design is French-roofed round-arched Victorian Gothic of a type, current in London in the sixties, which Richardson was to approach the next year in the Agawam Bank. The material is brick with stone trim, but castiron piers are conspicuously used on the ground storey. The quality, while inferior to that of the Western Railroad offices, is distinctly superior to Hathorne's later and now destroyed Springfield City Library, opposite the Unity Church. The Institution for Savings, even with its present mutilations, would be far more readily accepted by critics as an early work of Richardson's than either the church or the office building he was then erecting in Springfield. In other words, Hathorne's building makes plain that Richardson's direction was at this time so little clearly defined that others who were to arrive nowhere appear in retrospect to have known better whither American architecture was headed.

All drawings for the Western Railroad offices are lost. But the facade and the memories of Springfield people do not suggest that there were any remarkable features of plan or section. Indeed, a commercial building at this date, unless castiron was prominently used, rarely showed important innovations beyond the increase in height taken care of by the high basement and the French roof. Although Hathorne used iron piers on the ground storey of the Institution for Savings, the first large castiron front in Springfield was not built until 1875, when the heyday of the castiron front was already over. Springfield was unusually conservative in this, for the first castiron front in New England had been built, as has been said in an earlier chapter, in Worcester in 1854 by Elbridge Boyden. The elevator, moreover, introduced in the Fifth Avenue Hotel in 1858, was not used in an office building anywhere in America before 1871, when the Equitable Life Assurance Building in New York was completed.

Fortunately, although we lack the drawings for the Western Railroad offices in Springfield, we still have Richardson's unsuccessful competition drawings for this Equitable Building (probably prepared in late 1867, since the building began to be erected the next year from the winning designs of George B. Post). These show a commercial project of much greater interest than the one in Springfield. The building was to be much larger and taller, with a central light court surrounded by metal supports. (Fig. 8). It is thus considerably more advanced technically than the Western Railroad offices. It also makes clear that Richardson, even though he later did very little to further development, was not blindly prejudiced against the conspicuous use of metal in the interiors of masonry buildings. This is almost the only instance in which he planned to avail himself of metal to any significant extent.

The metal supports, although delicate, are rather complicated in design. They recall most closely the strange forms used by Baltard at Saint-Augustin. For on the one hand they are unlike the classical elegance of Henri Labrouste's Bibliothèque Nationale,[1] and on the other they lack the functional simplicity of Hittorf's Gare du Nord.[2] Al-

[1] Not finally opened until 1869, but undoubtedly known to the architectural world of Paris before Richardson left.

[2] For whose design the engineer Reynaud may have been more particularly responsible.

though the projected use of metal here is not very handsome, it does have a lightness and gaiety more suggestive of French than of American work in iron.

It has been considered a misfortune that circumstances did not lead Richardson to develop his style further in this direction instead of taking a line which was rather reactionary technically. Had he found an engineer of imagination with whom he could collaborate, instead of the sound but conservative builders, Norcross Brothers, who executed most of his later buildings, his work might have been better balanced and more central to the currents of his time. Yet had he advanced in the direction of lightness and openness of structure, the resultant visual effect would undoubtedly have been contrary to his personal taste. It might well have raised havoc with the personal style he was already on the way to creating. The mid-nineteenth century required powers of cultural and technical digestion even more Gargantuan than Richardson's famous ability to absorb rich food and champagne. On the whole, men were justified in limiting their diet somewhat arbitrarily, as did such great English Victorians as Ruskin and Morris.

The exterior design of the Equitable Building project bears little relation to the scheme of the interior. (Fig. 8). It is on the whole a more elaborate version of the Western Railroad offices: more elaborate because it was a project and also because it was intended to be executed, not in granite, but in the nearest obtainable substitute for French limestone—probably Ohio sandstone. The detail is less pure and less archaeological. It is indeed marked by rather arbitrary diagonal forms in the abrupt taste of the times here and in Europe. The design as a whole is, however, by no means florid. Considering the greater size, it would have been in execution rather less vigorous in relief than the Springfield offices. The entrance door is rather low and broad, with rusticated voussoirs, already somewhat "Richardsonian." But the delicate garlands on the top of the French roof recall the contemporary Neo-Grec-Louis-XV ornament of the private palaces of Paris or of Cendrier's stations.

77

The most important compositional device appears on the long side facade where two storeys of windows are grouped vertically under arches between piers. This was, of course, the essential device Richardson was to use in his mature commercial architecture, from the Cheney Building in Hartford of 1875 through the Harrison Avenue Ames Building in Boston of 1886, in order to give tall buildings a satisfactory coherence and scale. The device was known in France, as Guadet's Prix de Rome project makes evident.[3] But giant orders rising above a high ground storey to a main cornice surmounted by an attic served more usually in conventional architecture the same purpose of unifying the composition of tall buildings of six or seven storeys. The giant arcade was frequent in England at the time. There it was used in a more drastic and "Richardsonian" fashion than in Guadet's project, particularly for warehouses. As in the case of the vertical linking of the windows of the upper floors of the Western Railroad offices, Richardson may have seen the woodcuts of such things which appeared in the *Builder*.

V-6

The drawings for the Equitable are very handsome. The main floor plans are decorated with coloured marquetry and there is a fine combination of precision and free assurance in the rendering of the facade with light diagonal shading. At this date Richardson was probably still doing all his own drafting, and beside the tight or mussy renderings of his American contemporaries, his competition projects must have appeared extremely effective, even if they did not win the commission.

In October, 1867, when Richardson's first three buildings were under weigh, Richardson replaced George B. Post as the partner of Charles Gambrill.[4] This partnership was a practical means of sharing

[3] The monastic buildings are not very tall but the arches run the entire height of the wall as they do in Richardson's work not before the Harrison Avenue Ames Building and the Detroit Armory. As Schinkel's project for the Berlin Staatsbibliothek suggests a generation earlier, the inspiration for this device as used by Guadet was in the early Romantic rationalism of Durand.

[4] The competition drawings may follow this event, as Post's winning design was presumably later than his breach with Gambrill.

office space and building up a joint office force. It doubtless had real existence in a business way, but it involved no more merging of artistic personalities than Richardson's occupation of space in the offices of Littell. Indeed, the artistic personality of Gambrill was so dim that almost no glimmer of it has come down to us, particularly as he had only three commissions of his own during the eleven years he was in partnership with Richardson. The drawings which remain from the time of Gambrill's partnership with Post are rendered with an almost mathematical stiffness. They offer a type of Victorian Gothic design so reduced to the American vernacular that they are, if possible, even more commonplace than Littell's work.

Gambrill's Edward Stimson commission in Dedham, October, 1868, was only the remodelling of a Colonial house and singularly devoid of interest. (Fig. 17) . The walls are lined off with a thin, puritanical half timbering; the roof is French, with a curious flip outward at the eaves which Richardson was also to imitate, with more success, from the popular English saddle-back roof. The porch, the cornice and the dormers are decorated with thin wooden crisscrosses hardly worthy of the name of gingerbread. Only the entrance gate, now largely destroyed, has any of the complexity and vigorous vulgarity of design associated with the more lusty vernacular of the time. The walls of the house have of late been stuccoed over the clapboards between the half timbering, and the porch has been reduced to a small glazed enclosure at the front door; but the general effect has not been seriously changed.

V-7

A set of earlier drawings by Gambrill for a house for Mrs. Mary King shows slightly less vertical proportions and wider windows. This project also has an asymmetrical plan and mass not obtainable with the Colonial shell of the Stimson house. Yet, even so, it hardly reaches the level of the Sanford, now Covell, house in Newport, built in 1870 (by a local builder ?) in exactly the same cardboard half-timber style with the same saddle-back mansard.[5]

[5] No documents are available on Gambrill's Jonathan Sturges house built in New York in 1869-70.

The latest Gambrill house, that of Dr. Tinkham in Owego, New York, is hardly more than a simplified version of Richardson's Andrews house of 1872 in Newport. It is even closer to the first houses Charles F. McKim built when he left the Gambrill and Richardson office in 1872 to work for himself.

It is unlikely that Richardson owed anything positive to Gambrill, even at the very beginning of their relation, beyond purely practical information about American conditions and assistance in setting up and training an office force. But, considering the marked deterioration of Richardson's design between 1868 and 1870, it is not impossible that the more experienced Gambrill supported him in disregarding his clients' presumable demands for more conventional Gothic or Renaissance design. As a result, Richardson may have come to feel that American laymen barely knew one from the other; and on the whole preferred the crude to the suave, and the bizarre to the archaeological.

But, by this time, in Richardson's work, the refining influence of remembered European standards of execution in serious architecture had, in any event, begun to drop away. He was beginning to form the habit of depending for suggestions on the poor woodcuts in the English magazines, without any careful critique of what their gashy lines stood for. This loosened up the correct if somewhat personal taste which he displayed in his first three buildings. Anyone who has spent some time in Europe and then returned to America can appreciate the way certain foreign standards of taste drop away after a year or two, just as the power to speak foreign languages goes rusty.

Richardson, if he were to function effectively as an American architect and not as a returned expatriate, had to descend, at least briefly, to the nadir of taste and critical judgement of his compatriots and contemporaries. Only so, when he rose again, could he hope to carry them with him or at least drag them after him. Poor as his first buildings now appear, almost indistinguishable from those going up beside them, they were still too good for the late sixties in America.

This can hardly be said of the house in Boston built for B. W. Crowninshield.[6] This was commissioned in 1868 and completed in 1870. Richardson did not take much personal interest in the design of houses before the late seventies, according to Mrs. Van Rensselaer, but that does not excuse an edifice hardly superior even to Gambrill's Stimson house. The walls of the Crowninshield house are of the flattest, deadest, hardest red bricks, set with almost invisible joints, inferior even to French brickwork of the period. The roof is exactly the same as that of the Stimson house. But it has even uglier dormers.[7]

The bare windows with the single central muntin follow the bald new vernacular type which had come into general use since the Civil War.[8] The windows are tall, narrow and curiously spaced. The pair on the right side of the house breaks the symmetry quite arbitrarily, while those on either side of the entrance door are reduced to mere slots. No mouldings surround the windows, and the lintels above, although elaborately chamfered at the bottom, are flush with wall surface and decorated with the sparsest incised ornament, already more Eastlake than Neo-Grec.

V-8

Amid all this barrenness, which might be considered as a sort of conscious *sachlichkeit* or structural rationalism, there are the most fantastic stubby twisted columns of uncut bricks with sprouting capitals on the corners of the rectangular bay-like projection above the entrance. These are completely unrelated in size or proportion to the contiguous windows. There are also insets of tiles in pale blue and green and white, quite out of harmony with the strong red of the bricks. These tiles are set diagonally in bands at the cornice and in a cross-shaped pattern over the door. One chimney breaks through the

V-9

[6] Like Rumrill, a fellow member of the Porcellian Club at Harvard.

[7] They are presumably intended to harmonize with and merge into the main mass by continuing on the top the slope of the upper roof and by repeating on the sides the slope of the lower roof. This is a laudable enough intention which Richardson worked out very successfully later in his mature style.

[8] This had developed probably as a simplification of the sash windows imitating casements with heavy central muntins, used rather widely in the fifties to replace the Greek Revival nine-pane sash.

V-10

mansard just to the right of the central dormer, while the other chimney seems to be screwed on to the middle of the bay window at the left by a round tile plaque at the base. The two contiguous houses on Dartmouth Street, which may or may not be by Richardson, continue all the worst features of the corner mansion with a clustering of the peculiar dormers above their bay windows which is even more oppressive.

The corner location of the Crowninshield house permitted the use of the typical city house plan, one room wide, three rooms deep, with light from the side and an entrance in the center of the depth. Except for the accident of location, therefore, the plan in no way differs from other ordinary city houses of the day.

Attentive and sympathetic examination of this building may possibly arouse a grudging admiration for its originality, its relative simplicity and the handling of the bay window at the left end as an enrichment of the general mass. But there is no work of Richardson's so little rewarding in aesthetic satisfaction as well as historical interest.

The Dorsheimer [9] house in Buffalo, also commissioned in October, 1868, of whose exterior appearance no documents can be found, showed more ingenuity of plan.[10] ~~(Fig. 16)~~. The entrance was at a level below the main floor. The large living hall was at the rear, opening on a court, with a wide staircase rising at one end opposite a large fireplace at the other. Although the arrangement of this house at the front—two small corner rooms with a narrow entrance hall between—was con-

[9] William Dorsheimer received an honorary M.A. degree from Harvard in 1859, the year of Richardson's graduation. This very possibly established the contact between them. Dorsheimer was also in part responsible for two later major commissions of Richardson's: the Buffalo State Hospital of 1870, and the Albany State Capitol of 1876. He was a leading citizen of Buffalo, a Congressman, and later Lieutenant-Governor of New York.

[10] There is just a possibility that these plans, which are marked "Sketches" and undated, are later and for another house, or for a remodelling of the original one. One is tempted, however, to accept them for what they are worth as indicating that even in 1868 Richardson could do better residence work than the Crowninshield house.

ventional enough, the L-shaped plan introduced a type which Richardson was to develop with much success later. It had its prototypes in the better *maisons particuliers* of Paris with their large rear courts. But the great living hall, with a fireplace ingle-nook at one end and a monumental staircase at the other, was derived from English practice in country houses, if not in city mansions. The large dining room placed in the ell was not unknown in other American city houses of the time.

Insofar as one can judge merely from the plan, even the exterior design must have been superior to that of the Crowninshield house. For the windows on the Dorsheimer house were well arranged in three groups of three lights in the main storey, with the middle one slightly bayed out. On the floor above there are five groups, all of two lights except the center one, which was single and wider. Toward the court there were much larger windows of many grouped lights.

In May of the same year, 1868, Richardson had been commissioned to build the North Congregational Church in Springfield. On account of various vicissitudes, notably a change in site, the church was not actually built until 1872-73. Critics, beginning with Mrs. Van Rensselaer, have attributed the executed design to the year 1872 rather than to 1868, on the grounds of the definitely Romanesque type of detail. This seems to exaggerate somewhat the importance of such detail in Richardson's work. Otherwise the church does not seem so late.

The plan is undoubtedly more advanced than those of the early churches, for it has a large transept, a side porch, and a stair turret on the tower. However, this seems to be a complication and perfection of the earlier plans, in the advance toward the Brattle Square Church in Boston, 1870, rather than a return, after four or five years, toward the earlier type. (Fig. 26). The mass composition is of the English parish church type with the tower near the crossing, as at West Medford, and a pointed stone spire. The roofs descend low on the sides. V-12
This treatment, with the lack of emphasis on the west facade, is quite

unlike Brattle Square or Trinity, Boston, or the Buffalo project published in the *Architectural Sketch Book* in 1873.[11]

The feature which is most difficult to accept as of a date previous to 1872 is the tall stone dormer. But this may well have been added in execution in 1872-73. Undoubtedly most of the carved detail was at that time brought up to the standard established by the Brattle Square Church, although all the detail was not necessarily re-designed later. The flush lintels with chamfered mouldings on the under side were used in cruder form on the Crowninshield house. Therefore, while it is necessary to believe that the more Romanesque forms of the columns, capitals and round arches, as well as the very superior quality of the random ashlar in Longmeadow stone, were all due to the later execution, it is probable that the scheme, with the slight differences the new site made necessary, was essentially unchanged from the first designs of 1868-69.

The high dormer and the blocky Norman capitals may even be considered flaws in the execution of the early scheme, and the round Romanesque arches debatable improvements compared with the very straightforward treatment of the west end and the side porch. This bare structural treatment is certainly comparable in theory, though infinitely superior in effect, to that of the openings on the Crowninshield house.

A perspective study published by Mrs. Van Rensselaer looks almost like the work of an imitator—Stephen C. Earle of Worcester, for example, who copied this church in building the Park Congregational Church in Norwich, Connecticut, in 1873. Round arches are used in the sketch in all the places where lintels appear on the church as executed. No indication is given of the source or the date of this sketch. It looks as if it were a more advanced study prepared at the time of the actual building in 1872 and discarded in favor of a closer approximation of the earlier design of 1868.

The interior of the North Church is bare and unfinished, with a

[11] Vol. I, no. 4, Pl. XVI. The designs may well have been already in existence for a year or two before publication.

very clumsy confusion of beams supporting the barrel-shaped roof. There is too much light, since the windows were never provided with good stained glass. Finally, the space composition itself is careless; as if, in the absence of funds to provide decoration, it had been neglected in the later execution, if not in the earlier studies.

The Agawam Bank in Springfield was commissioned in April, 1869. (Fig. 13). Like the Western Railroad offices, this has been demolished. In this design Richardson broke away from the suavity of his first buildings quite as definitely as in the Crowninshield house, but with more justifiable effect. The mansard roof, the quarry-faced granite walling, the high basement, even the quoins and the cornice, are repeated almost without change from the Western Railroad offices, which, by this time, had been completed and had met with favor. But the character is wholly different. Exposure to the designs in such English magazines as the *Builder* and to the contemporary practice of such men as his partner, Gambrill, had strengthened his natural preference for robustness and weakened his respect for conventional precedent.

If the Western Railroad offices were still essentially French, although not exactly Second Empire in the American sense, this is definitely English, although far from typical Victorian Gothic. The rock facing of the quoins of the Railroad offices is here used for the whole basement storey, with segmental arches over the windows quite in the manner of the downtown buildings of the late fifties in Boston. Heavy rock-faced voussoirs form round arches over the windows on the main floor, but they are too rugged and heavy in proportions to suggest any longer the plates of Grandjean de Montigny. The rock-faced arches on the two upper floors are segmental pointed. Under these arches are tucked colonnettes, short enough under the arches of   V-13
the main storey, but, on the upper floors, so stubby as to be barely discernible except as a mussy confusion of the window outline.

These deplorable colonnettes are happily omitted on the side facade. But there the arrangement of the openings is rather awkward.

This is perfectly regular on the front, with two doors side by side in the center to which low steps with small solid balustrades ascend. But on the side there are three openings in the center as far apart as the openings on the front, flanked by slightly wider wall spaces, and then there is a line of openings near the corners. It is hard to believe that the plans if they were now in existence would make plain any practical necessity for an arrangement which produces such bad space divisions on the exterior.

A string course at the level of the third storey sills echoes unnecessarily the heavy horizontal line of the cornice. This is simpler and more blocky than that of the Western Railroad offices. The roof has a single shorter slope, less subtle and less well proportioned to the whole mass than the taller broken slope of the earlier mansard. The dormers have pointed gables and corner columns suggesting the civil Gothic work of French architects of the time, particularly Duc's reconstruction of the Conciergerie in the fifties. The plates of this in the *Encyclopédie d'Architecture* Richardson may well have seen if he had not observed the building itself when he was in Paris.

But the building as a whole with its square proportions, crude monotonous scale and hybrid detail, is like nothing so much as the type of commercial building frequently published in the English *Builder* in the late fifties and through the sixties. The English examples may be described as Victorian Romanesque or, more accurately, perhaps, as round-arched Victorian Gothic. The Agawam Bank is almost as unhappy a hodge-podge as the Crowninshield house and rather more pretentious and assertive.[12] Beside it, Hathorne's Savings Bank Building represents scholarly correctness in the use of the round-arched Victorian Gothic. But the differences are so great that no influence need be deduced.

Some have thought that the Agawam Bank was important because it represented Richardson's first turning toward the Romanesque. This is unjustifiable, for it is quite unlike any earlier Romanesque

[12] A more elaborate perspective project for this building exists. Because of the richer detail it appears more conventionally Victorian.

work in America or in France and equally unlike his own personal Romanesque style which appeared almost fully developed in his designs of the next year. It is doubtful if Richardson or anyone else thought it was Romanesque at the time.

It is worth mentioning that the City Hall in Springfield (now destroyed) had been built by Leopold Eidlitz in 1854-55 in a very creditable, rather cardboard-like South German Romantic Romanesque. It was one of the newest, most prominent and soundest buildings in the city, well built of brick with Longmeadow cut-stone trim and neat if uninspired detail. Yet Richardson's work of the sixties in Springfield shows no influence either from this or from the more varied Romanesque work of Eidlitz in New York, where he was already one of the leading architects.

There are two probable reasons for this. On the one hand, Richardson, with his French training, was insulated against the achievements of men like Eidlitz or Russell Sturgis who owed their training to Germany and continued to draw their European inspiration from there and not from France. Furthermore, by this date, Eidlitz, like Sturgis, had succumbed to the opportunities offered for work in the English Victorian Gothic and hence his Romanesque work was no longer a matter of current fashion. It belonged with Schulze's work at Harvard back in the old pre-war time, which always seems dim and old-fashioned, however sweet, after a war is over. If there is anything Romanesque about the Agawam Bank, it is a subconscious echo of Schulze's Boylston Hall, itself very debatably Romanesque.

The building, however, has its importance. In it Richardson experimented with boldness as he did with barrenness in the Crowninshield house. Furthermore, while the building might superficially appear to belong, in the broad sense, to the American Second Empire manner, Richardson had now really accepted the hegemony of the English Victorian Gothic. It must have been clear to him after this that the last traces of conventional Classicism, still present in this design, would have to be purged from his style if he were to achieve a consistent new integration. Finally, he had built something not unworthy to stand in the City of London. That was an ambition he could well put behind him.

The few virtues of the Agawam Bank have perhaps been sufficiently implied in analyzing it; but they are more conspicuous if one does not look at it so carefully and so hard. To a casual glance, it must have had certain granite qualities of solid mass and strong regular proportions which tend to disappear when it is studied in detail.

CHAPTER SIX

1869-1870

THE WORCESTER HIGH SCHOOL, which still stands, is an even more painful subject to Richardson's admirers. It was commissioned in November, 1869. As it was not finished until about two years later, even Richardson was possibly aware by the time it was done that it was not a success. Mrs. Van Rensselaer quotes at some length from a letter written to Richardson by another architect when the building was nearly done. This contemporary critic thought that, except for the green tiles (used somewhat as on the Crowninshield house and later removed), the Worcester people would "like it when they are used to it." They are now, of course, so used to it that they have largely forgotten it. But the contemporary architect's other detailed comments—which he thought possibly too subtle for the people of Worcester and which may appear over-subtle even today after the analysis of the two previous buildings—were quite justifiable criticisms.

A worse adjustment of roof and cornice hardly comes to mind. The tarred brick patterns, which fortunately do not appear in the earliest photographs, are worse than "poor and flat," as such makeshift polychromy always is.

They are notably inferior in scale and interest of pattern to those of Butterfield in England, from which they presumably derive. They look like savage tattooings on the bright red brickwork, which is, itself, almost as dead and mechanical as that of the Crowninshield house.

Were they merely a late and drastic attempt to rescue a design already gone sour in the eyes of its creator?

In the absence of drawings it is impossible to decide whether the "corner pavilions are much improved from the sketch." Bad as these turrets are in themselves, and badly related to the rest of the composition, their saddle-back roofs do have the air of being drawn directly from the woodcuts in the *Builder;* hence they appear very feebly superior to the hybrid general composition. It is even perhaps true in the exact formula of the contemporary critic that "the tower promises to be stunning." Much the same type of towers, designed a year or two later for the Buffalo State Hospital, fulfilled the promise.

The prime virtues of the High School lie in its plan, which is very elaborate for a school of the period. (Figs. 19a, 19b). The ground floor has a large "Play Room" in the center, with coat rooms and toilets on either side for girls and boys. This provides gymnasium and locker space taking up one quarter of the volume of the building, an amount amazing at that date. The main floor contains a library and two small laboratories, as well as classrooms and an office for the principal. The second floor has lounges and washrooms for both men and women teachers as well as six good-sized classrooms. The mansard floor has a large auditorium and four smaller rooms.

The exterior expresses almost nothing of this complexity of plan. The entrance porch in the front is, indeed, the width of the entrance hall, and the three projecting flat bays on the rear correspond to the three large rooms on that side, but that is all. This whole educational hive is otherwise merely surrounded by four walls and covered with a mansard. Apparently the process of designing the facades was carried out by Richardson in an architectural vacuum, without thought of the interior. The French roof fits halfway down over dormers like those on the Crowninshield house. The corner towers cut awkwardly through the main cornice, while in width they are less than half that of the end sections of the plan. These useless features are also quite out of scale with the exterior, conceived as a single mansarded mass. (Fig. 14).

The tall and narrow windows in the basement and on the main floor are grouped below segmental brick bearing arches, not elsewhere repeated in the design. The windows of the second floor are single, placed in a continuous regular rhythm unrelated both to the groups on the floor below and to the interior room arrangement. The dormers, at least, repeat this rhythm above the cornice line.

In front of the main mass, and quite apart from it in conception, rises a tall pile of rather effective vertical motifs. At the base there is a reversing double staircase more monumental than that of the Western Railroad offices; then comes a wide portico of three bays with square brick piers, ugly capitals of rather abstract carving and heavy lintels with notched chamfering. These lintels mask real brick vaults behind. Above the porch rises a svelte square brick shaft with thin buttresses. At the top of the shaft a clock is set in a lozenge of black bricks, and, above that, there is a plain round arch of tall proportions filled with heavy slated louvers. Finally, there is a corbel table cornice with minute square corner turrets supporting a very sharp tall spire. This is broken at two thirds of the height by an open wooden frame. Above that is a saddle-back roof like those of the corner towers.

The stairs and the porch, although crude in detail, are not unimpressive; the tower, with its stylized verticalism, is indeed a picturesque tour-de-force. Bell towers of this general type are frequent enough in the Late Mediaeval towns of Northern Europe. Richardson had a purely pictorial conception of such a feature. The tower was evidently intended to be seen from a distance, silhouetted against the sky as in a lithograph or an etching. As such, it must once have been very effective on its hillside site rising above the mid-nineteenth century city. Today, unfortunately, with the tall buildings of the main street rising in front, it can hardly be seen at all.

Such a visual effect was inspired more by the sketches of old towers in publications like the English *Architectural Association Sketch Books* [1] than by comparable French and English projects for modern

[1] This he very probably subscribed to from its beginning in 1867, since the entire first series and the second series to 1883 are in his library. The volumes

work. There were several of these in the *Croquis d'Architecture* [2] and many more in the regular English magazines which he must have been seeing at this time. The measured drawings in books by the younger English architects which Richardson may well have possessed as early as this, such as Nesfield's *Specimens* of 1862, would have inspired a similar conception.

VI-1   The force of Richardson's professional training and of the Worcester School Committee compelled him to provide an adequate educational structure before he sought a decorative silhouette. In his churches there had been no such conflict. It had been easy at once to evolve a picturesque composition and to satisfy the practical program. He evidently did not yet hope or expect to achieve much interest in VI-2 the general outline of his commercial buildings and his houses.

Richardson's increasing contact with his American colleagues and with their favorite English sources, on the one hand, and, on the other, his dimming memory of the atmosphere of serious state architectural activity in France, now led him to seek a new aesthetic goal for which his formal training offered no adequate preparation. Like the Agawam Bank, begun the same year, the Worcester High School clearly brings his period of preparatory work to an end. Only the creation of a personal style could resolve to his own satisfaction the dilemma in which he found himself. He was trying with one kind of excellent training to satisfy practical ends as that training dictated. At the same time he was seeking pictorial effects such as those he saw in English sketches of real mediaeval work, and which he undoubtedly assumed were actualized with success in modern English buildings.

The architect who visited the Worcester High School was able to see clearly enough the vicious symptoms of Richardson's dilemma but

are all stamped with his monogram, but it is impossible to say that he received them as they came out and did not at some later date merely buy all the back numbers, as the monograms, of course, date from the time of the binding.

[2] This also he probably had from its beginning in 1866, as Volumes 1-22 are in his library today, although without his monogram, probably because of a later rebinding. It seems unlikely that he or his successors would have acquired back numbers at any later date.

not that dilemma itself. The absence of intelligent local criticism forced Richardson to find a solution within the resources of his own temperament and training. Such a dilemma, at this time, was common to most of his compatriots. Indeed, for them it was infinitely more serious: their professional training was inadequate and such local traditions as they might have inherited had been frittered away in the previous decade. Yet, in a way, perhaps they suffered less than he from a dilemma of which they were hardly aware. Their architectural ambitions were less exalted and most of them were content to wander into further confusion for another five or ten years until eventually they accepted new archaeological disciplines, or, without much real comprehension, solutions of a type Richardson had in the meantime worked out for himself.

Of buildings designed by other architects at this time only one demands particular mention in this connection. The often excellent Victorian Gothic churches have no great critical interest. But Russell Sturgis, in building Farnam Hall at Yale, really accomplished a tentative resolution of contemporary problems of style. In this college dormitory, the unassertive varied rhythm of the windows outlined by simple brick mouldings is admirable. Admirable also is the way the general mass is enriched and varied with simple projecting features, like the round stair towers on the rear and the porches on the front. Even the ornament is restrained and original. As in Philip Webb's remarkable house in London, designed for Lord Carlisle the previous year, the mediaeval character is inherent in the sound craftsmanship and not superimposed as applied decoration.

Sturgis had approached the aesthetic problem of the day on the basis of his German training, with intelligent reference to the best contemporary English work. The result was not unlike what Richardson achieved ten years later in building Sever Hall, his first work at Harvard. But even Sturgis himself can hardly have appreciated his exceptional accomplishment in Farnam Hall much before he built the contiguous Lawrence Hall in 1883 in a similar manner. In Durfee

Hall and Battell Chapel, built at Yale in the early seventies, he strayed back into more conventional paths of the Victorian Gothic.

If we are tempted to judge Richardson harshly for his work of 1869, we need only compare it with the old Yale Divinity School begun the same year by Hunt, following his second return from Paris. Here, as in Richardson's case, an architect of sound French training attempted to compose within a visual silhouette derived from the English Victorian Gothic, forsaking the conservative Second Empire style he was using with such success in the Lenox Library in New York, 1869-77. In these Yale buildings, of which the whole group was not finished until the early eighties, there is no such touch of authentic pictorial vision as in the Worcester High School; no such groping expression of solid mass and sturdy materials as in the Agawam Bank.

Of Richardson's Cordova Exposition Building, commissioned in November, 1869, executed in wood in New York in the early spring of 1870, and taken down and reerected in the Argentine, no documents are discoverable. The loss is hardly to be considered great. Even in France at this date such a small pavilion would probably have been but a hodgepodge of crude gingerbread, like Davioud's chalets in the Bois de Boulogne. It is unlikely, though not impossible, that Richardson found the resolution of his essential dilemma in such a small and ephemeral construction. As in the case of Paxton's London Crystal Palace, which was an amplification of the earlier Chatsworth palmhouse, exposition buildings rarely offer real architectural innovations. They serve generally as sounding boards for innovations hitherto unknown to the public. Thus, in the Chicago Fairs of 1893 and 1933-34, Academic Classicism and European Modernism were made familiar to the general American public.

The remodelling done by Richardson at the Brunswick Hotel in
VI-3 New York in March, 1870—his only New York commission—is also lost to us.

Several house projects in the sketch books, of which a few drawings remain, must date from the years just before 1870. They are, for the most part, quite devoid of interest. Such work is only identifiable as Richardson's by the personal style of the draftsmanship and the more or less L-shaped plans with very ample living halls like that of the Dorsheimer house.

Of these, only one exists in a form worth discussing. This is a project for a house for Richard Codman.[3] The free drawing and elegant lettering of a sketch plan of this house, with brown-tinted walls and short green shadows, is unmistakably Richardson's. So, also, is the arrangement of the rooms. (Figures 15, 16). The large hall runs through the center of the house, with an enormous fireplace at the rear and stairs rising in a large ell to the right. The drawing room   VI-4 lies to the left and the dining room to the right, with the offices in a blunt rear wing. In many other respects, the house is only too much like Gambrill's work of this period. The roof is of the mansard type, though without the saddle-back flip at the eaves; the walls are sub-divided by thin chamfered half timbering, and, in one of several   VI-5 alternative elevations, the windows are indicated as of the same vernacular type as in the Stimson and Crowninshield houses.

But the project has other virtues beside the excellent plan. The composition is low and intelligently varied. The mansard comes down to the top of the ground storey all around, except for a higher two-storey block on the right. The windows are many and well distributed with small diamond panes. A wide bank of five on the front wall of the dining room is divided only by the width of the half timbering in the best Late Mediaeval way. The half timbering is simple, but not so widely spaced as to be ridiculous. If it is not a part of the actual construction of the house, at least it bears some relation to the under-lying framework. The brackets supporting the porch roofs and pro-jections are chamfered in section and awkward in pattern, but they are simple and not inexpressive structurally.

If executed, this would hardly have been classified with the work of 1868 and 1869 in quality. Perhaps, therefore, it was done a year or

[3] Codman was a fellow-member in the Porcellian Club although he did not graduate from Harvard until 1864.

two later. But the type of draftsmanship and the Gambrill-like half timbering suggest that it must certainly be earlier than the Andrews house in Newport, begun in 1872. Perhaps, as in the case of the North Congregational Church, it was worked over for several years, say from 1869 to 1871, although never brought to execution.

The preparatory period in Richardson's career was over by the time he made the designs for the Brattle Square Church competition in the spring of 1870. At least one more building—the Phoenix Insurance Company in Hartford, commissioned in 1872—was still very tentative and ungainly in design. By 1870, however, the first period of his maturity really began. Thenceforth, he knew clearly what he was attempting to do, and other people began to recognize his personal style, or thought that they did.

Richardson, of course, was not always able to accomplish what he attempted. Moreover, other people—clients, assistants and imitators—must have been perpetually disconcerted to find that they could rarely grasp quite what he was attempting until his buildings were completed. But from the age of thirty-two he was an architect of the first rank. He had relative failures as well as successes, but he no longer produced work which has to be explained almost entirely as the result of undigested outside influences or hypothetical internal conflicts. The intrinsic aesthetic value of his mature style remains, of course, debatable; but after 1870 it is no longer debatable whether his architecture constitutes material worth consideration for other reasons than the purely historical one of tracing a process of growth.

In 1870, Richardson's partnership with Gambrill had been in existence for two years and a half. The arrangements of this must have been quite stabilized. Richardson had also acquired his first assistant, who was to remain with him as an associate all his life. Charles Rutan joined the office in 1869, at the age of eighteen, as an untrained office-boy. He became in time as much of an engineer as Richardson felt he ever needed. He was never a designer. The office had at this time some half dozen commissions of Richardson's in various stages of completion and at least one of Gambrill's as well. In June, 1870, a more effective draftsman joined the office: Charles F. McKim, who had just returned from a brief study at the Ecole des Beaux Arts in Paris, following an even briefer stay in Russell Sturgis' office in New York. At this time, Richardson had been married for three years, and was still living on Staten Island with his wife and children.

These are material facts and they indicate that his life was settled, his success sufficient, and his psychological and professional maturity established and running smoothly when he was thirty-two. This was a not inconsiderable thing for a man who had spent, under great difficulties, more years than most on his education and who had to start again in his own land after a forced beginning elsewhere. Richardson had, however, a buoyant personal temperament and a healthy fondness for the society of others. Fortunately everyone liked him, and admired him for many reasons besides his architectural ability.

Other factors in Richardson's situation in 1870 are more hypothetical, but the evidence concerning them can at least be weighed. First, there is the growth of his library to consider. We do not know exactly what books he had when he returned from Paris;[4] but we can be fairly sure he had none published after 1865 and few published after 1861, the year when his money began to give out. Yet some books were doubtless given to him after he ceased buying, particularly at the time of his departure from Paris. As has been said, most of the English Romantic works on Gothic architecture, the similar French books, such as Taylor's *Voyages Pittoresques,* and various elementary archaeological handbooks were almost certainly in his possession on his return from Paris. He had at least a few photographs, certainly those of Guadet's *Prix de Rome* project and also Gerhardt's, which are dedicated to him with the date 1865.

But Richardson was using his books less and less as he paid more attention to contemporary magazines. There were no real American architectural magazines at this time, and very little architectural ma-   VI-6

[4] Beyond the three inscribed *Paris,* which have been mentioned earlier.

terial was published in general magazines. Therefore we may fairly assume that he saw some English magazines, either in the offices in which he worked or elsewhere. Evidence has already been presented to suggest that he studied the *Builder,* which was the cheapest and oldest, although in many respects the poorest. The only English magazine preserved in his library is, as has been said, the *Architectural Association Sketch Book* from Volume 1, 1867.

Whether he subscribed or not, he also must have seen the French *Croquis d'Architecture.* He was undoubtedly anxious not to lose contact entirely with the French associations which had meant so much to him, even though the work of the contemporary English architects was increasingly sympathetic to his developing tastes.

Perhaps the most noticeable thing about the foreign magazines of the late sixties, both French and English, is the absence of the archaeological documents and modern designs of fourteenth century Gothic style which were the favorites of leading mediaevalists in the forties and fifties. The attention of the younger men, to judge from the material of which they made sketches and measured drawings, had turned definitely away from the High Gothic to the late, and, in ecclesiastical architecture, more particularly to the early Middle Ages. Considering the number of more or less Romanesque churches begun in Paris during the early sixties as well as Guadet's *Grand Prix* design of 1864, it is not surprising to find the early volumes of the *Croquis d'Architecture* full of projects that are Norman or Syrian. Yet there is almost the same predominance of the Romanesque in the archaeological material of the *Architectural Association Sketch Book* at this time. For modern churches, however, the English in the late sixties continued to favor the early Continental Gothic or the English Perpendicular, rather than the Norman or some variant of the Continental Romanesque. Such English executed work as can even vaguely be described as Romanesque is chiefly commercial. It is, moreover, of a corruption comparable to Richardson's own Agawam Bank and Worcester High School or Hathorne's Springfield Institution for Savings, usually with mansard roofs and other modern French features.

VI-7

The healthiest and most promising architectural current in England, represented by the work of Webb, Nesfield,[5] and Shaw, was leading away from the Continental High Gothic favored in the early sixties toward the vernacular Late Gothic. In other words, the most advanced Englishmen were generally approaching the Queen Anne,[6] of which Nesfield's Lodge in Regent Park, built in the mid-sixties, has been considered the first illustration. This hardly appeared as yet in the illustrations of new buildings in the magazines, and it existed only by implication in the preoccupation of the draftsmen of the *Archaeological Association Sketch Book* with details of late mediaeval craftsmanship.

VI-8

It is impossible, of course, to know definitely just which material Richardson admired most in the contemporary magazines of the late sixties. When he went to England in 1882, the one architect in whom he expressed an interest was Burges, who had just died. His interest in Burges may have been due to a vivid memory of Burges' Law Court project.[7] This vigorous and varied design included mediaeval features borrowed from various countries. Burges' version of the tower of the

VI-9

[5] Nesfield's book of *Continental Sketches,* published in 1862, was probably in Richardson's possession in the late sixties, as has been said. When Burges' similar book came out in 1870 and Norman Shaw's in 1872, Richardson presumably acquired them very shortly after their appearance. Although among Richardson's photographs there are interiors by Shaw executed in Chelsea in the seventies, these were probably not purchased until 1882. There was nothing available in Nesfield's book or Shaw's to indicate the particular direction in which these two men, following on Webb, were developing the manner which was soon to be known as "Queen Anne."

[6] The Queen Anne was so-called not because it represented an imitation of the monumental architecture of Wren's followers and of Vanbrugh in her reign (this came only later in the eighties and nineties), but because the latest traces of regional vernacular traditions were to be found in the simple rural building of the early eighteenth century. It was these traditions which the leaders of the movement hoped to revive. In practice, their more advanced work of the late sixties and seventies would generally be better described as an imitation of the Carolean vernacular of the seventeenth century, even though many of the specific features most frequently imitated were actually Tudor and of late sixteenth century origin.

[7] Published in the *Builder* of March 4, 1867.

99

Palazzo Vecchio, for example, Richardson in his turn modified for his Hampden County Court House of 1871. This English architect's simplified Gothic designs for warehouses are also not without their parallel in Richardson's later commercial architecture. When published in the magazines in the sixties and seventies, they may already have attracted his particular attention.

VI-10

More certainly, Richardson must have seen and admired the buildings of Trinity College in Hartford designed by Burges in the seventies. These, although Gothic in detail, are more comparable in spirit to Richardson's characteristic work than anything else of the date in America. Richardson was, as we know from his letters, disappointed in Burges' own house when he went to see it in the early eighties. But the presumption is that he had been drawn to Burges a decade earlier, finding then in the man Kenneth Clark describes as the "brilliant, play-acting Burges" an ambition and an attitude toward the Middle Ages which seemed rather similar to his own. Richardson also saw Morris and the later Pre-Raphaelite circle in 1882.

Richardson was already giving up the style in which he was trained in Paris. He was clearly attracted toward the mediaeval and the picturesque. In looking through the magazines, he might well have felt, more strongly than if he had been in direct contact with French or English contemporary architecture, that for modern ecclesiastical and even monumental work the Romanesque offered sounder inspiration than the High Gothic of the earlier generation of mediaeval revivalists.

The general standards of execution and of taste indicated by the magazines were still so low that Richardson need not have been ashamed even of his own worst productions. It is quite possible to find parallels to all the faults of the Worcester High School in English work of the period. But a new special standard of craftsmanship in detail was being established in England, based on the study of the late mediaeval and even the early Northern Renaissance vernacular. The movement of the younger men was away from mere exuberance and vagary of surface decoration toward integrity of execution.

In associating himself with a general reaction against the High

Victorian Gothic, Richardson had a strength which even the best of the young English architects lacked. He really knew how to plan. He VI-11 recognized in the Norman and Syrian projects published in the *Croquis d'Architecture* designs of a type he had seen in construction in Paris. He knew them to be controlled by the discipline of planning he had learned to respect at the Ecole des Beaux Arts. No Englishman, whether a late representative of the local Classical tradition like Barry's son or Cockerell's, or even his own colleague at the Ecole, Phéné Spiers, could at this period of disintegration have quite the same understanding of this discipline. It would probably have been scorned as academic by Webb or Shaw. VI-12

So much can be plausibly deduced from a study of the magazines of the late sixties. When we come to the books in Richardson's library published between his return from Europe and 1870, we can draw conclusions with less certitude. It is possible that some were acquired only after the crystallization of his personal style in the latter year made them more desirable documents than the earlier books of Romantic Gothic archaeology he already owned.

De Vogüé's *Temple de Jerusalem*, published in 1864, and the first volume of his *Syrie Centrale*, 1865, were, perhaps, bought at this time.[8] Their existence in France, at any rate, sufficiently explains the Syrian character of much of the material in the *Croquis d'Architecture*. Texier and Pullan's *Architecture Byzantine*, 1864, of which the copy VI-13 in his library does not bear his monogram, was probably not acquired until much later and, perhaps, only by his successors. Dartein's *Etude* VI-14 *sur l'Architecture Lombarde* began to appear in 1865 in a French translation, and may have been subscribed to from the first. The French translation of Hübsch's *Altchristliche Kirchen* was issued in 1866 and was very probably in Richardson's possession by 1870, together with G. Rohaut de Fleury's *Monuments de Pise*, also of 1865. VI-15 The first volumes of Gailhabaud's *L'Architecture du V° au XVII°*

[8] But as the second volume did not come out until 1877, the year when the VI-16 characteristic Syrian type of arch rising from the ground makes its first appearance in Richardson's work, he may not have acquired the book at all until then.

Siècle, which began to appear in 1869, may also have been acquired at the time of publication.

Besides these works, all concerned with early mediaeval architecture, there may well have been added early a few less important books of more general or more detailed character, such as King's *Study of Medieval Architecture and Art,* 1868, of which only Volumes III and IV remain in the library, and Talberg's *Gothic Forms Applied to Furniture,* 1867. The only book comparable in significance with the listed works of Early Christian and Romanesque archaeology, is, however, Sauvageot's *Palais, Châteaux, Hôtels et Maisons de la France,* issued in 1867. This is in part concerned with the civil architecture of the Late Gothic and the Early Renaissance. It would thus complement the interest in the sixteenth century architecture of Northern Europe so evident in the English magazines and even noticeable in certain civil projects in the *Croquis d'Architecture.*

If, by 1870, Richardson possessed and was familiar with all these books or even a fair assortment of them, the character of the crystallization of his style which took place in that year is not surprising. The first contact with such inferior English magazines as the *Builder* had been disintegrating in its effect on Richardson's Parisian sense of style, as the first uncritical contact with a new foreign architecture is always likely to be. But books such as Nesfield's *Sketches* of 1862, Burges' *Architectural Drawings* of 1870 and Shaw's *Sketches* of 1872, and the point of view represented by the *Architectural Association Sketch Book,* were highly formative of sound taste. The mediaeval material in the *Croquis d'Architecture* served to clarify the possible relationship between the newer tendencies of English mediaeval revivalism and the less classical side of that Second Empire tradition in which he had been trained. There was never any likelihood of Richardson's going off on the Garnier path of florid Renaissance-Baroque exuberance, which was also represented in this magazine.

Richardson in 1870 was thus in a position to create and impose a personal style of more or less Romanesque inspiration with Late

Gothic overtones such as actually began to take form in his work at this date. He knew himself to be successful and capable of pleasing clients with almost anything he cared to offer them. Thus he could safely break away from the repetition of the formulas which were most respectable. He had learned the possibility of picturesque perspective composition in his churches and of sober dignity in his civil buildings. His first attempts to combine the two had been unsuccessful, as he undoubtedly knew better than anyone else. But he had found out certain essential things about his personal tastes: above all, that they could not be satisfied in the slipshod fashion which served most of those around him. He wanted rugged masonry, and he knew it could be better obtained with American building materials than with French. He wanted polychromy, but he already began to suspect that it could not be obtained in monumental building merely by daubing bricks with tar or sticking on colored tiles.[9]

He aimed to develop plans for complicated buildings which were symmetrical and functional in the French tradition, and he knew now that this would not produce the picturesque mass composition possible to free design in perspective in the English tradition. After the Worcester High School, it was clear that the difficulty could not be solved by the arbitrary imposition of a pictorial silhouette on a symmetrical plan. Both elements would have finally to be accommodated to one another without sacrifice of their individual virtues.

Essentially, Richardson's difficulties at the end of the sixties were those of all his compatriots who tried to found a personal or a national style and were not content to work arbitrarily in the Victorian Gothic at one time and in the equally Victorian Second Empire at another. The problem of the day was to combine two contradictory manners that were both justly admired, however badly they were imitated. More than this, the problem was to establish an architecture that was not merely new and different: everyone could and did experiment with the new and different until, in America, originality in architecture

9 Although he did that once again, more chastely, on the Phoenix Building in Hartford designed in 1872.

received a bad name which it has hardly lost yet. What Americans really sought in 1870 was not so much the novel or the peculiar manner they generally achieved, but something aesthetically sound and yet distinguished by its own life and power of development.

The relative modernity of Wight's Mercantile Library in Brooklyn, completed in 1869, or of Hammatt Billings' Cheney House in South Manchester, Connecticut, done in the same year, would hardly have been possible in the fifties. But neither the High Victorian Gothic of the one nor the simple mansarded style of the other is of greater significance or excellence than the work in the earlier Gothic or Renaissance manners which had lasted through from the fifties. The favored new manners of the late sixties, moreover, had not at all advanced in the early seventies before the panic of 1873 brought the post-war building boom to an end. Except in Richardson's work—then at its lowest point in quality and intrinsically inferior to the buildings just mentioned—or in Sturgis' Farnam Hall, there was nothing new in American architecture which held promise for the future. The only encouraging sign was the complete confusion and disintegration of the vernacular, which Richardson was not the only trained and sophisticated architect to share. From such an abyss there was no way out except upward.

VI-22

Only Richardson found in the early seventies a means of combining the disparate and even contradictory qualities the age demanded. The taste, not merely of seventy-five years later, but, more significantly, of ten years later, rejected all but Richardson's work of these years, on the basis of everything known of the great architecture of the past and everything hoped for in a great national architecture of the future.

Richardson alone was able to enter the depression of the mid-seventies with other ideals than those to which the nation turned at the end of the Civil War. He thus did not have to spend the years of relative inactivity in penitence and undirected experimentation on paper. For it is in such ways that most architects, who, by the accident of circumstances, have been the profiteers of a boom, are forced by the retributive forces of economics to occupy themselves during a depression. Richardson, on the other hand, could devote himself to the amplification and the perfection of a personal style first formed during the last years of prosperity.

PART III

EARLY MATURITY

1870–1877

CHAPTER SEVEN

1870-1871

RICHARDSON was very fortunate in the opportunities that came to him in 1870. He won two out of the three competitions he entered. As indicated by the relative inferiority of the Phoenix Building in Hartford, designed in 1872, he would not yet have been ready to find his way out of his difficulties in every type of work. But churches, public institutions and civic buildings presented problems for which he had either experience or special training.

His Brookline Town Hall competition project, which failed to win, should be discussed first: the other two buildings designed in this year were undoubtedly modified in execution in the following years. The Brookline design is known to us only from a small perspective sketch in Mrs. Van Rensselaer's book. (Fig. 17). The massing is picturesque and even asymmetrical in detail. The late mediaeval silhouette is really the outline of the whole building and not merely of an attached tower, as at Worcester. The central part of the facade has a low loggia of pointed arches above which are the mullioned windows of the principal hall. This arrangement follows a conventional French scheme and is obviously suited to the function of the building. Over this broad central section of the facade, a curved saddle-back hip roof rises from a heavy corbelled cornice to the belfry crowning the ridge. A great stone-mullioned dormer breaks the front of this roof. The side sections of the facade have plainer cornices at a lower level and flatter roofs. A large corbelled chimney on one side balances a corbelled turret above a stone balcony on the other. High pointed gables rise from the middle of each of the end facades.

Such a design might almost have appeared in the *Croquis d'Architecture* at about this time.[1] It would, in a general way, have been suitable for an Hôtel de Ville in Northern France. The asymmetry of the corner motifs, here quite incidental, would, however, have been avoided in France; the detail might well have been French Renaissance or even Louis XIII rather than Gothic. There is little specific English influence in this project; the planning and the resultant massing are too compact, the scale is too large, and the asymmetry too superficial. The modification of the French type is more personal than Victorian Gothic.

The design is most Richardsonian in the indication of rugged masonry and simple dark and light polychromy. But the breadth of treatment and the lack of dependence on carved detail for interest are also characteristic. Significant, too, is the essential unimportance in the total effect of the documents from which he casually drew. This total effect is not Romanesque, except in feeling, and the elements borrowed from the High Gothic and the Late are so stylized as to be barely recognizable. This Town Hall, if executed, would undoubtedly have been worthy of Richardson's canon as his earlier works are not. Even more than in the case of the Codman house it is a real loss to the sum of his work that this project was never carried out, particularly since the execution would have covered several years, and he would undoubtedly have improved the design in many particulars.

The first competition which Richardson won in 1870 was for the Brattle Square Church. This was to be erected on a prominent corner of Commonwealth Avenue in the new Back Bay district of Boston. It offered a much greater opportunity than the two churches he had built
and the third which he had already designed but did not execute until

---

[1] Compare, for example, the project by A. Lalanne for a Petit Hôtel de Ville in *Croquis d'Architecture*, 1868, Vol. III, no. 12, Fig. 5.

1872-73. The demands it made upon the architect were greater; so was the publicity which would follow if it were a success.

The setting of the Brattle Square Church resembled those of the churches on the new boulevards in Paris rather than the settings of Richardson's earlier work in semi-suburban Springfield and West Medford. But whereas the Paris churches were assured of a main frontage on the boulevards and were often isolated by streets at either side to emphasize their character as public monuments, this site was a corner one so shaped that it was natural to place the entrance on the side street. The corner placing of the tower, which the site suggested, and the resultant asymmetrical mass composition, intended to be seen in perspective, were, however, no longer unfamiliar to Richardson. By this time, indeed, such a site was probably more sympathetic to him than one in the middle of a block. He may or may not have liked the houses that were going up in the vicinity (they were hardly inferior to his own Crowninshield house which was just reaching completion nearby) : the scale of his church and the isolation offered by the corner site made it possible to disregard them.

Except for Bryant and Gilman's Arlington Street Church of 1861, which followed the style of Wren and Gibbs, the new Boston churches of the sixties in the Back Bay were all Gothic. They usually occupied corner sites and had walls of Roxbury Puddingstone with yellow sandstone trim and a little brownstone for accents, like Ware and Van Brunt's St. John's in Cambridge. In using these materials, rather than the Longmeadow stone of the Springfield church or the boulders of the Medford church, Richardson was merely following the practice he had already established of availing himself of local materials.

The Brattle Square Church was definitely Romanesque in character and not Victorian Gothic, the first work of Richardson's of which this may be truly said. The talented and rather obscure A. C. Martin also used Romanesque detail in this year in designing the First Church, Congregational. The chances are, considering the distinctly personal VII-3 character of the work of both, that there was no influence either way. Except for the pointed arches on the Brookline Town Hall project,

Richardson had used no real Gothic forms before except in his churches. Round arches of mediaeval, if scarcely Romanesque, character had been prominent on both the Agawam Bank and the tower of the Worcester High School. He had also shown, on the Crowninshield house and the Worcester High School, a distinct fondness for heavy masonry lintels flush with the wall surface and heavily moulded beneath. Similar lintels are prominent on the Commonwealth Avenue facade of the new church. (Fig. 18).

The Romanesque detail on the Brattle Square Church is anything but scholarly. Its sources, where ascertainable, are usually modern. If Richardson already possessed the works on early mediaeval archaeology mentioned at the end of the previous chapter, he certainly did not copy their plates very accurately. The capitals of the front porch are rather cold and regular in design, although cut with a certain vigor. In conception they represent a somewhat Neo-Grec stylization of Norman types, but they were evidently executed by workmen trained to imitate the naturalism of the Victorian Gothic. The cutting underneath the lintels is mostly a meaningless notching similar to but simpler than that used at Worcester. The prototypes of this detail are perhaps to be sought as much in crude Norman work as in the English Victorian Gothic, but the effect is certainly not characteristically Romanesque. The solid panels at the top of the lintelled windows are apparently a device to use windows of a certain size and yet obtain a taller unit of composition, a French rather than an English type of fudging. This may have a specific foreign prototype, but it is certainly not mediaeval. The cross of pilasters applied over the tracery of the rose window on the front was used by Daumet on the facade of the Sanctuary of the Ecce Homo in Jerusalem.[2]

The other rose, with its clumsy plate tracery, recalls the Norman rose added in the restoration by Lord Grimsthorpe of the south

[2] Published in *Croquis d'Architecture*, 1866. Vol. I, no. 9, Fig. 1. As it appears again on Leclère's Grand Prix design of 1868 for a Calvary, the motif was evidently conventional in the Second Empire Romanesque and already familiar to Richardson in Paris. The Norman detail mentioned above can also be closely paralleled in French work of the sixties.

transept of St. Albans Cathedral in England. The plate tracery at the top of the tower arches is equally rudimentary if less crude. The simple but very vigorous corbelled cornice of the tower is an Italian mediaeval motif frequently reflected in more Gothic guise in the work of Burges and others in England. The other features of the detail are equally removed from the exact imitation of ancient Romanesque forms and can usually be paralleled in such contemporary French Syrian-Romanesque work as Vaudremer's St.-Pierre de Montrouge. (Fig. 2). This was begun well before Richardson left France, and was furthermore presented in many plates in the *Croquis d'Architecture* after its completion in 1867.

If this detail were all that was new about the Brattle Square Church, it would be of little more importance than Martin's First Church in Cambridge—a mere Romanesque variant of the dominant Victorian Gothic. Its highly individual quality does not even derive from the use of materials. (This is, indeed, less rugged and less insistently stony than on the previous churches or even the Agawam Bank.) The significant character of this church derives from fundamentals. These fundamentals are what distinguish one style of architecture from another: the proportions of exterior mass and of interior space; the relative importance and placing of the elements, structural and ornamental, which break up the main surfaces.

The interior is very different in spatial effect from those of the Unity Church and Grace Church, West Medford. Not only is the plan cross-shaped—a short nave provided with transepts of the same width and almost no chancel, as at the North Church; in addition, the walls are rather high. This allows plenty of room for galleries, which were added in 1884 to improve the acoustics, as Richardson had from the first suggested. The timber trusses of the ceiling are simple and structural in design.

The geometrical simplicity of the nave and cross arms offers a monumental interior admirable for a Protestant service and more interesting than the plain aisled rectangle of the Unity Church. Whatever Richardson may have planned in the way of wall paintings to com-

VII-4

plete this interior, thanks to the fact that the Brattle Square congregation found themselves unable financially to complete the church there is nothing today but magnificent space, a prime architectural quality which few appreciate unembellished. The First Baptist congregation, who later acquired it, merely added the galleries and a Sunday School wing at the rear. The pulpit and organ treatment, although probably original, is rather bare.

The exterior mass of the church encloses simply and clearly the interior space. A roof of moderate pitch limits the mass at the top, framing the great rose windows to perfection. The high walls have no buttresses or other projections to break the continuity of the surfaces. These wall surfaces, of quarry-faced Roxbury Puddingstone laid in random ashlar, are more beautiful than those of other contemporary churches because they are larger and plainer. Victorian Gothic walls were in general badly cut up by structural and ornamental features. The subdued chord of mottled grey-orange walling and grey-beige trim, with occasional accents of darker and lighter sandstone in the broad banded arches, produces a distinctly finer effect than the stern masonry of the earlier churches or the violent, cheap polychromy of the Worcester High School. Yet the means are more conventional. The very crudeness of the detail has its value, for such detail distracts the eye less from the main pattern of openings in the plain wall and the varied texture and color of the Puddingstone.

Around the main mass are grouped subsidiary features, more elaborately detailed since they are nearer the observer's eye. The arched porch on the front and the small pavilion at its left end, which is better designed and more French, are not very striking except in the use of Romanesque detail.

The most conspicuous feature is properly the tower. (Fig. 25). It occupies the actual corner in plan and forms the climax of the perspective silhouette. This tower has always been more admired than the church as a whole. Indeed, in 1881, money was subscribed by a group of citizens to preserve it for the city of Boston, whatever might become of the rest of the fabric.

The relations between the church and the tower are somewhat tenuous. But, since the model is obviously the completely detached Italian campanile, and not the English parish church steeple, the fault in this relationship lies, not with the general mass of the church, but with the tower itself, which should be more isolated. The tower is open at the base to provide an inappropriate and perfectly useless carriage porch. Yet this tower, of course, even more than that of the Worcester High School, is really meant to be seen alone and from a distance. Then the carriage porch at the base and the awkward relationship to the church are no longer noticeable.

The upper half of the tower is an extremely ingenious and original creation. The great belfry arches in two orders are perfectly scaled to the whole and yet very like those on the Worcester tower. The frieze of the Sacraments, with trumpeting angels at the corners, was modelled by Bartholdi after a sketch by Richardson and executed *in situ* by Italian carvers. Bartholdi was certainly not the equal of Rude or Carpeaux as a sculptor; but the effect of this particular sculpture, considering the scale and the distance from which it must always be seen, is equal to that of Rude's Marseillaise on the Arc de l'Etoile or Carpeaux's Dance on the Paris Opéra. The gilded metal trumpets of the angels, who give the church its popular name of the Holy Bean-blowers, accent the corners of the silhouette against the sky in the most brilliantly picturesque manner conceivable.

Yet on top of this frieze Richardson successfully returned to the simplicity and structural quality of the lower part of the tower. Above the strongly shadowed corbel table there is a plain roof of moderate pitch, not quite a flat Italian roof and certainly not a Gothic spire.

Although Richardson never did anything much like the Brattle Square Church again, here he turned the corner of his career.[3] The rest of his great work could easily follow from this beginning. All the analysis which has preceded, however, does not in the least explain

---

[3] There is, in the magnificent plain side wall toward the alley, a horizontal group of windows with light metal posts supporting the long lintel. This ranks high as a technical innovation, but is quite without parallel in his later work.

how this masterpiece came to follow so closely after the Worcester High School. At any rate, it was the remarkable impression made in Boston by the Brattle Square Church which at once brought Richardson an invitation to enter the important competition for Trinity Church.

The competition for the Brattle Square Church was won in July, 1870. Its construction went on during several years. In the absence of competition drawings it is impossible to say if the present design was effectively settled upon from the first. Probably the project was considerably modified and improved in 1871 before the construction was really under weigh. It is somewhat curious, therefore, that the admirers of Charles F. McKim have never claimed that the crystallization of Richardson's style in this church was due, at least in part, to the influence of this young assistant who entered Richardson's office in June—after the competition designs had been sent in but before the results were known.

McKim was not just an untrained office boy like Rutan. He had behind him a Harvard education, a brief experience in Russell Sturgis' office in New York, three years of study at the Ecole des Beaux Arts, and, in addition, more travelling, particularly in England, than Richardson had been able to afford. He returned to America on account of the Franco-Prussian War. Richardson already expected to win the Brattle Square competition and was glad to take him on because such well educated draftsmen were unknown in America. McKim probably selected Richardson's office because only there or in Hunt's would the advantages of his education be fully appreciated. He was placed in general charge of the drawings for the church, and he might, therefore, have had almost as much authority as Richardson had when he studied the Hospice d'Ivry for Théodore Labrouste.

McKim came direct from Paris and undoubtedly refreshed Richardson's memory of what his French colleagues and friends were doing. He was also a more convinced mediaevalist and readier to accept the full gospel of Viollet-le-Duc. More familiar with contemporary English architecture than Richardson, and for a long time afterward more

VII-5

VII-6

influenced by it, he could correct the impressions Richardson drew from contemporary English architectural magazines with his knowledge of what the new buildings in England actually looked like.

Richardson was nine years older than McKim, already distinctly successful, and with a marked personal taste which had by this time profoundly modified even the stylistic discipline he brought home from France. McKim's personal tastes did not fully develop before the eighties. In 1870, they were negative and critical rather than positive and creative. It is hardly likely that in the two years before McKim branched out on his own he should have directed the main line of development of Richardson's art. Yet the more professional quality of the work of 1870-72 is probably due in considerable part to the fact that in McKim Richardson had at last a properly trained draftsman who, in the French fashion, knew how to translate sketched ideas of plan and facade composition into finished drawings. In the previous years all the drafting was either done by untrained assistants, or by Richardson himself, never a happy arrangement for a designing architect who must deal primarily with his problem as a whole.

The other commission which Richardson obtained in competition in the seventies was no less important than that for the Brattle Square Church. But the execution dragged out over a long period of years and the history of it is more complicated even than that of the church. Fortunately the existence of many drawings make it possible to know VII-7 with some accuracy the changes that were made from the original competition project. This commission was for a large lunatic asylum in Buffalo, now known as the State Hospital, according to the present-day euphemism. The programme was comparable in scale to that of the Ivry Hospice des Incurables, and was of the type for which Richardson's training particularly prepared him.

If, in the Brattle Square Church, he could return so successfully from the unfamiliar English Gothic formula to something nearer the Romanesque churches of the Second Empire of Paris, it would seem as if for this project he had only to adapt to American conditions the type of institutional design of which he saw so much in Paris. Something might perhaps have been expected comparable to Vaudremer's excellent and more or less Romanesque Santé Prison, to which the *Croquis d'Architecture* had devoted its plates for years. But if Vaudremer was the most Richardsonian architect of France, Richardson was by no means an imitator of Vaudremer. He may not even have admired his work. At any rate, the Buffalo State Hospital, as executed, is far less like the Durandesque Romanesque of Vaudremer's prison than the Brattle Square Church is like St.-Pierre de Montrouge.

The general plan of the State Hospital, adopted by the managers on August 25, 1870, and approved by the governor on September 16, is practically identical with the executed buildings: a main central pavilion in front, flanked by receding wards like a V of birds in flight. (Fig. 19). The wards are T- and H-shaped and connected by quarter-circle galleries. The low service buildings form a subordinate group in the court at the rear.

This general plan was determined by Dr. Joseph P. Gray, the head of the existing State Lunatic Asylum in Utica. According to tradition, it was based on the scheme of similar French institutions. It also follows very closely that of the older buildings of the Connecticut State Hospital in Middletown, begun in 1867 by Sloan and Hutton, and it VII-8 was therefore of a type already known in this country. Although the institution in Middletown has mansard roofs and Renaissance (*sic*) detail, it is of random ashlar in Portland brownstone, the natural building material of the region. It is possible that the material as well as the plan used in Buffalo may have been suggested by the earlier Connecticut buildings.

The site had been given by the city of Buffalo in 1869, and the committee of ten managers was appointed by the governor and authorized to proceed in obtaining an architect in April of the following year. The board first met on May 26. The competition for an architect, if it was a competition, must have been highly informal. It was decided almost at once that Richardson should be the designing architect—probably at the suggestion of Dorsheimer, whose house he was just completing—and that A. J. Warner of Rochester should be the supervising architect.

The two apparently prepared the first plans together. F. L. Olmsted, who was to determine the placing of the group on the terrain and lay out the grounds, inspected the site together with Richardson and Warner, in January, 1871. At the same time they entertained proposals for the building stone. This was to be a brown sandstone from Hulburton Quarry in Orleans County: more like the Portland stone used in Middletown for the Connecticut State Hospital than the Longmeadow stone Richardson had used in Springfield. Excavation started in June, 1871.

By the end of that year the plans and elevations were definitely determined upon, in the form illustrated in the *Proceedings in connection with the Ceremony of Laying the Cornerstone,* September 18, 1872. This differs hardly at all from what was eventually executed. At the time of the laying of the cornerstone, the walls of the main building and the first two wards to the right were laid to the top of the basement. These were the only three units for which complete plans had then been finished.

In this same year, for the sake of economy—the three pavilions under construction were expected to cost about $3,000,000—it was decided to substitute brick for brownstone in building the three outer pavilions. When the pavilions on the left side were built, the two nearest the main building were of stone, the others of brick. This repeated the scheme of the first half, which had been completed in the main by 1878. Patients were not received until 1880 and the formal opening of the main building did not take place until November 15, 1881. Even then, however, all the left hand pavilions were not finished, although these followed, without modification, the design of those built through the seventies.

In examining this group of buildings today we are thus not seeing a design of the summer of 1870 carried at once into execution. But since the lithograph in the *Proceedings* of September 18, 1872, differs from the executed design only in the change to brick for the outer pavilions, we can be sure that, however long the execution eventually took, the final design is at the latest of early 1872 and probably of 1871.

There is, however, a general elevation which almost certainly belongs with the general plan of 1870. It is rather crudely drawn on tracing cloth and probably was not the one submitted to the committee. (Fig. 20). In the design of the side pavilions this shows many of the worst peculiarities of the vernacular Victorian Gothic, in a form as corrupt as on the Worcester High School, if somewhat bolder.

The central pavilion is distinctly French, however, with its large rose window, not dissimilar to those of the Brattle Square Church, and its compact if clumsy mass. It suggests the chapels that often form the central unit of similar Second Empire public institutions.[4]

The next group of drawings, probably of 1871, is for the main building and the first two side wards only. These show no important general changes in plan. There is, however, a marked change in the entire conception of the central unit, and also a notable simplification of the design of the side units. The material was apparently not decided upon at the time of the earlier general elevation, but it is here indicated as of rough-faced random ashlar. (Fig. 21). The main building in these drawings is designed vertically and looks like an administration unit and not a chapel. The center of interest in the elevation is the entrance loggia of three round arches set between slightly projecting side bays. Two towers, which vary considerably in design, are set back at the sides of the mass. They are the dominating features of the three-dimensional composition.

The windows all have flat lintels and stone mullions of late Gothic character. There are relieving arches only over the three grouped windows in the end bays on the ground floor. The windows of the second and third floors in the center of the elevation are joined to-

[4] A. Vaudoyer's project for a Hospice de Refuge pour la Vieillesse, in *Croquis d'Architecture*, 1869, Vol. III, no. 11, Fig. 4, is very typical. The use of the Romanesque, at least, for the decorative features of the central unit, was quite as frequent in France at this time in such institutions as in churches, as has been indicated in Chapter II.

gether vertically. The main mass and the towers have machicolated cornices and a sort of *chemin de ronde* with square openings. In the central dormer there is a small rose window.

The left hand tower is a more chunky version of the Late Gothic type used at the Worcester High School, with two large lintelled lights under a segmental bearing arch. The corner turrets at the level of the *chemin de ronde* are round instead of square. The right hand tower has a stone coping around a flat platform and only one large square corner turret with a pointed roof. This rises to the height of the roof of the other tower. This elevation was doubtless actually drawn by McKim, but there exist two sketches by Richardson himself for the two towers. These are in the vigorously free but geometrical style of the study for the tower of the Church of the Unity. VII-9

In this stage of the design the heavy barge boards on the side pavilions are omitted, and the window forms are harmonious with those of the main building. The window panes throughout are small diamonds like those on the Codman house project.

The executed design which appears fully developed in the lithograph in the *Proceedings* of September, 1872, does not modify the essential conception as shown in the drawings just discussed. But there are many minor changes and a general simplification and adjustment of scale throughout. Instead of the incidental asymmetry of two towers, which balance but do not match, there are two similar towers with round corner turrets, and three mullioned lights without bearing arches. This is a distinct improvement. (Fig. 22).

Instead of a single gabled dormer with a rose window in the center, there is a large dormer with a hip roof flanked by two smaller side dormers of similar character. The windows of these descend into the *chemin de ronde,* and are covered with lintels and decorated with light engaged colonnettes. They are even joined together by lintels and colonnettes. This arrangement, which owes something to the François I style, is rather fussy and too small in scale for the rest of the composition. Perhaps it is an emendation by McKim.

The windows of the central portion of the facade are no longer tied together vertically. Thus, they are better related to the more domestic scale of the wings. Only those of the third floor have segmental arches. The lintels of the other windows have lost their prominent depending ears. This is typical of the corrections of the vernacular crudities of the late sixties which occur throughout the design.

The windows in the fixed transoms and the towers have small square panes. Those that open have plain double-hung sashes with central muntins in the wider ones. The inner order of the loggia arches has almost no impost; the outer order, as in the porch of the Brattle Square Church, rests on sturdy Romanesque columns engaged in the two central piers.

It was in 1871 that from imitation of vaguely ecclesiastical contemporary French models for the central unit, and from imitation of the crudest contemporary English civil vernacular for the wards, the shift was really made to a coherent use of the traditions of mediaeval civil design. The composition of the whole group became vastly simpler and more coherent, building up effectively to the emphatic vertical composition of the main pavilion. Furthermore, the design was scaled throughout in detail to rough-faced random ashlar so that its character became identifiably Richardsonian. The dilemma of the Worcester High School—that of providing both a highly articulated plan and a pictorial silhouette—was at last solved by broadening the conception of the picturesque and modelling the whole mass up to the towers very much as in the Brookline Town Hall project.

The State Hospital was built very slowly—doubtless funds for public welfare were difficult to obtain from legislatures between 1873 and 1878. It was also built very solidly, with brick partitions, iron staircases and heavy hardwood trim. Plain, though crude, this is still in fine condition. But if the institution was built over a long period of time, this was perhaps an advantage to Richardson financially. It meant that through the years when commissions were scarce for all American architects he had one which paid continuously and well. How well, it is hard to say; but his first payment when the work started was $5,000.

The outer wards, probably designed in 1872 but possibly modified in execution in the next few years, are of interest for the very marked superiority of the brickwork over that of the Worcester High School. The bricks are common and not pressed, rather hard but somewhat irregular in texture. They were originally of a strong salmon red, which even the grime of years has not made disagreeable. There are also patterns in tarred bricks, now washed off in places. But these patterns are simpler and better placed, so that they resemble Mediaeval or early Renaissance use of black burned headers rather than the gaudy fancies of Butterfield and his school.   VII-10

The low service buildings at the rear are very fine. Their exact date cannot be ascertained, but they may be considered as designed in 1871. They are broader, simpler and more characteristically Richardsonian than the central pavilion and the wards.

This building or group of buildings is not, perhaps, so fine intrinsically as the Brattle Square Church, but it is more important in that it opens the line of monumental designs for utilitarian structures along which Richardson was to advance furthest. The dark rough stone; the great scale; the simple detail largely of structural character and only generically derived from mediaeval precedent; the bold silhouette and the solid mass; the adjustment of the parts of a complex programme, not only in plan, but in an exterior composition that expresses that plan: these are, in the best sense of the word, Richardsonian. For they are Richardsonian in a way that his followers were rarely able to follow. Indeed, his great personal gifts, which have so little to do with the use of Romanesque forms and archaeological detail, are perhaps more visible in these early monuments than in the later ones which are superficially closer to the work of his imitators.

If there is one phase in the career of a great artist which is of higher interest than another, it is surely the one we have now reached in Richardson's case. The period of preparation is definitely over and yet the personal style remains in part to be created. This corresponds, for example, to the few years in the forties in Corot's career when he first turned from the exact rendition of nature to elaborate composition in the Classical tradition. This was before his personal style became so watered and sentimentalized that it could be indefinitely and uncreatively repeated. Richardson had still many mistakes to make, but not for another decade the deadly mistake of complacent self-repetition. His mind was still as elastic as in the late sixties, but this elasticity was now shaped and directed by a subconsciously clear intention. He had now definitely chosen certain lines, no longer French or English, but his own.

The Brattle Square Church may seem to indicate a return from English ideals in ecclesiastical architecture toward something nearer those of the Second Empire Romanesque. The Buffalo State Hospital, particularly as one examines the stages in the development of the design, appears to represent just the opposite tendency: a turning from French principles of composition to principles observable in the practice of Street or Burges in England or in that of such younger men as Webb and Nesfield and Shaw. But in both cases the change is only superficially from French to English or vice versa. Actually it is the adjustment within Richardson of outside tensions, an act of integration opposed to the centrifugal tendencies of the previous five years. Henceforth, in his executed work, elements and features were borrowed from foreign contemporaries as well as from the farther past, but the essence of the style was his own. The magazines that came into the office, like the archaeological books, provided stimulation and occasional documents of detail, but the architecture was no longer anything but Richardson's.

CHAPTER EIGHT

1871-1872

THERE exists an interesting project for a stone house which may be attributed to the years 1870 or 1871. The drawings are in the free geometrical style of the *Croquis d'Architecture*, but they are inferior to Richardson's own sketches. Like the elevations of 1871 for the Buffalo State Hospital, which they resemble, these are probably by McKim. VIII-1 They appear to be definitely later than the tight hard drawings for the Codman house.

The project is for an ambitious mansion of which the plans for the main floors are unfortunately lacking. The asymmetrical mass is composed about a prominent tower with a saddle-back roof. The style is not domestic, like the Codman house, but monumental. It has also about the last pointed arches Richardson was to use and some incidental columns with carved capitals at the window openings. The heavy but solid and dignified Victorian Gothic character resembles that of the house based on the best English models of Burges and others which the Reverend Francis Goodwin built in Hartford in 1870 with the collaboration of Withers.[1] VIII-2

Richardson's next executed building was the Hampden County Courthouse in Springfield. He obtained the commission for this in July, 1871, as the result of a competition. The first designs were, therefore, probably made in the spring of 1871, about the same time as the

[1] The Rev. Francis Goodwin was also instrumental in arranging that Burges should design the already mentioned new buildings for Trinity College.

second set of drawings for Buffalo. The general scheme is naturally closer to that for the Brookline Town Hall, but it is simpler and, on the whole, better coördinated.

The three arches of the front resemble those of Buffalo; but they are broader and lower, and without engaged columns. The mullioned windows above seem to express, as in the Brookline Town Hall, a central large room on the upper floor. As a matter of fact, however, on account of the necessary interior supports for the tower, there is no such large room here. These mullioned windows resemble those of Buffalo, but are more Late Gothic in character, with inconspicuous lintels and mouldings on the sides as well as at the top. The corner balcony on the right, which is not repeated on the left, recalls the incidental asymmetry of the Brookline project and also the perspective composition of the churches.

In the project published in the *New York Sketch Book*,[2] in general quite like the executed work, there is shown a rather crude corbel-table cornice and a saddle-back roof above with wide eaves projecting on wooden rafters. (Fig. 23). Broad wooden dormers with hip roofs were also indicated in this project. Richardson was compelled by the building committee [3] to change these elements materially in execution. The cornice on the building is now narrower, with nubby modillions alternating in size. There are stepped battlements at the edge of the roof instead of projecting eaves. The executed dormers are of stone, with gables and mullions of Late Gothic French type.

These changes in the upper part of the building, being rather small and fussy, are somewhat out of scale with the rest. They do, however, improve the silhouette as a whole by emphasizing the vertical, as does the later arrangement of the parts in the facade of the central pavilion at Buffalo.

The tower in the center of the front is the culmination of the design both in the project and in the executed building. It composes

VIII-3

VIII-4

---

[2] 1874, Vol. I, no. 1.

[3] Such intervention is hard to interpret: was it a matter of taste or of expense? It can hardly have been the latter, since the executed design uses more granite.

admirably with the main mass in spite of the bad adjustment in elevation. The type follows closely that of the Palazzo Vecchio in Florence,
as revealed in the Victorian Gothic imitation of Burges' Law Courts
project, published in the *Builder* in 1870. The proportions, however,
are lower and broader and there is really no shaft. While this tower,
like the Buffalo towers, may be agreeably seen from a distance and from
all sides above the building, it is really an integral part of the building
and not an attached independent motif like the Worcester or even the
Brattle Square Tower. (Fig. 24).

The plan of the building, now entirely changed, represents a
rather successful attempt to place a monumental structure on a deep,
narrow lot facing streets at both ends. It is I-shaped, with the facade
just described on one end pavilion. A very plain facade forms the
rear. This has regularly spaced mullioned windows in two storeys with
bearing arches in the masonry above the lintels of the lower row. Except
for the lack of a large room in the center of the second floor of the front,
which the fenestration suggests, the court rooms and offices were intelligently distributed and clearly expressed on the exterior.

By 1906 the building had become so inadequate in size that a very
drastic remodelling took place. This remodelling was done by Richardson's successors, Shepley, Rutan and Coolidge. They built at the same
time the harmonious Registry of Deeds to the right. But their remodelling of the old building was unjustifiably drastic and it all but ruined
the original qualities of the design. The addition on the east side does
no harm; but the removal of the high roof and dormers completely
spoils the mass composition. The three-dimensional relation of the
tower to the rest of the building is now as bad as its two-dimensional
relation in elevation. The rather simple rear entrance door is not offen-
sive, although it spoils the pure unaccented rhythm of the rear which
Mrs. Van Rensselaer rightly felt gave the greatest promise for Richardson's later development. But the division of the front windows by
heavy storey spandrels in the middle of their height completely changes   VIII-5
the original verticality of the composition so that the facade seems
cluttered and constricted. Finally, the inexcusable substitution of a

direct flight of stairs for the wide double flight before the entrance, and the equally pointless introduction of Italian Gothic tracery in the belfry, damage the scale and the breadth of the design to an almost unbelievable extent.

The difference in architectural quality due to these modifications, made only twenty years after Richardson's death by men who were his collaborators and pupils in the early eighties, provides an extraordinary demonstration of the sureness of his hand at this early date. It also indicates the almost total incapacity of his imitators and pupils to understand what really made his work so fine.

It is futile to weep over what is gone. We may be grateful that old photographs exist to show how the Hampden County Courthouse should be. It still has qualities that even drastic remodelling could not destroy. The material is the local Monson granite which Richardson had used before on the Western Railroad offices and the Agawam Bank. It is here all rock-faced except for the trim. The scale of the random ashlar is very large, particularly in the beautifully battered base and the square piers, but it is not as perfectly adjusted to the design as in his later work. The color is a cool rather light grey, enlivened by a light red mortar now largely covered by repointing. The red mortar was a very Victorian polychromatic device which here had its justification in relieving a little the more than legal sternness of the design and the material.

The trim is very heavy and crude, suggesting properly the difficulty of working granite. It is also extremely well scaled to the ashlar. The mullions are plain oblongs in section and yet quite delicate in effect; the lintels are chamfered, with simple mouldings above the tops of the actual window openings. Only the projections at the top of the battlements and the string course at the bottom of the second storey windows appear a bit trivial when executed in granite.

The carved pier capitals of the porch and the tower are magnificent. The simple rows of leaves are Romanesque in feeling and yet hardly archaeological. They are not at all realistic in the Victorian

Gothic vein, and yet their crudeness is obviously due to the difficulty of working the material and not to wilful archaism.

The relation between the monumental ground storey arches and the simpler mullioned windows above may perhaps be criticized unfavorably. It is, however, less serious a fault than the similar arrangement in a much more mature building like the North Easton Town Hall of 1879. The corner balcony breaks the otherwise complete symmetry and is hardly balanced by the slot-like window at the other side. This is an example of that rather childish desire to protest against French principles of order that appeared in a similar way in the Brookline Town Hall and in the Buffalo study of 1871. But the relation of the building to the Court Square was such that it would ordinarily be seen and approached from the corner where the balcony is. Finally, the ugly letters of the word *Lex* provide an almost ludicrously inadequate transition from the continuous wall surface of the main building to the tower which rises in the center.

All this negative criticism is to be taken as an indication that Richardson had not yet achieved perfect mastery of his personal style. But it is not necessary any longer to ask if this work be predominantly French or English. The major virtues of mass, scale, and distribution are the virtues of a very great architect, even if the evident minor vices are as obviously due to the carelessness of a designer still inexperienced. In the next few years, while this was building, Richardson learned to avoid many of his difficulties. But until we come to Sever Hall, designed in 1878, we hardly find anything in his work which is more consistently fine.

1872 was the year in which Richardson came into national prominence through his selection as the architect for Trinity Church in Boston. The commission for the Phoenix Insurance Building in Hartford came into his office in March, probably while he was preparing the first Trinity drawings. And the commission for the Andrews house in Newport dates from July, the same month in which his drawings for Trinity won the competition. These buildings were both completed well before the construction of Trinity was at all advanced, and are essentially earlier works.

As to the North Church in Springfield, executed in the years 1872-73, it only remains to ask one question: In comparison with the State Hospital and the Hampden County Courthouse, both designed in 1871 and in building through the same years, does this church illustrate an earlier or a later type of design? The answer is that it seems definitely to represent a slightly earlier stage of development; roughly comparable to that of the Brattle Square Church. If it was redesigned after 1868 it must have been in 1870-71 rather than in 1872.

The Phoenix Insurance Building, designed in 1872, is very disappointing. The brick is hard and cold; the patterns with which it is enlivened, although simple, are quite out of scale with the cut-stone trim. The unfortunate tile inserts have already been mentioned in connection with the earlier use of the motif.

The building is composed in three successive layers with little relation between them. One asks at once why, if lintels can cover the wide windows of the second floor, are arches needed below? The rhythm of the windows of the first two floors, while not quite as confused as that of the side of the Agawam Bank, contrasts unfavorably with the splendid regularity of the rear of the Hampden County Courthouse. The disagreeable weakness of the corners is, if anything, accentuated by the flat stone quoins. The top floor has a meaningless center gable and corner pavilions projecting only an inch or so. The silhouette of the top, with its fussy weak cornice, is as trivial as any by Richardson's contemporaries. This is one building of the seventies which hardly deserves a place in Richardson's canon.

But of course the Phoenix Building should not be compared with the three monumental buildings which have just been discussed, nor even with those earlier Springfield commercial buildings which had the advantage of corner locations and fine masonry construction. This was the most difficult architectural problem the age offered: the design of a facade, four or five windows wide and three to five storeys tall, in a street of half-urban, half-suburban character.

Men of an engineering turn of mind had been working with cast-iron in such buildings for more than two decades. The use of cast-iron still continued. But the catastrophes in the great fires in Boston and Chicago of the previous year, due in part to castiron, were already diminishing its popularity.[4] Yet in the next year, Putnam and Tilden in Boston produced a commercial structure with castiron walls that actually supported the interior skeleton, an important and forgotten step toward the skyscraper. In this somewhat "Romanesquoid" design with continuous vertical lines, they intentionally avoided masonry forms—in favor, it is perhaps just to say, of those of bracketted wood. This building [5] was superior to Richardson's Phoenix Building in almost every way.

But Richardson was not an architect of engineering turn of mind. He had made no architectural use of iron, except in his use of metal supports for the light court in the Equitable project of 1867, and the supports in the side window of the Brattle Square Church, which were hardly intended to be conspicuous. Moreover, he was working here for a fire insurance company which had almost certainly lost very heavily from the destruction of castiron buildings in the great urban fires of the previous year. It is quite understandable that the use of unprotected iron was quite out of the question.

In Paris, the problem of building a commercial facade of five or six storeys was never in the nineteenth century a difficult one. The scheme of composition was dictated in all but details by the existing building laws and by the design of the structures on either side or across the street. Good stone, moreover, was cheap enough to be conventional. In America, however, convention demanded the use of stone or a particular type of design less than it had in the mid-sixties when Richardson was doing commercial work in Springfield.

Such a problem defeated all the advance Richardson had made the previous year in the way of fittting a well articulated plan into an ex-

[4] Castiron loses its strength when exposed to heat. Many buildings therefore collapsed which the fires hardly touched.

[5] The designs were published in the *Architectural Sketch Book*, Vol. I, no. 11.

pressive and picturesque composition in three dimensions. Here the plan was all but non-existent—it is now so modified that one can only guess what it was originally. But the essence of good commercial planning was then, and still is, to have as few fixed subdivisions of the interior as possible.

The confusion of the third floor design is a pathetic attempt to introduce something expressive of unimportant internal subdivisions, something of the third dimension, and some variety of silhouette. But in trying to find virtues in this dubious composition the third floor is best disregarded. That at least surely belongs in the uncanonical category of the Crowninshield house and the Worcester High School. Indeed, it is worse than they.

Yet the ground storey is not without vigour. And although the second story is as barren as the Crowninshield house, the wide proportion of the central windows, with their smooth, strong lintels, was a desirable reaction from the somewhat fortress-like fenestration of Buffalo and the Hampden County Courthouse.

No photographs or drawings of the American Merchants Union Express Company Building in Chicago can be discovered. This was not commissioned until September, 1872, but it was completed before Trinity was even started. Mrs. Van Rensselaer described it thus: "It is dignified and in many features very good and it shows a use of Romanesque motifs which entitled it to rank as the first of his commercial structures that can be called characteristic; yet it is still 'nondescript' rather than consistent in style." Wight, in his obituary notice of Richardson in the *Inland Architect* (Vol. VII, pp. 59-61), mentions the combined use of pointed arches, segmental pointed arches, and heavy lintels. This suggests a design more comparable to the Stone House project of 1871 than to the Phoenix Building. On the basis of such information, or of Montgomery Schuyler's words in *American Architecture* (p. 130), it is quite impossible to make any analysis of the design. It is quite possible that if we knew it today, there might be as much to say about it as about the other works of 1870-72 which have been discussed in the preceding pages at length.

During the summer of 1872, McKim, who had already obtained several personal commissions for houses, took office space in the same building with Gambrill and Richardson, and began to practice for himself.[6] He did not, however, entirely cease to work for Richardson until the latter moved his home and his personal office to Brookline in the spring of 1874.

Some time before October, 1872, Stanford White joined Richardson's staff, presumably to replace McKim. Baldwin, White's biographer, speaks of White's entering the office as an apprentice draftsman in Boston.[7] If this is correct, it would indicate that after the commission was received the drafting work on Trinity Church was at least in part transferred to Boston. Certainly, as White's letters to his mother indicate, there were frequent trips to Boston. McKim apparently stayed in New York.

White was at this time without architectural experience. Yet, since he stayed with Richardson longer than McKim, he perhaps learned more from him. He finally left Richardson in 1878 to travel in Europe. On his return he became McKim's partner. White had marked talent in drawing and painting. Within a few years he was an effective collaborator with Richardson in decorative detail and in house design generally. His first work in Richardson's office seems to have been the drawings for the Andrews house, which was commissioned in July, 1872.

The Andrews house was one of Richardson's most significant works, his first executed wooden house. It was, unfortunately, destroyed by fire some fifteen years ago. But although no photographs are extant, studies for the plans exist in several stages of development as well as

[6] This was in 1872, according to Mead. (*V.* Moore, Charles: *The Life and Times of Charles Follen McKim,* 1929, p. 40.) According to Moore himself (*ibid.,* p. 318), it was a year earlier. But the separation of McKim from Richardson was so gradual that the point is not important.

[7] Baldwin, Charles C.: *Stanford White,* 1931, Chapter V, *passim.*

two elevations. The drawing of these elevations lacks the professional quality of those that have been attributed to McKim, but there is a delicate, sketchy quality which exhibits in embryo the style of the drawings White made for Richardson in the next few years. Some of them are signed with his name. This picturesque type of rendering, resembling etching, continued for some years after White's departure as the standard manner of the office.

The plan of the Andrews house is an elaboration of the L-shaped scheme of the Codman house. (Fig. 28). Except for the ample fenestration, however, it is not particularly expressive of the wooden frame construction. The free general distribution is comparable to that of the large contemporary country houses of England. It is, indeed, rather inefficiently spread out, with many small rooms. But, as in the Dor-

VIII-10

sheimer house, there is a great living hall with a staircase and fire-place which could be treated with the monumental scale which appealed to Richardson. Except for this feature, which is paralleled in the Goodwin house in Hartford, the plan does not differ much from

VIII-11

that of the great granite château Hunt was building for George Peabody Wetmore in Newport at the same time.

It is the exterior design of the Andrews house which is exceptional and novel. (Fig. 27). The free picturesque massing does not depend for interest on ornamental accessories nor even center around a dominating tower. It is, however, rather chaotically varied in its asymmetry. The windows are arranged in generous groups related to the interior planning. They are all filled with decorative small diamond

VIII-12

panes. The continuous porch with its crude detail is vernacular in character and might well have been taken bodily from some Newport cottage of the fifties. It was, however, the use of the common shingle to cover the walls which proved epoch-making. As shingles would not weather properly under a porch roof, the walls of the lower storey were covered with clapboards, but in the general effect these were not conspicuous.

Shingles had all but passed from even rural vernacular use for over a generation. Soon after this they returned again to general favor. The best later houses of Richardson were covered with shingles and also those of McKim and White. Indeed, by the eighties, shingles were a ubiquitous feature in a new American domestic vernacular. Richardson's reintroduction of shingles, which had been so characteristic of the late seventeenth and early eighteenth centuries in America, was parallel to the contemporary revival by the most advanced English architects of the rural building methods of the time of Queen Anne. Indeed, one of the favorite devices of Norman Shaw, in particular, was the use of tile or slate hanging for upper storeys.[8]

VIII-13

Drawings of such houses would naturally be translated by an American eye into something quite comparable to the Andrews house; just as the drawings in Shaw's *Cottages* of 1878 were in the eighties regularly translated into American suburban framehouses with clapboards below and shingles above. It by no means follows that Richardson was doing this. For there were few documents of this sort of English work available in 1872, and none in his library. Later, however, in the designs White prepared for Richardson's houses in the next six years, the specific influence of English Queen Anne manor houses is very obvious.

VIII-14

It seems more plausible to explain Richardson's choice of shingles for the Andrews house on the basis of his general preference for rough-surfaced and expressive materials. Perhaps earlier memories of Colonial work played their part, but this house is certainly even less of a Colonial Revival design than those houses Richardson built in the eighties in which an early American quality is somewhat more evident. Both McKim and White were shortly to become absorbed with the imitation of the English Queen Anne and with the theoretically parallel imitation of the American Colonial. It is very important to emphasize from the first that although Richardson often drew suggestions from contemporary English domestic work and from the Colonial, he never imitated such sources any more closely than he imitated the Romanesque.

VIII-15

VIII-16

[8] Tile and slate hanging were themselves seventeenth century English translations into more permanent materials of an earlier vernacular use of wooden shingles.

The historical importance of the Andrews house is so great that it is very easy to neglect its real excellence. On the basis of Richardson's consistent improvement of his early studies during execution, we may well believe that the finished work was far more compact and simpler than the drawings. It may well have been comparable in quality to the Buffalo State Hospital, if not to the Brattle Square Church or the Hampden County Courthouse. Yet since even the studies are totally dissimilar in design to these others, except for the picturesque massing and the emphasis on the expressive texture of the building materials, this house illustrates the increasing breadth of his talent, as the Phoenix Insurance Building does not.

VIII-17

Trinity Church in Boston was commissioned, like the Andrews house, in July, 1872. However, as the commission was won in a competition, the original designs must date from the spring. The competition project, for which the drawings were made by McKim, was much changed during the next few years. The church was fairly begun only in 1874 after Richardson had moved to Brookline. (Fig. 31). The facade, as we see it today, is entirely different from the one completed in 1877. The porch, for which some sketches remain from before Richardson's death, and the present capping of the front towers in imitation of the crossing tower belong to the nineties.

These conspicuous external modifications, as well as the ciborium and pulpit which are equally prominent in the interior, were the work of Shepley, Rutan and Coolidge. It is necessary to emphasize that the present front is only partly Richardson's own work, since that is the most familiar aspect of the church. The conventional image of Richardson's work is based on this—his supposed masterpiece. But the image is an incorrect one. As the adjective "Richardsonian" is generally used to mean imitative of Trinity, and particularly of the facade which is so largely by his followers, it is not altogether paradoxical to say that Richardson's own work was rarely "Richardsonian." [9]

VIII-18

VIII-19

[9] Needless to say, the term has not been used throughout this book in this unfortunate sense except ironically, with the use of quotation marks.

To discuss Trinity as the design grew in Richardson's hands, it is desirable to begin with the earliest document. A photograph of a perspective, which evidently precedes that published by Mrs. Van Rensselaer, exists in the offices of Coolidge, Shepley, Bulfinch and Abbott. The date of this drawing is uncertain, but very probably it was done in the summer of 1872. The draftsmanship, although more finished than in the elevations of the Andrews house, appears to be White's rather than Richardson's or McKim's. It is, therefore, not likely that it is one of the actual competition drawings.[10] (Fig. 30).

As was generally the case, Richardson began a new project by following rather closely the last comparable building he had built, on this occasion the Brattle Square Church. But the scheme of the Brattle Square Church was much enlarged and elaborated in the Trinity project. The nave was slightly longer and provided with wider side aisles; the facade was flanked with low, square towers; and over the crossing was a large square lantern not unlike a rather squat version of one of the Buffalo towers. Above this square lantern rose, without any transition, a very tall octagonal tower with a pointed roof. This crowning feature indeed rose higher above the lantern than the nave roof did above the ground.[11]

[10] *The Architectural Sketch Book*, Vol. I, no. 1, July, 1873, has a project by Richardson worth comparing with this early project for Trinity Church, Boston. This unexecuted design for Trinity Church, Buffalo, is even more like the Brattle Square Church and may possibly date from 1872. The corner tower has a pointed round angle turrent somewhat in the manner of the early study for the right hand tower of the Buffalo State Hospital. There is another little turret behind the transept. These awkward features would very possibly have been omitted in execution. The baptistery with the turret at the right end of the front facade is very like the baptistery on the Boston church. The almost Byzantine interior has sheathed wooden barrel vaults and a shallow dome on pendentives over the crossing. A broad chamfered arch opens into the chancel. The effect is finer and more original than the Boston interior. If this interesting project had been executed, it would certainly have been of the quality of the Boston church, even if smaller and less impressive. The material was to have been buff sandstone with Medina brownstone trim.

[11] The suggestion that Richardson used the rather centralized composition instead of a long conventional Gothic plan because of the exiguity of the site is ridiculous. The composition is exactly that introduced in the Brattle Square

The apse was narrower than the choir and surrounded by an ambulatory. A large separate parish house was directly behind the church and parallel with the transept, to which it was connected by a low lintelled colonnade. On the lower part of the church there was very little detail and the whole effect was rather flat and crude as in the Brattle Square Church. The lantern and the tower, however, had engaged colonnettes and more recognizably Romanesque detail. The polychromy was simple, chiefly bands and checkerboards, and the walling was to have been of quarry-faced Roxbury Puddingstone.

The perspective published by Mrs. Van Rensselaer as the "Competitive Design" is so much closer to the executed work than to the drawing just discussed that it must have been mislabelled. It represents more probably the designs from which, on October 10, 1873, the contracts were let to the builders, Norcross Brothers. In this drawing, the chief changes in plan have already been made that were incorporated in the finished building. The parish house has been pushed to the side and its axis now runs parallel to the nave. The apse has been enlarged to the full width of the choir. The central tower is reduced to half the height in the earlier perspective and the right hand front tower—which does not show in the earlier drawing—is complicated by a square angle turret and a heavy arch projecting from the side of the base under a penthouse roof. (Fig. 30).

Although the detail of the central tower and the cloister colonnade was little changed, that of the apse and transepts was made more elaborate. On the apse there are buttresses and colonnettes between the windows and polychromy of a type that seems to be specifically Auvergnat [12] in the spandrels. This was to have been in polished granite of different colours. The rose windows have elaborate tracery of arches and colonnettes instead of simple plate tracery. Below them there are

Church, and there is considerable free space at the rear of the apse. It is even more ridiculous to suggest that such considerations led to the use of the Romanesque style. Square plans are not unknown in the Victorian Gothic nor are they characteristically Romanesque.

[12] This is the first use by Richardson of a characteristic detail from the Southern French Romanesque of Auvergne.

niches with statues, which were never cut, flanked by colonnettes some-what like those in the executed work. Even the lintelled windows at the base of the wall are richer and subdivided by colonnettes. Two narrowed arched windows with corner colonnettes replace the single wide arch with plate tracery at the side of the transept, and similar openings appear in the upper wall of the nave.

This later scheme is much richer than the first but generally in-ferior. On the one hand, there is an evident attempt to achieve more of the picturesqueness of the Victorian Gothic. On the other, there is evident a more precise study of Romansque documents than Richard-son had made when the Brattle Square Church was detailed. As the first volume of Revoil's *Architecture Romane du Midi de la France,* now in his library, appeared in 1873, it is just possible that the new detail and, particularly, the elaborate polychromy may have been derived from that.

The parish house, with its large mullioned windows, and the at-tached cloister are the best parts of this project as they are of the executed group. For the repetition of the simple Brattle Square mass-ing in the church itself is less close; and the lantern is no better incorporated with the rest of the composition, despite its less extreme proportions.

In the executed church the most notable improvement is in the design of the crossing tower. Norcross Brothers had found the early scheme beyond their power to construct. The story goes that La Farge sent Richardson a group of photographs, among which was one of the cathedral of Salamanca. Richardson sensed in the Salamanca lantern a possible solution of his difficulties and handed the photograph to White. White then made a drawing modifying the scheme to fit the new church.[13] The differences from the Spanish original are the greater height and the square plan. Indeed, the design of the earlier square lantern, with its round corner turrets and lintelled openings, is pre-

[13] White's study for the tower is at the offices of Coolidge, Shepley, Bulfinch and Abbott.   VIII-20

served almost without change. A further storey of arched openings was added above; then came the Salamanca dormers and octagonal tiled roof.

This is the most imitative feature on any building by Richardson. It is not without significance that the drawing was made by White and merely adapted as a termination for the original lantern designed by Richardson. The greater richness of detail and intricacy of design are characteristic of White's taste and are out of harmony with the simpler and more massive treatment of the lower part of the church. The tower is, nevertheless, a splendid culmination of the three-dimensional composition. But one must suspect that Richardson himself would eventually have designed something much more original, if White had not been so diabolically clever in adapting the Salamanca tower from the photograph.

The other chief changes in the executed design need not be attributed to White, although one, at least—the substitution of triple lights for the roses in the transept ends—was not an improvement. The increase in picturesque complexity in the parish house is balanced by the return to the simple, early form for the front towers. The increase in size of the baptistery between the transept and the choir notably improves the pyramidal effect from the rear. In building the church, rock-faced Milford granite with Longmeadow stone trim was substituted for the Roxbury Puddingstone. This had still been the intended material in 1873 but it had proved insufficiently strong. Until the grime of Boston settled like a pall over the rough surfaces of the granite, the effect must have been fine; even though the colour contrast was strong. The quarry-faced Puddingstone of the Brattle Square Church has weathered much more pleasantly. (Fig. 32).

The facade as left by Richardson was manifestly unfinished. The arrangement of the portal was rather like that of Saint-Gilles-de-Provence, but it was very simple and rugged, with bold, naturalistically carved foliage which can still be seen under the porch. Some sort of a porch was evidently intended from the first. Before Richardson's death, drawings were in existence, possibly based on his sketches, for an elaborately carved composition of the type actually built in the nineties. By the time these drawings were made, however, Richardson had seen Saint-Trophime at Arles, and he had begun to leave to his draftsmen the making of detail drawings with the assistance of photographs of old work. Even if the porch had been executed before his death, it would have been little superior to the glib archaeological exercise which now masks the original portals. At any rate, no porch was built at the time of the execution of the church, and the unfinished front must always have been the least satisfactory aspect of Trinity.[14]

An early section of the interior [15] shows that changes were made there as well as on the exterior after the construction started. In the early state of the design, four enormous masonry arches resting on compound piers were to have supported the crossing tower. The panelled wooden ceilings were to have followed the actual slope of the roofs with rather crude arched wooden trusses to support them. This was certainly very much more effective than the barrel roof—of trefoil section in wood and plaster with flat cross trusses—which now masks the tower arches and the actual slope of the roof. On the other hand, the polychrome decoration of the executed interior makes up for a   VIII-21
great deal. The changes made in the design during construction were as often advantageous as not.

[14] The "Competitive Design for a Village Church", published in 1875 in the *New York Sketch Book*, Vol. II, no. 10, follows on the whole the later designs for Trinity. Tall windows are grouped on the front and on the transept ends in place of the roses of Brattle Square. The facade is more coherent than that of Trinity. The great square crossing tower, with its tall pointed roof and corner turrets, rather overpowers the composition. The nave roof descends in a single slope to the top of the low aisle walls, with large wooden dormers instead of a clerestorey, making the proportions of the church itself even more squat. The detail is already much more archaeological. The Romanesque forms in the stone work and the Late Gothic forms in wood are insufficiently coördinated. This design would have been preferred in the eighties and nineties to the project for Trinity Church, Buffalo, but to modern eyes it is perilously close to slick eclectic revivalism. The contrasts of height and breadth in mass, and the quaintness in detail foreshadow the mannerisms into which Richardson's imitators fell soon after his death—if they did not desert the Mediaeval styles entirely.

[15] Published in the *Architectural Sketch Book*, Vol. I, no. 2, August, 1873.

141

The rector of Trinity Church was at this time Phillips Brooks, who soon became one of Richardson's most intimate friends. On account of his religious opinions, the interior was not intended for a ritualistic service. The large choir and apse were, therefore, not particularly useful. Brooks refused Richardson's suggestion that the altar be placed forward in the apse and covered with a ciborium, in the way that the space distribution made logical. (Fig. 33).

The interior is substantially intact, but if it is to be appreciated today it must be studied more than casually. At first you see only the conspicuous Early Christian ciborium of the nineties, to contain which the large chancel seems to have been planned. The worst French stained glass windows of the eighties and the smeary Burne-Jones colour of the somewhat better English windows also strike the eye at once. But if you stay inside the church until your eyes become adjusted to the dim light, you see something rather unexpected and not altogether unworthy of comparison with St. Mark's. For Trinity is still the "colour church" which Richardson intended and which, with La Farge's able coöperation, he achieved: not a muddy brown cavern with a gaudy white and gold ciborium and cheap windows of thin watery colour.

The La Farge windows in the facade are magnificent in colour and scale once the eye is adjusted to the key of their rich tones. They imitate no earlier glass, and yet rival the best of the past in their quality of low burning intensity. The design is rather derivative, but the feat of modelling plausibly in painted glass is surprisingly successful. A further adjustment to the darkness, and the assistance of artificial light make it possible to appreciate the general colour treatment of the walls. La Farge's figure panels are too dimmed by time to make any positive impression. But the general effect is splendid.[16]

VIII-22

VIII-23

[16] The work was done hurriedly, since no funds were available for the decoration until late 1876, a few months before the intended date of consecration, Feb. 9, 1877. La Farge was assisted by the young Saint-Gaudens, to whom some of the angels painted in the lantern are due. Some of the cartoons still exist in the cellar of Trinity.

The walls can be described as a dull terra cotta or strong orange-brown-red. With this is considerable gold, and even more of a rather dim blue-green, all of about the same middle value. There are some stencilled patterns, barely distinguishable for the most part, and up in the tower there are large conventionalized figures as well as small and almost invisible pictorial panels. The surfaces of the roof are also simply stencilled between the frequent dark brown beams. There are no rich materials, nothing throughout but the most commonplace textures of painted sand-finished plaster and varnished dark wood. The whole is undoubtedly dimmer and more harmonized by grime than when it was new. But, considering the lighting conditions, it can never have been as gaudy as a water colour sketch, preserved in the sexton's office, would indicate.

The decorative treatment is warm; it fills the atmosphere not with a glow like the windows, but with a sort of coloured mist. In this mist the bad French windows can be isolated as an irrelevance, and the Morris windows can be appreciated for their design, even if their colour is but a pale shadow beside La Farge's. The twentieth century windows, correct conventional exercises in French High Mediaeval design, serve only to show that the more we know about mediaeval art the less we are able to equal it. For many years this interior, like the exterior as Richardson left it, has really been seen by only a few people.

Trinity has become a mere landmark—like the Public Library opposite which McKim designed just ten years later, and which emphasizes by contrast all the faults of Trinity.[17] The Library is not altogether a better building, and yet it has the undoubted effect of throwing the church back into the mid-seventies when it was built. Peabody and Stearns' vernacular Brunswick Hotel behind Trinity, and the absurd round-arched Victorian Gothic Cluny Apartments by Putnam and Tilden opposite; the gaudy Italianate New Old South by Cummings and Sears at one opposite corner, and that clumsy Richardsonian parody, S. S. Pierce's Store at the other: all these completely

VIII-24

---

[17] This building is, however, the most Richardsonian thing McKim ever designed, to use the ambiguous adjective in its proper sense. *V*. Chapter XV.

engulf Trinity in the Brown Decades. Copley Square by its very topography grants the honors to the Library. Thus, the Copley-Plaza Hotel, which follows McKim's general line in an undistinguished way, seems a more proper monument for such a city square.

Richardson used later to wonder why, if the building committee liked what he finally built, they had ever selected his early competition drawings. In the interim, he had educated his building committee and himself so well that his design of 1872 came to seem incorrect and crude. As a matter of fact, he educated them too well. From the first they believed that the tower was the finest thing about the church, because it was copied from Salamanca.

VIII-25
But there were many reasons in 1872 to select Richardson's drawings. Over a generation earlier, another Trinity, in New York, had set a standard of Gothic design which had hardly been equalled. The newer Italianate sort of Victorian Gothic was already a decade old. There were many who could see that it was meretricious at best. The very fact that Sturgis and Brigham's Museum of Fine Arts was then rising in Italian Gothic brick and terra cotta on another side of Copley Square was to the contemporary mind one reason the more for avoiding that style. By contrast they could hope to emphasize the unique excellence of Trinity.

Nor were the first designs as poor as Richardson later thought. They were inferior to the Brattle Square Church, but they had something of its quality. Moreover, if one disregards the present state of the facade, Trinity is not so different from the first studies. It still appears somewhat incomplete and imperfect, but in an organic way: the bottom is younger than the top. If one looks first at the bold simplicity of the cloister and parish house, the crossing tower seems, by comparison, almost as overripe as the porch.

On the whole it was something of an accident that the prestige of this church and the obvious origin of its tower imposed on contemporaries a false idea. Richardson was not a revivalist who consistently sought his inspiration in specific Southern French and Spanish Romanesque monuments. But it was dangerously easy for young architects to follow the lead set by White, one of themselves, rather than by Richardson. Very few appreciated the authentic qualities of the body of the church and of the parish-house; almost none could hope for the cooperation of La Farge in elaborate schemes of interior decoration. But round arches and colonnettes and rock-faced stone anyone could copy, and within a very few years almost everyone did, particularly in ecclesiastical work.

Richardson was not by choice a church builder; indeed, after Trinity he only built two more churches. One of these is more a workshop imitation of his earlier work than an authentic creation. Although he aspired to found with Trinity an American style of architecture—as for a time he very nearly did—it was not one of the things of which he spoke most proudly at the end of his life. An advancing artist is never very much interested in his past work. Yet, even so, it is significant that the Courthouse and Jail in Pittsburgh and the Marshall Field Wholesale Store were the buildings which he felt to be his best work and by which he wished posterity to judge him.

The great significance of Trinity, for all its architectural excellence, lies chiefly in the publicity it gave Richardson and his personal style. Insofar as this publicity brought him new commissions of a sort better suited to his talents, it was most fortunate. Insofar as it provided a new ecclesiastical fashion which drove out the Victorian Gothic, it was in the end meaningless. An imitative fashion is flattering, but it brings a reaction. Ten years after Trinity was completed, this reaction had already found equally conspicuous expression in the Library which McKim was designing to be built across Copley Square. In the next few years, however, it was more important that Trinity established Richardson's personal reputation as America's leading architect.

As has already been said, Richardson moved his home and his personal office to Brookline in the spring of 1874. Here he found an eighteenth century house to which he added more and more drafting rooms as his practice increased. The special quality of his office was in large part due to the fact that it was an adjunct to his own house and that his draftsmen became almost members of the family. His relations with his assistants remained very intimate for some years, and his library was used by them even more than by him.

Settling in Brookline, Richardson renewed his contact with many of his Harvard friends. He was very fond of entertaining and the food and the conversation at his table were both of the highest order. No matter how hard he worked—and he worked very hard—he found time for his friends. He was as much sought after personally as he was in his professional capacity. Yet, although he might so easily have become the sort of American architect who owes his success to his social relations, a salesman of architecture rather than a designer and builder, Richardson had real artistic integrity. He was never tempted to think of architecture as contracts nor even as designs on paper. He always supervised the execution of his buildings closely and thus preserved a sympathetic sense of the quality of materials.[18]

Although he travelled a great deal for professional reasons, he travelled very little for pleasure. The trip to Niagara Falls and through the province of Quebec, which he took in 1875 with F. L. Olmsted and their two families, was afterward referred to as Richardson's "wedding journey." It is characteristic that he appreciated to the full the excellence of the vernacular stone farmhouses. It was perhaps fortunate, however, that he did not return to Europe until 1882. With the success of the archaeological treatment of the Trinity crossing tower to encourage him, the sight of the great Romanesque monuments of Europe might have tempted him to further copying.

Among the books Richardson probably acquired during the years Trinity was being designed and built, several deal with Romanesque archaeology. Revoil's *Architecture Romane du Midi de la France* has already been mentioned. It was undoubtedly very influential, if not as essentially formative as earlier critics of Richardson might have sup-

[18] At least until his work increased and his health declined in the last years of his life to such an extent that the supervision of almost all his work had to be delegated. *V.* Chapters XIII-XIV.

posed. The two volumes of Rohaut de Fleury's *La Toscane au Moyen Age*, published in 1873, and Street's *Brick and Marble in the Middle Ages*, 1874, indicate that Richardson was still quite interested in VIII-26 sources more in the Italianate Victorian Gothic tradition. Like the Romanesque material which continued to appear in the English magazines, the *Visit to the Domed Churches of the Charente* (published in 1875 by the English Architectural Association in honour of Edward VIII-27 Sharpe, and also in Richardson's library) gives sufficient proof that English architects were also examining the more richly carved Romanesque styles of France. Richardson's choice of documents was somewhat special. His own tastes were growing more precise, but they still remained within the sphere of interest of his English contemporaries, and his attitude toward such volumes was as free and unarchaeological as theirs. Bourgoin's *Les Arts Arabes*, of 1873, offered a more exotic inspiration for ornament, but it never had much influence on Richardson's executed work although he also acquired an abridged edition of Prisse d'Avennes' more monumental work on the same subject. VIII-28

Representing more conventional French sources, Bandol's *Eglises* VIII-29 *de Bourgs et Villages*, 1877, Eyries' *Châteaux Historiques de la France* (Vol. I, 1877; Vol. II, 1879), and Rohaut de Fleury's *Latran au Moyen Age*, 1877, balance the Victorian Gothic vision of Davie's *Architectural Studies in France*, also of 1877. None of these last books can have been in Richardson's possession early enough to provide inspiration for Trinity. But they indicate that his interest in the Middle Ages remained catholic and was by no means restricted, as so many have assumed, to the Romanesque of certain provinces of France.

No man's mind can be read from his library. Who does not buy books he never opens? Yet Richardson was not a student of the past, but a practicing architect. The books he bought do have significance. In most cases they must have been ordered from abroad at considerable expense. When they arrived, perusing them must have offered the relaxation Richardson had no time to seek in trips to Europe, or even in trips through his own country. But his French training did not encourage the exact repetition of documents. Indeed, the very fact that in Paris the art of the Middle Ages was a sort of not too secret vice led him to consider the Romanesque features he was using as a personal vehicle of expression. Therefore he felt quite free to bend them to his own temperament. Moreover, although the adaptation of the Salamanca lantern did solve the particular problem of covering the crossing at Trinity, it threw everything else out as he must soon have seen. Hence he was never again tempted to borrow a specific feature from the past in this same way.

But the study of mediaeval work encouraged him to achieve a greater consistency and integrity of personal style. The fact that his own work is really so little like the Romanesque does not mean that he misunderstood the Romanesque. Rather his understanding of it was so deep that he realized the futility of imitation. Nor did his particular admirations direct his borrowings. The existence of the Rohaut de Fleury book in his library does not necessarily mean that he especially admired the Pisa group of Romanesque buildings before he saw it in 1882. Very possibly, the book may not have been bought until that time. But certainly the Pisa buildings find no echo whatsoever in his work either before or after 1882. He continued, moreover, long after his own work had ceased to resemble the Victorian Gothic, to revel in the same ancient monuments which had inspired Butterfield and Street. To the creative architect there is inspiration in the principles of construction and composition illustrated by any sort of fine building, an inspiration far more profound than any that can be found in documents which are only copied, and never really studied.[19]

[19] In an interesting discussion with Le Corbusier, the peasant building of the Sahara which he had just seen was compared in detail with the peasant building of Donegal in Ireland which I had just seen. Both types of vernacular threw light on problems of modern construction and style.

CHAPTER NINE

1873-1877

RICHARDSON was fortunate, in the mid-seventies when building was slack, to have the two large commissions for the Buffalo State Hospital and Trinity Church. These continued until better times came again. But he was not totally without new work in the years 1873 through 1877. Houses were commissioned in 1873 and 1874; an important business building in 1875; and, in the same year, the complicated story of his relations with the Albany State Capitol began. Finally, in 1877, two libraries were commissioned.

Since it was with the building of Trinity that Richardson and his supposed revival of the Romanesque became conspicuous in the American architectural scene, it is well to examine in some detail at this point the stylistic tendencies of the depression years. Since little building was actually executed at this time, it is fortunate that many projects were currently published. It would be difficult to find projects of an earlier period, due to the absence of serious magazines devoted to architecture.[1] But, fortunately, in the mid-seventies two new and superior architectural magazines appeared, with the particular purpose of showing the projects which the younger architects were then designing if not building. In the *Architectural Sketch Book*, published 1873-76, and the *New York Sketch Book*, of 1874-76, can be found Richardson's two church projects already mentioned, one house project—they are otherwise completely unrecorded—and, in addition, the first publica-

IX-1

---

[1] There were some magazines, but they were very poor.

tion of his executed work. Henceforth, particularly after the 1880 republication in book form of the plates from the two *Sketch Books,* it was possible for architects to imitate his work even if they had not seen it.

The first certain examples of his influence have been mentioned: the imitation of the Unity Church in West Springfield by Eugene C. Gardner, in 1870, and the imitation of the North Congregational Church by Stephen C. Earle in the Park Congregational Church, Norwich, Connecticut, in 1873. Earle followed the Brattle Square Church in designing Christ Church Cathedral in 1874. This was a free version of the Richardsonian original and quite an excellent work. After the appearance of the *Sketch Books* and the established prestige of Trinity, there are more examples. Some, indeed, are rather hard to recognize when they derive from published projects and not from executed work.

IX-2

No one can examine today these volumes and the first volume of the *American Architect,* which began to appear in 1876, without observing three or more new types of design which were not in use in the late sixties. There are to be seen, first, a considerable group of designs which can no longer be described as round-arched Victorian Gothic even if they are hardly Richardsonian Romanesque. Second in importance, is the imitation of the most advanced English work. The English Queen Anne in its first and still mediaeval form appears frequently, together with most of the picturesque accessories, such as small bay windows, turrets, flat half timbering, patterned shingle work and small paned windows, soon to be ubiquitous in the American domestic vernacular of the eighties. Finally, there are a few measured drawings of old Colonial work and two interiors by McKim which were Colonial in intention and even recognizably so. These are the first graphic signs of the revival which was to succeed the Queen Anne in residence architecture.

IX-3

IX-4

With these nostalgic crocuses of the spring of the "American Renaissance" should be grouped the projects in different types of academic Renaissance design made by Ware's pupils in the architectural classes at the Massachusetts Institute of Technology. These same students were, indeed, also responsible for the measured drawings of Colonial church spires in Boston. There were even a few projects for buildings by established architects which approached the type of Renaissance monumental design which eventually succeeded the Richardsonian Romanesque. Predominantly, however, the material in these magazines is still Victorian Gothic, with a small selection of belated General Grant designs.

IX-5

The dying General Grant manner, which had rivalled the Victorian Gothic in the sixties, was merging imperceptibly with a more academic manner inspired by Paris or by Walter's work on the Capitol in Washington. But this academic manner, used less and less even for public buildings, was without an apparent future until Hunt and McKim and White took hold of it a decade later. One of the better examples of this still official style was the winning design in the competition of 1874 for the Providence City Hall by S. J. F. Thayer, a typical man-of-all-work among post-Civil War architects.

There is also the curious design by the young firm of McKim and Mead submitted in this competition.[2] This merits detailed discussion. The general composition, with the battered base and the central tower, owes more than a little to Richardson's Springfield Courthouse. On account of the projecting corner bays and the still further projecting entrance porch, it is much more complicated and less massive. The general scheme, indeed, is rather French and academic, with low roofs and an attic over the pilaster-decorated second storey, and a rusticated basement and first storey. But the hybrid detail, with prominent broken pediments, and the very large windows are due rather to English influence. There is a suggestion of the more developed and urbanized Queen Anne represented by Norman Shaw's New Zealand Chambers of 1873, which had been published in the *Builder*. McKim, indeed, in his very early work and in projects published in the seventies—to

IX-6

[2] The firm is thus proved, despite the confused testimony of Charles Moore (in *Life and Times of Charles Follen McKim,* Boston, 1929, Chapter V, *passim*), to have been in existence well before 1878.

which his biographer makes no reference—foreshadows the characteristic direction his firm took in the late eighties and nineties more
clearly than he was to do in the houses he designed with White between 1878 and 1883.

The early work of George B. Post, who had been Richardson's
predecessor as Gambrill's partner and who was to be one of the most
successful and least original New York architects of the eighties, is
also illustrated in the *Sketch Books* with an exceptional design of the
mid-seventies. This is a domed Renaissance building for the Williams-
burgh Savings Bank which might easily have been prepared in the
nineties. Indeed, it prefigures McKim's famous Columbia Library.

The best of the classical designs in these magazines is Hunt's Lenox
Library of 1869, whose conservative Parisian excellence has already
been mentioned. It is curious and even unfortunate that it had so
little influence.

The best of the more mediaeval designs are those by Russell Sturgis:
the already mentioned Farnam Hall of 1869 at Yale (wrongly labelled
Durfee), and a group of houses on 57th Street, New York, built in
1875. These are of surprising excellence. The windows are well grouped
in projecting flat bays, the cornice line is vigorously horizontal, and
the detail has a suavity which suggests the best work of the next decade.
These are, of course, not typically Victorian Gothic.

Yet even the typical Victorian Gothic was still producing in the
mid-seventies some of its boldest and most original monuments. William A. Potter's polychromatic South Congregational Church in Springfield, for example, dates from 1872-74. (It is, however not in the
Sketch Books.) With its fine tower and enormous rose window this is
undoubtedly superior to Richardson's North Congregational Church.
The same may even be said for the Harvard Street Church in Brookline,
built in the same years by his brother, Edward T. Potter. The forms
of this are more conventional, but the subtler harmonies of pale, almost
lavender brownstone, cream sandstone, and yellow-green Serpentine,
now made freshly visible by sand-blasting, are pleasanter than the
violent polychromy of the Springfield Church. It is further worth

remarking that in these years, W. A. Potter designed several Gothic post offices. Ware and Van Brunt's Worcester Union Station and Atwood's Holyoke City Hall are further good examples of Gothic design, both of all but Richardsonian scale and simplicity. These are illustrated in the *Sketch Books*.

The Romanesque work illustrated is generally not as good as the Victorian Gothic designs. But many of the best of these were, as a matter of fact, executed in the previous decade. Of those alternative designs offered in competitions in the seventies which may be fairly compared, the round-arched types are slightly superior although they rarely won. It is characteristic that the very commonplace Gothic scheme for the Brown University Library by Hartwell and Swasey was executed instead of the simpler and more monumental Romanesque design by W. A. Potter. Just as today, the architectural taste of universities was a decade or more behind the times.

Although the use of the round arch must be due in part to Richardson's success at Trinity, the usual type of design still derives rather more from the English commercial work of the previous decade and the round-arched Victorian Gothic used by Eidlitz, then one of the leading architects in New York. Of this, one good example, the Bowery Savings Bank, is twice illustrated. It is, however, of greater interest that J. C. Cady, in his project for the Tribune Building in New York, made use of a compositional device Richardson had introduced in his Equitable project of 1867. In this otherwise feeble design prominent round arches cover vertical rows of windows rising almost to the full height of the building. The idea must have been derived from the already mentioned English warehouses. This project is, however, less rationalistic and original than Hunt's ugly accepted design, which still stands although it has been enlarged to twice its original height. Had this project of Cady's been executed it might appear epoch-making IX-8 For it certainly comes as close as anything of Richardson's to Sullivan's early skyscraper designs.

It is evident in studying the magazines of the time that the American architectural world was teeming with ideas in the years of inactivity during the mid-seventies. The Queen Anne designs of Oakey and Jones and others are several years earlier than the first successes in this vein by McKim and Mead. Moreover, McKim's Colonial detail was, in these years, both freer in detail and more correct in spirit than the treatment he developed in the mid-eighties after the Queen Anne interlude. Various types of academic design have also been mentioned which were to come to fruition in the late eighties and nineties.

McKim's houses of these years were more influenced by Richardson's Andrews home than by the English Queen Anne. The house for Frank Blake, Jr., at Newton Lower Falls, is typical. The proportions are rather low and quite asymmetrical, but the tower is almost buried at the juncture of the main block and the service ring. The lower storey is clapboarded; the upper shingled as on the Andrews house; but there is a broad band of scalloped shingles around the middle. Most of the windows have large panes filling the whole sash. Only those in the tower and the dormers have large lozenges, and these are by no means as effective as the small diamond panes Richardson intended to use even as early as the Codman project of 1869. The broad barge boards with round holes in them are like those Gambrill used on the Oswego house of 1874 for Dr. Tinkham. Even more they are like those on the project for the Wilkeson house at Bridgehampton, which should also be attributed to Gambrill rather than to Richardson.[3] The porte-cochère on the Blake house is absurdly prominent and throws the rest of the house into obscurity. Certainly if the facts were not known, this house would be attributed to some uneducated builder working around 1890 and never to McKim, the impresario of the American Renaissance.

It must be admitted that Richardson's own house, built for Benjamin F. Bowles in Springfield and commissioned in May, 1873, is hardly better. This was, indeed, Richardson's last really inferior work.[4] It

[3] Illustrated in the *New York Sketch Book*, Vol. II, no. 8.

[4] That is among his early work. Of course some of the late work of the office for which he was barely responsible personally was very poor. This may usually be considered semi-posthumous. *V*. Chapters XIII-XIV.

hardly rose above the general level of his compatriots, and that level had risen very little since he designed his first executed house for B. W. Crowninshield five years earlier. There exists a study, possibly in White's draftsmanship, which must be for this house. It is of interest only as indicating that the design, as so often with Richardson, was much changed and improved before execution.

The Bowles house is of brick like the Crowninshield house, but it occupies an isolated suburban corner site. The polychromy of the brickwork is of the simple type, with a few plain black stripes and a broader diapered band below the second storey windows. This treatment is almost identical with that of the brick pavilions of the Buffalo State Hospital, probably determined upon at about the same time.

The mass is square, with a high pointed roof flipping out at the eaves as on the project for the Hampden County Courthouse. A tall dormer with a similar roof rises on the front above the asymmetrically placed entrance porch. This porch is simple, with round brick arches and open-work brick balustrades on top. The service wing is inconspicuous in design. But, at the rear corner of the main house, there is a large oblong bay window covered with a low slanting roof. Above this a rather Queen Anne half-timbered gable with two overhangs breaks the main roof. The windows throughout are narrow and coupled under segmental arches, as at Buffalo. Only the windows in the gable and dormers have small panes.

IX-10

Almost all the features of this house can be paralleled in contemporary projects by other architects published in the *Sketch Books*. Its chief Richardsonian quality was in the solid compact massing, or, as Mrs. Van Rensselaer doubtless justly informs us, in an expanse of plain brick wall at the rear. Unfortunately this does not show in the only discoverable view of the house. The building was demolished about ten years ago, and the absence of a plan makes it impossible to discuss the interior arrangements. There is a sketch plan in Richardson's draftsmanship for a client initialed B. This may well be an early study for this house: it is very similar to the Andrews plans and does not conform to the Bowles house as executed.

It is very possible that considerable responsibility may have been delegated to White in the exterior design of this house. But the design is of so little individuality that the question is not important.

But it is interesting to question to what extent the next house Richardson built is to be considered the design of White. The William Watts Sherman house in Newport, commissioned more than a year later, in September, 1874, is more like the houses White built in the early eighties than it is like Richardson's later domestic style. A connecting link exists, moreover, in a design for a house for James Cheney made in 1878, just before White left Richardson. This drawing is signed by White and has the characteristic detail of the houses he built in the next few years, after he had joined McKim: glass beads set in stucco and turned porch screens. (Fig. 42). These things Richardson nowhere used.

According to the testimony of Mrs. Watts Sherman, Richardson did not consider the interiors of her house to be complete when he finished it. He advised that they should be elaborated by White. Thus, White redecorated the library and redesigned the dining room fireplace in the years just before 1881.[5]

The delicate mixture of Queen Anne eighteenth century feeling, and elements of *Japonisme* in the library detail has points of resemblance to that of the fireplace in the living hall. The Jacobean fireplace in the dining room is a larger and somewhat more archaeological version of the type used in Mrs. Sherman's bedroom. The earlier interior detail is, therefore, almost certainly of White's design also. On the exterior the free use of cut shingles of varied forms, the small scale of the half timbering, and, above all, the painted patterns on the stucco panels are far more characteristic of White's work than of Richardson's at any period. The embellishment of the interior of this house, of which the construction began in 1875—to judge from the date on the

IX-11

[5] It is necessary to indicate the date in this fashion, since the biographers of White and of McKim generally give only the date of the last payment for each commission. The probability is that White undertook this work soon after his return from Europe in 1879.

chimney—was ultimately completed by White at Richardson's suggestion: presumably because White had been responsible for the interior and exterior detail from the first. The plan and the general composition were as certainly Richardson's.

The house as it exists today is in a magnificent state of preservation. But it has been much enlarged. The long left-hand service wing was added in the style of the original by Dudley Newton, a Newport architect, about twenty years ago, and it actually improves the composition. The side and rear were modified and enlarged by White. This was probably done at the time of the redecoration of the library, as the more delicate and Japanese detail on the barge boards of the smaller side gable would indicate. At various later dates Dudley Newton made further changes on the rear, always with a close approximation of the original detail. But the massing from the front is clearly Richardson's, whether it is studied in the perspective published in the *New York Sketch Book* in 1875 or as it exists today. (Figs. 36, 37).

No original plan exists on paper. But the plan, as far as it can be reconstructed today, is of the type which Richardson began to use in the Codman house project six years earlier: ell-shaped with a large living hall extending from front to rear. The arrangement, if somewhat more conventional, is also more practical. For the staircase is opposite the entrance rather than at the rear. The rear wall of the hall is one large window divided only by stone mullions. This is now darkened by the conservatory outside. The fireplace is tall and hooded.

This room has not much detail of the more delicate type which would naturally be attributed to White except in the incised ornament on the fireplace. The woodwork throughout the room is of dark mahogany. The heavy spiral bannisters, the plain chamfered posts of the staircase, and the deeply beamed ceiling, are, indeed, even more Richardsonian as executed than they are in the sketch published in the *New York Sketch Book*. This sketch, although unsigned, was almost certainly drawn by White. The remarkably beautiful glass in the windows at the front, in half-naturalistic, half-conventional flower patterns of strange acid colour, is by La Farge. (Fig. 38). This must

157

have been his first work for Richardson, done probably when they were planning the decorations on the interior of Trinity. The La Farge glass in the transoms at the rear of the hall and in the dining room is inferior—muddier in colour and less conventionalized in design. Probably this belongs to the period of White's work five years later.

IX-13 The handsome green and gold library to the right of the living hall is entirely White's and was finished in 1881; the white and gold drawing room in the wing behind was decorated by the firm of Allard under White's supervision. The dining room behind the staircase is also probably largely of White's design. The fireplace is definitely his and differs markedly from an early sketch which shows a sort of inglenook beneath a flat Tudor arch. This room was almost doubled in length when Dudley Newton built the service wing.

Upstairs, the hall, with the small-scaled Queen Anne cabinet work of the long bay window across the front and the delicate flower patterns painted on the small leaded panes in grey and yellow, is almost cer-
IX-14 tainly White's work, but of the period of the original construction. The main bedroom in the ell is panelled in a sort of free and refined Jacobean style with richly figured redwood. This room is ingeniously lined with closets and drawers behind movable panels. The delicacy of the ornament again suggests that this was entirely White's work. It is known to be of the period of the original construction.

The exterior of the house is in every way a surprising advance over the Bowles house and even over the excellent Andrews house. The
IX-15 Queen Anne character is chiefly due to the half-timber and stucco detail, which may be attributed to White. But the broad sweep of the composition and the prominent gables, as well as the use of stone for the ground storey, are in the Mediaeval tradition of Shaw's best houses
IX-16 of the early seventies, such as Preen and Pinner.

The colour harmony of pink granite random ashlar walling and rather orange sandstone trim must have been very like that of Trinity as it was originally. It is not altogether the more agreeable today for lacking Trinity's grime. The shingles and the other woodwork above are, however, well weathered to that extraordinarily beautiful silvery grey which wood attains only near the sea coast. For once, even the patterned bands on a roof, that favorite and dubious Victorian Gothic device, are not a blemish. Indeed, the pattern cut shingles are in general very cleverly distributed and quite unlike that awkward band around the second storey of McKim's Blake house. Even the red painted patterns on the stucco panels are not as tawdry a conceit as the broken glass to which Stanford White was so addicted a few years later.

The main fluted chimney stack on the crest of the roof is splendid. But the library chimney on the front is quite different as it is today from that in the published project. It was probably rebuilt at some later time and made taller, as the rather commonplace design suggests.[6]

Extremely ingenious is the way in which the thin American beam ends appear at the projection below the second storey. Like the use of shingles in places of tiles, this frank translation of a European Late Gothic structural feature into modern American methods of wood construction is more in Richardson's than in White's manner. The thin curved brackets under the top projection of the front gable are, however, exactly of the type which passed from White's later work into the American Queen Anne vernacular. The high sash division of the IX-17 double-hung windows was continued in White's later houses but, fortunately, not in Richardson's. It may be justified here as an attempt to echo the placing of the stone transoms of the grouped windows of the hall. But it was wisely disregarded in the treatment of the small paned windows of the front gable. The compromise of using plain panes in the lower sash and small squares above, which passed into the later vernacular, had already been initiated by Richardson in the Buffalo State Hospital. The porte-cochère is inconspicuous and far superior to the one by McKim on the Blake house. The actual front doorway with its Corinthian pilasters is not Richardson's.

The Watts Sherman stables are well designed in the style of the

[6] The date 1875 which is cut on a stone block set in the brick of the chimney would, of course, have been preserved.

house, but they are rather more intricate and picturesque in composition. Screens of turned spindles appear as in much of White's work five years later. These, like the incised ornament on the barge boards resembling that on the main gables of the house, are rather bolder in scale than White's characteristic work. Yet the stables are probably almost entirely White's.

American architects were to occupy themselves frequently in the following fifty years with various attempts to reproduce in a modern American country house the Late Gothic manor houses of England. Of these attempts the Watts Sherman house is by no means the most plausible as archaeological reconstruction. But it is certainly the most successful in translating the type into American terms. To appreciate fully its excellence, it should be compared with other houses built at Newport in the seventies. Hunt's Wetmore house, which has already been spoken of in relation to the Andrews house, has a monumental quality in its solid granite mass to which Richardson properly did not aspire in his country houses. But Hunt was building the first and perhaps the best of his Newport palaces, while Richardson's Watts Sherman house, although really a mansion, was still, not too paradoxically, a "cottage".

The Nathan Matthews house of 1873 by Peabody and Stearns, although larger than the original Sherman house, was also a "cottage". Peabody and Stearns were the young Boston architects who were to be leaders of their profession in the next two decades and among the more successful imitators of Richardson's monumental masonry style. Yet this Matthews house has all the vices of the American Victorian Gothic domestic vernacular: confused massing, a conglomeration of different materials, and quantities of the crudest sort of gingerbread. It does, however, preserve the piazzas of the earlier "cottages" as Richardson's Sherman house did not.

The Watts Sherman house was even further above the general level of professional achievement in house design in the mid-seventies than Trinity was above contemporary churches. It was also more significant. It prepared the way for the rise in the general level of the domestic vernacular that came in the next decade.

Several house projects by Gambrill and Richardson are published in the *Architectural Sketch Book* and the *New York Sketch Book*. One of these, that for Dr. Tinkham at Owego, N. Y., was executed, and is stated by Mrs. Van Rensselaer to have been by Gambrill alone. (~~Fig. 48~~) . It closely resembles McKim's Blake house. Although smaller than either, it is about half way between that and the Watts Sherman house in style.

Another much more elaborate project, which was never executed, is for a house for Rush Cheney in South Manchester, of about 1876. This is very obviously not Gambrill's. But the detail is definitely White's: glass beads set in stucco, delicate turned porch posts, and thin curved brackets. Richardson in this year was occupied with the IX-21 construction of the Cheney Building in Hartford. After the success of their collaboration on the Watts Sherman house, it would not have been surprising if a similar project was left almost entirely in White's hands. (Fig. 41). The composition is less compact than in the Sherman house, more whimsical and more commonplace, as McKim, Mead and White's houses of a few years later were to be. The drawing, although unsigned, is surely by White, who signed the very similar drawing for the James Cheney house project two years later. But, like the Watts Sherman house, the executed building would undoubtedly have been more Richardsonian than the drawing. Moreover, the broad massing, the ample fenestration and the restraint in the use of detail certainly are not White's. Richardson had in White an able assistant, the best he ever found; but White still worked under his direction.

In the case of two other house projects, similar questions of attribution arise. The project for Samuel Wilkeson in Bridgehampton, Long Island, is almost certainly Gambrill's. Neither the symmetrical composition nor the cut-off gables are Richardsonian. The barge boards cut with circles are quite like those on McKim's Blake house and very similar to those on Gambrill's Tinkham house. The turned porch columns are very commonplace, almost exactly like those used by the cheapest builders in the eighties and nineties. The wash drawing does not even appear to be by White. Yet this project, like the Tinkham house, is very superior to all other wooden houses of this period except Richardson's. It is, however, not superior to the higher level of the best domestic architecture of the next decade. Whether or not Gambrill ever influenced Richardson in the sixties, there can be no question that Richardson influenced Gambrill in the seventies. It would also appear that Richardson's influence at this time reached McKim through Gambrill.

IX-22

A further house project published in the *New York Sketch Book* in 1875 is for Arthur W. Blake. (Fig. 40). This is almost as certainly Richardson's as the Wilkeson house is Gambrill's. The delicate rendering, like an etching, is surely by White's hand; the mass is well centralized; and the barge boards and half timbering are simplified versions of similar detail on the Watts Sherman house. The spaces above the curving branches at the top of the porch posts are not filled in as on the Andrews house. Just such supports as these are characteristic of Richardson's railroad stations of the eighties.

This Blake project was considerably smaller and simpler than the Watts Sherman house and the Rush Cheney projects. Hence, it is rather more like the wooden houses Richardson built after 1880. As there was far less of White's intricate detail, this would also have been a better model for the designers of "cottages" in the eighties. Unfortunately it did not catch the eye in the same way as the gayer detail of White. The extraneous gables and the octagonal bay window rising into a turret were appreciated and imitated rather than the compact mass, the plain shingle-covered walls, and the sturdy porch detail.

No plans were published with any of these projects. It would have been interesting, particularly in the case of the Blake house, to know how Richardson at this time adapted his larger house plans with their generous rooms to the exigencies of a small suburban dwelling. There is, however, a plan of the project for the James Cheney house. (Fig. 42). This has already been touched on so often that it may as well be disposed of here, although it is dated 1878. This plan is not so well arranged as that of the Watts Sherman house. The hall is only lighted from above the stairs. It forms an unnecessarily ample entrance way rather than a real living area. The drawing room is small and awkwardly L-shaped. There is so much more of White's detail on this and there are so many small gables that the project must be largely of his design. This is almost proved by the fact that when James Cheney actually built a few years later he called on White and not Richardson.

IX-23

This project, prepared just before White left Richardson for good, should be considered the first of White's houses rather than the last which Richardson designed in wood in the seventies. The next house Richardson built, the Trinity Rectory in Boston, begun in 1879, is of masonry and different in almost every respect. The James Bryant house in wood which Richardson designed in 1880 is even more dissimilar. After the departure of White, Richardson found his own direction again in house design. He completely threw off the influence of the Queen Anne which was certainly present in the Andrews and Watts Sherman houses.

IX-24

It is not to be regretted that Richardson left the Queen Anne to McKim, Mead and White. They exploited it more thoroughly than it deserved in the following years. It is to be regretted, however, that Richardson lost White's assistance. For White was exactly the collaborator he needed for domestic interiors. White, moreover, did better work under the direction of an older and more architectural mind than later in a partnership of equals. After he lost the Richardsonian discipline, which made even the James Cheney project superior to most of his later work, he was little more than a gifted and imaginative exterior decorator. Later he accepted from Wells and McKim the archaeological discipline of the Italian Renaissance.[7]

This is probably the first time it has ever been suggested that White's parting with Richardson was anything but the decisive step in a triumphant architectural career. Yet in retrospect it appears that he left the position of a one-eyed minister to become king among the

IX-25

[7] *V*. Chapter XII and Chapter XV, *infra*.

blind. Even if he had seen it thus, perhaps he would have made the step. But Richardson still had sight enough so that after he lost his one-eyed premier he got on for some years with the assistance of the blind.

The next building begun after the Watts Sherman house was a very fine and interesting one. Richardson had done no important commercial work since the sixties. Neither the Phoenix Insurance Building in Hartford nor his American Merchants Union Express Building in Chicago can ever have been very striking. But the Cheney Building in Hartford, commissioned in September, 1875, was the first step toward the Marshall Field Store in Chicago, designed ten years later, which Richardson and all his critics have agreed was one of his greatest masterpieces.

The Cheney Building is very monumental and conspicuously Romanesque, yet it is also a sound commercial design. Richardson had just been acclaimed as the designer of America's greatest modern church avowedly in the Romanesque style. He was an exponent of the theory that the Romanesque was the most proper source of inspiration for modern America, as Robert Dale Owen had claimed in the forties. Such a general theory was absurd, as those who took it at its face value soon demonstrated; but it was not absurd for Richardson. He made even plainer here than at Trinity that he could approach modern problems in a spirit not wholly dissimilar to that of the men of the twelfth century, making innovations as great as theirs, all the while that he tried to use their forms.

According to the project in the *Sketch Books,* the building was originally to have been built in brick with stone trim. Rather fortunately for the monumental spirit in which it was designed, rock-faced brownstone ashlar was substituted for the brick, with bands of buff sandstone in the arches and buff sandstone trim. Time has pleasantly softened this polychromy and weathered the brownstone to a very rich tone and texture. As indicated by the considerably earlier Gothic cathedral across the street and most of the masonry buildings in Hartford dating from before the Civil War, this brownstone was a natural local building material, quarried nearby. It was also being used at this time, in a very similar way, at Trinity College in the execution of Burges' imported designs.

This was one of the few characteristic buildings designed by Richardson before 1882 in which brownstone was the predominant material. Its ubiquitous use by his imitators has obscured the fact that he generally preferred granite walling, reserving the dark stone for trim. By using local materials as much as he could in his early buildings,[8] Richardson was assured of some sort of harmony with existing masonry buildings. His successors foolishly imitated all over the country his use of the Longmeadow- and Portland-type stones which were most available in Springfield and Hartford. Then they reacted against the resultant gloom by turning to Bedford limestone and buff brick. But for this the shocking alternation of dark and light in the cities of the last fifty years would not be so ubiquitous. Then perhaps the work of Richardson and his imitators would not have seemed by 1900 the products of a dark age which preceded the bright dawn of an "American Renaissance". The effect of the Boston Public Library on Trinity is a familiar case in point. The contrast of the commonplace nearby department stores of limestone and buff brick with the Cheney Building in Hartford is even stronger. But they have little formal plastic design and the Cheney Building has the support of Christ Church across the street. Therefore eyes once focussed on the excellence of the Cheney Building can always see it clearly. Perhaps in time Americans will learn to see that the light-coloured later buildings are but sepulchres and not to be associated with a rebirth.

The general design of the Cheney Building is almost as elemental as its worn earthy colour. The most meretricious feature of the project is the asymmetrical treatment of the two upper corners. This is a superficial trace of Victorian Gothic influence, the gesture of one trained in symmetry who must display his freedom from it. In the

[8] Longmeadow stone and Monson granite in Springfield; Roxbury Puddingstone in Boston; brownstone here, etc.

executed designs this is less conspicuous. Instead of the gable which appears on the left in the project, the left upper corner repeats that on the right, except for the taller windows and the pointed roof which is hardly visible from the street. The slight modification of the design in these corner bays serves to emphasize that the building is a solid mass and not a mere flat facade. Yet their projection is very slight. (Fig. 43).

The scale of the building is enormous. By joining storeys together vertically, in the way projected for the Equitable Building in 1867, the seven storeys of the structure are reduced to two superimposed arcades and an attic. The five ground storey arches are very wide and high, with the mezzanine windows above their springing. The intermediate masonry piers are sturdy and yet rather surprisingly narrow. The two porches are supported by short columns on brackets which are somewhat Victorian Gothic. But these trivial motifs serve to tie the corner pavilions into the main block very ingeniously and the carving on them has the Gothic naturalism and somewhat angular vigour of the best work on Trinity.

The great banded arches have thin and unnecessary drip moulds. In the elaborate string course above, the lower part is fluted and classical, the upper foliate and Gothic. Despite this disparate detail, the effect is Romanesque in feeling. The second arcade of the design includes three floors, with the windows of the third somewhat drastically forced into the top of the arches. The arches in this stage are coupled over each of the lower arches. The change in the proportions of the openings from square to vertically oblong is Romanesque enough but not altogether happy. The imposts of this arcade and the string course above are all more richly carved than the distance from the eye altogether justifies. The attic storey is the most delicate in scale and also the most elaborate. In the end bays there are three arches to the two of the arcade below, and there are four in the middle section. Coupled colonnettes alternate with single colonnettes, all with bossy capitols. The bracketted cornice stops somewhat awkwardly against the corner pavilions. The balustrade, with its small square panels of

1. Hospice des Incurables, Ivry, Seine, by F.-M.-Theodore Labrouste. Administration Building and Ward, 1862-65.

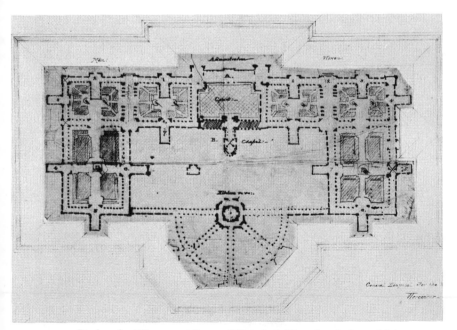

2. Project for Worcester General Hospital. Plan sketch, late 1860's.

3. Church of the Unity, Springfield. Exterior, 1866-69.

4. Church of the Unity, Springfield. Early elevation sketch. 1866.

5. Church of the Unity, Springfield. Interior, 1866-69.

6. Grace Church, Medford. Exterior, 1867-69.

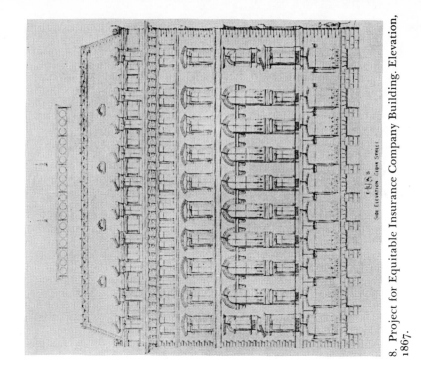

8. Project for Equitable Insurance Company Building. Elevation, 1867.

7. Western Railway Offices, Springfield, 1867-69.

9. Richardson's own house, Arrochar, Staten Island. Exterior, 1868.

10. Dorsheimer House, Buffalo. Exterior, 1868.

11. Project for house. Elevation, dated Aug. 10, 1868.

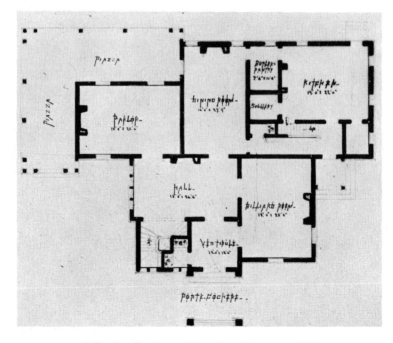

12. Project for house. Plan, dated Aug. 10, 1868.

13. Agawam National Bank, Springfield. Exterior, 1869-70.

14. Worcester High School. Exterior, 1869-71.

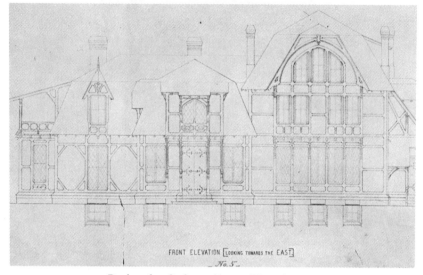

15. Project for Codman house. Elevation, c. 1871.

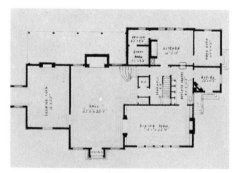

16. Project for Codman house. Plan,
c. 1871.

17. Project for Brookline Town Hall
Perspective Sketch, 1870.

18. Brattle Square Church, Boston. Exterior from N.E., 1870-72.

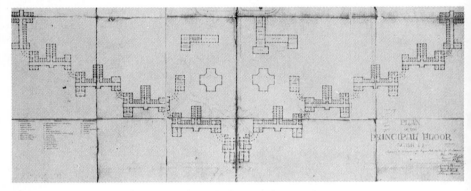

19. State Hospital, Buffalo. Original plan, 1870.

20. State Hospital, Buffalo. Original elevation, 1870.

21. State Hospital, Buffalo. Elevation Study, 1871.

22. State Hospital, Buffalo. Administration Building, 1872-78.

23. Hampden County Courthouse, Springfield. Early perspective study, 1871.

24. Hampden County Courthouse, Springfield. Exterior, 1871-73, before alteration.

25. Project for Church in Columbus, Ohio. 1871-72.

26. North Congregational Church, Springfield. Exterior (1868), 1872-73.

27. Andrews house, Newport. Elevation, 1872.

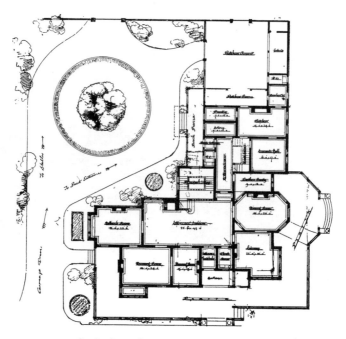

28. Andrews house, Newport. Plan, 1872.

29. American Merchants' Union Express Company Building, Chicago. Early perspective, 1872.

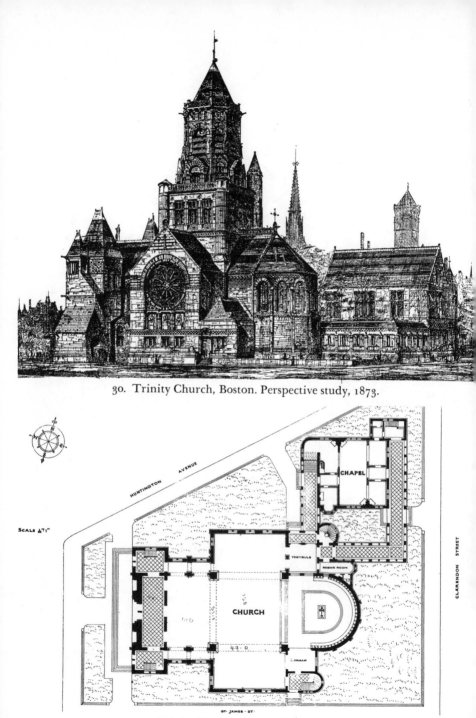

30. Trinity Church, Boston. Perspective study, 1873.

31. Trinity Church, Boston. Plan, 1873-77.

32. Trinity Church, Boston. Exterior from South East, 1873-77.

33. Trinity Church, Boston. Interior, 1873-77.

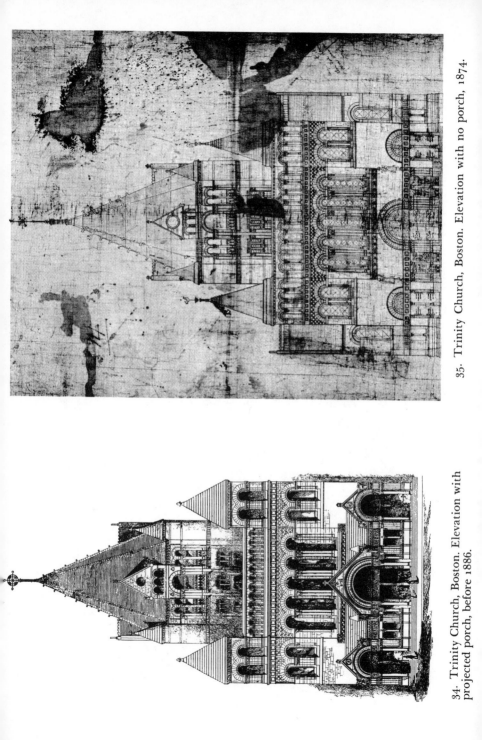

35. Trinity Church, Boston. Elevation with no porch, 1874.

34. Trinity Church, Boston. Elevation with projected porch, before 1886.

36. Sherman house, Newport. Perspective, 1874.

37. Sherman house, Newport. Exterior, 1874-75.

38. Sherman house, Newport. Hall, 1874-75.

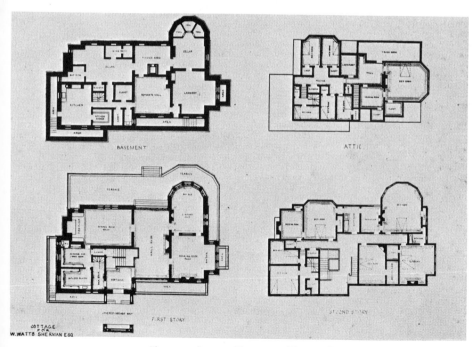

39. Sherman house, Newport. Plans, 1874.

40. Blake house, Newton Lower Falls. Perspective, 1874.

41. Project for Rush Cheney house. Perspective, 1876.

42. Project for James Cheney house. Perspective and plan, 1878.

43. Cheney Block, Hartford. Exterior, 1875-76.

44. New York State Capitol, Albany. South elevation study, 1877.

45. Project for Cheney Block Annex.

46. Ames Memorial Library, North Easton, Fireplace, 18~8

47. Winn Memorial Library, Woburn. Exterior, 1877-78.

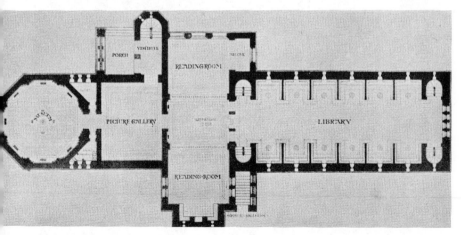

48. Winn Memorial Library, Woburn. Plan, 1877-78.

49. Ames Memorial Library, North Easton. Exterior, 1877-79.

50. Ames Memorial Library, North Easton. Interior of stack wing, 1877-79.

51. Sever Hall, Cambridge. Front, 1878-80.

52. Sever Hall, Cambridge. Rear, 1878-80.

53. Ames Memorial Town Hall, North Easton. Exterior, 1879-81.

54. New York State Capitol, Albany. Senate Chamber, 1878-81.

55. New York State Capitol. Court of Appeals, fireplace, 1881.

56. Ames Monument, Sherman, Wyoming, 1879.

57. Rectory of Trinity Church, Boston. Exterior, 1879-80.

58. F. L. Ames Gate Lodge, North Easton. Exterior from North, 1880-81.

59. F. L. Ames Gate Lodge, North Easton. Exterior from South West, 1880-81.

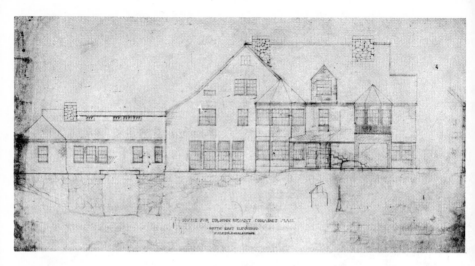

60. Bryant house, Cohasset. Elevation, 1880.

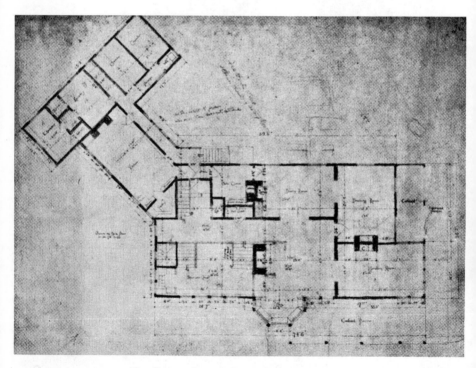

61. Bryant house, Cohasset. Plan, 1880.

62. Bryant house, Cohasset. Exterior from S.W. 1880.

63. Bryant house, Cohasset. Exterior from S.E. 1880.

64. Crane Memorial Library, Quincy. Perspective sketch of rear, 1880.

65. Crane Memorial Library, Quincy. Front, 1880-83.

66. Metal bridge in the Fenway, Boston, 1880-81.

67. Stone bridge in the Fenway, Boston, 1880-81.

68. City Hall, Albany. Exterior, 1880-82.

69. Higginson house, Boston. Exterior, with Whittier house by McKim, Mead & White to the right, both 1881-83.

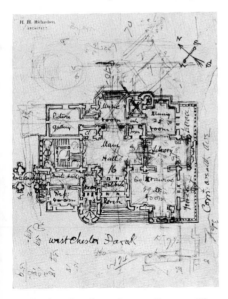

70. Project for Ames house, Boston. Plan study, 1880.

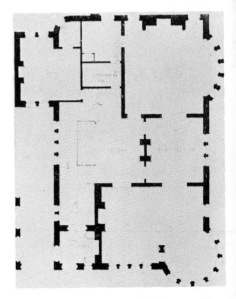

71. Anderson house, Washington. Plan, 1881.

72. Anderson house, Washington. Perspective, 1881.

73. Anderson house, Washington. Entrance, 1881.

74. Brown house, Marion. Exterior, 1881-82, with later changes.

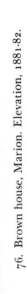

76. Brown house, Marion. Elevation, 1881-82.

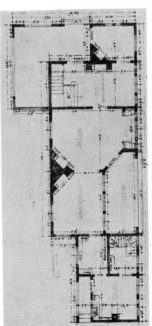

75. Brown house, Marion. Plan, 1881-82.

77. Boston & Albany Station, Chestnut Hill. Exterior, 1883-84.

78. Boston & Albany Station, Auburndale. Exterior, 1881.

79. Austin Hall, Cambridge. Exterior, 1881-83.

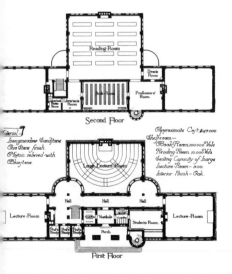

. Austin Hall, Cambridge. Plans, 1881-83.

81. Ames Building (Kingston and Bedford Streets), Boston. Exterior, 1882-83.

82. Stoughton house, Cambridge. Exterior, 1882-83.

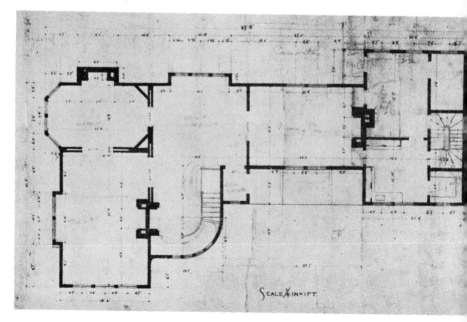

83. Stoughton house, Cambridge. Plan, 1882-83.

84. Channing house, Brookline. Exterior, 1882-83.

85. Sard house, Albany. Exterior, 1882-83.

86. Project for Episcopal Cathedral in Albany. Perspective, 1883.

87. Emanuel Church, Pittsburgh. Exterior, 1885-86.

88. Billings Library, Burlington. Exterior, 1883-86.

89. Converse Memorial Library, Malden. Exterior, 1883-85.

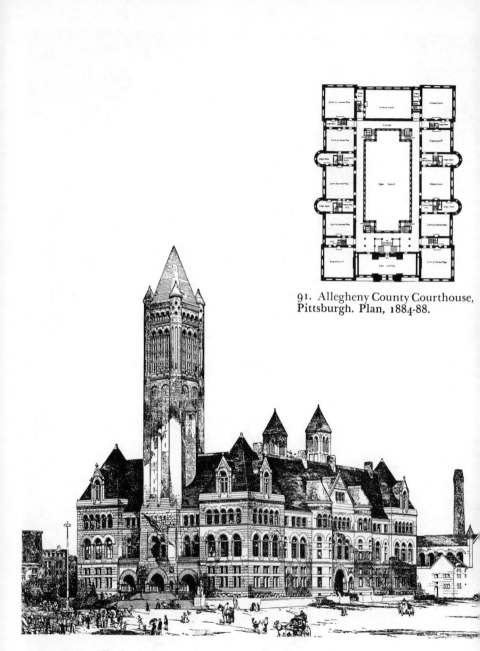

91. Allegheny County Courthouse,
Pittsburgh. Plan, 1884-88.

90. Allegheny County Courthouse, Pittsburgh. Perspective, 1884-88.

92. Allegheny County Jail, Pittsburgh. Exterior, 1884-86.

93. Allegheny County Courthouse, Pittsburgh. Court, 1884-88.

94. Allegheny County Courthouse, Pittsburgh. Court, 1884-88.

95. Marshall Field Wholesale Store. Exterior, 1885-87.

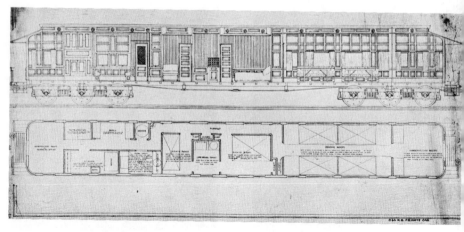

96. Project for private railroad car. Plan and section, 1884.

97. Marshall Field Wholesale Store. Perspective project, 1885.

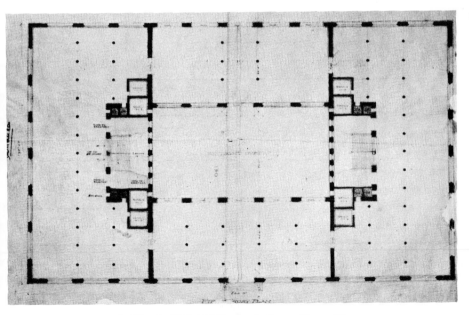

98. Marshall Field Wholesale Store. Plan, 1885.

99. Paine house, Waltham. Exterior, 1884-86, with later baywindows.

100. Paine house, Waltham. Stairway, 1884-86.

101. Adams and Hay houses, Washington. Elevation study, 1884.

102. Hay house, Washington. Entrance, 1884-86.

103. Hay house, Washington. Hall, 1884-86.

104. Gurney house, Pride's Crossing. Early perspective sketch, 1884.

105. Glessner house, Chicago. Exterior, 1885-87.

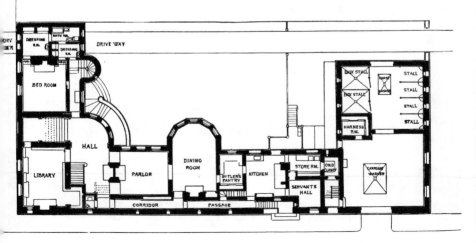

106. Glessner house, Chicago. Plan, 1885.

107. Lululund, Bushy, Middlesex. Exterior. 1886-94.

108. MacVeagh house, Chicago. Exterior, 1885-87.

109. Warder house, Washington. Exterior, 1885-87.

110. Gratwick house, Buffalo. Exterior, 1886-89.

111. Potter house, St. Louis. Exterior, 1886-87.

112. Ames Building (Harrison Avenue),
Boston. Exterior, 1886-87.

113. Chamber of Commerce Building,
Cincinnati. Exterior, 1886-88, in construction.

114. Union Station, New London. Exterior, 1885-87.

Queen Anne character, is the least Romanesque feature of the building, but it is not as successful as some of the more Romanesque features. It was, nevertheless, quite as frequently imitated by the Romanesque Revivalists in the next decade.

It is clear that Richardson now knew how to compose with the Romanesque as well as he ever knew how to compose in a more classical style. But he was still uncertain how to terminate a design at the top without prominent roofs. He was also too ready to sacrifice interior convenience to a predetermined exterior pictorial effect in the fenestration. Yet the Cheney Building is distinctly more advanced and more significant than Trinity.

This building has been almost entirely reconstructed inside as it is now a department store. Originally, there were five deep stores on the ground floor, with masonry party walls between. A light court surrounded by grouped windows in masonry walls was at the rear. There were very few interior castiron supports and none in exterior walls.

Since there has been so much adverse comment in the discussion of the Cheney Building, it is worth stating categorically, to balance the critical record, that it is certainly one of the very finest buildings in the world dating from the mid-seventies. Like the Watts Sherman house, IX-28 its qualities are more conspicuous today than when it was built. In the hierarchy of Richardson's work they are both at least the equal in standing of the more famous Trinity.

Richardson's confused and tragi-comic relationship with the New York State Capitol in Albany started in 1875. This monument had been begun in 1867 in the full blow of post-Civil War prosperity. The architect was Thomas Fuller, best known for his Victorian Gothic IX-29 capitol at Ottawa. The Albany design was not Gothic, but, according to contemporary opinion, "Italian Renaissance". It combined the pavilioned plan and mansard roofs of the Anglo-American Second Empire style with the more academic giant porticos of Walter's wings IX-30 on the Capitol in Washington. It was to have cost $4,000,000. By 1875, $7,000,000 had already been spent although the building was only

167

two storeys above ground. In a time of depression it is not surprising that a drastic change of administration was deemed necessary.

In 1875 a new Capitol commission was appointed, of which Lieutenant-Governor William Dorsheimer was the most important member. This new Commission appointed an advisory architectural board, consisting of Frederick Law Olmsted, Leopold Eidlitz and Richardson, to give its opinion as to what should be done about completing the building. After a thorough examination the board offered its report in the form of a wholly new project. The advisors soon found themselves appointed Fuller's successors, which was undoubtedly what Dorsheimer had intended. He had employed Richardson for his own house in 1868 and had probably been connected with the work which still continued on the Buffalo State Hospital, on which Olmsted had also advised.

IX-31

The new project was almost entirely the work of Eidlitz, a much older architect than Richardson and better known at this time. In the perspective [9] it appears that the already built basement and first storey of Fuller's design were to be preserved practically unchanged. The next storey above this was not very different, although the giant porticos were entirely omitted. But the top storey throughout and the upper part of the pavilions and turrets were indubitably Romanesque, even if rather more Victorian than Richardsonian. There were long arcades, with colonnettes at the corners of the windows, and much surface polychromy. The mansards were made inconspicuous between the tall steep roofs of pavilions and towers. The culminating feature was a great square tower rising from within the building and topped by an octagonal lantern and dome.

The impetus to propose such a mediaeval design came, doubtless, from the Connecticut State Capitol. In the competition for that a few years earlier, most of the designs were Victorian Gothic, including the winning one by Richard M. Upjohn. The Romanesque was an old love of Eidlitz, as we have seen. Its round arches could also be used with less impropriety above the classical arches of Fuller's work.

[9] Published in the *American Architect* for March 11, 1876.

Richardson's own new style apparently influenced the accepted design very little, although he may have been responsible for the ruggedness of the detail on the eastern approach and the central lantern.

In the next year work began under the new scheme, Richardson's actual commission dating from February, 1876. Apparently the exterior was to have been jointly executed by Richardson and Eidlitz; in the interior, however, there was a definite division of labor roughly from southeast to northwest. Thus Richardson was to design the Senate side, except for the front corner staircase which is by Eidlitz, and Eidlitz the Assembly side. The rear, with the great Western Staircase and the State Library, was to be Richardson's. Olmsted was, of course, only a general advisor whose taste was highly esteemed. (Fig. 54) .

But, as the change of architects took place, considerable criticism arose in the profession and also in the legislature. While the controversy continued, with committees of architects testifying before the legislature, the upper storeys were being built on the north side in a modified version of Eidlitz' original Romanesque scheme. Suddenly the style was legislated back from Romanesque to Renaissance. Thus, when Richardson came to build the upper storeys of the southern facade, he was in a quandary. He eventually found a solution by using classical detail treated in a somewhat crude manner recalling the Provencal Romanesque. He also provided dormers of rather clumsy François I character. (Fig. 44).

The exterior of the Capitol, in spite of all this interference and compromise, is not as bad as might be expected. The mere size of the white granite mass capped by the tall red roofs which finally replaced the mansards, is impressive. The stylized detail, whether intentionally Renaissance or intentionally Romanesque, has a rugged character suited to granite. There are occasional sections, such as the upper walls inside the court, which are really excellent.

The problem was, of course, hopeless. It could no more be solved by continuing the style of General Grant's day through the late seventies and eighties—as was done in the case of the appalling Municipal

Building in Philadelphia—than by changing to anything which could be described in the parlance of the times as "pure" Romanesque. Even the exterior, moreover, was not finished within Richardson's lifetime. Quite certainly the best part of the exterior is the western facade. This is, at least in part, the work of Isaac G. Perry, a local architect who finally completed the Capitol in 1894, using a more Richardsonian style than Richardson himself was permitted to apply in the seventies.

Whatever importance his work on the exterior of the Albany Capitol had for Richardson lay in defining his own type of Romanesque design as distinguished from that of the older Eidlitz. He also learned that the effect of picturesque silhouette and sturdy mass which he sought could be obtained with a combination of stylistic reminiscences as unrelated as the Romanesque and the François I. Mediaeval sixteenth century features had already appeared in his work: the dormers on the Hampden County Courthouse, for example, and many other details on the Watts Sherman house. But these were not combined with classical forms. On the Capitol, however, in designing François I dormers to harmonize with the Romanesque storey below, Richardson found that he could easily make any sort of detail individual in character. It was worth while, just as he was coming to associate the Romanesque so closely with his personal taste, that he should be brought to realize that there were other sources from which he could quite as well take suggestions for his own use. Otherwise he might shortly have become what others thought he was and what he even sometimes claimed to be: a Romanesque revivalist merely, and not a really great nineteenth century architect.

Inside the Capitol the pink marble wainscoting in the corridors, with mouldings and carved bosses of grey stone, alone calls for mention. This is characteristically rich and vigorous detail of the mid-seventies. But Richardson's real achievement was to be the Senate Chamber, just as that of Eidlitz was the Assembly Chamber. The Senate Chamber was not designed until 1878 and belongs definitely in the next period of Richardson's work. So also do the Governor's Room and the Court of Appeals. The Library and the Western Staircase were not begun until the end of his life and the Library has since been burnt out. The elaborate staircase as executed is predominantly the work of Isaac G. Perry, as is also the lush and monumental eastern approach, an impressive "Richardsonian" feature. This work was finished in the late eighties and nineties, but the eastern approach at least is not without considerable individual character.

A proposed addition to the Cheney Building in Hartford was published in the *American Architect and Building News* for 1877. (Fig. 45). This was not executed, but it is a rather interesting and significant design. The structure was separate from the main building, to which it was attached by a bridge over an alley. Only the ground storey was of stone, with a very wide segmental arch over the bayed shop window. Above this, the second floor had three arched windows in brick and the third and fourth, five. The steep roof was at right angles to the street, with a half-timbered dormer. On one corner was a tiny bay window turret corbelled at the base and with a pointed roof.

IX-32

This is Richardson's most Queen Anne project in masonry. The delicacy of scale and the picturesqueness of the dormer, the corner turret, and the bridge, with its twisted columns, suggest that the design was in large part White's. In the treatment of the upper floors, however, the avoidance of unnecessarily monumental scale, and the continuity of the fenestration are excellent. The panels in the third floor spandrels were apparently to be of carved brick like those used a year later with such success on Sever Hall.

IX-33

This building would not have been very harmonious with the Cheney Building itself and, of course, it was not as important. But it serves to link the developments of the mid-seventies with the brick monuments which are so conspicuous in the work of the succeeding five year period.

One other monument remains whose design belongs in the series which began in 1870, previous to the opening of the period of complete mastery in 1878.[10] This is the Winn Memorial Library in Woburn,

[10] The North Easton Library was commissioned only a few months later than the Woburn Library, but the design definitely belongs to the next period.

Mass., commissioned in competition in March, 1877, and hence wholly designed and probably under construction in that year. In this, the first of his great series of libraries, he established the characteristic plan he was later to perfect. This plan provided for the various functions of the building in a natural asymmetrical way and yet permitted real monumentality of composition. The Winn Library is certainly not one of his best works. Yet in some ways it represented almost as important a creative act as the Brattle Square Church, with which the period of the seventies had opened. All that Richardson had learned from the French about planning was now dissolved in his own personal command of functional arrangement. All the boldness and freedom he had been absorbing from the English, little by little, was also translated into his own terms. His bold relief, his vigorous expressive massing, his polychromy are here at their most intense. The great fault is that everything is developed at once. Hence the effect is strident, as in much of the best contemporary Victorian Gothic work. The polychromy struggles with the rock-hewn surfaces; the porch, the tower, and the gable are each too individually designed; the octagonal art gallery at the right is like a strayed chapter house, quite unrelated to the rest of the building. Only when we look away from all these brilliant and aggressive features to the stack wing do we see the really essential qualities of the best Richardsonian design: the simplicity, the poise, the adaptation of feature to function with little regard for precedent, the precisely balanced yet asymmetrical composition. (Fig. 48).

The long row of little stack windows, separated by colonnettes alternately single and in pairs, is held together as a horizontal unit by the heavy lintel above, which is also the lower member of the cornice below the roof. This arrangement is what is most truly original. The porch and the tower are Romanesque variants of English Victorian Gothic design; the Auvergnat marquetry on the gable beside the octagon, quite out of scale with the banded arches, is an ill digested fragment from Revoil. The tower is too vertical, the rest too horizontal; the whole a sort of compilation, recalling Butterfield and without his perverse mastery. (Fig. 47).

Yet the relation between the ranges of the arcades on the front gable is far better than on the Cheney Building. And the carving throughout is far more vigorous and spirited than on most later work.[11] The interior, particularly of the stack wing, with its wooden barrel roof and sturdy wooden grouped supports, is as fine as in his best later libraries. In the later libraries it is as if he took this design and moulded it together, reducing the individuality of the separate parts, solidifying the whole, and simplifying the detail. Later he could do this between his first project and the execution. In 1877 he still had to learn by building. Here the process of creation is half complete; later we only see the completed process, unless we examine early studies.

The years between 1870 and 1877 are perhaps the most important of Richardson's career. They established him justly as the most brilliant American architect of his day. Later he was to do far more work and far more finished work. But the series of buildings built between the time he was thirty-two and the time he was forty have a freshness that is later lost. These are also perhaps the most profitable of his works to study. In them we can piece together his personal style step by step, almost as he found it himself. In detailed examination their virtues are the more remarkable for being associated with equally conspicuous vices. His work is almost done before our eyes and the contribution of his most able assistant, White, can be determined with some accuracy. Later, when he was doing much more work than in these years, there is rarely the same personal quality. His office staff learned to be "Richardsonian"; the machinery of production became smoother, the results were usually easier to foretell.

Yet none of the buildings before 1878 are, perhaps, among his very greatest. They are generally more interesting than altogether fine. The course of his genius was still rising. Had his career ended here, books would hardly have been written about his architecture.

[11] In general the bold naturalistic carving of the mid-seventies, which is far more Gothic than Renaissance, is superior to all but the finest work around 1880.

PART IV

ACHIEVEMENT

1877–1883

CHAPTER TEN

1877-1879

RICHARDSON had not been very busy through the seventies. After 1872, only in 1877 did he have more than one new commission in any single year. But by 1880 the number of his new commissions had risen to five, one more than in the last pre-depression year. Within a few years he had twice as much work each year. As his popularity increased, therefore, he could not give to all his work the same attention he had lavished on the few commissions of his early maturity. A critical study must distinguish between the really creative work, still almost wholly his own, and other commissions which the office staff developed under his supervision. This distinction is not very important, however, before 1883. It was, indeed, in the five years between 1878 and 1883 that Richardson did most of his finest and most finished work.

Philip Webb, the one English contemporary architect who is really comparable in distinction to Richardson, saw very clearly that the standard of his work could not be maintained unless he restricted the number of his commissions. In his long career, extending from the design of William Morris's epoch-making Red House in 1859 to his retirement in 1900, he averaged only a little more than one commission a year. Thus he only needed to maintain a very small office, usually with no more than one responsible draftsman. The later reputation of one of these assistants, W. R. Lethaby, as an archaeologist and a critic, is indicative of the extent to which these men became disciples.[1]

[1] Lethaby was also Webb's biographer. *V.* Lethaby, W. R.: *Philip Webb and His Work*, Oxford, 1935. This also has a few illustrations of his work, at least more than are available elsewhere.

Webb kept down the number of his commissions by refusing bluntly those that did not interest him and even those on which he thought the client would not be sufficiently adaptable to his rather dictatorial ways. Richardson would have been well advised to have been more selective in accepting architectural work, particularly after he lost White, the only assistant he ever had who was at once sympathetic and individual.

It was not impossible for one man to control five new commissions a year, together with the projects that were not built, and the completion of earlier work which was also occupying the office. But it is obvious that no single architect could handle up to a score of jobs, as Richardson eventually was doing, without delegating to someone the responsibility for many.

It is easy to understand why Richardson never restricted the amount of his work, except by charging a rather higher fee than other architects and by warning prospective clients that his way of building was expensive. The buoyancy of his temperament, which had stood him in such good stead in the sixties, made it psychologically difficult for him to turn down opportunities. Probably, also, it would have been financially inconvenient to refuse commissions. He lived very amply, and there is every reason to believe that he, like many American architects, treated his professional earnings as income rather than principal. Even when he knew he was dying, in the mid-eighties, he gloried in the amount of work that was going on in his office. Although he knew well enough that the Pittsburgh buildings and the Marshall Field Store were the things he wanted time to complete, he never saved himself, and often disobeyed medical orders. He might have prolonged his life considerably and lived to do other work as fine or finer than the Field Store if he had not so readily accepted himself as a sort of legendary hero. With a psychology like that of his contemporaries in business, increasing ill health left him bent but unbowed, unwilling to turn away a single suburban railroad station, even if he himself could never hope to draw a line of its design.

As long as White remained with Richardson a certain amount of delegation was not dangerous to the quality of his production. For the two worked together in a really effective coöperation. White, under Richardson's general supervision, was at his best in houses, while Richardson undoubtedly preferred more monumental work. Even with Langford Warren, who succeeded White as chief assistant, things could go on not too badly. Warren had taste if little imagination, and his archaeological leanings did not often affect Richardson's executed work. Richardson, around 1880, still had time both to initiate the conception for each project and to redesign it entirely when Warren's drawings misinterpreted his intention.[2] But, as the commissions poured in a few years later and the office filled up with young men from Professor Ware's classes at the Massachusetts Institute of Technology, the situation changed. Rutan, who had been with Richardson so long, took charge adequately of technical matters, but there could really be no effective lieutenant in matters of design.

For all Richardson's expansiveness and the unusually complete and continuous contact with the office force which everyone testifies he preserved to the end, a certain dilution of his personal style was bound to take place. This is only very slightly visible in the work undertaken before his trip to Europe in 1882. But it is necessary even in the years just after 1878, which were his most mature and most fruitful, to be on the lookout for indications of the presence of increasingly uncomprehending hands in the office.

The men in the office were not unsympathetic to Richardson's style. Indeed, left to themselves, they tended to produce exaggerated parodies, like all followers *plus royalistes que le roi.* But they were, of course, much younger. They had known neither the stimulating stylistic confusion of the sixties in America, nor the sound traditional training which the Ecole des Beaux Arts still offered when Richardson was in Paris. They came from the new American architectural schools or from other architects' offices. Architecture to them was designing on paper. Style was something borrowed out of the past from books, or, worse, from photographs which were becoming more available. Their

[2] For example, the Trinity Rectory. *V.* Chapter XI.

taste was not, like Richardson's, wrought personally out of surrounding chaos, but something learned almost by rote. In their ideology, the Richardsonian style had to be a Romanesque Revival if it were of any worth at all.

In recalling the documents already in Richardson's library and noting the new acquisitions made from this time on, it is not enough to consider the inspiration they could offer to a great creative mind. The facility with which the men in the office could crib from them must perpetually be borne in mind.

For cribbing was in increasingly good repute about 1880. Richardson's older rival as America's leading architect was Richard Hunt. And the most spectacular example of Hunt's outright cribbing was
X-1   his W. K. Vanderbilt house in New York, begun in 1878. This was as conspicuous and as generally admired as Trinity Church. Even Trinity, moreover, offered the precedent of its crossing tower taken from Salamanca. Such precise imitation of documents had hardly been known for a generation. Archaeological correctness was not a vice of the period after the Civil War even in Gothic design. Whatever else it was, the Victorian Gothic was consciously interpretive, rather than imitative, of the art of the past.

There is little to indicate that Richardson himself ever came to seek "correctness" of style. There is nothing to justify the contention that in the seventies he desired to be a Romanesque Revivalist in the sense of the earlier Gothic Revivalists of the forties, or even of the imitators of the Renaissance styles who came after him. It is true that the source of certain details can be traced with some precision to the plates of Revoil's *Architecture Romane du Midi de la France*. But even these borrowings are probably more due to White than to Richardson himself. Nor were Romanesque sources the only ones from which Richardson drew inspiration. His use of French Renaissance detail on the Albany Capitol, of tall Late Gothic dormers elsewhere,
X-2   and of Queen Anne detail on his houses, all indicate that he by no means restricted himself to the study of Southern French Romanesque design in the mid-seventies.

Although the polychromy on Trinity is specifically Auvergnat, and the general feeling perhaps more like that of the richly decorated schools of Southern France than the cruder and more structural schools of the North, even within the Romanesque Richardson's borrowings in these years may be traced to a considerable variety of sources. The banded arches on the Cheney Building and the Woburn Library were doubtless Auvergnat in inspiration; but earlier, on the Brattle Square Church, they had certainly been of Victorian Gothic origin and hence ultimately Italian. His carved detail, at first French Second Empire Norman or Syrian, was later even less archaeological. That on the three preceding masonry buildings, the Cheney Building, the Albany Capitol and the Woburn Library, was far more closely related to the vigorous naturalism of the best English monumental work of the time than to the Romanesque of any school of the past.

The source from which Richardson drew the most assistance in the seventies was still the modern architecture of England, at this time growing suaver and more eclectic as the Queen Anne movement gained force. There is hardly a building by him in the seventies that would not be considered rather typically late Victorian Gothic if only its arches were pointed and its masonry less rugged. This is particularly evident in the case of the Woburn Library, as has already been pointed out. Richardson's personal style was chiefly characterized by a predilection for massive walls, lintel-covered openings, and broad low arches, none of which is particularly derived from the Romanesque. The most characteristic type of arch, which he began to use only in late 1877, was specifically Syrian.[3] Even his solid mass composition is rarely related to Romanesque types of mass composition, except in the special case of the crossing tower of Trinity.

The formation of Richardson's style took place when he designed the Brattle Square Church and the Buffalo State Hospital. Trinity, as has been implied, was something of a side track. His style, however, continued to develop through the seventies, reaching complete maturity by about 1878. The special qualities of his best late buildings

[3] Derived undoubtedly from de Vogüé's *Syrie Centrale*.

are restraint and precision of scale. Yet the scale he was achieving in the mid-eighties, at the end of his life, was not so very different from that of his work in the mid-seventies. Relative unrestraint is more characteristic of his middle years. Only the increasing respect for symmetry, which begins to be evident from 1878, is an innovation in his late work, and that is a reversion to his French training rather than a really new development. The exaggerated pursuit of asymmetry in architecture is a sign of youth, quite as out of place in the work of mature genius as its exaggerated avoidance.

There can be no certainty as to the exact dates when the great majority of Richardson's books came into his possession. About three-quarters of them bear publication dates earlier than 1878. His library was roughly completed, it may therefore be assumed, just about the time his personal style came to full maturity. He did not need many more books after 1878 because he did not need much more outside inspiration. Even so, his office force had a better supply of documents to imitate than existed in most other architects' libraries.

The most important new work, probably acquired at this time, is Léon Palustre's *La Renaissance en France*. The first part of this, issued in 1877, may well have been bought to supplement Sauvageot imme-diately on its publication, when the François I style appeared the best compromise to satisfy the requirements of legislated Renaissance in Albany. In later years he found much inspiration in the massing of sixteenth century French architecture, although he almost never again used any Renaissance detail. Hunt, however, undoubtedly owed to Palustre the possibility of carrying out the W. K. Vanderbilt house in the François I style with a wealth of "correct" detail. This house was completed in 1881, just too soon to profit from the second volume of Palustre, which appeared in the latter year.

Of the other books in Richardson's library with publication dates up to 1883, very few are of a type specifically useful to a practicing architect. The acquisition of Stephenson's *House Architecture*, pub-lished in 1880, probably reflects the development of his interest in domestic design with the many new commissions of 1879 and the

X-3

X-4

immediately following years. This provided a source for much of his Queen Anne interior detail. But Eidlitz' *Nature and Function of Art* X-5 is a dedicated tribute from a collaborator, not the proof of a sudden passion for theory. The acquisition of Pennethorne's *The Geometry and Optics of Ancient Architecture* and the Archaeological Institute of America's *Report of the Investigations at Assos,* both of 1882, implied no repentant desire to return to classical forms. They serve only to show the breadth of Richardson's cultural interests. Only the large monograph on St. Mark's, of which the first volume appeared in 1881, left its mark on his work, and that chiefly after 1883. This was probably X-6 subscribed for when he was in Venice in 1882.

The increasingly archaeological character of Richardson's detail after 1880, in contrast to the more vigorous and original carving of the seventies, is probably due to the attempts that were made to educate the executants. The carvers of the Evans firm, who carried out so much of Richardson's work, were from this time on frequently shown photographs of mediaeval work. Richardson's intention was undoubtedly that they should emulate its quality. But they learned only too well to make lifeless forgeries. Within a few years they had quite lost whatever personal touch they once had.

The greater pressure of work also made it necessary for Richardson to leave the design of detail almost entirely to his draftsmen. After 1880 he had no time to train them personally, as he had trained his first assistants, McKim and White. When White left, there remained no one in the office with real imagination and taste in matters of detail. Richardson was forced to send his men to books and photographs in self-protection; archaeology was at least better than botched imitations of his own earlier ornament or Americanized Queen Anne fantasies. His own efforts were restricted to essentials: the study of plans with his clients; the study of massing in perspective; the general disposition of features in elevation; the choice and expression of materials; and the supervision of execution.

How many photographs of architecture Richardson owned before he went to Europe in 1882 there is no way of telling. But the great bulk of the existing collection he must have brought back with him at that time. The particular signs of photographic inspiration of detail certainly grew much more evident from then on.

Richardson hardly intended to practice "productive archaeology". But the general inability to understand and appreciate his personal style for what it was—the misapprehension that it was merely a Romanesque Revival—is somewhat justified by the "correct" detail on his late buildings. Lewis Mumford, in the *Brown Decades,* points out that. Richardson protected himself against the possible recriminations of his clients by a specific statement in the circular explaining the character of his services: ". . . I cannot, however, guarantee that the building . . . shall conform to his (the client's) ideas of beauty or taste, or indeed to those of any person or school." Although undoubtedly Richardson was an advocate of the use of Romanesque models, he realized with how little respect for archaeology he drew his own inspiration. His work was so readily acclaimed as Romanesque only because his generation knew next to nothing about the ancient monuments in the style.

Curiously enough, Richardson's work was derided for being Romanesque by the succeeding generation also, which knew little more of the style. In my own case, indeed, a generation later still, the appreciation of Richardson's originality began at Harvard with the surprising discovery that the real Romanesque was rarely Richardsonian. The study of the architecture of the early Middle Ages under so brilliant and subtle a historian of art as Kingsley Porter made clear how little Richardson owed to that period of the past.[4] Later, the appreciation

[4] The great illustration of Richardson's essential originality and the wide field of reference from which he drew suggestions was Sever Hall at Harvard, begun in 1878. It was the Syrian portal of Sever which I left to learn from Kingsley Porter—in Hunt's Greek Fogg Museum—what the styles of the early Middle Ages really had been. It was no longer possible for me to believe Sever was Romanesque, not even as Romanesque as Schulze's nearby Appleton Chapel, which had been Richardson's own first illustration of the style. In the same way, no one at Harvard since Charles H. Moore's day had believed that Memorial Hall was appreciably Gothic.

of his debt to the Early Christian art of Syria, to the sixteenth century styles of Northern Europe, and even to the American Colonial, prepared the way for the obvious truth that he was not a revivalist in any proper sense of the word at all. Richardson, in developing his personal style, was ready to find inspiration in any part of the past that appealed to him. The Romanesque was perhaps most useful. On account of his French training, the Renaissance and the Classical styles seemed sterile and worn out. On the other hand, the Victorian Gothic had already taken the bloom off the inspiration to be derived from the styles of the thirteenth and fourteenth centuries.

Typical of what two generations of Americans were to mistake for an accurate imitation of the Southern French Romanesque was the North Easton Library. This was built for the Ames family as a memorial to Oakes Ames, whose memory was already quite otherwise embalmed in the pages of American history. The North Easton Library was commissioned in September, 1877, and the design is therefore at least six months later than that for the Woburn Library. It is much quieter in design than the earlier monument. The plan is very similar but more compact. It lacks the octagonal wing, which is such an undigested feature of the earlier design. The massing is consequently much simpler. One short broad gable projects on the front of the long low main block of the building. The rather plain tower is almost too inconspicuously placed at the inner angle of this projection. Although the stone roof of the tower rises to a rather sharp point, the other tiled roofs have a low pitch with only a slight upcurve at the eaves. The battered foundation is lower and less prominent than that of the Hampden County Courthouse, which, in some ways, this building recalls more than any intervening work. (Fig. 49).

While the Cheney Building and the Woburn Library were largely of brownstone, the walling here is of rock-faced Milford granite with rather less Longmeadow trim than there is on Trinity. Since in the country there is little grime, this building remains rather light in colour. Hence, it appears today more as Richardson intended it than does the gloomy bulk of Trinity.

The best feature of this Library, as at Woburn, is the row of windows in the stack wing. The most conspicuous feature of the design, hitherto not found in any of Richardson's work, is the very low arch rising in Syrian style almost from the ground. The cavernous appearance of this characteristic feature, so often imitated by the Richardsonian school, almost suggests some Freudian motivation in the subconscious. Yet the detail on this arch is neither Syrian nor related to poor Oedipus. The zigzags are, indeed, rather definitely Norman, although lacking in the proper boldness. Otherwise there is very little carved detail on the exterior: only capitals with crockets of the early French Gothic type. The corner gargoyles are of a sort of Pre-Raphaelite Mediaevalism too picturesque and too realistic to have any source other than the vivid imagination of Stanford White. Except for the marquetry designs on the gable ends, which are as Auvergnat as those of Trinity and the Woburn Library, there is nothing here which derives from the Romanesque of Southern France. On the rear, plain lintels cover most of the windows. The only important feature is a wide mullioned bank of five lights in the reading room. This is of the simplest Late Gothic type.

The interior is very simple. (Fig. 50). The stack wing is slightly superior to that at Woburn, perhaps, but really very little changed. The reading room has square-panelled wainscoting with bands of thin reeding about the windows. This was to become a commonplace of the vernacular in the next decade. The wooden detail should possibly all be attributed to White, and may be inspired either by Stephenson's book or by the Colonial work White saw in the summer of 1877.[5]

X-7

But the exuberant stone fireplace, although out of character with its domestic setting, is a very original work of decorative art. It was probably developed by White in detail, but the scale is Richardsonian. This fireplace is not in the least archaeological. The design is rather

[5] On the "famous" trip he took along the North Shore with McKim and Bigelow in search of seventeenth and eighteenth century houses.

in the best Pre-Raphaelite decorative tradition of the Morris firm in England, executed with great boldness and realism. The parts are put together rather chaotically, so that the general composition is not satisfactory, but the pomegranate trees rising from the vases make a very fine ornamental relief. Equally excellent are the branches of bay and oak so unexpectedly framing the matter-of-fact medallion of Oakes Ames. (Fig. 46).

If this fireplace is the product of White's decorative invention, much might have been expected of his later collaboration with Richardson. (It was just at this time that White began to collaborate with Saint-Gaudens on the pedestal for the Farragut statue, which was, perhaps, his finest minor work.) Richardson later produced one monumental fireplace which is finer than this: the one in Austin Hall, but even that hardly has the same promise, although the execution is more suave. Since Pre-Raphaelite inspiration was so fruitful in decoration, it was a pity that Richardson rarely turned in this direction again—or White, either, for that matter. Even these two men, who could have most profited from another decade of freedom in decorative art, soon lost the habit of imaginative invention. Ornamental detail, however, is not one of the more important elements in great architecture.

The North Easton Library may be seen today much as Richardson left it, somewhat overshadowed by the bolder and less successful Town Hall he began two years later. The only change is the wing inconspicuously added at the rear a few years ago to provide more stack space. Only the Woburn Library, among the many Richardson built after 1877, was large enough to provide space for the books needed for general reading in the twentieth century. Yet, when these libraries were built, they seemed to many extravagantly large for the still undeveloped reading tastes of the public. The North Easton Library was built by the heirs of two of the most famous and, indeed, notorious magnates of the period. Nevertheless, the Ames family and Richardson here served not the special interests of the new magnates but one of the best general tendencies of the time: the increasing desire for informal education. It was significant of Richardson's position as a man of his own time that he built more and better public libraries than churches.

After the exuberance of the Woburn Library the North Easton Library is perhaps a little bare. But Richardson was learning that continuity of surface was of essential importance for the effect of rugged mass in which he was interested. Therefore he omitted drip moulds above the arches and violent banded polychromy. Even on the entrance arch he flattened the Norman detail so that the whole wall surface might appear to curve in at the porch. As a reaction from the excessive verticality of certain features at Woburn, the effect here is rather too horizontal. The roofs are too low for the solid bulk of the masses they cover; the entrance arch looks as if it led to the basement. But the random ashlar of the granite walling is so handsome that one does not regret the long low expanses of it. The restraint in the use of carved detail also enhances the quality of the materials. This is not a great building, but it was a desirable corrective to the pyrotechnics at Woburn. For Richardson, as for any architect building at the end of five years of depression, dullness was safer than brilliance.

Sever is unassertive but not dull. Above all others it is the building in which Richardson achieved complete maturity of style. Commissioned in October, 1878, it was the first work he undertook after the severance, in the same month, of his more and more meaningless partnership with Gambrill. But even before this, both the Buffalo State Hospital and the Albany Capitol commissions had been given to him personally and not to the firm.[6] Sever was also the first building entirely designed after White's departure for Europe. This may explain the greater simplicity of Sever compared to the somewhat similar treat-

[6] After Richardson moved his personal office to Boston in 1874, White was increasingly a real collaborator such as Gambrill had never been. But the contribution of White to Richardson's more monumental work seems to have been negligible except in the case of the Trinity crossing tower. The arrangement with Gambrill must have left him in charge of the decreasingly important New York office. The New York office may have continued to handle work distant from Boston, like the Buffalo State Hospital, even though it was not a commission of the firm. But no important designing for that project seems to have been done later than 1873. Gambrill did no work of his own after the mid-seventies.

ment of the brickwork on the Cheney addition project of the previous year.

The common red brick of which Sever was built, and the general proportions and the symmetry are Richardson's sincere tribute of respect to the eighteenth century building of the yard. Wisely he forgot the polychrome and picturesque style of Ware and Van Brunt's new Memorial Hall across the street, the Gothic and Jacobean designs of their Matthews Hall and Peabody and Stearns' Weld Hall, built at the beginning of the decade. The late Romanticism of the seventies had damaged the consistency of the eighteenth century college architecture far more than Schulze's early Romanticism of the fifties, when Richardson was in college. Only Ryder and Harris among contemporary architects had tried to preserve the old style in building Thayer Hall. This is a simple but pompous pseudo-Georgian pile, too tall for the old buildings and of a hard red brick with beige sandstone trim.

Richardson borrowed few features of design from the Colonial tradition—only the large pediment on the front and the smaller one over the rear door. He could do far better than copy. Long ago he must have sensed the fine quality of mass and the excellence of the brick-work of the early buildings in the yard. The quality of mass he emulated to perfection. Brick of eighteenth century quality was no longer made, but at least he found a common brick of a fine rich red. Perhaps unadvisedly, he used red mortar and orange-red tile roofs, as if after the orgy of polychromy at Woburn the previous year he wished to show what could be done with one colour alone. The windows are   X-8 arranged in large groups. Their regular spacing provides the chief decorative interest of the composition. The few ornamental features introduced were certainly neither Romanesque nor Colonial.

The exterior of this building displays such superb craftsmanship that it is a distinct disappointment to discover that the interior construction is somewhat shoddy. Richardson was still too much a Romantic to care as much for solidity that did not show—an engineering virtue—as for solidity that did.

The plan of Sever is very similar to the excellent one of the

Worcester High School. But here the plan is almost ideally expressed on the exterior. In deference to the symmetrical design of the old buildings, however, the presence of a large classroom at the left hand end is indicated only by the absence of windows on the north facade. The narrow offices are marked by bay windows. These continue the whole height of the walls and are capped with roofs steeper in slope than the main roof. Their somewhat tower-like appearance is the only really mediaeval element about the design. The most conspicuous fault is the entrance, which, like that at North Easton, is Early Christian rather than Romanesque or Gothic. This low Syrian archway is so deeply recessed as to suggest walls of more than twice the actual thickness. The mouldings in cut brick which surround it are also much too heavy in scale. The segmental arch used on the Cheney project would have been far more satisfactory. (Fig. 51).

Moulded brick is skilfully and properly used around the windows. The small roll moulding on the jambs and below the flat arches over the top is unnecessary but effective. The windows in the central bay of the front and at the corners have rounded corners cut in brownstone. Elsewhere these wedges of stone are unmoulded, an awkward if inconspicuous detail. The precedent for this treatment appears to have been a modern German house in Paderborn by Guldenpfennig, published some years before in the English *Builder*.[7] The ultimate source, however, was rather the general sixteenth century North European brick style to which the Queen Anne architects in England were turning very frequently at this time for ideas of craftsmanship. Suggestive of Queen Anne design, also, but of a different type, is the elaborate ornament cut in the brick of the pediment. This is more Renaissance, or even Baroque of a rural sort, than Romanesque, and is very similar to much contemporary English detail to be seen in the *Builder*. The cornice is of a hybrid character also, at once early eighteenth century and Romanesque in scale. The rather widely spaced carved bosses in the carved brick frieze are more vigorous and naturalistic.

The treatment of the rear, although more complicated, is even

[7] Vol. 28, May 14, 1870.

X-9

better than that of the front. The flat arched doorway in the center, with its simple pediment, is of Queen Anne inspiration, but in the best late Stuart vernacular tradition. It accords better with the flat-arched structural pattern of the windows than the heavy and bare Syrian arch on the front. The slightly bulging bay above, supported on brick corbelling, emphasizes the solidity of the total mass of the building far better than the central bay on the front which projects so abruptly above the entrance. There is, moreover, no need of a crowning pediment, so that the cornice line remains unbroken. The different heights of the windows of the first and second storey on this side are, of course, due to the staircase in the center. The long dormer in the roof effectively lights the attic and echoes in design the long low proportions of the whole building. (Fig. 52).

In the distribution of the fenestration on both the front and the rear, the larger groups of windows at the top terminate the rhythmic arrangement more subtly than the low arcade at the top of the Cheney Building. The windows in the towers, however, are rather narrow and the single lights near the corners also break the rhythm in a way not entirely justified by the plan. Against such minor faults of consistency, which appear only on careful study, may be set minor virtues which the same careful study brings to notice. For instance, the fluted brick chimneys are the finest Richardson ever designed. The detail in the cornices is marvellously adjusted so as to use the brick in a fashion at once simple and rich. The window panes are not tiny, and yet they are so associated with the heavier transoms that the windows do not seem holes in the wall.

This is without question one of Richardson's greatest works of architecture. It is, moreover, an almost unique masterpiece of the incredibly difficult art of building in harmony with fine work of the past and yet creating a new style for a new day. The architects of the next generation who worked at Harvard were not even aware of the need of such a new style. Ever since 1888, when McKim designed the Johnston Gate with the avowed intention of "bringing Harvard back to bricks and mortar"—what, pray, had Richardson done at Sever? [8]—, the fine old buildings of the Harvard Yard have been swamped with parodies. The worst offenders, perhaps, have been Richardson's own successors.

At last, however, in designing the new Biological Laboratories, the same firm—of which Richardson's grandson, Mr. Henry Richardson Shepley, is a partner—has faced squarely the difficult problem which Richardson solved for his own day at Sever. The Biological Laboratory is certainly not the best example of contemporary style in America. But when it was erected a few years ago, there was in the field of college architecture in America no building of comparable significance, just as there was none at the time of Sever.[9]

The Albany Senate Chamber, which belongs to exactly the same years, is very different from Sever. It was the richest work of architecture Richardson ever executed, and it quite lacked important innovations in composition.[10] The plan was largely predetermined by Fuller's original scheme for the building and even the size and arrangement of the windows in two rows was fixed by the necessity for keeping even storey levels on the exterior and a consistent rhythm. The placing of

[8] He had used a red mortar, to be specific, which McKim used through the early eighties, but which would not have seemed correctly Colonial to him in 1888. McKim's successors in 1934 were using red mortar again in a "Georgian" building at Wesleyan University.

[9] Sturgis, the excellence of whose Farnam Hall at Yale in 1869 has been mentioned, did not improve upon Sever when he built Lawrence Hall at Yale five years later. Out of deference to his own earlier work (a deference which later Yale architects have never shown), he was content to repeat Farnam almost without change.

[10] According to the testimony of a letter written by White to Saint-Gaudens in May, 1878, just before his departure to join the sculptor in Europe, he and Richardson had just "tackled the Albany Senate Chamber, and between [them] cooked up something pretty decent." (*V.* Baldwin, *op. cit.*) Richardson, encouraged by White, then thought of employing Saint-Gaudens to do the decorative sculpture, an arrangement which should have been very happy. But the blank panels above the fireplaces are still waiting for a sculptor. Although the first designs of the Senate Chamber are to be dated late spring, 1878, it was not finished until 1881, a year after Sever. It must have been much modified, in execution. It seems proper, therefore, to consider it later than Sever.

the galleries behind great arcades above the side lobbies was both ingenious and effective. But the situation of the main doorway on the axis of the interior wall forced Richardson to set the president's desk against a window on the outside wall. Thus the Senators' chairs faced the light, which was distinctly awkward. The two fireplaces can hardly have been needed for heating at this period. They would, moreover, have been quite inadequate in so large and tall a room. Yet these two large motifs flanking the entrance door divide and destroy the axial emphasis. In spite of these serious practical and aesthetic defects, the room remains effectively monumental. (Fig. 54).

Above all, the materials are sumptuous in texture and rich in colour. The lower walls are covered by tall screen-like settee backs of mahogany and leather. These are rather small in scale, but they were harmonious with the other furniture designed by Richardson, the rest of which has now unfortunately been removed. Above the settees the walls are of unpolished pink Knoxville marble of a dull neutral tone. At a higher level on the north and south walls the rather large square panels are of golden Mexican onyx, selected for variety of colour and pattern, and framed by plain slightly convex bands of yellow Siena marble. At this level on the east and west walls open the great arches of the gallery. Resting on heavy columns of highly polished red-brown granite, these arches are sheathed with voussoirs of Siena marble, selected, like the onyx of the wall panels, for variety of colour. The mouldings, the enormous carved capitals, and the balustrade, which bows out rather awkwardly between the columns, are of unpolished Knoxville marble, like the lower walls. Above the panels and the arches the walls are covered with gilded and embossed lead. The elaborate all-over pattern is so small in scale as to provide a rich texture and little more. The very heavy beamed ceiling of oak is supported on carved consoles of marble. Thus, except for the settees which line the walls, the scale is monumental throughout. The colour is also beautifully scaled from the pale grey-pink of the dull Knoxville marble through the richer yellows and browns of the onyx, the Siena marble, and the gilding of the walls, to the dark yellow-brown oak of the ceiling, and the red-brown of the granite columns. The mahogany and the leather of the furniture were the deepest notes of all.

The panels on the chimney breasts of Knoxville marble were never carved. These features, therefore, seem unduly heavy and bare. But on the whole there is a consistent and rather Byzantine luxury such as Richardson had only been able to imitate in paint with La Farge's help at Trinity. The carving of the string courses and capitals is rather fresh and Pre-Raphaelite in design. In execution the finish is not high enough, however, and what in sandstone would be accepted as strength and ruggedness, in marble appears crudity and even incompetence.

The pre-existing difficulties were so great in carrying out the Senate Chamber that it is a pity Richardson did not elsewhere have as ample resources. The use of colours is not pyrotechnic as at Woburn. The richness of effect can be compared very favorably with the boiled-vegetable dullness of tone in Eidlitz' Assembly Chamber, begun and finished slightly earlier. The Assembly Chamber was a much larger room with four enormous columns in the corners. It is undoubtedly more monumental in general design and scale than the Senate Chamber, even now that the original stone vaulting has been replaced with a flat beamed ceiling. But the dead neutral masonry is not sufficiently enlivened by the arabesques at tiny scale that are cut in the stones of the arches and spandrels, nor even by William M. Hunt's painted lunettes, which are washed out in colour and quite unarchitectural in conception. Eidlitz' work throughout the interior of the Capitol remains Victorian Gothic in spirit and is quite lacking in the suavity of Richardson's.

Richardson carried out some other work at the Capitol in the years before 1883. In the Executive Chamber the fireplace bears the date 1880. The Court of Appeals was finished, like the Senate Chamber, in 1881. This has now been transported bodily into a wing especially built for it on the rear of the old State Hall. Both of these fine rooms are less varied in colour and naturally less monumental than the Senate Chamber. The walls are panelled in rich brown oak, not as yet to be described as golden, with only a very little marble and onyx. Most of the panelling is of rather conventional early eighteenth century type, like that in the reading room of the North Easton Library, but better executed.

The happiest idea in the Court of Appeals was a very simple one: that of arranging the series of portraits of justices in a sort of frieze above the wainscoting. The general excellence of the room can only be compared, among Richardson's later interiors, with the living hall of the John Hay house. The Executive Chamber is less elaborate, but also dignified and impressive.

The ornament in the Court of Appeals calls for particular mention. (Fig. 55). The fireplace is set in a sort of wide inglenook of Siena marble and Mexican onyx under an arching beam of oak. The decorative reliefs, carved in oak above the beam, have great swirling bosses, more suggestive of Sullivan's ornament of the nineties than of the marble carving in the Senate Chamber. The execution is more finished X-11
and smaller in scale, as befits work in wood. Although the effect is Byzantine, these reliefs are hardly archaeological. Yet with this precedent for a Byzantine effect established (probably by Richardson's own hand now that White had left him), the office force thenceforth was naturally tempted to crib similar detail from the photographic plates in the monograph on St. Mark's which Richardson acquired for his library in the next year or two.

In the profusion of the carving around the fireplace and on the nearby oaken clock, of which Richardson was equally proud, there is a disturbing variation of scale which contrasts with the sound architectural design of the room as a whole. Richardson, by nature a gourmand, frankly enjoyed such richness of effect; but he did not know how to control himself when he began to elaborate.

On the whole, the relatively inconspicuous carving on Richardson's buildings of the early seventies is better than that of the buildings of the early eighties to which far more thought was undoubtedly given. Ornamental invention in America was breaking down at this time. X-12
Within a few years White also took refuge in the imitation of Quattrocento and Cinquecento ornament. Only in the almost vernacular

"Richardsonian", of which Perry's work on the Capitol after Richardson's death is an example, did something of the old Victorian Gothic gusto continue, translated into the swirling bosses of Richardson's ornament of 1880-81.

Yet perhaps Edward Colonna, working in the mid-eighties on the design of private cars in Dayton, Ohio, derived as much from this as from the broom plant which was his avowed inspiration. Colonna's work was the opening phase of the ornamental manner which was to flourish in Europe in the nineties as *Modern Style*. This is known to Anglo-Saxons as the Art Nouveau. The beginnings of Sullivan's characteristic ornament of the nineties, moreover, can be found in his still Richardsonian work of the late eighties. Richardson, who loved ornament, was really no ornamentalist. Hence he was finally satisfied in his last years with archaeological ornament. Yet, through such work as the Court of Appeals fireplace, he perhaps played his part in the initiation of what was perhaps the last great ornamental style of the Western world. His work was, at least, one of several alternative links between late Pre-Raphaelite and early Art Nouveau decorative design.

X-13

CHAPTER ELEVEN

1879-1880

IN 1879 Richardson received two new commissions from the Ames family. One was for a monument commemorating the completion of the Union Pacific at Sherman, Wyoming; the other was for a town hall in memory of Oliver Ames, to be built beside the Library at North Easton. F. L. Ames, by this time, was one of his immediate circle of friends.

The monument in Wyoming is a two-stepped pyramid with a blunt, pointed top, all of great blocks of random ashlar. (Fig. 56). It is decorated only with a simple well placed inscription on the front and two square bronze plaques of Oakes and Oliver Ames designed by Saint-Gaudens on opposite sides. This is perhaps the finest memorial in America. Against the background of the Rockies, it is like an abstract mountain itself. Richardson, who at Albany seemed to have forgotten his passion for rugged grandeur in a welter of polychromy and ornament, here, as in Sever Hall, returned to fundamentals. Solid masonry mass and fine sculpture were enough. For the medallions he chose the best young sculptor of the day, whose name was just about to be made famous by his Farragut statue, already designed but not unveiled until XI-1 1881.

But if the monument in Wyoming is one of Richardson's least known and most perfect works, the North Easton Town Hall in memory of Oliver Ames was both widely studied and unworthy of his genius. It is an awkward and aggressive pile, perhaps successful as a part of Olmsted's picturesque treatment of the hillside, but not as architecture. (Fig. 53). The Library had a real purpose in the North Easton community; the Town Hall had none, for the town meetings were held at Easton. Today it is not open at all, since the exiguous staircase in the corner turret makes the use of the upper hall too great a fire hazard. This tower, like that at Woburn, is exaggeratedly vertical in relation to the rest of the mass and looks quite as inadequate as it actually is. It is obviously a mere pictorial embellishment like the Worcester High School tower. The contrast of the light granite and dark Longmeadow stone of the tower with the plain brick walls of the main block is also far too great.

On the other hand, the great arches of the front loggia are too low and horizontal for the general proportions of the building. This arcade, with its stubby columns, recalls less the new Syrian entrances of the nearby Library and of Sever Hall than the Unity Church narthex of 1866 or the Agawam Bank windows of 1869. Its only virtue is in the splendid vigour of the masonry. But the monumental scale is totally inappropriate to the brick walls and simple brownstone detail of the storey above.

The treatment of the two ends of the building is quite disparate. At the right, behind the tower, is a large dormer of timber and tile-hanging in close imitation of Norman Shaw's idiom. At the other end, the mass is terminated by a low pitched gable. The roof of this gable descends below the main cornice line and is quite unrelated to the tall saddle-backed hip roof of the main portion of the building. A prominent Late Gothic dormer with more or less Romanesque detail breaks the center of the main roof. This, as well as the general disposition, is taken over with some exaggeration of scale from the unexecuted project for the Brookline Town Hall of 1870. But the composition here, although much more developed and personal in character, is inferior even to that early study. The formal discipline of the French official tradition was now almost lost. To judge from this building alone, Richardson would appear to have forgotten in the course of the decade

almost as much of what he once knew as he had learned from the
Romanesque and the Queen Anne.

The real virtues of the North Easton Town Hall are in the general
massing and the treatment of the upper storey. In its best elements it
is a bolder and somewhat more mediaeval version of Sever. The brownstone mullions and lintels of the windows are admirably handled and
the spacing, except in the section at the left end, is remarkably happy.

But it was the more conspicuous but inferior qualities, the adaptation to a picturesque site [1] and the piquancy of exaggerated characteri-
zation, that appealed to the taste of the time, as they had at the Unity
Church twelve years earlier. This was one of Richardson's most generally admired buildings and perhaps the most widely emulated. The
arbitrary asymmetry in the subordinate parts, the abrupt shifts in scale,
and the combination in one building of exaggeratedly vertical and exaggeratedly horizontal elements were all copied by imitators for more
than a decade. The use on the same building of Romanesque and sixteenth century forms, only superficially harmonized, and the violent
and unmotivated juxtaposition of heavy rock-faced stone masonry with
brickwork and wooden construction were also to be characteristic of
the worst practice of the Richardsonian school.

Like the Phoenix Building of 1872, the North Easton Town Hall
was a lapse and almost an anachronism, certainly not up to the standard of Richardson's best years. But the American public has always
had an unerring flair for what is just behind the times. Second-rate
architects, moreover, are everywhere carried away by inferior expres-
sions of strong personal style. This building was at once selected as
Richardson's choicest. The practice of a school was based largely on
its vices, while its virtues and the greater but comparable virtues of
Sever were hardly emulated at all.

---

[1] F. L. Olmsted collaborated with Richardson on this work. The splendid
naturalistic treatment of the rocky hillside and the great stairs rising through the
ledges are very fine indeed in themselves, and more truly Olmsted's than
Richardson's. But they are not very flattering to the more conventional treatment of the site of the Library just below.

The Rectory of Trinity Church was built on the corner of Newbury and Clarendon Streets in Boston as a residence for Richardson's friend, Phillips Brooks. It is a much less ambiguous and far finer design than the North Easton Town Hall. Commissioned in April, 1879, and finished during the following year, it must also have been designed at about the same time as Sever Hall. Indeed, it closely resembles Sever. The Rectory is the first of a series of excellent houses built by Richardson in the eighties.

Several preliminary studies exist for the Trinity Rectory. The general arrangement, with the entrance in a recessed porch on the middle of the long side, did not change appreciably between the early studies and the final execution. In all the stages of the design the drawing room is at the front, and the dining room at the rear, with the hall and the stairs between. This, indeed, the narrow site made necessary. But the studies for the elevation indicate three successive states in Richardson's conception of the house. The first is still almost Victorian Gothic, with saddle-back gables, projecting eaves and even black brick patterns. The long segmental arch over the recessed entrance porch is of dark and light stone voussoirs. Only the windows in this project are at all like anything on Sever. This study, although a geometrical elevation and not a perspective, appears to be in Richardson's own draftsmanship. For there is a very free expressive quality in the pencil work and more vigour than in White's renderings.

The perspective of a later state of the exterior is a rather finished sketch in brown ink, probably in the draftsmanship of H. Langford Warren, in these years Richardson's chief assistant. This is probably also of his designing, for it is definitely Queen Anne, small in scale and highly finished, with a profusion of detail not unlike that White used on the house projects of the previous years, although less imaginative. The only Romanesque features are a plain round arch at the entrance, rather broad and low, but not of the special Syrian type, and the Auvergnat marquetry in one of the gables. The dormers and the balustrade at the edge of the roof are of French Late Gothic type "correctly" detailed, and the half timbering in the gables is quite

Tudor. The whole resembles the work of the younger Englishmen of the time, such as Ernest George and Peto, and is not Richardsonian in any sense of the word.

But the executed design is characteristic of Richardson at his best. (Fig. 57). Even today, with a third storey, which damages the broad low proportions, added beneath the old roof, the house is unmistakably his. This is not merely because of the heavy brownstone Syrian arch over the recessed porch. Indeed, this over-monumental feature is, as at Sever, the least fortunate part of the composition. The best features are very similar to those of Sever: flat-arched windows, surrounded by a simple cut-brick moulding, evenly although not altogether symmetrically arranged, and vigorous cut-brick panels which form the chief embellishment. The plastic treatment of the Clarendon Street end, with the bay window and the chimney, while a little confused at the cornice line, is a development of the effect Richardson was already seeking in the Crowninshield house ten years earlier.

The brownstone is less sparsely and spottily distributed here than on Sever. The gables and dormers are very expressive of the interior distribution. Even the colour effect is rich and mellow, the softer brick has reacted well to city grime as the hard brick of the Crowninshield house did not. Among the best features of the design, although quite incidental, are the small-paned double-hung Queen Anne windows.

The interior is not very interesting, and is now in rather poor condition. There is vague Queen Anne trim of a simple sort. Only the drawing room inglenook bears any elaborate embellishment. This embellishment is less successful than that of the Albany Court of Appeals. The diapers suggestive of Muhammadan art were doubtless essentially the design of Warren or some other draftsman who had dipped into the books on Arabic decoration in the library. On the other hand, the large-scale studies for the exterior brick carving are still in the best Pre-Raphaelite manner. While these studies are probably not of Richardson's own draftsmanship, the executed work is certainly one of the best examples of his ornament. Only the detail XI-4 of the brownstone arch is cold and archaeological and without personal character. Altogether, this is one of Richardson's best works, domestic in scale, yet dignified in handling, a better model for urban house design than most of his later and more sumptuous masonry mansions.

The year 1880 was in many respects the most interesting and successful year of Richardson's career. The earliest new work initiated in this year was the Ames Gate Lodge in North Easton, for which the commission entered the office in March. F. L. Ames, as a close friend of Richardson's, allowed him great freedom, and this small building was from the first recognized by discriminating critics as one of his most personal works. It remains one of his finest, in which every feature shows the mark of his own taste in its most individual form.

XI-5

This is much more than an ordinary gate lodge. It was intended to serve as a guest house for the overflow from the mansion which John A. Mitchell had enlarged for the Ames family a few years earlier. The wing on the left of the great arch was to serve only as a sort of orangery and therefore gave Richardson the opportunity for a solid and almost defensive-looking wall toward the road. But the larger wing on the right provided service quarters and a living room downstairs, with a sitting room and four small bedrooms upstairs. The plan of this wing is compact and most of the rooms are very small. But the upstairs sitting room is attractively cozy. The corner fireplace became a surprisingly effective feature. There is a screen of woodwork to separate it from the entrance passage, which does not appear in the plan. Another pleasant thing on the second floor was the small corner porch with the whimsical arrangement by which water could be drawn directly from the well below.

But it was not the interior distribution that brought the Ames Gate Lodge its fame. It was the massive exterior, almost as much a man-made mountain as the more abstract pyramid in Sherman, Wyoming. The construction was of boulders, much more boldly used than in the early church at West Medford, and trimmed with rock-faced Longmeadow stone. The walls are so low and battered that the lodge looks like a great glacial moraine roofed and made habitable. The pseudo-natural features in the Romantic gardens of the eighteenth century, such as the artificial volcano at Wörlitz and the great grottos at Ludwigslust and in the Potsdam Neuer Garten, were not dissimilar. Even more it suggests the work of some legendary Icelandic hero in a romance by William Morris. Richardson was here not content with the twelfth century; he seemed to be seeking his inspiration back in the time before architecture took form. (Fig. 58).

The great arch, the most conspicuous feature of the front, has long rock-faced voussoirs of varicoloured stone. For once the Syrian form is admirable, since it echoes the rock-pile shape of the whole. The window mullions and lintels are great rough monoliths splendidly scaled to the walling. The boulders throughout are selected so that the largest come at the base, while at the top of the stair tower and the chimney they are no larger than cobblestones. The roof is of the strong orange-red tile first used at Sever Hall. This covers the mass in a continuous low slope, with the dormers barely breaking the roof, like half-closed eyes. The dormers were the final extreme solution of a problem which had interested Richardson more than a decade earlier when he had designed the Crowninshield house. Such dormers, emphasizing the general mass of the roof, were very successful on this exceptional building. But in general they were less satisfactory than the more straightforward treatment of the dormer on the rear of Sever.

The inner side of the Gate Lodge is neither so elemental nor so compactly composed as the outer. (Fig. 59). The tower at the end of the plant-house stands out rather too much from the general mass. The band of windows in this wing is, however, even finer than the more elaborate treatment of the same motif on the libraries. The two porches, set behind monolothic piers in the corners of the lodge itself, are magnificently scaled to the boulder walls. The windows on this side are larger than on the front, and the projecting arch in the center has the wooden supports shown in the Blake house project but here very low and rugged in scale. The most elaborate feature is the two-storey well-house with cut brownstone trim. There are low arches with bosses cut on the lintels above the second floor openings. This is a curious detail, apparently of sixteenth century French origin, used also on the inglenook windows of the Trinity Rectory and rather out of place here.

Inside the second storey porch is some carving recalling the trip to Sherman, Wyoming, Richardson made the previous year with F. L. Ames and Saint-Gaudens in connection with the monument there. This delicately naturalistic ornament with its curvilinear stylization recalls the pedestal of the Farragut statue which was just being executed from White's and Saint-Gaudens' designs. It also makes one thinks, as does this building as a whole, of the work of Gaudì in Barcelona. The spirit of his best work in Parque Güell, begun in 1900, is certainly more similar to that of the Ames Gate Lodge than to the general European Art Nouveau style. The Cellers Güell by Gaudì's disciple, Francesc Berenguer, are even more an aspect of the same desire to give to architecture the quality of a natural object, or, more precisely, of a pile of stones shaped by the force of gravitation.

But if the exterior of the lodge brings to mind such far and exotic things, only lately rehabilitated by the Surrealists, the one important interior, the upstairs sitting room, has rather the quaintness of the backgrounds in Kate Greenaway's illustrations. However, the deep blue-green colour of the Queen Anne panelling and the free asymmetrical distribution of the room have none of the fussy prettiness of the work of Ruskin's young lady protégée. It is altogether practical and masculine, suitable for a room labelled "Bachelor's Hall" on the plan.

This was a very exceptional sort of house, but in this, even more than in the Trinity Rectory, Richardson found the basis of his later and more American domestic style. The simple broad masses with low but conspicuous roofs, the asymmetrical plan, the interesting wall surfaces of natural texture, the freely placed small-paned sash-windows, the simple sturdy porch detail, the occasional round projections: all make their appearance here, as well as a simple sort of Queen Anne interior trim, lacking the imaginative virtues of Stanford White's, but more suited to ordinary rooms. Nothing could be further from the James Cheney project of two years earlier. But that, as has been said, must have been largely White's work. Henceforth, for a few years, Richardson's country houses are wholly his own and the most consistently original of his productions.

But it was some time before even a few other architects had the sense to appreciate this and to follow him intelligently in this direction. In general, only the boulder walling was imitated from this design. Thus, cobbles, used for porches and basements, became a prominent and usually inappropriate feature of the vernacular of the next decades. It was not until another five years after Richardson had illustrated his new American type of country house in larger and less exceptional examples, that his wiser disciples began to understand what he had been doing. Then it was already too late. For by that time the Colonial XI-6 Revival of McKim, Mead and White was the rising fashion in American suburban architecture. For a really national type of modern design the spurious nationalism of sentiment was preferred. In this field as in others, the possibilities of a sound tradition based on Richardson's practice came to a rapid end.

The other house designed in 1880, that for Dr. John Bryant in Cohasset, Mass., was commissioned in September. The Bryant house would hardly have been designed as it was had not the design of the Ames Gate Lodge come first, very different though they were. The Gate Lodge is perfectly preserved and only partially obscured today by planting. Excellent early photographs of it are also available. The Bryant house, however, is almost impossible to envisage in its original form in the absence of such early photographs. One of the later owners XI-7 enlarged it very considerably in the style of the original; Thomas W. Lawson rebuilt the stables after a fire and made further changes in the house itself; finally, the present owners, Boston College, have thrown out several new dormers. No one of these modifications alone would have been very serious. But with the present growth of the trees around the house, it is now quite impossible, except from the rear, to photograph or even to see any aspect of the house strictly as Richardson intended it to be. Fortunately, pencil plans and elevations exist.

The site is a magnificent one, even finer than that of the North Easton Town Hall. The narrow end of the house faces the sea on a wooded promontory extending into Cohasset harbor. The land at the other end of the house slopes down again. The original entrance was from a lower level, in the carriage passage under the service wing at the rear.

The plan of the house was never very satisfactory. (Fig. 61). An unnecessarily large area was given over to a stair hall separate from the living hall. In front, toward the water, were two rather small rooms, one set behind a porch. But all these rooms, as well as the dining room side of the living hall opened into one another with broad sliding doors. This was at least a step in the direction of larger rooms and more open planning, developing the practice of the mid-century, when front and back drawing rooms were so often arranged to be thrown together. There was a long but narrow covered porch on the south in addition to the smaller one on the east. But the total piazza space was much less than in the ordinary summer cottages of the mid-century or Richardson's Andrews house of 1872. Although primarily for summer use, this was a mansion rather than a large cottage. In this respect, English

Queen Anne influence had not been entirely for the best.

It is the handling of the mass of this house and the absence of any arbitrary detail that make it remarkable. There is here nothing Romanesque, Late Gothic, or Queen Anne. No feature of the design is borrowed from the European past, nor even from the legendary and prehistoric eras which the Gate Lodge brings to mind.

The L-shaped plan which Richardson always preferred for houses is here much modified. The main oblong block of the house is everywhere two rooms thick; the service wing, on account of the declivity of the ground, is carried obliquely over a bridge at the rear. The effect of mass is as simple as at the Ames Gate Lodge. But as the house was larger and the surfaces smoother, Richardson provided more variety in the shape. The main block is covered with a roof of 45° pitch, its gable facing the sea. At the other end, a sort of penthouse sweeps down lower from a cross gable: the basement at the rear is wholly above ground, and the height would otherwise have been excessive.

Toward the sea a two-storey porch is set in front of the main gable under a low pitched roof. A subsidiary gable projects toward the sea at the left hand corner. The fenestration on this facade is ample and regular. There are four windows in a bank in the lower storey of the left hand projection and two wide windows above. In the third storey of the main gable are four more windows in a bank above the porch, with one square one up in the peak. There are also large French windows opening onto the porch. The one-storey porch on the long southern elevation has a low sloped roof like that of the two storey porch toward the sea. (Fig. 60). This porch extended from the corner toward the sea, back as far as the large two-storey bay window. The half-octagonal roof of this bay conforms to the slope of the cross gable to which it is attached. There is also a smaller bay on the second floor above the porch, with a similar half-octagonal pointed roof. Between these bay window roofs a large plain dormer breaks the slope of the main roof. The fenestration on this side is more confused but also more extensive than on the front. In addition to the bay windows, which are almost all glass, a wide bank of four tall windows lights the stair hall to the left; the other windows are of varied but more conventional sizes and shapes.

The two other elevations and those of the service wing are less important in the general composition. But the wall rising almost three storeys at the rear is rather magnificent in a wooden country house. The kitchen in the bridge has a bank of six windows toward the stables. This is a remarkable feature, which must be the longest horizontal band of fenestration ever used in a house up to this date. The whole treatment of the service bridge suggests the twentieth century audacities of Le Corbusier in ferro-concrete.

The house above the stone basement is all covered with shingles. But the magnificent shingle walls have none of the cut patterns used in such profusion on the Watts Sherman house. The plain shingling of the walls also covers the great roofs, out of which project five big chimney stacks of rough stones. The windows have regular small panes with heavy eighteenth century muntins, but the number of panes varies with the size of the windows. Thus an even scale for the fenestration is established throughout, except in the transoms of the staircase windows, where the fixed panes are smaller. But the size and shape of the windows are varied to fit the needs of the rooms within. The basement

XI-9 walls of rubble are a conspicuous feature of the rear and of the entrance bridge because the ground level is so much lower than on the east and south. The stones, however, are not so large and rough as to be inharmonious with the shingles above.

In using shingles all over the surface of the house with no trim except the narrow mouldings around the windows, Richardson was undoubtedly inspired by the shingled farmhouses of the eighteenth century. Yet their magnificent qualities of simple mass and texture are emulated without any direct imitation of eighteenth century design except in the scaling of the windows. Richardson had, of course, begun to use shingles as early as the Andrews house of 1872. But in the house designs of the mid-seventies, only the Blake project approached this

XI-10 in simplicity. The rest are essentially English Queen Anne houses translated into American terms, probably because of White's collaboration.

At the Ames Gate Lodge and at Sever, Richardson had learned to develop the intrinsic qualities of materials other than rock-faced random ashlar. Now he tried his hand again with one of the favourite materials of the early national vernacular, omitting all decorative embellishment. As Sever drew sustenance from an early love for Hollis and Stoughton, so the Bryant house depended on a sympathetic appreciation of the essential virtues of Colonial wooden architecture and not on archaeological imitation of detail. If the architects of the Colonial Revival had only understood this,[2] they might really have developed a new national tradition in domestic architecture.

It is the absence of decorative detail on the Bryant house which

XI-11 [2] W. R. Emerson had, to some extent, on the Proctor house of the previous year in Milton.

was disappointing to the taste of the eighties and which seems so remarkable today. The porch supports, for example, are not columns. Instead they are thin piers covered with shingles, thus continuing the treatment of the walls and not standing out as isolated features. These thin piers express exactly the thin frame construction and not the weight of stone or brick masonry. Yet they also avoid the abstract linear quality of the gingerbread supports of the second quarter of the nineteenth century. This detail is a prime example of Richardson's power of expressive invention at this time, far superior to all White's pretty turned work.

The strong narrow mouldings around the windows are the only finished wooden detail except the actual muntins of the window panes. These mouldings frame the windows sufficiently and yet remain a part of the window pattern, not a border around it, barely breaking the continuous textured surface of the shingled walls. Later, Richardson usually painted such mouldings a strong dark green to bring them even more into harmony with the darker tone of the shingles. Here apparently they were always white, to flatter the greyish stone basement and the silvery colour which the shingles could be expected to take on beside the salt water. Since the conspicuous window muntins with which they were associated had to be painted for preservation, the mouldings around could not very well have been left unpainted to weather with the shingles, like the larger-scaled trim on the Watts Sherman house. In the eighteenth century even very rustic houses rarely avoided altogether the use of painted trim with shingle walls. But if one looks at old farmhouses it is evident that shingles appear richer in texture and less dirty when associated with a minimum of smooth painted trim.[3]

[3] McKim, Mead and White, Emerson, and many others who were already using shingles by this time, avoided the difficulty either by painting the shingles and the associated wide trim the same colour or, more frequently, by painting the trim a grey-brown very close to the tone of the shingles. But thus they lost something of the beauty of the unbroken weathered shingle texture. Generally also, the other architects used clapboards on the lower storey as Richardson had done on the Andrews house in 1872. This combination was not flattering to the

The Crane Memorial Public Library in Quincy, commissioned in May, 1880, is without question the best library Richardson ever built. Though superficially somewhat more Romanesque in feeling, it is no more a close copy of ancient precedent than the Ames Library. It is, however, altogether as improved a version of the Ames Library as that was an improved version of Woburn.

The whole building, from the front, forms a single low mass whose outline is not broken by the gable over the entrance. The stair turret is much shorter and smaller, a practical rather than a decorative feature. Its roof is associated with that of the gable, to which it is attached quite as in the case of the Bryant bay window. The eyelid dormers in the tile roof are like those on the Ames Gate Lodge, but less suitable here. (Fig. 65).

XI-12   The band of stack windows on the right runs the entire length of the wall from turret to corner. Curiously modern is the way in which this corner is treated. For only the thickness of the end wall lies beyond the windows at the end. In a masonry building seen in elevation, this appears a fault of design. When seen in perspective as it was designed, however, it represents in conception a very advanced step away from traditional design. The way the great Syrian arch of the porch was pushed to one side by the stair turret is also a fault only in elevation and is, indeed, hardly appreciable in perspective. This arch, as in so much of Richardson's work at this time, is the most inharmonious and awkward feature of the whole, and yet the thing which seems most to have struck contemporaries.

Besides the band of stack windows carried the full length of the wall, Richardson's other great achievement in this design has to do with fenestration. Almost the whole masonry wall of the reading room, as well as that at the end of the stacks and in the gable at the rear of the building, consists of enormous windows subdivided by narrow

shingles, even when the shingles as well as the clapboards were painted. The combination of materials is usually only a substitute for the conventional use of masonry on the lower storey in the Queen Anne manner, such as Richardson's on the Watts Sherman house.

stone mullions and transoms. This was an extension of the principle of the large window used on the rear of the North Easton Library. The very simple mouldings of these mullions recall the handling of the trim in brick at Sever and in wood at the Bryant house. These window walls are certainly not Romanesque and they are Late Gothic only in inspiration.

As much cannot be said for the three arches in the top gable. They are both Romanesque and "Richardsonian", in the conventional sense, like the entrance arch. Except for the capitals below these arches and those of the colonnettes of the stack windows, there is, however, no carved ornament. The capitals are still quite as much Gothic as Southern French Romanesque, but rather less vigorous in design than those on earlier work. The stone gutter spouts at the corners are, on the other hand, very original. They are freely conceived in the third dimension in a way that recalls the best applied art of 1900.

The favorite Milford granite is better balanced with the Longmeadow trim than at North Easton. The contrast is overemphatic only in the bands in the gables, but even this motif is in better scale than Auvergnat marquetry would have been. The battered base sets the mass up above the ground almost like a Greek temple on its stylobate. By strict expression of function and material Richardson made asymmetrical design formally monumental instead of merely picturesque. This was a very rare achievement in the long history of architecture.

Yet the holograph sketch for the rear [4] makes plain how similar was Richardson's original vision of his monumental masonry buildings to that of wooden houses like Dr. Bryant's. (Fig. 64). Such a sketch of mass and fenestration might quite easily have been carried out as a shingled house instead of a stone library. The continuous gable roof, with the penthouse extension at the rear, and the projecting gable rising at one end of the rear wall are obviously inspired by charac-

[4] Now much changed by the wing added by W. M. Aitken in 1908. Aitken was selected to do the remodelling because he had worked on the drawings in Richardson's office when the building was first built. It is curious to observe how he lost all the solidity and verticality of Richardson's proportions in the superficially respectful addition.

teristic seventeenth and eighteenth century farmhouses. No one would think of calling the Quincy Library a Colonial Revival building. It incorporates, however, as the sketch makes evident, the essential qualities of the early American vernacular as only Richardson knew how to do. Only through the detailed analysis of which these last chapters have been so full can Richardson's real method of creation in such a case be made clear.

The interior of the Library was more sumptuous than those of the earlier libraries. The general treatment of the stack room was, however, similar, as was also the general distribution of the plan. The most elaborate feature was the fireplace in the reading room. This was of wood, not stone, and rather confused and "Eastlake" in design. The elaborate carving, based on the flora of Quincy, is much less archaeological than that on the exterior. This fireplace was at the time enormously admired. Even the clumsy twisted colonnettes flanking the chimney breast were frequently imitated. Yet it is much less successful than the simple mantel in the "Bachelor's Hall" of the Ames Gate Lodge.

The most interesting decorative work here was done by La Farge in the windows. The somewhat murky opalescent panels, with monograms and publishers' devices, which are now in the windows at the rear of the new stack, were pieced out with new work when they were reinstalled in 1908. These are conspicuously a product of the "Brown Decades" in colour, although they harmonize well with the rich medium-brown woodwork. The later Crane Memorial Window to the left of the fireplace is in La Farge's pictorial Tiffany church window manner and is quite out of keeping with the building. But in the window to the right of the fireplace is a small panel which is perhaps La Farge's most beautiful work in glass. It is at once like a mosaic and like a relief. The flesh of the figures is, for example, of rough-surfaced pink quartz. The effect is of a jewel of Byzantine splendour, quite unlike any glass work of any other period.

When Richardson used the assistance of La Farge and Saint-Gaudens, at this time at the height of their powers and very sympathetic to his ideals, he was served as few nineteenth century architects have been. It is a pity he had to leave so much ot his ornamental carving to the Evans firm. He could, and did eventually, train Evans and his workmen to forge Romanesque and Byzantine detail. But of what value would have been the work of even the master forger of modern times, Dossena, compared to the enrichment La Farge and Saint-Gaudens were ready to provide. America, in these years, came near to that marriage of the arts which later professional schools have tried in vain to develop. But the forces of the day were too centrifugal to employ regularly an architect, a painter and a sculptor together. Richardson was no more able than William Morris in England to bring the arts together in a synthesis. La Farge continued to paint isolated pictures—often, alas, on windows—and Saint-Gaudens made independent statues. Later, each of them only once collaborated with an architect anywhere near as successfully as they had with Richardson. The chancel of the Church of the Ascension in New York is a distinguished joint work of La Farge and White. The Adams monument in Washington, on which Saint-Gaudens worked with White, is also excellent. But White's decorative contribution after 1880 was never again what it had been on the Farragut pedestal. Only in that minor early work did he show a creative power comparable to Richardson's.

XI-13

The bridge in the Fenway, commissioned by the Boston Department of Public Works in April, 1880, continued Richardson's professional association with F. L. Olmsted, with whom he had worked at Buffalo, Albany and, lately, at North Easton. Olmsted's early work in Central Park in New York, begun in the fifties, was still almost purely Romantic. Central Park was then beyond the urban frontier. It was still, therefore, an embellished open area, not an oasis in the desert of the city, but, rather like the great contemporary private parks of Prince Pückler-Muskau at Muskau and Branitz. In the Fenway, however, Olmsted was attempting to correct the tendency of American cities to ruin in their rapid growth all the assets of natural beauty in their vicinity. The Fenway is now hopelessly inefficient as an artery between the city and the suburbs for streams of motor traffic. But in the last quarter of the nineteenth century it was a remarkable example of a new and more intelligent attitude toward the problem of large-scale urban planning and landscape design. For all its meandering, the Fenway was a creative experiment. This is far more than can be said for the schemes of city beautification at the end of the last century and the opening of our own.

XI-14 Richardson's bridge is really two. One is a low Puddingstone arch across the water course. (Fig. 67). This is all gracious and varied curves, yet imitative neither of natural objects nor of the masonry bridges of the past. The other is a metal bridge over the railroad tracks and a street. (Fig. 66). The latter has the advantage of complete matter-of-factness. This Richardson achieved perhaps the better because he was not himself much interested in engineering. He allowed the engineer (probably Rutan or the engineers of the Boston and Albany Railroad) to design the metal trusses that carried the roadbed. Then he supported the ends of those trusses in the plainest possible way over a wide break in the Puddingstone wall which curved with the road from the masonry bridge. There is one central masonry support, also. On the sides he provided a simple balustrade of decorative ironwork. That was all.

Richardson had the sense to realize that metal construction, like masonry or wood, had its own principles. At Sever, the Ames Gate Lodge and the Bryant house he had used brick and boulders and shingles without embellishment. Now he did the same with metal. The result is inconspicuous, but hardly more so than the stone arch. For that is also quite without ornamental detail. The latter is harmonious with the curves of the landscape, quite as the metal bridge is appropriate to the straight lines of the railroad.

Fortunately the model of the stone bridge was appreciated and followed in this park and many others in the next decade. Yet in our own day, in the magnificent new parkways leading into New York—which represent the extension in the twentieth century of Olmsted's original idea for the Fenway—architects lacking Richardson's sense of fitness have returned to the picturesque mediaeval models used for park bridges by the early Romantics. Yet no American architect before the last few years would have left a span as Richardson left this metal bridge: exactly as it had been designed by the engineers. The range of Richardson's talent and his capacity to cope directly with the problems of the more modern world is made evident in this work in the Fenway. What a pity no one realized this at the time. It is significant that even Mrs. Van Rensselaer fails to mention the metal bridge in the Fenway.[5]

The Albany City Hall is one of Richardson's most Romanesque designs. It was commissioned in November, 1880, just as the main building campaign on the Capitol was reaching completion. It is a much more successful development of the early scheme of the Brookline Town Hall project than the excessively picturesque North Easton Town Hall designed the previous year. The construction is of Milford granite and Longmeadow stone throughout, and the taller proportions are more clearly expressive of a public building of several full storeys. The tower in itself is really magnificent, although the corner placing may be criticized as inharmonious with the symmetrical design of the nearby Capitol. The detail is rich but not too profuse. It is, indeed, rather more original than that on the Quincy Library; it has the plastic freedom of the detail in the Court of Appeals and yet is bolder, to suit the masonry exterior. The most unsatisfactory feature is the gable in the center of the facade. The late Gothic type was still not wholly translated into Richardson's personal idiom. (Fig. 68).

The building is most effective from the side, although the prison and the bridge of sighs shown in the early sketch are not in existence. (Fig. 79). The simpler treatment of the mullioned windows on the rear and the sides is more consistent with the rock-faced walling than

[5] This bridge is the best argument that could be offered, in addition to the Harrison Avenue store designed in the last months of Richardson's life, that had he lived longer he would have found as early as did Sullivan an appropriate architectural expression for skyscraper metal skeleton construction.

the carved decoration on the front. The functional arrangement of the windows is interesting and very skilfully composed. The grouping of the lights in the three main bays of the side is an ingenious approach to real openness of design in masonry construction.[6]

In general, however, this was a sound but uncreative Richardsonian design. Such a type his more intelligent followers could learn to repeat with almost equal success. Although the largest and most conspicuous, it is the least important work of the year. But at least the picturesque was disciplined into monumentality better than at the North Easton Town Hall, if not as well as at the Quincy Library.

There are certain projects almost certainly of 1879-1880 which are of considerable interest. The best known was for a Memorial Arch in Buffalo. (Fig. 80) . The perspective shows a noble arch of square proportions in typical Richardsonian masonry. A frieze and corbel table, like those of the Brattle Square Church Tower, surround the top. A slight pencil line suggests a possible high roof. The conception is comparable in effectiveness to the Sherman monument although much richer and more urbane.

The project for a mansion for Oliver Ames on the corner of Commonwealth Avenue and Westchester Park (now Massachusetts Avenue) exists in a holograph sketch plan and several studies—one of them signed by Langford Warren. This is rather larger and more sumptuous than the masonry mansions executed in the next year. The preliminary sketches for the elevations seem to indicate the use of rock-faced masonry throughout. The effect is almost as monumental as the Albany City Hall. These sketches do not coincide exactly with the plan. The plan is elaborately axial although irregular. There is an enormous cross-shaped hall, but the other rooms are rather small and the general

[6] At the end of the decade a similar treatment was effectively employed by Jenney on his best skyscraper, the second Leiter Building in Chicago. Like the metal bridge in the Fenway, but in a very different way, this side facade also suggests that if Richardson had lived, even his very first use of metal construction (which would probably have been the Ames Building on Court Street in Boston, the commission for which his successors received in 1889) might have been superior to Sullivan's Wainwright Building of 1890.

distribution is not good. The bold drawing is undoubtedly by Richardson himself. (Fig. 70).

The exterior studies are very tentative and not drawn by Richardson. The segmental recessed porch is like that in the early study for the Trinity Rectory. The stair turret at its side is almost a copy of that at the rear corner of the Albany City Hall. The corner turret on the second floor is a trivial Late Gothic feature like that on the Cheney addition project. The best features, the banks of mullioned windows on the front and the curving bay rising two storeys with a tower roof, are mediaeval in origin but skilfully adapted to modern domestic use. Another sketch (signed by Langford Warren) would hardly seem to belong to the same project were it not labelled. The porte-cochère is drawn directly from the Norman porch at Canterbury. These drawings, like those for the Trinity Rectory, indicate how the underlings adapted both archaeological cribbing and earlier Richardsonian features to his plans. He finally pulled together the whole, as the assistants were not able to do, by his personal conception of mass composition. This is clear in the holograph sketch of the rear of the Quincy Library.

More interesting than the Ames house is the project for an apartment house of which several slightly differing plans exist. This was to be built for B. W. Crowninshield on the lot next to that selected for the Oliver Ames house.[7] The plan is rather skilfully disposed about a central court. Thus, there would have been more light than in the deep apartments of the new and disgraceful "dumbbell" type actually erected in this decade on Commonwealth Avenue as well as in slum districts. A thumbnail sketch suggests two gables over the round-cornered wide bays on the facade, with a high hipped roof over the whole. Richardson's work would be the wider in range had this or a similar apartment house been executed. Even the project, however, is of great value as a suggestion of possibilities his early death left unexplored.[8]

[7] This was eventually built by Karl Fehmer in the François I style—like Hunt's W. K. Vanderbilt house in New York, but all of brownstone.

[8] A house project for a client named Borland seems to date from 1881. It is smaller than the Higginson house on Beacon Street but very similar. *V.* Chapter XII.

CHAPTER TWELVE

1881-1883

THE F. L. HIGGINSON house on Beacon Street in Boston was commissioned in February, 1881. The C. A. Whittier house next door, by McKim, Mead and White, completed in 1883, was designed at the same time. The fact that the two houses were to stand side by side was taken into consideration by their respective architects. This was rather exceptional in nineteenth century America. Although the Higginson house has Late Gothic features with Romanesque detail and the Whittier house is definitely François I in style, the roofs are of the same high pitch over both houses and the cornices are of similar weight. Both, moreover, have ground storeys of brownstone and brick walls above with a great deal of brownstone trim. (Fig. 69).

How much Richardson lost when White ceased to be his chief draftsman is evident in a comparison of these two houses. The house by McKim, Mead and White is distinctly the better of the two, despite its more archaeological character. The elaborate detail, of which there is a profusion, is exquisite in itself and beautifully placed, while the more restrained detail of the Higginson house appears by contrast clumsy and hybrid rather than original. The fenestration on the Whittier house is slightly more ample and far more rigidly organized. White and McKim also preserved better the continuity of surface on their house by using smooth- instead of rock-faced Longmeadow stone with the brick. Yet the dormer and the tower extend the surface plane of the lower wall in front of the roof in a way that diminishes the effect of solid masonry mass. The less projecting tower on the house by Richardson is better welded into the whole plastic mass. But as it is of stone throughout, the Higginson tower appears too heavy for the brick walls of the rest of the facade. Richardson's clumsy Late Gothic dormer is definitely inferior and more like the work of later imitators.

The studies for the Higginson house, of which several are in existence, appear to be all in the draftmanship of Langford Warren. The inferior quality of the executed work may be largely due to the fact that Richardson did not supervise this design as closely as he did other work of this year which, for one reason or another, interested him more. Yet one of the elevation sketches is certainly distinctly superior to the executed design and much more like Richardson's best work. (Fig. 89) . For this sketch indicates the use of stone throughout and shows, instead of the executed excrescence, a plain horizontal dormer with five windows like that on the rear of Sever. The lower but more massive corbelled cornice in this sketch is also superior to that executed.

In part the faults of the final design may be judged to have arisen from an attempt to meet the young architects next door half way. The sixteenth century dormer, the wider and flatter cornice, and the use of brick for the main walls, all harmonize more with the Whittier house. By this gracious gesture of architectural courtesy Richardson's style, which was already so completely integrated and individual, lost more than that of McKim, Mead and White gained. But if the Whittier house be compared with their Ross Winans house in Baltimore, designed at just the same time in the François I style, it is easy to see that the colour harmony of brownstone and brick on the Boston house is richer and the three-dimensional composition simpler and clearer.

The essential difference between the work of Richardson and that of his pupils, at the time when the resemblance was superficially closest, is clearly visible in these two houses. The solid plastic mass of the Higginson house, as shown in the early sketch, has almost no detail. Without being horizontal in composition it is well related to the ground by the marked batter of the base. On the other hand, the smooth, rather flat surfaces of the Whittier house suggest volume rather than mass, and the proportions are quite vertical. Both houses have somewhat unrelated pictorial accessories: the Whittier house a projecting porch awkwardly jammed between the corner of the house and the tower; the Higginson house a little bay window stuck onto the right side of the facade. The little bay window does not appear on the earlier study and was doubtless added to continue the line of the dormer on the facade.

To McKim and White the evident superiority of their finished design to that of Richardson must have seemed to vindicate their consistent use of François I precedent. This they certainly handled much more personally than Hunt had on the W. K. Vanderbilt house, which had just initiated the vogue. Although in the end they also went along the way of archaeology and Renaissance order, it is curious that in such work of the next few years as the Third Senior Society Building in New Haven, the Narragansett Pier Casino, and St. Peter's Church in Baltimore, they came to show more respect for Richardson's taste and achievement than they did here. With the building of these houses, however, Richardson and everyone else saw that his pupils were now rivals. Moreover, their vision was already more adapted to the vogue of the time for greater lightness and smoothness than that of the builder of the Ames Gate Lodge. Contemporaries could not be aware, as we are, that Richardson was building for the ages and McKim and White only for the eighties. But, in such a masonry city house, the new firm undoubtedly built better for the eighties than Richardson, now depending increasingly on his office staff, could always build for the ages.

A small study for the Higginson dining room shows the new sort of small-scale interior detail of Queen Anne inspiration used so successfully in the "Bachelor's Hall" of the Ames Gate Lodge. In this sketch a panelled inglenook, in which the fireplace was set, extended XII-1   the whole length of the wall, as in the Dorsheimer hall of 1868 and the Watts Sherman dining room in the early sketch of 1874. The marble subframement of the fireplace opening is low and broad and simple. The wooden panels are small and varied. There is carving only on the brackets supporting the cross beams. This ornament is hardly more than an enrichment of the gun stock curve. Below the ceiling are grilles of turned wood, of which a cruder version was used in the Quincy Library. These are delicate and original if rather fussy in character. Perhaps this interior was left largely to the draftsmen. Certainly here, and indeed in all but a few of the later house interiors, there is a certain contrast between a simple general composition, characteristic of Richardson at his best, and the extraneous grille work and Romanesque detail. The character is already different from that of the Trinity Rectory interiors, broader in scale and yet with ornament that is less original. The question is of more importance in the case of the Hay house and the Paine house, where the quality effect is higher. XII-2

The N. L. Anderson house in Washington was commissioned in May, 1881. Like the Higginson house, this has been demolished, but the original drawings are all in existence and make plain that it was much superior to the Boston mansion. The corner lot and the less urban character of Washington permitted Richardson to design the house as an isolated mass. Thus he avoided the particular problem of the row house which must share its mass with its neighbors. At the same time he kept the scale domestic and did not attempt the monumental effect of the Oliver Ames project.

The plan is compact but the interior disposition is without particular interest. (Fig. 71). The parlor, with the corner bay window, is only too obviously of the type which was ubiquitously repeated at small scale in the vernacular house building of this decade. The corner bay is not large enough to provide a partially separate living space attached to the main room, as does the corner bay of parlor in the Paine house in Waltham, begun three years later. The hall also is too small for a living room, yet too large merely for an entrance.

But the exterior of this house is very fine. (Fig. 72). It is all of brick, and quite as devoid of features specifically reminiscent of the past as Sever Hall. The composition is freer and there is less decoration than at Sever. Even the round corner tower holds its place on the exterior better than the orangery tower of the Ames Gate Lodge. The other polygonal tower on the side is very superior to the similar one on the Higginson house. Like the bay windows on the Bryant house, these towers increase the plastic interest without becoming separated from the main mass. The cut brick panels with coats of arms are inferior in vigour to those of Sever Hall. (Fig. 73). But the bands of octagonal bricks and of basket-work patterns at the entrance and at the top of the wall provide an ingenious and novel sort of decoration. The bricks around the windows are moulded only with a curved chamfering. This house hardly resembles the Trinity Rectory in effect of mass or distribution of parts. Yet the quality of the two is rather similar and both are among the finest as well as the earliest of his masonry houses. The omission of brownstone trim and of Syrian arches and Romanesque detail was, however, an advance comparable to that he had made with wooden construction in the Bryant house.

Another house begun in 1881, that for the Reverend Percy Brown at Marion, Mass., is entirely different. It was commissioned in October. Although the cost is said to have been only $2,500, it is the equal in quality of such a large house as Dr. Bryant's in Cohasset. Like the Bryant house it is of frame construction covered with shingles. But it emulates the rural eighteenth century vernacular even more closely, since a gambrel roof descends to the top of the first storey and is broken by several small dormers. The windows are all of small panes, but of varied sizes and shapes. The porches are set back inside the main mass. Their shingled supports are thus a part of the main wall plane, but slightly curved out in silhouette to form brackets at the top. The shingles above and below the windows are cut with saw-tooth edges. This is the only ornament on the house. (Fig. 76).

The house has been somewhat enlarged by its present owners, the Hosmers. But the original character of the design is in no way damaged. If anything, it is enhanced by the new gambrelled gable at the right of the front. The porches have also been increased in size, but absolutely in the original style. (Fig. 74).

The original plan is rather cut up for such a small house. Although the parlor and dining room are separated only by a wide door frame, one large ell-shaped room would have served as well the two purposes. XII-3 The tiny study was useful for the clergyman's literary work. (Fig. 75).

A small perspective study of this house, probably by Richardson himself, recalls that of the rear of the Quincy Library. The resemblance to the Colonial vernacular is obviously much greater. But the traditional forms are quite as completely modified and adapted for this small wooden summer cottage as for the library in masonry. Fortunately, the quality of this adaptation was not unappreciated at the time. As Lewis Mumford was perhaps the first modern critic to point XII-4 out, the gambrelled and shingled cottages built along the New England seacoast in the next decades, from the designs of many different architects and even by local contractors, are the best modern wooden domestic architecture the Eastern States have yet had. If conventional frame construction is used in small houses, it is hard to see how anything intrinsically as satisfactory can be developed. Of course, now that we have come to expect wider expanses of glass than can be harmoniously fitted into shingle walls, and roofs that can be used as terraces, such design is no longer compatible with the characteristic contemporary style forms. The adaptation to wooden construction of such features, developed in connection with more modern types of construction, is at best a compromise, however. The visual charm of the Richardsonian seaside cottage style at its best can hardly be equalled.

From its low hill of grass this tiny house set against magnificent trees looks out over the Marion harbour. The shingles are a natural grey; the trim, of which there is no more than on the Bryant house, is dark green both inside and out. How few, seeing it with the later and more pretentious imitations nearby, realize that this house is one of the vital monuments of American architecture! For it establishes Richardson's right to consideration as the great American architect far better than Trinity or the Albany Capitol. It was a far more significant thing to have set a sound model for the domestic vernacular than for more monumental buildings.

223

The first of Richardson's railroad stations for the Boston and Albany is of similar significance. The Auburndale station was commissioned in 1881 and is the best he ever built. This first station was almost certainly of his own personal design. It may be safely assumed that most of the later ones were produced by the office staff and barely seen by Richardson. Indeed, some of the stations built just after his death on the same suburban line by Shepley, Rutan and Coolidge are more comparable to this first example than are the last stations designed before his death.[1] It is the latter which look more typical of the work of the new firm.

The Auburndale Station is no more than a long low rectangle of rock-faced granite covered with a roof. The doors and windows, surrounded by rock-faced Longmeadow stone, hardly break the massiveness of the composition. A bay window from the ticket office facing the tracks is the only projection. The oblong interior is subdivided into men's and women's waiting rooms, with the ticket office in the center and a baggage room at one end. (Fig. 78).

On the right hand corner of the front there is, however, an open carriage porch. This is supported on heavy square wooden supports branching out at the top, like those on the Blake house project five years earlier. The porch continues along this end and then follows the track some distance beyond the further end of the station. The low roof of the station was originally of red tiles, but is now unfortunately of process shingles of poor colour and scale. This roof descends over the porches without any break. The arching of the eaves and the roof at the sides of the carriage porch is the only decorative effect.

Richardson's power of mass composition is perhaps nowhere more evident than here. The elemental quality of masonry mass, here purified of all the accidental features of the Ames Gate Lodge, is more moving than almost any other thing in fine architecture.

This station is not, as Lewis Mumford has suggested, well lighted inside. Sheathed in dark wood and with only a few windows in the low side walls, it is distinctly dark, bare, and depressing. Indeed, it is

[1] The Allston Station, by Shepley, Rutan and Coolidge, is particularly fine.

quite inferior in amenity to many small stations of the sixties and seventies which were certainly not the work of great architects. But this is no terminal in which crowds must spend hours. It is merely a place where commuters take tickets and board trains in the morning and return again at night without ever lingering in the interior. Its function is almost as symbolic as a monument. The exterior must catch the eye and make plain that this is where the train stops. So Richardson designed it almost as he designed the abstract pyramid of stone at Sherman, Wyoming, which symbolized the meeting of the Union Pacific lines.

The Brighton station, commissioned in July, 1884, is even simpler [2] than that at Auburndale, but the porch arrangement is less successful. On the other hand, the Palmer station, commissioned next after Auburndale in August, 1881, is very different from these suburban stopping places. Here the station lies in a wedge between two different railroad lines. It is, therefore, completely surrounded by porches and can hardly be apprehended as architecture from the outside at all. In order to admit adequate light to the various different services of the interior, there are large dormers at the end and also several more in a range down each side. The external effect of these heavy dormers, which were repeated later on the Framingham station and on that at Holyoke, is not altogether happy. They seem to weigh down the continuous low slopes of the roof, which continue over the porches to rest on light wooden supports. The arrangement at Palmer, with the dormers on the side tapering in size toward the narrow end, is more interesting and more expressive than that of the symmetrically placed dormers on the other two stations of the type. The windows under the porches are joined in mullioned and lintelled groups. Arches are used only in the broad end, and there is almost no carved detail.

[2] The later stations fall into two groups. Those that are similar to the ones designed in 1881 are all discussed in this place. The other group is discussed in Chapter XIV.

The North Easton station for the Old Colony Railroad (later the New York, New Haven and Hartford) was commissioned in November, 1881. On this the eaves are bracketted out on wooden beams on the front and sides. This provides shelter all the way around in place of the porches of the other stations. These relatively light wooden brackets are distinctly out of scale with the heavy but unmoulded Syrian arch of the carriage porch, repeated over the grouped windows at either side. On the Chestnut Hill station, commissioned in April, 1883, the similar arches of the carriage porch continue the plane of the side walls of the station and the main roof sweeps down over the porch. (Fig. 77). This is a better arrangement. The train side of this station is less successful. The wooden supports to the porch are rather spindly, and the low wooden gable which lets light into the interior is also out of scale. But on the whole this is the only other small station really comparable in quality to that at Auburndale.

The Dairy Building, commissioned by the Boston and Albany Railroad in November, 1881, has been destroyed. To judge from the drawings that still exist, it must have been more like the Anderson house than the early railroad stations in character. It is of brick, very simply treated. The arches are used only constructively, not as ornament. Indeed, there is no detail at all. The mass is well composed with a wide gable at one end and small gabled dormers repeated indefinitely down the side. Richardson obviously appreciated that in industrial design repetition of the bay unit was essential. Appropriate visual interest could better be obtained thus, and by the use of sound, simple proportions, than by the centralized composition and varied features suitable in monumental and isolated buildings. Only the tall roofs and the gables still recall his picturesque predilections. Until Frank Lloyd Wright designed the Larkin Administration Building in Buffalo in 1905, there was perhaps no industrial work, even by Sullivan, at once so simple and straightforward in character and of equal architectural interest.

The largest commission of 1881[8] was that for Austin Hall in Cambridge. This was intended to house the Harvard Law School. The commission entered the office in February. There are two separate sets of drawings for Austin Hall. The earlier shows a plan scheme essentially asymmetrical and very complicated and picturesque in massing. The asymmetrical stair turret, modified and handled more like the bay windows on Sever, is the only trace of this early conception that remains in the finished work.

The difference between the first and the second set of studies is so great that the earlier should be considered almost as a project for a different building. The superiority of the second scheme, which was finally executed, is marked. Richardson had a real power of self-criticism in his work, and was ready to turn to a quite different conception if the first failed to develop into a satisfactory composition.

The existing plan of the first scheme is a mere sketch in Richardson's own hand. The arrangement of the interior can be easily read from the elevations. The entrance through a triple porch was to be in the middle of the long side and flanked by two towers. The right end of the building was to contain the library. This section rose a storey higher than the rest. The end of the building was bowed out somewhat like the central section of the rear of Sever, enriching the mass and increasing the interior space. This tall, rather solid wing was covered with a hip roof. The rest of the building was slightly narrower and covered with a long roof ending in a gable at the left. On the rear facade the porch and the towers were naturally omitted.

Of the drawings for the front elevation of this scheme, the only one of real interest is the small one which, like the plan, is holograph. The others represent the conception as worked up by the draftsmen—in one case, certainly by Langford Warren. In Richardson's own pencil sketch

[8] The Pruyn monument in the Rural Cemetery outside Albany, commissioned in October, 1881, is not of much interest. It is a flat slab of polished pinkish granite, slightly slanted toward the front, with moulded edges and a little weak foliate carving at the corners. The inscription is well arranged, with a cross in the upper left hand corner and four incised panels of foliage between the arms. The carving and even the lettering has naturally become dirty and clogged.

the triple porch has gables like the porch later proposed for Trinity. This picturesque feature is more Gothic than Romanesque. In the developed elevations it was discarded as unsuited to the general massiveness of the building. In the first sketch, the taller tower at the right of the porch is quite simple, forming an effective transition between the tall mass of the library and the low porch. The plastic effect was further enriched by an attached turret. At the other end of the porch was a lower tower, rising no higher than the cornice level of the main roof.

The fenestration is only indicated in the early sketch. A band of windows of the type used on the Quincy Library is suggested on the lower left. On the upper right, the wall of the law library, practically the whole space is filled with square lights separated by mullions. The more developed elevations make plain the impossibility of composing the symmetrical and horizontal motif of the triple porch with the two vertical stair towers of different height on either side, and of combining all these features effectively with the main masses behind. All the faults of the designs of the Woburn Library and the North Easton Town Hall were concentrated here in these applied features. The problem of composition could only be solved by beginning over again. Of course, the real reason for beginning over again probably lay in difficulties in the plan of which we have no knowledge. For this represented a much more complicated functional problem than the two earlier buildings just mentioned.

The new scheme for Austin appears in a holograph sketch plan which may date many months or, just as possibly, only a few days after the first. The library wing, with the main lecture room under it, was here moved around to the center of the rear. Thus the whole arrangement could be made symmetrical. (Fig. 80). What is, perhaps, the most interesting elevation sketch of the considerable series based on this plan does not even have a stair turret on one side of the front. This is in many other respects more advanced than the executed design.

The two one-storeyed wings, as in the executed building, have

228

long bands of windows like those on the stacks of the public libraries Richardson had just built. These wings have hip roofs. The main roof, however, is gabled, with a taller hipped projection in the center to cover the library at the rear and a lower broader gable in the middle of the front. In the executed work, the roof of the main section of the building is considerably hipped and higher, so that there is no break in the main ridge. The front gable is omitted. (Fig. 79).

The chief superiority of this sketch elevation is in the fenestration of the main mass. The double band of square lights below the cornice is broken by pilasters into groups of three. In the executed work, the lights are coupled, with heavier piers between the pairs and colonnettes instead of plain mullions between the single lights. In the central portion above the porch, the sketch shows groups of three oblong lights, corresponding to the square lights of the band at the top. At the ends of the higher portion of the facade are three large square windows with small panes, simpler and more open than the arched openings used at this point in the executed design. Below these great openings are smaller windows in two storeys, to light the low offices on the left. On the other side, a broad mullioned and transomed bank of lights serves a larger room. This functional asymmetry was preserved in execution.

Except for the minor detail of the colonnettes and pilasters in the banks of windows, there was nothing Romanesque in this stage of the design except the rich inset loggia. The arches and intermediary lintelled bays of this followed closely the scheme of St.-Gilles—the first familiar feature of Southern French Romanesque architecture imitated by Richardson. In the drawing this portal is lighter and better scaled   XII-5
to the windows above than as executed.

The final designs were an improvement over the sketch perspective in the handling of the main mass, but they were less original and more Romanesque in detail. The profusion of Romanesque detail—and Southern French at that—on a building freer and more open in conception than Sever, must be explained largely in terms of Richardson's working conditions. He himself did not turn to the Romanesque,

229

except for general inspiration. But the draftsmen, in working up the detailed drawings, filled in with Romanesque detail where they had neither sense enough to be content with fine stonework nor imagination enough to think of original devices.

Austin is broadly conceived in terms of a light-yellow sandstone base, dark Longmeadow walling and broad lintels and cornices of light stone at the top. The profusion of banded arches, dark and light diapers and Auvergnat marquetry in bluestone is incidental. The scale of the polychromy is more delicate than at Woburn but the effect was originally as gaudy. The colour is certainly not as beautiful nor really as rich as the plain Puddingstone of the Brattle Square Church or the Fenway Bridge. Yet, Richardson was possibly justified in setting the key high, since time has nearly reduced the whole to a succession of grimy browns.

The arrangement of the executed interior has been suggested in discussing the facade. The two low wings contain lecture rooms; a third, larger one is in the wing under the library at the rear. Quarter-circle projections in the corners between the wings facilitate circulation and provide additional light in dark corners. The central part of the building is occupied by offices and by the students' room, which lies behind the larger mullioned window. The stair turret made it possible for the Dean to reach his offices on the second floor directly from the outside.

The rear facade of the building is matter-of-fact, retaining all the virtues of the early perspective study for the front. The square lights of the windows are grouped between plain mullions in a varied but orderly way, as on the Palmer station. The dark ashlar walling is broken only by the light-coloured string course between the storeys and the heavy lintel and cornice at the top.

The solid end wall of the building is, however, embellished with a broad checkerboard band. There is also a great panel of light stone. On it the Harvard arms are surrounded by rich waving foliage not dissimilar to that on the panels over the Court of Appeals fireplace in Albany. The bossy Byzantine capitals of the porch are of similar character and were much admired and imitated. They are, however, inferior in conception and execution to the crude crocketted capitals Richardson had been using until the previous year. They contribute to an effect, not merely of solidity and mass, but of actual clumsiness in the whole design of the porch. The attempt at the main openings to express, and even to exaggerate, the full thickness of the masonry is like the treatment of the low Syrian arches at Sever and Quincy. This contrasts unhappily with the more straightforward treatment of the windows.

The fireplace in the Austin Hall library, on the other hand, has decoration which, in detail of design and execution, represents the highest point of Richardson's achievement in ornament. (Fig. 99). The great rich corbels of stone supporting the mantel are carved all over with foliage and fruit in the freest and most naturalistic way. The effect is of Chinese jade carving enormously enlarged, or, even, at some remove, of the quality of the ambulatory capitals of Cluny. Mr. C. M. S. Niver, properly a little shocked by the latter comparison, points out that this ornament is really no more than a skilful translation into stone of the best late Pre-Raphaelite graphic ornament—the sort found in the Kelmscott Chaucer or even Morris wallpapers. Indeed, it follows this source more closely, perhaps, than the North Easton fireplace. Such graphic ornament was the best of the period and the translation is able if not completely plastic in detail. But by this time, Richardson's feeling for mass demanded, as in the bossy capitols of the portal, that the whole ornamental composition should be plastic rather than its individual parts. With such naturalistic delineation, the full rendition of the single leaves and fruits in the round might, indeed, have been unarchitectural. XII-8

It is said that the workmen on this building were imported from England. One can hardly believe that American carvers could have cut stone with such suavity, however fine the original design. Certainly it is superior to all other execution of ornament Richardson was able to obtain, except from Saint-Gaudens.

Although less original and less forward-looking than his other buildings of these years, Austin Hall is certainly one of Richardson's greatest works. Richardson repaid his debt to Harvard by constructing the only two buildings in Cambridge worthy to stand with those of the eighteenth and the first decades of the nineteenth century. To compare it with its nearest neighbor in time and in space, Peabody and Stearns' Hemingway Gymnasium, is to realize his absolute superiority to his contemporaries. The leading Boston architectural firm of Richardson's generation, Peabody and Stearns, was still as far beneath him as when it built the Nathan Matthews house in Newport just before his Watts Sherman house.[4] This brick and brownstone gymnasium is of a strange monumental Queen Anne, pompous and picturesque in the worst manner of these years. Only when Peabody and Stearns became Richardson's devout imitators, shortly after this, were they able to approach him even superficially in quality.

The period of Richardson's highest general level of achievement was drawing to a close while Austin Hall was building in the years after 1881. But the concluding period of mass production and uneven quality does not really begin until 1883. It seems definitely to have been associated with the trip to Europe he made in the summer of 1882. Certain buildings that were largely designed during his absence, such as the Sard house and the Kingston and Bedford Street Ames Store, are undoubtedly inferior to his work of the preceding years. Two wooden houses, however, one commissioned just before his departure, and one commissioned in February, 1883, belong rather with the work of 1880-1881 of the same type. At the expense of exact chronological sequence, discussion of them may be appropriately introduced at this point, as in the case of the railroad stations which followed closely the type of the first one at Auburndale.

As the house for Mrs. M. F. Stoughton in Cambridge was commissioned in June, 1882, the final drawings probably date from just after

[4] This is a trifle unjust or, at least, inexact: the Nathan Matthews house was designed a year before the Andrews house and completed two years before the Watts Sherman house was designed; Hemingway was exactly contemporary with Sever.

Richardson's return from Europe. This is one of his most successful works and is, perhaps, the best suburban wooden house in America. It is comparable only to the finest of Frank Lloyd Wright's. It has been somewhat changed at various times. Mrs. Stoughton's son, the historian, John Fiske, remodelled the second storey of the service wing as a library, putting in the group of diamond-paned windows in the upper left end of the Brattle Street facade. The later owners, Dean Hurlbut and Mrs. Hurlbut (who still occupies the house) also made considerable additions on the rear. These do not modify the perspective view of the front of the house, which still follows closely the early holograph sketch except for the later library window.

In many ways the mass composition is developed further than that of the Bryant house. On a flat site it was desirable to introduce more varied interest into the lay-out of the house itself. The plan is L-shaped, as usual, with the entrance at the inside corner leading into a large living hall. (Fig. 83). The stairway rises toward the front of XII-11 the house in a circular tower-like projection, effective both inside and out. This tower-like projection is completely merged with the general mass, so that even its roof is barely distinguishable from the continuous slopes of the main roofs. The drawing room and the original library are in the short end of the L, with bedrooms above. The roof of this wing runs parallel to the side street and ends in a gable on the front. The long end of the L contains the dining room. On the front there is a two-storeyed loggia, somewhat more subtly treated than the porches on the earlier Bryant and Brown houses. The head of the L has a cross gable over the short service wing.

The facade toward the side street is now much lengthened by the new entrance at the rear. It was always somewhat confused by bays and dormers, like the side facade of the Bryant house. The roof is now covered with process shingles which are too small and dark and even in texture. But these are required in place of wooden shingles by modern urban building codes. The split cedar shingles with which the lower walls have been recovered are, on the other hand, rather too large in scale. The trim is still of the original dark green.

The windows are of the type used at Cohasset and Marion, with small regular panes and heavy muntins, but of various sizes and shapes. The holograph sketch indicates that Richardson saw these as continuous banks, which in execution were subdivided for practical reasons into separate double-hung windows. The upper loggia was not originally glazed. (Fig. 82).

The interior of this house has been almost completely changed by Mr. Pierre La Rose, who redecorated it in the present century. The original library, whose walnut panelling was brought from an older house, is certainly not of Richardson's design. This alone is unchanged. The dining room, however, retains its small Queen Anne panelling and a fine, very broad fireplace. The original detail of the stair rail, on the other hand, is thin and hybrid, unworthy of the magnificent space composition in which it plays the most conspicuous part. In justice to Mr. La Rose, who showed no great respect for the original interiors in his redecoration, it must be admitted that such detail can hardly be of Richardson's personal design.

Richardson was primarily an architect. He gave of his best to the really architectural problems of house design. But he did not ordinarily spend much effort on interiors. It is unfortunate that Mrs. Stoughton could not have had White decorate the interiors as the Watts Shermans had, at Richardson's suggestion, a few years earlier.

The house for Dr. Walter W. Channing in Brookline was commissioned in February, 1883. The Channing house was somewhat smaller than the Stoughton house, but it has since been enlarged toward the rear, very much as was originally intended. Except for the symmetrical placing of the windows this addition is in the original style.

The Channing house is square in mass, not L-shaped, and the tower, if one should call it that, is a mere plastic enhancement of the front corner. It also provides a larger and better lighted, if awkwardly shaped, reception room within. The plan is very compact, and not too much space is given to the stair hall.

The preservation of the original shingles on the walls and roof immensely enhances the general effect. Certain details are inferior to the subtle perfection of the Stoughton house. The string course carried around the house above the first floor windows is pointless since there is no change in materials between the two storeys. It also cuts very awkwardly across the stair window. Under the eaves, the lambrequin-like projecting band of shingles with saw-toothed edges is a similar complication. This was more simply and effectively used at Marion. The cut-shingle patterns on the lower part of the corner bay recall White's work. The use of single panes in the lower sashes, so characteristic of the Colonial Revival vernacular of the next decade, spoils the consistency of scale. The diamond-paned windows to the right of the door, and the small bay above are later changes that certainly do not improve the total effect. The very simple inset entrance, and the boldly designed stair windows are, however, distinctly new and effective. (Fig. 84).

The great virtue of this house is the way it is set on a rising slope among magnificent trees. Richardson followed here the best Romantic principles in placing his building in the landscape—more so than when he actually collaborated with Olmsted at the North Easton Town Hall. The solid, simple mass, so richly plastic, all soft grey with touches of dark-green trim, fits perfectly into the setting of hill slope and varied foliage. It is clearly visible as architecture and yet harmonious with nature. For all the minor faults, to be attributed probably to the draftsmen in the office, the Channing house is a work of high quality whose threatened destruction is a minor tragedy. This and the Stough- XII-12 ton house might so easily have been the model for several decades of sound suburban building, just as the Brown house was for so many seaside cottages. But its virtues were too fundamental to be seen. A generation which chiefly appreciated detail found here almost no detail to copy. Instead they turned for inspiration to the work of the brilliant young firm of McKim, Mead and White, who were building enormous wooden mansions in the summer social capitals of the East instead of suburban houses for doctors in Brookline and for the mothers of historians in Cambridge. The latter and not the former were of the type and size to which the American middle classes then and now aspire. But the eighties were increasingly impressed by millionaires.

By 1880 the Victorian Gothic was almost over in America. What use of English Gothic forms for churches still continued was now suave and archaeological, based on the work of English architects like XII-13 Pearson and Seddon. While the Queen Anne progressed toward an imitation of the forms of the seventeenth and eighteenth century in civil work, most English church architects remained faithful to mediaeval design, only seeking a higher standard of craftsmanship and a new accuracy of feeling and form. An early American design of this type is C. C. Haight's project for St. Luke's Cathedral in Portland, Maine, published in the *Sketch Books* of the mid-seventies. In his civil work of the same period at Columbia, Haight approached a similar revivalistic excellence. But the movement which was later to develop as almost a second Gothic Revival—restricted to ecclesiastical and educational design—did not really make its appearance generally until the maturity of Henry Vaughn and the opening of the career of the young firm of Cram and Goodhue around 1890.

The influence of Richardson's monumental style began to be felt in the mid-seventies. But the direct influence of Richardson and the Romanesque Revival in general was less conspicuous in the opening years of the eighties than the emulation of the Vanderbilt houses in New York and of the early work of McKim, Mead and White.

The rather solid twin houses on Fifth Avenue, built for W. H. Vanderbilt and his daughters by the Herter Brothers in 1879, were XII-14 still of brownstone. They were also symmetrically disposed, with rich naturalistic bands of carving contrasting oddly with the thin Renaissance pilasters.[5] But from the first, and for all the amazing hybrid splendours of their interiors, these mansions must have looked old-fashioned beside the new François I design of the W. K. Vanderbilt house, a few blocks away. This was executed by Hunt, in light-coloured

[5] The Herter Brothers assured contemporaries the style was "Greek Renaissance" (*sic!*). The carving has since been scraped off.

236

Indiana limestone, for the remarkable woman who, as Mrs. O. H. P. Belmont, was to retain her prominence in American life in one way or another for two generations. The Cornelius Vanderbilt house by XII-15 George B. Post was first erected at the beginning of the eighties and enlarged later. Built of brick, with light stone trim copied from the Louis XII wing of Blois, this followed the lead set by the W. K. Vanderbilt house. What were Higginsons and Andersons and Ameses beside Vanderbilt, in setting a vogue in the last decades of the nineteenth century? New England and the West might on the whole prefer the more sober style of Richardson, but even in Boston, the Oliver Ames house by Karl Fehmer, built instead of Richardson's project, was not the only François I château on Commonwealth Avenue. And Mrs. Nathaniel Thayer, whose social importance in Boston was more than comparable to Mrs. W. K. Vanderbilt's in New York, had a house by Peabody and Stearns which was distinctly Flemish Renaissance in detail although still of brick and brownstone. In New York, of course, Fifth Avenue was soon lined with sixteenth century châteaux: Hunt himself built the most splendid for the Astors and the Gerrys. Ogden Goelet's "Ochre Court" in Newport, and, above all, Alfred Vanderbilt's "Biltmore", both by Hunt and considerably later, continued to show that such French precedent could be even more magnificently followed in the country than in the city.

All this new megalopolitan splendour of the eighties had little more to do with the development of American architecture than the similar châteaux which the Rothschilds and the Pereires were building in France. McKim, Mead and White, in the Whittier house in Boston and the inferior Ross Winans house in Baltimore, were slightly more successful than the rest in combining the early French Renaissance style with elements already acclimated to America. Such work is, however, of minor interest and significance compared to the less archaeological work they were doing at the same time. Their many summer houses of wood, built in the late seventies and early eighties, were a development of the type McKim had used in the mid-seventies. On this crude American Queen Anne skeleton was imposed the rich imaginative complication of mass and detail which White had begun to evolve in the projects for the Cheney houses, designed while he was still with Richardson.

The earliest group of houses is at Elberon, N. J., where some go back to the mid-seventies before White had left Richardson and joined McKim and Mead. The best example there is the Moses Taylor house, a translation into delicate semi-Colonial, semi-Queen Anne house detail of the mid-century Swiss chalet type with two-storey porches on three sides.

The Cyrus H. McCormick house at Richfield Springs has more imaginative detail by White. The delicate turned gingerbread on the porches is elegant and original. But the stucco panels, with vases of flowers and spider webs outlined in broken bits of colored glass, are certainly neither. This incredible mosaic work,[6] which White had proposed for the decoration of the Cheney houses, was used with greater virtuosity on the Chapin house in Providence. The latter is one of the most startling examples of White's capacity as an exterior decorator, if hardly as an architect, at this time.

Of the many Newport houses of these years, the best are the Isaac Bell, Jr., house on Bellevue Avenue and the Robert Goelet house on the cliffs. The Bell house has a massive general composition, finely turned posts and very little whimsical detail. The Goelet house is much larger, with a symmetrical disposition of tower-like bays, and yet, also, a tendency to ramble pointlessly in several directions. But finer than any exterior is the dining room at "Kingscote"—now the Armstrong house—which has been mentioned earlier. This is the equal in quality

---

[6] Although at this period there is less obvious influence of Colonial detail in the work of the firm than in McKim's work of the mid-seventies, it is interesting that there was American seventeenth century precedent for the use of broken glass patterns set in stucco. An example is preserved at the Essex Institute. When McKim and White and their comrades took their "famous trip" in search of the Colonial along the North Shore in 1877, perhaps Ben Perley Poor at Indian Head showed them such fragments and pieces of seventeenth century turned work as well.

of any comparable room by Richardson. For it is splendid in scale and distribution, and equally splendid in its use of materials: marble, Tiffany glass, mahogany and cork. At the same time, it is restrained in the use of detail and almost devoid of archaeological reminiscence.

The Newport Casino is another excellent shingled work of these years. The symmetrically disposed facade toward the street, and the simple treatment of the rear galleries and the theatre building beyond the tennis courts are particularly worth remarking. It is of interest that Richardson had in his collection a group of photographs of this Casino as well as a photograph of the Bell house and two other similar houses by his pupils. As he possessed almost no other illustrations of the work of his American contemporaries, this would seem to indicate that he found these buildings the worthiest of their day.[7] The fact that this early work of McKim, Mead and White represented a development parallel to his own, rather than an imitation of his style, illustrates the breadth of his judgement. Richardson was wise enough to realize the hope of American architecture lay not in imitation but in emulation of his work.

The more monumental work of McKim, Mead and White is, for the most part, not of the interest of the wooden houses. Nor did Richardson possess photographs of it. The Tiffany apartment house in New York, 1882-84, was considered very "Richardsonian" in the eighties. Actually, it is almost entirely in the spirit of Norman Shaw's best urban work of the seventies. Only the low broad entrance arch and the rock facing of the stone basement derives from Richardson. XII-17

Only one design of these years is at all Classical. This is a clubhouse project of 1879 which was never executed. The upper part of the building is regular in composition with symmetrical Renaissance features. But the ground floor is asymmetrical and imitates Norman Shaw's work.

McKim, Mead and White were not alone in the early eighties in developing the sort of American Queen Anne which was very soon to

[7] There is also a photograph of a small bank in Albany by Russell Sturgis, of picturesque Late Gothic character with a corner turret.

239

become the basis of the general vernacular. It was by no means evident as yet that Richardson's personal style was to be widely and stupidly imitated. That a violent reaction was about to arise from an apparently sympathetic quarter, the offices of McKim, Mead and White, would have seemed immensely unlikely. During these few years in the early eighties, America had not merely one great architect, but a group apparently allied in direction. A national consistency of style, such as had been lost in the decades before the Civil War, seemed on the verge of attainment.[8]

In the spring of 1882, the strain of his increasing work had begun to tell on Richardson. His energy spent itself in a never ceasing preoccupation with architectural problems. The little holograph sketches, in which the essentials of plan and composition were worked out, were most frequently done while he was in actual conference with clients, when he was on trains travelling to supervise buildings in execution, and in bed. Yet he was also strenuous in his relaxation, always hospitable and always with his friends, whose interests were often very diverse from architecture. As his weight increased, his expenditure of energy did not diminish and the testimony of contemporaries consistently emphasizes the forceful dynamism of his character.[9]

This spring of 1882 was the high point of his career. For five years, since the completion of Trinity, he had been generally accepted as America's leading architect. In one type of building after another he had more than equalled his creative achievement of the early seventies. He had made himself as much at home with wooden construction and with brick as with rock-faced granite. He had faced all the isolated architectural problems of his day and offered solutions which were at once contemporary and, in the best sense, traditional. In the work of McKim, Mead and White he could see his influence encouraging originality, while the rise of an imitative Richardsonian school was not so far advanced as to give him pause.

[8] *V.* Chapter XV for the reaction that began in the next few years.

[9] It is rather interesting that when he was too tired and ill to continue his social life in the spring of 1882, he found amusement in the detective stories of Gaboriau.

The picture of his character cannot be improved over that painted by Mrs. Van Rensselaer in 1888 when the living memory of him was still warm and vivid. But it is possible to see more clearly now than she could, that when his health broke down and he was sent to Europe, he left behind perhaps the happiest moment in his whole career. The problems of the skyscraper, which he was not to live long enough to face, had not arisen. The academic point of view was still in abey- XII-18 ance. The choicest commissions of all sorts were still coming to his office. The inferiority of his office staff was not yet too evident. Richardson could go to Europe as few Americans have ever done, justly assured of his absolute eminence.

PART V

LATE WORKS

1882–1886

CHAPTER THIRTEEN

1882-1884

IN THE summer of 1882 Richardson returned to Europe. It was his first, and last, visit since leaving Paris in 1865. His companions were Phillips Brooks and two other clergymen, as well as a young architect named Jaques from his own office. He went first to London, where he visited specialists and received encouragement about his health.

In London he spent little time on architecture. He did not like Streets' new Law Courts. This is not surprising, as they had been designed in 1866 and only begun eight years later. When they reached completion in 1882, the design was therefore a decade and a half behind the times. He was also disappointed by the house built by Burges for himself. This he was able to see, although Burges had just died. Nevertheless, he brought home photographs of its theatrical mediaeval interiors. He also acquired photographs of the interiors of Norman Shaw's Chelsea houses, whose fine eighteenth century vernacular design had already influenced his work. He passed a pleasant half day with Morris at the Merton Abbey works and met at his house the members of the later Pre-Raphaelite circle. With Morris and William de Morgan he was much at home; Richardson and Morris had perhaps more similarity of temperament than either shared with his ordinary associates. It is a pity, particularly for Morris, that they could not have collaborated.

Richardson found the newer Queen Anne houses, now more and

more what modern Americans would call "Georgian", lacking in interest and individuality. His judgement was just enough, although the streets they filled were better for this standardization than those which Richardson's American contemporaries cluttered with their early Queen Anne idiosyncrasies.

In France, the Gothic interested him very little. At Clermont-Ferrand he was excited by the crude Romanesque of Notre-Dame-du-Port, and with some difficulty acquired many photographs of it. At St.-Trophime he expressed the fervid wish that his builders, Norcross Brothers, and Evans, who executed his architectural carving, might have been there. It is doubtful if the visit would have improved their work; certainly the photographs he brought back to them did not.

He found St.-Gilles less interesting. It was too finished and classical for his taste.

In Italy as in France, Richardson spent the great part of his time getting photographs of Romanesque churches. He thought the Pisa group the finest thing he saw in Europe. A generation of tourists echoed his opinion, as a later generation were to echo Henry Adams' opinion of Mont-St.-Michel and Chartres. In Florence the architecture of the Bargello, so curiously like his own work of the early seventies in feeling, was a great pleasure to him. The pictures in the museums naturally made a strong impression also. Rome he never saw, perhaps out of respect to his renunciation of the Prix de Rome implicit in his not becoming a French subject in the sixties. But he went to Bologna and spent half a day in Ravenna. The tomb of Theodoric there was the closest he was ever to come to the Syrian architecture he had studied in de Vogüé's books. He also saw "Saint-Apollinaire-en-Classe, vieille usine désaffectée de Dieu," in the just words of T. S. Eliot. Fortunately this had not yet been rebuilt by archaeologists.

In Venice, he was a less strenuous tourist, enjoying and indulging himself as any sensitive visitor must. The amazingly contrasted qualities of the facade of St. Mark's and the Piazza are never better appreciated than over a peach ice at Florian's while the band is playing. Even Ruskin had gone to balls in Venice. At the Murano glass works, lately revived by the demands of an English public brought up on *The Stones of Venice* and the products of Merton Abbey, he saw exactly the sort of rich and varied colouring he had sought in the Albany Senate Chamber. The interior of St. Mark's must, however, have depressed him. In spite of all that he and La Farge had been able to do in Trinity, what was it but a feeble *pochade* beside the authentic Byzantine splendour which six centuries of later mosaicists had not been able to spoil. For this was and still is the most beautiful church interior in the world as regards colour. Did Richardson feel the humility of an authentic genius in his own day before the accomplishment of nameless generations?

Spain was the country with whose Romanesque architecture he felt most at home. He measured brickwork and found the joints thicker than the bricks; he saw stone voussoirs eight feet long which he imitated later on the Pittsburgh jail. The ambulatory of Avila gave him the scheme he used in the project for the Albany Cathedral. At Salamanca he saw the lantern, which the contemporary world considered his most fundamental inspiration, and of which before this he had seen only the poor photograph La Farge sent him.

He travelled rapidly through Spain, without the entourage of clergymen, and returned through Poitiers. There the Late Gothic houses pleased him as much as Notre-Dame-la-Grande. In Paris, where he had not stopped on his way to Italy, he sought his old friends. Guadet, Gerhardt and the others were impressed by his success, but they were naturally not persuaded to relinquish their official style and achieve a more personal expression. Perhaps, indeed, they had the better of the argument. Richardson's genius might have towered even higher above their talent had he risen from the level at which French official architecture still stood in the sixties—instead of from the abyss in which American architecture then wallowed. On the other hand, without the American architectural desert from which to take off, he might have been all his life an anonymous agent of the vernacular, like most of his French friends; or, at the best, like Guadet, the mere codifier and expounder of existing theory.

XIII-3

247

Although Richardson was so active in acquiring photographs, he realized their limitations as very few American architects were to do for two generations. Of St.-Gilles, for example, he wrote: "To think that I have seen it and felt its influence so differently from the way one does from photographs." But Richardson's later work was chiefly affected indirectly through this acquisition of photographs of the buildings he admired. These photographs were far more dangerous documents for his draftsmen and his carvers than the lithographs and engravings in the older books. The sight of original old work should have opened his eyes to the superiority of the detail he had worked out himself. Actually, it rather inhibited his powers of invention in the field of ornament. As he grew ever busier he became more satisfied with detail best described as bad photo-sculpture of old work.

On the other hand, the study of old buildings, however brief, made him realize how rare extreme elaboration was in mediaeval work. Ruskin's influential criticism, which emphasized in architecture the applied arts of carving and polychromy, was obviously based on an erroneous premise. In monumental masonry design Richardson's detail henceforth was sparser, as well as duller, than in his preceding work.

Earlier in his career such a trip might have done him much harm. But by this time, although he did not perhaps altogether know it, his mind was really closed and his act of creation complete. Nor was his head turned by the fact that he must have seen clearly that he was the greatest architect in the world. He must have sensed that it was a world in transition. European architecture was to find itself shortly, when Mackintosh in Glasgow and Wagner in Vienna and Van de Velde in Brussels each began to found his personal style.*

"Barcelona did not interest Mr. Richardson as much as some of the French towns, but he was very tired," Jaques wrote in a letter quoted by Mrs. Van Rensselaer. What would he have thought of the Surrealist Casa Vicens in Barcelona just completed by the young Antonio Gaudí? One can hardly guess. The iron grille he would cer-

XIII-4

XIII-5

* On the Continent at this time Cuijpers' Amsterdam Riksmuseum, begun in 1876, would probably have been most sympathetic to Richardson, if he could have seen it.

248

tainly have appreciated. It was not dissimilar to the railing he had used on the Fenway railroad bridge, but it was much more powerfully original. Gaudí in 1882 was at a point in his career comparable to that in Richardson's when he designed the Crowninshield house in 1868. His best work came considerably later. He was closest to Richardson's personal style in certain earlier student projects and, again, when he first reached maturity in the design of the Casa Güell, 1885-89.

XIII-6

It is unfortunate that Richardson had every reason to consider the Europeans old-fashioned as regards architecture in the early eighties. Who can blame him if he found more life in the Romanesque than in the work of contemporary French and English architects at this date. The underground path, which may have led to Europe in the nineties from Richardson's ornament of this period in the Albany Court of Appeals, has been mentioned, although it is purely hypothetical. But Richardson saw nothing of the new currents which were just about to bend iron and even stone into strange naturalistic forms. Not only was no one a better architect than he (neither were most of the men of the next decade) : no one as yet exemplified architectural ideas any newer than his.

XIII-7

The changes in his work after 1882 are rarely for the better. But it is not necessary to blame them on the lack of fresh inspiration in Europe at this time. They are more obviously due to over-production in his own office. Richardson's style was too completely matured to be much affected by external influences, but he could not escape the influence of the conditions under which he worked.

Beginning with the summer and autumn of 1882, when Richardson was away, symptoms of decline begin to be evident. This decline was not in his own creative power of design but in the general level of the executed work, produced in cooperation with an office force lacking full comprehension of his personal style. The increasing substitution of accurately copied archaeological detail for freshly conceived forms, although the most obvious, is the least serious of several symptoms.

Although detail determines the classification of most nineteenth century architecture, it is usually the weakest and least interesting feature of the whole. It is wise, therefore, to discount detail in considering nineteenth century architecture. In the absence of ornament of really creative quality, even a modern eye may prefer decoration which is safely archaeological to that which is dubiously original. This was certainly the attitude of most young architects in the eighties, and very justifiably, considering the unfortunate character of the detail designed by most of the preceding generation. The contemporary attitude of estimating the excellence of nineteenth century architecture in terms of its freedom from all detail is a false one. Some of the finest buildings of the nineteenth century, like the Crystal Palace, have almost no detail, but some others, like the Houses of Parliament, which are, perhaps, equally fine, are loaded with it. Richardson's later work is less interesting where the detail is conventional, but, judged as a whole and not as a compilation of parts, it is not necessarily inferior.

If the late nineteenth century had resembled in the condition of its architecture the early eighteenth or the early twelfth century, the lack of an authentic detail, of which designers and workmen were equally masters, would have been serious indeed. A real Romanesque church or a Rococo palace with poor detail is lacking in a vital matter. But the nineteenth century was more like the late twelfth century or the seventeenth. Important new architectural development was a matter of innovation in structure and in general composition. Even as in the Baroque, detail of too high an intrinsic quality might be considered a disadvantage, throwing the design out of focus by attracting attention to individual features which should only be seen in relation to each other. In the case of McKim, Mead and White in the early eighties, and occasionally in the case of Richardson himself, preoccupation with achieving a maximum of interest in ornamental detail led to a loss of quality in the total architectural effect.

A more serious symptom of decline, not unrelated to the sparseness of the archaeological detail, was a sort of sterilization of Richardson's earlier exuberance. This begins to be apparent in the Sard house of 1882. The dryness of the masonry of the Sard house is not really comparable to the increasing simplicity and restraint of the new work in other materials. The brick and shingle houses are, on the contrary, still bold and vigorous. They represented no loss of vitality in Richardson's style, of which vitality was one of the chief virtues.

Even the tendency represented in another building of 1882, the Kingston and Bedford Street Ames Building, was less dangerous. To repeat earlier successful designs without really improving them was ominous, after the hitherto continuous advance in Richardson's power of creation: but it was not as ominous as the dilute dullness of the Sard house.

The conditions under which Richardson was now working forced him to depend more and more on his draftsmen. After the Channing house, designed in the spring of 1883, and before his death in the spring of 1886, over thirty separate commissions passed through the office. Of these almost twenty remained unfinished at the time of his death. More work was begun in the last three years of his life than he had undertaken before the year 1880. Indeed, the number of his buildings which must be considered at least partly posthumous exceeds that of all his early buildings down through Trinity Church. It is more remarkable that half a dozen buildings of the final years of his career are among his greatest works than that so many are inferior. Even among the unexecuted projects, not counted in the above statistics, there are some excellent designs dating from this period.

The Grange Sard, Jr., house in Albany, commissioned in January, 1882, is a wider and lower version of the Higginson house, all of brownstone. The late Gothic motif over the narrow entrance to the recessed porch is very archaeological and out of character with the smooth-cut lintels over the second storey windows. The bulging parapet of the entrance porch was fairly libelled by contemporary children as "the Sards' bath tub". But if this feature is somewhat exuberant, the composition as a whole is dry and over-refined. (Fig. 85).

For the first time in Richardson's work the masonry is arranged in alternate broad and narrow courses instead of the characteristic random ashlar. The unmoulded mullions are too thin. Thus, the surfaces are poor and flat in quality. This house is certainly not Romanesque or Late Gothic as a whole, nor is it characteristic of Richardson's personal style as we have come to know it in the work of the preceding years. Was Richardson attempting to modify his treatment of stone walls to accord with the flatter effect appropriate to the shingled walls of the Bryant house and the brick walls of the Anderson house?

A large part of the preparation of the final drawings for this house must have been done while Richardson was in Europe. Its unexpected character is almost certainly due to the office force. These younger men were undoubtedly as much influenced by the slicker surfaces and greater delicacy of Hunt's W. K. Vanderbilt house and McKim, Mead and White's earliest urban work as by the new standards of "correctness". The fenestration is ample in detail and well arranged. The plan is satisfactory and the composition skilful. Yet the house would hardly be taken for Richardson's own work if it were not definitely documented. This is the first of the group of works which must be set in a category apart. It does not wholly belong to the canon of Richardson's work, because it is so markedly influenced by the taste of his assistants.[1]

The commercial building built for F. L. Ames, at Kingston and Bedford Streets, Boston, commissioned in March, 1882, is no more.[2] It burned a decade later and was replaced by a building which follows the original rather closely. This is by Shepley, Rutan and Coolidge.

---

[1] Of the remodelling undertaken for Miss Edith Mason in Newport, probably in 1882, nothing remains but a plan. The actual house has been demolished, and the plan offers no features of interest.

[2] Another Ames building of this date, identified by Mrs. Van Rensselaer as on Washington Street, was never erected, according to the records of Coolidge, Shepley, Bulfinch and Abbott, and those of the F. L. Ames Estate. The Ames Building, now on Washington Street, by Shepley, Rutan and Coolidge was built in 1889. A few rather indeterminate studies in the sketch books suggest that the work to which Mrs. Van Rensselaer refers was an intended remodelling, as they only show the upper floors. These are rather more delicate and open than the executed building on Kingston and Bedford Streets, and do not look as if Richardson himself had had much to do with the design.

The first Kingston and Bedford Wholesale Store was surprisingly like the Cheney Building of seven years earlier. It must have been finally studied while Richardson was away in Europe. The relations between the different storeys are better handled than in Hartford, and the solid massing is effectively emphasized by the curving site. There are no corner pavilions, but, instead, a curiously broken rhythm in the lower arcade. The chief differences are the use of brownstone through- XIII-9 out, ill advised in the middle of a grimy city, and the tall dormers of rather hybrid type, with Late Gothic outline and Romanesque detail. (Fig. 81).

This building does not advance beyond the Cheney Building toward Richardson's ultimate achievement in the field of commercial architecture, the Marshall Field Wholesale Store, begun in Chicago two years later. It is rather to be considered a repetition by the office force of a type already established. The building by Shepley, Rutan and Coolidge which soon replaced it is, actually, in some respects superior. For it profits by the example of Richardson's own latest and best work in the field.

The competition project for All Saints Cathedral in Albany, which Richardson began at least to think about while he was in Europe, was the most elaborate design of his whole career. It was the only design for an important church later than Trinity. Richardson's early admirers usually regretted that this church was never built. But Mrs. Van Rensselaer, with her usual acuteness, saw that the work he actually executed in the succeeding years was more significant. Richardson naturally regretted the loss of the commission. He had, however, made little attempt to conform to the restrictions of the programme and he soon recovered from his disappointment. A more conventional Gothic project by an English architect named Gibson was selected. Curiously enough, Gibson set to work building Richardsonian Romanesque houses as soon as he arrived in Albany.

Mrs. Van Rensselaer emphasizes, in discussing Richardson's Cathedral drawings, the "scholarly" treatment of the "pure" Romanesque. Indeed, it is to the fact that the design was "Romanesque," when the programme called for Gothic, that Richardson's loss of the commission is in part to be attributed. To modern eyes the design, while certainly not very original, will hardly appear so "scholarly" and, above all, not "pure" Romanesque.

Certain features have identifiable Romanesque origins, such as the rather Auvergnat ring of chapels, serving as vestries, around the chevet. (Fig. 86). Nevertheless, even the more vertical version of the Salamanca tower over the crossing is really twelfth century Gothic in silhouette. For the scheme of the original with its corner turrets and gables is, of course, exactly that of the earliest and finest Gothic spires of Northern France. Otherwise, the church is in every way French Gothic in conception, except for the omission of the nave vaults. This is characteristic enough of the English Gothic favored by the Protestant Episcopal Church in America. The interior elevation of the nave, with the vaulting shafts and the colonnettes grouped about heavy round piers, is as characteristically Gothic of the twelfth century as the domed rib vaults of the aisles. The disposition of the facade is, as it were, a half-way stage between the Abbaye-aux-Dames and Notre Dame, not unlike Saint-Denis. Except for the Auvergnat chevet and the Spanish crossing, both types in use in the late twelfth century, this might be a hypothetical reconstruction of a major cathedral somewhere in Southern England of about the date of the choir of Canterbury.

These drawings are the natural fruit of Richardson's trip to Europe. They represent a vain desire to vie directly not with his own contemporaries, who, he saw, were no match for him, but with the builders of the twelfth century, with whom he felt a natural kinship. It was a waste of his time. This archaeological exercise was of assistance only to his draftsmen in providing the kind of training they wanted. But at least it got the virus of the Middle Ages out of Richardson's system.

The Billings Library at the University of Vermont in Burlington was commissioned in April, 1883. This is the sort of compilation of features from Richardson's own earlier works and projects such as his successors were to continue making after his death. It is almost a typical

"Richardsonian" work in the sense of being apparently a characteristic product of his school rather than of his own hand. For it is all of brownstone, like the Kingston and Bedford Street Store and the Sard House. Richardson had not used dark stone alone, without a good deal of lighter trim, since the North Congregational Church ten years earlier. Indeed, in that decade he had used it only three times: for walling in the Cheney Building, Austin Hall, and the Woburn Library. (Fig. 88).

The octagonal end and the tall open tower are improved versions of the prominent features of the Woburn Library, his first and poorest work of the type. The turrets at the end of the band of stack windows were not used on any of the three earlier libraries nor on the similar wings of Austin Hall. All of these earlier buildings represented advancing steps in his development as this does not. The pairing of two towers of different heights beside the entrance was tried and discarded in the first project for Austin Hall. The awkward relationship between the broad low Syrian arch and the slim arcade above is to be equalled only in the poorer work of imitators. The sparse detail is almost all imitated from earlier buildings except that of the great arch, which is flat and dead. In the terms of the criticism of Italian painting, this is obviously a workshop piece.

The excellent little station at Chestnut Hill, commissioned at the same time as the Billings Library, has already been mentioned; as well as the very bare and symmetrical station at Holyoke, another workshop piece, commissioned in November. The Framingham station, commissioned in October, 1883, is a better and somewhat more personal work. The dormers are lower and more interestingly disposed. There are also some inconspicuous subsidiary units, covered with shingles, which give a pleasant variety to the general effect.

Emmanuel Church in Allegheny City (now part of Pittsburgh) was commissioned in August, 1833. Although it is very small and simple, it is certainly one of Richardson's best later works. It is a small aisleless rectangle in plan, with the apse partially cut off from the nave by banks of organ pipes on either side. Under the dark wooden roof, XIII-11 the marble reredos with its bands of Cosmatesque mosaic appears bright and rich. In the altar niche are two angels in mosaic flanking the cross. The statues in the niches at the side are inferior, but the general decorative effect of the apse is delicately sumptuous.

The church is lighted on the sides by groups of three arched windows and by rather stunted slate-covered dormers half way up the roof. The facade, which is of brick like the sidewalls, is very effective. The plain high gable follows the lines of the roof. At the base there are three wide low arches which are nevertheless not of the Syrian type. The imposts of these arches are great rock-faced blocks of brownstone. The broad archivolts of five bands of brick voussoirs are flush with the basket pattern brickwork at the springing of the gable. Above this band are three arched lights, rather taller in proportion than the entrance arches, with banded voussoirs. A slot window with a flat brick arch completes the composition. (Fig. 87).

The patterns in the brick are simple throughout but they give a varied texture to the plain facade. Bands of vertical bricks run across at the bottom and top of the windows, and the bricks at the edge of the gables are at right angles to the slope. These are bonded, in late mediaeval fashion, with triangles running into the wall. There are further ingenious details, such as the batter of the base and the curved cut-brick projection which covers the end of the cornices of the side walls. The stone finial is the only detail of doubtful quality. Altogether this church is very superior to most of the more considerable work Richardson designed in this year.

The best large building of this rather uninspired year is the Converse Library in Malden. Here the earlier library type was effectively modified to an L shape. There is a Trustees' Room in the short arm of the L and a loggia opening on the wide terrace which fills the angle. This terrace is surrounded by a plain wall which provides an effective base for the building. An octagonal stair turret with simple detail is set at the intersection of the two wings. The reading room windows rise to the full height of the wall, adjoining the typical window band of the stacks. At the other end, this band comes up against a more substantial turret than at Burlington. The material is Longmeadow stone throughout, except for the rather minute pieces of Serpentine in the simple marquetry of the front gable. (Fig. 89). The interior is very like those of the earlier libraries; but the oak is now golden and the detail Byzantine and rather mechanical. The exterior detail is also quite archaeological. The drip moulds over the arches, unused in the previous years, are to be regretted, as they break the continuity of the surface.

XIII-12

Yet, altogether this is a fine building, more refined in scale and less clumsy than the work of the seventies. It is not seriously marred by the symptoms of decline so evident in the Burlington Library, even though it is somewhat dryer in treatment and more "correct" in detail than his best work of the immediately preceding years. The greater precision of composition, the reduction in the apparent weight, the success of the walled front terrace and ingenuity of the relation between the horizontal stack windows and the vertical reading room window certainly make up for a great deal. The omission of contrasting trim, moreover, is appropriate to the more completely integrated composition, as it was not at Burlington.

The large project for a casino and theatre in Washington may be attributed to about this date. (Fig. 109). The distribution of the parts is excellent. The more or less Byzantine scheme of the auditorium, with its low dome on pendentives, is not found elsewhere in Richardson's work. The facade is well designed in stone and brick. The suggested surface decoration of the interior approaches Sullivan's work of the end of the decade in the Auditorium in Chicago, yet the project seems to have been largely developed by draftsmen. It is a rather conventional application of the Richardsonian style, such as many imitators tried in the next few years.

Several other projects, probably of 1884, never came to execution; but they have little individual interest. The Willimantic station design was an enlargement of the North Easton scheme, with the windows grouped under low arches. The Corning house was to have been of cobblestones on the lower storey and shingles above, like the Paine house executed in the next few years. The plan and the one slight elevation sketch suggest a well composed asymmetrical mass more compact than most of the later houses.

XIII-13 The project for the Buffalo Y. M. C. A., on a triangular lot with larger corner towers, exists in an interesting holograph plan which Mrs. Van Rensselaer mistook for that of a library. The perspective appeared first in an English magazine. At this time Richardson objected to the publication of his projects, knowing how much he was able to improve them in execution. How it reached England is not clear. The plan was excellent, but the exterior was "Richardsonian" in the worst sense. It must have been even more the work of draftsmen than the Washington project.

More interesting were the projects for cars for the Boston & Albany Railroad. The simple wooden trim, the ample distribution—the natural expression of the discomfort Richardson, with his enormous bulk, must have suffered in travelling—were certainly very superior to the contemporary treatment of the problem. Perhaps they were also superior, as regards the interior, to the aluminum paint and red piping of the newest cars of our own day. But the wooden exteriors, although simple, were heavy and clumsy, without the mechanical elegance obtainable with steel. These designs for everyday transportation units are to be contrasted with the luxurious yachts for which Stanford White was responsible: Richardson was not so much the purveyor to a millionaire class as his younger rivals were becoming. (Fig. 96).

The year 1884 saw the beginning of one of the monuments of which Richardson was proudest. The Allegheny County Buildings in Pittsburgh were commissioned after a competition in February. The XIII-14 project must, therefore, have been first studied at the end of 1883. This was an enormous work, the largest Richardson had undertaken alone since the Buffalo State Hospital, and almost as sumptuous as the Albany Capitol on which he was still working. The original contract price was over $2,000,000. This must have been exceeded before the buildings were entirely completed. Richardson lived to see the jail complete, and the final drawings for the courthouse had all passed through the office before his death.

The jail is more successful than the courthouse; but it was, of course, a much simpler thing for Richardson to design. The eight-foot XIII·15 voussoirs he had admired in Spain appear here, but the general impression is more like the granite buildings of the fifties in downtown Boston. The granite wall around the jail yard is one of the most magnificent displays of fine material in the world. (Fig. 92). The warden's house, with its lintelled windows set into one corner of this wall, is more effective even than that of Dance's famous old Newgate Prison in London. The towering end walls of the cross arms of the jail itself are equally impressive. The side walls are cut by tall arched windows, like the sides of Guadet's Hospice, but even bolder in scale.

The octagonal central lantern and the square front tower, although splendidly scaled to the rest, reflect somewhat too specifically the fortified towns Richardson had seen the year before in Southern France. Some of the other little turrets are also an unnecessary complication, but they serve as ventilators. The bridge of sighs is at once barren and fussy beside the magnificent main entrance with its eight-foot voussoirs and pairs of narrow flanking lights. But these are minor faults.

Here, for once, Richardson had the opportunity to be as massive as he desired and, at the same time, perfectly expressive of the purpose of the building. The quality of the chimney shaft is rare in any age. But in the nineteenth century, which built so many smokestacks, this is perhaps the only one whose beauty is intentional and really architectural in the fullest sense. This plain cylindrical shaft rising above the solid wall, with its curious angles in plan, is of an abstract quality hardly dreamed of by twentieth century architects. Yet it is also absolutely material in its practical usefulness and its massive rock-faced granite.

The courthouse, in its general distribution, is a sort of reduction of the scheme of the Albany Capitol and an enlargement of that of Sever Hall. (Fig. 91). The four large corner pavilions, with roofs rising above the main roof, the great tower on one side, and the high dormers recall Albany, as does the arrangement around a central court. The projecting round bays for the smaller rooms, rising like engaged turrets, are very like those of Sever. By placing the lobbies and stairs in the four corners of the court, Richardson avoided corridors on the upper floors and made it possible to light some of the court rooms on both sides.

The court is all of great blocks of rock-faced granite and has no carved detail. Great arches flank two sides, scaled like a Roman aqueduct. Beneath these main arches other lintelled and arched lights are grouped. At the top of the projecting lower storeys, which support terraces, are rows of smaller arches, three to each of the great arches below. Above the set-back are more arches and, above them, lintelled windows below the cornice. The end walls have four storeys of medium-sized arches and coupled lintelled windows at the top. The arches in the corner towers follow the line of the stairs.

This is a sort of engineering in masonry simpler even than the exterior of the Marshall Field Warehouse begun the next year. It is as effectively open as the jail wall is effectively closed and impressive because of its enormous scale and its expressively varied rhythm. (Figs. 93, 94).

The exterior is perhaps slightly inferior. (Fig. 90). The contrast between the square corner pavilions, which are too large to be towers, and the round bays, which are too small, is not improved by the central gables and the tall dormers. The heavy base demanded by the main tower makes the front facade actually heavier in appearance than the jail. This, far more than the elemental treatment of the court, provides precedent for the elephantiasis of the architecture of so many of Richardson's imitators. The earlier arrangement, with the tower rising on the court side, would have been more satisfactory.

There are significant changes from Richardson's earlier practice in the treatment of the exterior of the courthouse. These are indicative of the increase in formality in design at this time. The symmetrical arrangement of this building is perhaps merely coincident with the acceptance of the Renaissance discipline by McKim, Mead and White at just this time. The use of light-coloured granite throughout, without XIII-16 Longmeadow trim, was unknown in Richardson's work since the Hampden County Courthouse. This, like the use of brownstone throughout XIII-17 at Malden, makes plain that he was tiring of exterior polychromy and consciously initiating the monochrome manner of treatment McKim, Mead and White were so soon to impose on American architecture generally. In the jail, with its magnificent rough granite surfaces, this was desirable. But the exterior of the courthouse, perhaps, has a certain impoverished look like the earlier and equally monochrome Sard house.

This effect is of small importance. As Richardson was aware, the Pittsburgh atmosphere soon turned the walls to an even tone of blackish grey.[3] More serious is the character of the masonry, with very narrow courses alternating with rather wide courses in the fashion first used on the Sard house. This gives a monotonous horizontal pattern to the walls, fortunately not imitated on the jail or the great tower. It may have some constructive significance in bonding the walls together more solidly. But it certainly seems to reflect the rise of a more XIII-18 mechanical feeling for design, associated with the substitution of wash renderings for the free pen work of Stanford White and Langford Warren. This newer sort of rendering was probably introduced to the office by John Shepley and Charles A. Coolidge, who came to take Lang- XIII-19 ford Warren's place at this time. In it the walls were very pale and the windows washed with black ink. Thus they looked like holes in the wall, exactly the thing Richardson had previously tried to avoid by the use of small-paned windows.

The detail on the exterior of this building is very restrained, but also very archaeological. The rich rough material is quite without XIII-20 smooth-cut detail like that on the jail or in the court. Nor is there a profusion of free ornament as on Austin Hall, but rather an effect of stiffness and coldness completely lacking in Richardson's previous

[3] The buildings have just been sandblasted, so that for a few years they can XIII-21 be seen as they were designed. Richardson, himself, suggested the desirability of occasional washing.

work. On the top of the tower, at the furthest point from the eye, the detail grows more elaborate. But it is the tall shaft of the tower between the cornice of the main building and the belfry storey, with its rounded projections at the corners and in the middle of each side, which is XIII-22 the best thing on the exterior. (Fig. 90).

The side elevations, however, have great distinction when seen as a whole. The lintelled openings in the lower storeys are of the type introduced on the side facade of the Albany City Hall. They are here used in a much more consistent way. The great arches of the main floor really give a remarkably open effect. The lintelled windows below the cornice and in the gable are of the library stack type. The low vaulted entrance lobby has a Piranesian grandeur very superior to the intricate interweaving of the half flights in the Western Staircase of the Albany XIII-23 Capitol, as it was planned at this time. (Fig. 115) .[4]

Except for a group of suburban railroad stations and several houses, the only other commission of 1884 was that for a Baptist Church in Newton. Although this was not received until October, the church was finished well before Richardson's death in the spring of 1886. But even though it was finished within his lifetime, it is to all intents and purposes a posthumous work. There are early studies by Mr. Coolidge, completely in the English Norman parish church style which McKim, Mead and White were using at this time for a church at Stockbridge. Nothing could be much less Richardsonian than these.

The execution, by contrast, looks like the work of some Western imitator who grasped only the worst idiosyncrasies of Richardson's XIII-24 developed style. (Fig. 116) . The polygonal tower has all the fussiness of the one at Woburn and rests awkwardly on a square base as if it had been designed for some other building. While the tower is tall and slim, the church itself is broader and lower than the North Congre-

[4] It is possible to consider that the lush decoration and the freer curves Perry used in executing this staircase are superior to the latest designs made in Richardson's lifetime. The stairway was, in conception, so much more ornamental than practical that such excess is more appropriate than Richardson's relatively restrained project.

gational Church in Springfield. The interior proportions are even more oppressive, although the decorative effect is somewhat richer. The porch is like a parody of that of Austin Hall, with the more conventional contrast of heavy dark trim and light granite walling broken up by badly scaled marquetry. The gable of the facade behind is both bare and cluttered, with an unbelievably crude half rose window and a strange Queen Anne projection at the top of the gable. But enough of description. It is obvious that when Mr. Coolidge's drawings did not please Richardson, some other draftsmen worked the design out in a way superficially more Richardsonian. Already Richardson was too busy, apparently, even to see and criticize all the work that went out from his own office. What if the arrangement of the baptismal tank was ingenious in its plan, as Mrs. Van Rensselaer remarks, and the whole church built for remarkably little money? It would have been better for Richardson's reputation if it had never been built at all.[5]

The same is true of most of the little stations at Brighton, Waban, Woodland, and Eliot, all commissioned in the same month as the Newton church, and that at Wellesley Hills, commissioned in July of the next year. Of these, only the Brighton station, whose relative excellence was mentioned earlier, and that at Wellesley Hills were completed within Richardson's lifetime. The Wellesley Hills station has round projections at either end of the side and very wide sheltering eaves instead of porches. It is moderately successful, as is the similar one at Waban. The Woodland station is smaller and more original, with plain monolithic piers supporting the corner porches.

None of these is superior to those Shepley, Rutan and Coolidge continued to build in the next few years, and none of them shows in any way the marks of Richardson's own personal thought. The line of suburban stations which began so brilliantly at Auburndale petered out at Brighton three years later. Over-production already was lowering the level of production in Richardson's office. Had he lived, his reputation must soon have suffered from such work signed with his name.

[5] The Dartmouth College Chapel, a close copy of this Newton Church by Faxon, is actually better.

CHAPTER FOURTEEN

1884-1886

RICHARDSON had had eight new commissions as early as 1881. It is not surprising that in the next year, when he was away in Europe for several months, the symptoms of decline in his work became manifest. The office then learned to go on without him, and he developed the assurance that they could thus carry on. Had new commissions later diminished, a return to the earlier situation, with Richardson correcting and redesigning everything done in the office, might have been possible. But instead of diminishing, new commissions poured in, in greater numbers than ever, in the last two years of his life.

The fatal habit of delegation once initiated, Richardson became a sort of executive in the business sense. He had no partner, but he was the head of an architectural firm; and the firm produced almost automatically at a rate no one creative personality could keep up with. The distribution of responsibility for the changes in taste and the lapses of judgement that are so manifest in all the work of 1884 cannot be precise. In justice to his office force, however, it must be said that Richardson was really responsible and not they. If they made final decisions about less important work without consulting him, they were only attempting to save his energy for the Pittsburgh buildings, about which he cared most. If he had attempted to control in detail all the work going on in the office at once, his creative energy would have been frittered away. In spite of his enormous vigour and power of decision, the pace was impossible. It was no longer necessarily true, as it certainly had been earlier, that any work from his office was better than similar work by imitators. The level of the vernacular as a whole had perhaps not risen appreciably, but the quality of the work of trained architects had certainly improved. Most of the clients who came to Richardson for domestic work in 1884 would have got nearly as good work from McKim, Mead and White, and even from several other young architects.

Richardson's tragedy was not his early death: it was his excessive popularity, which led to over-production. The tragedy of the great individual genius is often enough due to too general an acceptance of that genius. A universal demand for the product of one man cannot be supplied except with counterfeits. Whether or not those counterfeits are signed with his name is of no importance. They are no longer really his. The very different cases of Rubens and Corot in their later careers both illustrate this point. When a great individual like Richardson begins to fail, the whole justification of his individuality is lost. For personal genius is not transmissible.

The men in Richardson's office, after McKim and White had left, may have been among the ablest young architects of the day; but they could not possibly produce his personal work. When they imitated his personal manner they were little better off than imitators in other offices, now that his work was so widely distributed and so amply published. When they used their own judgement, they diluted his per- sonal expression with foreign elements, even if their judgement was excellent, as it may very often have been. Thus, the situation was really tragic, since there was no solution.

Richardson as a great individual had raised American architecture from the slough of the late sixties. But the very fact of this individuality set a limit to the height which he could reach single-handed. At the same time, his natural belief in the value of personal expression in architecture and of personal inspiration from the art of the past was a dangerous doctrine for men who were not in the least geniuses. It was also something of an anachronism in an age whose appreciations were superficial and whose problems were increasingly technical.

In this very year, 1884, the first skyscraper was built in Chicago by Major Jenney, a man who was essentially a technician and not an artist. The Home Insurance Building was a ludicrous parody of Richardsonian Romanesque design, totally misunderstood and barbarously expressed. But the immanent destiny of American architecture of the next half century lay in that building and not in Richardson's mansions nor in his jail. The rising age of commercial expansion and hurry demanded a new technical method. But that new technical method was not necessarily sound, any more than the age it served. Richardson worked best at a slow tempo and with the characteristic methods of earlier ages. Fortunately, he was able to do so. His clients were those who had won such success or inherited such fortunes that they could seek refuge in the illusion of recreating an earlier and nobler age: whether in the twelfth century in Europe, as Henry Adams did quite consciously, or in the Colonial period in America, out of vague ancestral piety. Yet Richardson offered them better than they asked. For he knew how to make modern houses out of the elements of castles and farmhouses. In the best libraries, at Quincy and Malden, and in the best railroad stations, at Auburndale and Chestnut Hill, the very simplicity of the problem brought out his essential creative force. But he could not and would not repeat himself. The Burlington Library and most of the later railroad stations were hardly his work at all.

Like a legendary hero, he lived for new problems, dreaming of ice-houses and river boats to conquer while the smooth machine of his office turned out the late buildings to which his name was signed. The problems presented by the amenities of late nineteenth century bourgeois living: good medium-sized suburban houses, pleasant suburban stations, nice small libraries for an increasingly educated democracy— these he had already solved, even if his work still left untouched many more serious and, perhaps, insoluble problems. "For the great transcontinental railroads he built a monument to graft; for the prophet of the decline of Western civilization, a refuge—opposite the White House; at a time when America's living accommodations, the basic architectural need, were at their lowest." Thus might the cynic write with partial justice. For in 1879 the invention of the dumbbell tenement made possible the erection of slums of whose degradation the earlier nineteenth century had not dreamed. While Richardson built isolated houses for the more affluent, even they began to take refuge in the simpler tenement life of the new apartment houses. For at least one such building he made a project. But today, fifty years later, the urban housing of America is barely ameliorated. What could one architect have hoped to do?

It is not necessary that a great artist should grasp directly the whole of his time. Art is what is to be made and that is determined by forces over which the artist has no direct control. Even the future is not always right. Apartment housing may be an impasse; the skyscraper almost certainly is. In those problems he had handled, Richardson had set a higher standard, perhaps, than any architect of his generation in the world. Sever Hall might have been sufficient inspiration for a whole generation of college building, and the Quincy Library for small public edifices in all the towns of the nation. In his two smaller wooden houses, he had shown that a simple free treatment of shingle-covered frame construction could be applied at any scale and not merely to country mansions. At the other end of the scale, the Pittsburgh courthouse made plain that a great civic structure could be at once monumental and practical. Few architects in any age have done as much and he was to do still more.

Among his later work, one building stands supreme: the Marshall Field Wholesale Store. Of his later houses, which failed in general to maintain the standard of his best years, the Glessner house has the finest masonry exterior of any he ever built, and the interiors of the Paine house and the Hay house are, in their way, equally superior. The canon of his work was not yet complete, despite all the poor work that issued from the office in the last two years of his life.

The Paine house, commissioned in January, 1884, was left materially unfinished on Richardson's death. So many things are extremely fine about it that it need not be considered posthumous. The original conception, however, was considerably modified in the execution. Plans and a perspective dating from 1884 make plain what the original conception was like. As the work was carried out, the plans were changed only in minor details, but the completed exterior is quite different.

There was an older house on the site, dating from the late sixties. This house was largely, but not completely, swallowed up in the new construction. The greater part of the old house became a service wing, but the dining room and an "Autumn Parlor" remained. (~~Fig. 117~~). The chief feature of the plan, as usual in Richardson's larger houses, was a great living hall. Although this extends the full width of the house, it is rather inadequately lighted. But the great fireplace in the hall, with wide onyx facing, is very handsome, despite the spindly mantel, with its feeble Romanesque-Byzantine carving like that in the interior of the Malden Library. Side of the fireplace is a round bay window and a sort of nook, partly cut off from the rest of the room by a grille of turned wood. Diagonally opposite the fireplace corner is the staircase, rising with several landings into the polygonal bay formed by one of the towers of the garden facade. This great feature is a splendid example of Richardson's virtuosity in the design of stairs. They pour down into the room like a mountain cataract, and even the turned spindles of the balustrades and the small square panels look well seen against the light. For the lack of light in this room is not altogether unfortunate. (Fig. 100). The brown woodwork, with the orange-red plaster walls, stencilled with great Japanese symbols, forms a rich harmony beneath the great structural beams of the ceiling.

XIV-4

The better lighted "Summer Parlor", with its golden-yellow woodwork and light green-blue plaster walls, would not be so effective but for the great beauty of the fireplace, which is entirely of peach-coloured marble. This is at once ample and delicate, as the later type of woodwork rarely succeeds in being. The planning of this room is interesting. The corner bay in the tower is so large as to form almost a separate room and not a mere corner projection. (~~Fig. 120~~). Otherwise the distribution of the interior is not of great interest, except for a small sitting room arranged in the bay under the stair landing, and the landing itself, which is large enough to form a pleasant morning room.

The exterior of the house was originally intended to have a high hip roof with domed roofs over the towers. The actual treatment, with a very low gable and flat roofs on the towers, is certainly superior. The use of boulder masonry for the tower storey of the main house and the entire height of the towers is also effective. Otherwise, the changes in the executed work are unfortunate. The most serious is the substitution of windows with plain lower sashes and upper sashes having side bands of small panes for windows entirely of small panes, such as were used in the houses of the early eighties. The transoms of the lower storey windows are even more graceless. The Colonial Revival design of the Palladian window in the end gable is as inexplicable as the swooping hood at the northeast corner, which emphasizes the division of the general mass into horizontal layers by the combination of boulder walling below and shingles above. Yet the garden facade, although sadly disfigured now, with wooden bays between the stone piers of the loggia, remains one of Richardson's happiest and most original compositions. Although the second storey loggia is too delicate in scale, like most of the woodwork of the mid-eighties, the dissimilar towers are beautifully balanced, and the long low dormer in the roof is even more satisfactory than that on the rear of Sever. (Fig. 99).

XIV-5

It is hard to estimate the extent to which this house should be considered Richardson's own work. For the peculiar virtues, quite as easily as the peculiar vices, might be in part the contribution of the young men of the office force. The windows are probably due to the justifiable request of the client for large panes through which to see the splendid view; the interior wooden detail, the Palladian window, and the spindly posts of the second storey porch look more like the work of the office force. But surely no one but Richardson himself can have been responsible for the general composition of the garden facade, for the planning of the two great rooms, and for such features as the parlor fireplace and the long dormer, which are new in Richardson's work and yet in his best tradition.

The two adjoining houses in Washington for John Hay and Henry Adams were also commissioned in January, 1884.[1] Together they form a single composition. Since they are destroyed, it is not possible to discuss them as fully as the Paine house. The Paine house had a very beautiful country site, already selected for the earlier house. But Richardson developed the new house to take the fullest advantage of the location on the crest of a rolling hill against a bank of pines. It cannot be said that he availed himself as appropriately of the corner site of the Washington houses, across Lafayette Square from the White House.

XIV-6 The idea of combining the two contiguous houses in a single mass composition was excellent, but the shaft in the storey levels was awkward. Moreover, the regularity of the fenestration in the smaller Adams house, juxtaposed with the irregularity of the fenestration in the Hay house on the corner, divided the composition quite as much as if the two houses had been designed by different architects.

The Hay house is certainly very inferior to the other Washington house of brick, that for the Andersons, although the Anderson house is similarly designed in perspective view from the corner. An early study indicates that the two new houses were at one time intended to be built of rock-faced yellow sandstone with brownstone trim. (Fig. 101). Possibly, with the richer texture of the stone, the surfaces would not have appeared so bare, and the towers—which appear so arbitrary and out of scale in the brick—might, like the towers on the Quincy Library and Austin, have seemed enrichments of the main mass rather than excrescences on it.

But it is still smaller faults which ultimately established the inferiority of the design. The use of plate glass throughout makes of the windows mere holes in the wall surface. Small panes would have been in better scale with the brick and given interest to the surface texture. The failure to group the windows into banks or to make each window large enough to hold its own in the design is even more serious. (Fig.

---

[1] It is unfortunate that the tablet, erected by the Washington Chapter of the D.A.R. in the hotel on the site of the Hay-Adams houses, gives a date for these houses some years after Richardson's death.

+88). An early sketch elevation of the Hay house shows the use of brick and of small-paned windows of rather square proportions, regularly although asymmetrically placed. This is very much better than the executed design, in which the vertical windows are arranged without any consistent scheme other than a roughly symmetrical placing in an asymmetrical mass composition.

The Adams house, with its regular bands of windows, is better composed, although the treatment of the two lower floors almost suggests that it is two houses rather than one. It represents an advance over earlier city houses in the more ample fenestration and the avoidance of arbitrarily picturesque features. But even this facade was more dignified and in better scale in the earlier elevation intended for execution in stone.   XIV-7

The plans of these houses are not remarkable. The towers of the Hay house are not really useful as they are in the Paine house, but merely the arbitrary features they appear to be on the exterior. The redeeming achievement in these houses is the great hall in the Hay house. This is finer than the Paine hall in composition, and superior in luxury of tone and texture to the Albany Senate Chamber. (Fig. 103). In this Richardson's powers are shown to the full.[2]

Are the faults in these houses Richardson's, or are they due to the office force? The Syrian entrance arch of the Hay house seems merely to have been repeated from the Trinity Rectory; but most of the faults are of such an essential nature that they cannot be attributed only to unsupervised drafting. The early pencil sketch was right in spirit, the   XIV-8 others are profoundly wrong. Were the Glessner house not still to follow, it would appear that Richardson was again losing interest in house design.

[2] The interior woodwork of the Hay hall is in existence, as it was put in storage by Mrs. James W. Wadsworth, John Hay's daughter, when the house was demolished. A museum could hardly obtain a better memorial of Richardson's monumental interiors than by reinstalling this room. Certainly the portal and the fireplace from the Warder house, preserved in the National Museum, are not to be considered Richardson's work, and the detail saved from the Marshall Field Store is of no particular interest.

Of the relative failures of the year 1884, the Hay-Adams houses were not the last. The Gurney house in Pride's Crossing, commissioned in November, was practically finished before Richardson's death. It cannot, therefore, be considered as in any literal sense posthumous. It has been so modified since, with a spotted slate roof and a slated gable in the middle of the garden front, that it seems today hardly more than a crude parody of the Ames Gate Lodge. Early studies suggest a simpler and more graceful design, with cobblestones on the lower storey and shingles above, and a rather simple oblong mass which might have had something of the quality of the Paine house. (Fig. 104). But for all the magnificence of the boulder-walled terrace on the rocky site, there are such faults in the treatment of the roof, with the end gable awkwardly broken by a chimney, the bold crude eaves, and the bulbous dormers, that this can never have been a successful house.

Interior studies which exist for this house show detail almost Colonial Revival in character, with white painted woodwork. Except for the proportions, these drawings, which are rendered in water colour, are totally unlike anything of Richardson's. Like the trim in the Stoughton house, many wooden details in the Paine house, and the stair railings which are too delicate for the rest of the Hay hall, these studies suggest that Richardson supervised his ordinary interior domestic trim hardly at all in the eighties. Perhaps wisely, he reserved his strength for matters of really architectural scale, such as fireplaces and stairs.

The smallest building built by Richardson in 1884, the Ames Gardener's Cottage in North Easton, was commissioned in March. It is, perhaps, the only thing that can be compared in quality with the Pittsburgh jail. It should have been a model for American suburban dwellings: so skilful was Richardson in giving interest to the mass by the rounded projection at one corner and the porch, and in retaining otherwise the most regular arrangement of plain windows in a plain shingle-covered wall. (Fig. 125) . Instead, of course, vernacular builders attempted to load on to cottages of this size all the decorative features of McKim, Mead and White mansions. A community of houses like the Ames Gardener's Cottage would still be superior to any isolated housing yet executed in America.

The year 1885 brought Richardson his last great opportunities. The Glessner house and the large New London station added two fine works to the canon, each the best of its type he had built. But in the Marshall Field Wholesale Store he was offered a commercial commission of sufficient size and importance for him to establish a new standard of design the very year after a new type of construction had been introduced in the field. This new standard of design was associated, as in all of Richardson's work, with traditional methods of construction. But in the next few years it helped Sullivan to find an architectural expression for the new skeleton type of construction.

XIV-9

The Marshall Field Store was commissioned in April, 1885, just a year before Richardson's death. This and the Pittsburgh courthouse were the two buildings Richardson esteemed the most important of his career. As regards the Field Store, he was certainly correct. The building was destroyed a few years ago to make room for an outdoor parking garage. It was really sacrificed to the urban congestion the skyscraper had created. It is futile to suggest that this building should have been preserved and all the blocks around torn down to display one of the greatest monuments of architecture in America. The first skyscrapers, the Home Insurance and the Tacoma, have been torn down as well. These three monuments, historically among the most interesting buildings in America, should have made Chicago a center of pilgrimage for all who are interested in architecture. The money and the effort that might have saved them was poured instead into the temporary structures of an ironical "Century of Progress" exposition. Pointless piety has preserved of the Marshall Field Wholesale Store only the carved capitals, things absolutely without value or interest in this period of Richardson's career.

XIV-10

The Field Store was a solid block of masonry supporting walls, with an interior court surrounded by masonry supporting walls, and the main interior partitions of masonry. The isolated interior piers and the floor beams were, however, of metal. (Fig. 98). In a building of only

XIV-11

seven storeys, it was not necessary to replace the solid exterior walls of masonry with the hybrid type of masonry and metal wall introduced by Jenney at the Home Insurance Building, which was just reaching completion. The Home Insurance Building is taller; but the semi-self-supporting masonry sheathing of its walls is little thinner than the masonry of the Field Store.[3] The advantages of developed skyscraper construction, with the external sheathing intentionally supported entirely on the metal skeleton, first appeared in the Tacoma Building by Holabird and Roche, two young men trained in Jenney's office. The Tacoma Building was not begun until after Richardson's death, and even that still had two rear walls of bearing masonry.

In a masonry building as low, relatively, as the Field Building, the fenestration could safely be made at least as ample as it was in the Home Insurance Building. It remains a question whether the general run of buildings ever should have been raised to greater heights, if American cities had been properly planned and the building laws sufficiently detailed and intelligent. But the question of the height of buildings did not lie with the architect; it lay with the client. The pressure came from the rise in land values. The architect could point out that to build with masonry much higher than seven storeys meant sacrificing light and space in the lower storeys; thus, perhaps, he lost the job. Or, if he were a technician, like Jenney and the younger men around him in Chicago, he could advise a new type of construction without the disadvantages of masonry.

Richardson was not reactionary technically in building the Field Building as he did: he was just short of the forefront of technical advance. Had he built a building of equally advanced construction even two or three years later, he would have used the early skeleton type introduced in the Tacoma Building. His successors, Shepley, Rutan and Coolidge, in building the Ames Building on Washington Street

[3] Apparently it might have been thinner than it was. For the skeleton almost entirely supported the masonry sheathing. But as Jenney was still feeling his way, he could not be sure of this. It was determined when the building was taken down.

in Boston, were the first to bring the new skyscraper construction to that city. This was in the same year, 1889, in which Bradford Lee Gilbert first used skeleton construction in New York for the Tower Building on Broadway. XIV-12

Richardson in his maturity was not interested in new materials but, rather, in preserving the integrity of traditional construction in the face of the cheap and shoddy makeshifts of his contemporaries.[4] It would have been altogether incredible had this building shown even the hybrid advance of Jenney's Home Insurance Building. In retrospect, we can see that the essential step in the invention of the skyscraper was taken by Jenney. But to contemporaries, the combination XIV-13 of metal and masonry in that building may justly have appeared a shoddy makeshift. For the part the metal played in supporting the exterior walls was only determined with accuracy when the building was taken down. The Home Insurance was not, therefore, a scientifically studied engineering solution: it was the product of the same homely ingenuity which placed hidden flying buttresses under the aisle roofs of the Abbaye-aux-Dames in Caën in the early twelfth century. Had Richardson been an engineer himself, he might have advanced directly in the Field Store to the developed principle of skeleton support used by Holabird and Roche in the Tacoma Building. But it was the part of prudence not to adopt the uncertain method of the Home Insurance Building which, as far as anyone really knew, might come tumbling down at any moment.

But if Richardson was not here creative technically, he was, perhaps, never more creative artistically. (Fig. 95). The idea of grouping several storeys under arches had been used first in the Equitable project of 1867. It had been developed, with lavish use of mediaeval detail and a complicated rhythm, in the Cheney Building, ten years before the Field Store. In the court of the Allegheny courthouse, the scheme

[4] The fires of the seventies had discouraged the use of iron and postponed, for a decade after the elevator made possible greater heights, the application of the principles already clear in Putnam and Tilden's Boston castiron building of 1873. In the meantime, methods of fireproofing metal construction were much improved.

was already beginning to be simplified and freed from archaeological reminiscence.

The sure dependence on sturdy masonry for a rich effect, and the simplification of the rhythm make the exterior of the Field Store very superior to the court of the Pittsburgh building. There is almost no detail. The only carving that can be seen from a distance is the crocketted cornice. That is Gothic and not Romanesque in inspiration, and yet is vigorously and crudely cut, to be in scale with the whole mass which it terminates. This ornament, which is so truly architectural, must be compared with the pilaster capitals on the Hampden County Courthouse fifteen years earlier.

The rhythm of the first four storeys is absolutely even except for the wide corner piers. These assure the solid massive appearance of the building in spite of the very large proportion of window space. These broad corners entail some sacrifice in the interior, but they give the building a unity of effect which is lacking in the Pittsburgh courthouse with its corner pavilions. The rhythm of the two upper floors is doubled and that of the attic quadrupled. By providing a low basement storey with segmental arches, and by subdividing the windows of the main floors with stone pilasters to support the intermediate stone floor spandrels, the weight of the design at each level of the composition is exactly proportioned. The plain corners and the heavy cornice frame the whole design and emphasize the solidity of the total block which needs no visible roof. Here Richardson finally escaped from the picturesque and achieved the highest type of formal design.

Beyond this there is very little to add. The square blocks of stone in the spandrels of the great arches are not varied in colour; the pilaster capitals are hardly carved at all. But the scale of the masonry is gradually reduced from the enormous boldly rock-faced slabs of red Missouri granite which form the basement, to the small square blocks in the spandrels. The red sandstone of the walls above the basement gradually decreases in roughness. Although not of light stone, like most of Richardson's latest work, this building need not have been gloomy if it had been sandblasted from time to time like the Pittsburgh courthouse. The unmoulded voussoirs are of adequate size but not exaggerated as on the Pittsburgh jail. The lintels are proportionately heavy. The windows are properly of plate glass, since they are recessed from the arcades. The walls thus form an open cage, not a continuous surface. There are many other subtleties of omission and commission which express the personal assurance of a great architect at the height of his powers. But there is almost nothing for imitators to borrow. The design is so elementary that any attempt to copy it was bound to be inferior.

Sullivan's first attempt, in the Auditorium Building begun two years later, magnificent though that is, is a case in point. In 1888, in the Walker Warehouse, however, he passed beyond imitation, drawing inspiration and not precedent from the Marshall Field Store. With this design he was well on the way to his first skyscraper style. A year later Jenney, in the second Leiter Building, also found inspiration in the Field Store. Without using any arches, in frank terms of masonry-sheathed skeleton construction, he came very close to repeating Richardson's triumph. But the sense of proportions of his designers was not fine enough. Had Richardson lived, he might have built, in the next few years, something like the second Leiter Building but altogether superior in the subtleties only a great architect appreciates. Such a work would have been superior even to Sullivan's Wainwright Building. XIV-14

The Glessner house in Chicago, commissioned in May, 1885, is, in its way, as fine as the Marshall Field Wholesale Store. It is, of course, XIV-15 by no means as significant historically. The plan is very ingeniously arranged in an L around a court, with many of the rooms opening on the court. (Fig. 106). Thus, the exterior is justifiably very solid, to shut out the surrounding city, with a few large windows only on the front. There is no polychromy on the exterior and almost no carved ornament. The whole effect, as in the Stoughton house, is in the simple solid mass of grey granite. (Fig. 105). The tower, indeed, like that of the Stoughton house, barely appears on the exterior at all. Richardson had never, even in the Pittsburgh jail, used granite so magnificently. On the court side, unfortunately, the bricks have turned almost black with grime, while the Joliet stone lintels have thrown off the grime and remained too white.

XIV-16 The interiors are very poor; only the dining room fireplace still has something of the amplitude of Richardson's best work. But the interiors must be largely posthumous. Like most of the new work started in 1885, the house was not finished until some time after Richardson's death.

The New London station, commissioned in September, 1885, was hardly even begun before Richardson's death. (Fig. 114). But the design is so different from that of the earlier stations and so excellent, that it must have been closely supervised. It is, in many respects, an improved version of Sever Hall. As befits a more utilitarian building, it is, however, somewhat dryer and more bare than Sever. But the treatment of the brick patterns in the gable is as good as on Emmanuel Church, and the shape and scale of the entrance arch are distinctly superior to that of Sever. The slight projection of the second storey all around the station is, on the other hand, rather pointless. The fenestration is ample and well organized. The colour effect of the exterior has of late been much improved by sandblasting.

The Warder house was commissioned in March, earlier than the Marshall Field Store and the Glessner house. But it is a far less personal work. The commission is definitely known to have been largely in the hands of Shepley and Coolidge. One may well wonder if the substitution of smooth-faced cream-coloured sandstone for the more characteristic rock-faced brownstone or granite was not entirely due to the influence of the younger men. This, and the deeply recessed plate glass windows give the design a rather bald look. This bald look is generally associated with the reaction against the rich colours and varied textures of the seventies, at just this time making its appearance in the influential new work of McKim, Mead and White.

The proportions, and even certain individual features, like the very pointed tower and the loggias on the rear wall of the court, derive more directly from sixteenth century French work than anything Richardson had ever done. (Fig. 109). At the same time, the detail is very flat and delicately Byzantine, both inside the house and out. The portal, now rather stupidly preserved in the National Museum, was detailed by John Galen Howard.

The plan is well arranged, with a small court in front and a sunken carriage drive passing through to the rear under the side wing. The main rooms opened into one another in a fashion once novel in Richardson's work but now commonplace. The very elaborate interior trim was almost certainly designed without Richardson's supervision, if not after his death. There is a curious contrast between the heavy scale of the masonry arches and the extreme delicacy of the carved ornament in the woodwork. A comparison with interiors only slightly anterior, such as the Hay hall or the Paine parlor, makes evident the great difference between Richardson's noble vision of interior architecture and the elaborate interior decoration now provided by his assistants and successors. The parlor mantel of white holly is nevertheless preserved in the National Museum as an example of Richardson's work.

Even if this house must be largely credited to the new firm of Shepley, Rutan and Coolidge, who completed it, it is worthy of a late place in Richardson's canon. For it is far better than the clumsy Hay house as a mass composition of a new and more delicate type.[5]

A little fountain in the very center of Detroit was commissioned by the J. J. Bagley Estate in April, 1885. It is simple and solid in effect, with rather vigorous detail for this late date, but it lacks the monumental simplicity of the Ames pyramid in Sherman, Wyoming. (Fig. 135).

The MacVeagh house in Chicago, commissioned in July, 1885, and the J. R. Lionberger house, commissioned in November, are certainly more largely posthumous works than the Warder house. Since they were both of rock-faced granite, they are, of course, superficially more

XIV-17

[5] The Warder has been moved but not destroyed. On its new site at 2633 16th Street, the present owner, Major Patten, has made it into an apartment house. The interiors have for the most part been dispersed. But, except for the portal, the facade is intact.

"Richardsonian." The court facade of the MacVeagh house is very like that of the Warder house. The Lake Shore Drive facade, with the corner towers tied into the main mass by the loggias between and the roof above, is more original. (Fig. 108). But the balancing of one round tower with another which is octagonal is more arbitrary than on the Paine garden facade, and the proportions of the whole are indeterminate, neither clearly horizontal nor clearly vertical. The rock-faced granite walls are much less rich in effect than those of the Glessner house. The frequent plate glass windows are even more blank-looking than in the smooth masonry of the Warder house. There is a further confusion of effect here, due to the juxtaposition on the same facade of matter-of-fact domestic windows and monumental arched openings. The sparse detail of flat Byzantine character is probably to be attributed to John Galen Howard.

Comparing this house with the Glessner house, also built in Chicago and, nominally, by the same architect in the same year, one realizes clearly the unreality of the conception of architectural responsibility in America. If the Glessner house is Richardson's, this is not— at least, not in the same sense. Nor has the MacVeagh house virtues of its own, such as can be granted the Warder house. It is, of course, still superior to the Richardsonian work which was being done in Chicago at this time even by such architects as Adler and Sullivan and Burnham and Root, but that is saying very little.

As to the J. R. Lionberger house in St. Louis, it is a small parody of the MacVeagh house, false in scale and more like a tomb than a residence. (Fig. 133) . In those busy last few months of his life, perhaps Richardson never saw the plans at all. At any rate, he never went to St. Louis.

The I. H. Lionberger house, designed in the early spring of 1886, was not considered by Mrs. Van Rensselaer a work of Richardson's. It is, however, superior in plan and composition to the J. R. Lionberger house. (Fig. 142) . The treatment of the brickwork, with the projecting upper storey, is very similar to that of the New London railroad station. It is, probably, almost entirely the work of Coolidge and Shepley, but certainly in a very good late Richardsonian spirit.

Curiously similar to these two houses is the Cincinnati Chamber of Commerce building, for which Richardson had won the competition in August of 1885.[6] The construction of this building was not begun until after Richardson's death, but the final designs, which were a slight improvement over the competition designs, had all passed through the office during his lifetime. Even so, one can hardly believe that this project ever received the personal attention given to the Pittsburgh buildings or the Field Store. The treatment of the mass has the indeterminate quality of the MacVeagh house. The towers are too tall and narrow to be merely great bulges on the corners, and yet they are not incidental enough to be mere decorative turrets. (Fig. 113). The high roof covers the trusses supporting the office floors above the great hall. Thus it has a practical purpose. But it is so broken up by dormers, like those on the Kingston and Bedford Street Ames Store, that it fails to hold the whole composition together.

The division into storeys is far less happy than in the Pittsburgh courthouse or the Field Store. The solid masonry of the towers is so regularly coursed as to have none of the Titanic quality of the Pittsburgh jail or the courthouse tower shaft. If this is essentially of Richardson's own design, it would have to be acknowledged that his powers were now declining. It is inferior even to the North Easton Town Hall, whose vices at least have piquancy. The elephantine "Richardsonianism" is below the level of the effect attained by his best imitators. Richardson was being worked to death, and his work was dying even before he did. In this sense, the Cincinnati Chamber of Commerce can be called posthumous. Its destruction by fire was no great loss.

The remaining works prepared in Richardson's office before his death are more literally posthumous. He was very seriously ill in the

[6] According to the jealous legend of the local architects, Richardson won because he entertained the committee so well. If there was what then seemed improper influence, we may feel sure it was more the quality of the conversation than the quality of the champagne which led to Richardson's selection.

fall of 1885, and forbidden to travel. At the same time, he continued working and entertaining quite as he had always done. Most of the commissions later than the Glessner house were undertaken at a time when he was in no condition to give of his best. His visits of supervision to the buildings in construction had to cease. His office force, in putting through drawings he had no chance to revise, was saving him efforts that he could not make. To a large extent, they thus saved him at the expense of his reputation. To rescue that reputation it is necessary to explain in some detail the conditions in the office in the spring of 1886. Fortunately, the only detailed records of the office are of just that period.

About twenty men were employed in the office at this time. Including projects which never came to execution and the large Springfield railroad station, which was not actually commissioned until after Richardson's death, there were about twenty-five pieces of work in various stages of completion in the office during the early months of 1886. Richardson's final illness really began in March. He was then sent to New York and to Washington for change and rest. Very soon he came home and went to bed, never to rise again.[7] The buildings he talked about in these last weeks were, as has already been said, the Pittsburgh courthouse and the Field Store. He was intensely interested in the work of the score of men in his office downstairs, but, of course, he could not control it in detail. Those buildings which he had studied during the previous years and whose designs were well advanced before his illness of the autumn of 1885 all have at least a claim to be considered his. But those that were newly studied later than that, even if he, himself, occasionally studied them in part, were not really his— they were, rather, the first works of his successors, Shepley, Rutan and Coolidge.

The Armory Building for the Bagley Estate was commissioned in December, 1885. It is possible, therefore, that the early study, somewhat in the spirit of the Dairy Building of 1881, was, at least, passed

[7] He died of Bright's disease on April 27th.

by Richardson. In simple designs of this sort the office force was able to continue Richardson's best manner better than in more monumental work, which required both creative imagination and restraint. (Fig. 136).

The wholesale store on Harrison Avenue in Boston, to be built for F. L. Ames and to be occupied by J. H. Pray and Sons, was commissioned in January, 1886. It ranks as one of Richardson's finest works, although he probably did little more than indicate a general type of solution. This was a less conspicuous monument than the Marshall Field Store and the embellishment was undoubtedly restrained by economic considerations. (Fig. 112). The corbelled cornice used here had been considered and, fortunately, rejected for the Field Store. It is more suitable on this design, although it restricts the light admitted to the top floor. But the simplification of the arcade scheme is probably due to the use of brick instead of stone. This is foreshadowed in the competition design for the court of the Pittsburgh courthouse. In many ways it is an advance over the solider treatment of the great monument in Chicago. As Lewis Mumford pointed out in the *Brown Decades*, Richardson, or his office force, seemed to have seen ahead to the possibilities of design which Sullivan was soon to work out with metal skeleton construction. Although the construction is still of masonry, the effect is less heavy than that of Sullivan's Wainwright Building. For the bays are very wide, the lintels very light, and the piers as thin as possible. Even the window reveals are reduced.[8]

It is unlikely that such an ultimate development of the masonry building formula was due solely to the office force. The buildings of the next years, designed by Shepley, Rutan and Coolidge, are never as simple and rarely as light. This must be considered Richardson's

[8] The avoidance of subsidiary arches recalls the treatment of English ware- XIV-18 houses in the sixties. It is more appropriate in a vertical composition than it would have been for a horizontal oblong block. In this connection, it is interesting to compare the Walker Warehouse of 1888 by Sullivan, in which the verticals conflict somewhat with the horizontal base and the general proportions, with his Schiller Building, which is definitely a tower.

last great work. It is, at least, the last work from the office in which his own genius shines.

The commission for the Herkomer house, also of January, 1886, is known to have been the result of a bargain between Herkomer and Richardson. Herkomer was to paint Richardson's portrait, and Richardson was to provide drawings for remodeling and enlarging Herkomer's house at Bushy, England. Herkomer found in Richardson's work a type of Romantic mediaevalism which appealed to him more than that of the English architects a generation earlier—more, even, than that of such as Theodor Fischer, a generation later. The house is all picturesque silhouette, and the archaeological detail in the early elevations is obviously the work of draftsmen throughout. It was not completed for many years, and, of course, the construction was not supervised, even by Shepley, Rutan and Coolidge. The executed detail was largely redesigned by Herkomer. Thus the result is hybrid and barely to be considered Richardson's at all. (Fig. 107).

XIV-19

The house commissioned by Dr. J. H. Bigelow in Newton, also in January, has distinctly Richardsonian qualities of the best sort. The long low massing and the plain shingled wall surfaces, although painted red, are in the best tradition of the wooden houses of the opening years of the decade. (Fig. 140). But if the general effect is Richardsonian, the more conspicuous details are not. The roof of the front block of the house is much sharper than Richardson himself ever used on his shingle houses, and the little front turret is a ridiculous imitation in wood of a feature of French château architecture. This Richardson would never have executed in his best years, although it is not unlike the turrets on the Cheney addition project and the Oliver Ames house.

The Potter house in St. Louis Mrs. Van Rensselaer did not consider Richardson's. The office records, however, prove that it was being studied throughout the early months of 1886. It is less novel than the Bigelow house, and follows more closely the lines of the Stoughton house. (Fig. 111). Like so much of this late work, it is rather bare and not compactly planned. The details, such as the porch supports, are, however, authentic in treatment, and the general effect is not unworthy of Richardson's name. It is certainly simpler and less awkward in composition than even the best shingle houses of the next few years by Shepley, Rutan and Coolidge.

The Gratwick house in Buffalo, on the other hand, has most of the faults of the succeeding masonry buildings of Shepley, Rutan and Coolidge. It was commissioned in February. The rock-faced granite walls were rather dry and devoid of detail, although of monumental scale. The parts, although excellent in themselves, are not well composed. It is more of a fortress and less of a house than Richardson's good earlier houses in masonry. There is also a certain conflict between the general massiveness and the ample fenestration. Its destruction is no great loss. (Fig. 110).

The Nickerson house in Dedham has often been considered Richardson's and was doubtless discussed by Richardson with Mr. Nickerson before his death. But the commission came to Shepley, Rutan and Coolidge. The building must be considered one of the earliest and best of their works. The amplitude and balance of the design is an improvement over the Gratwick house. The fortress-like character is also more appropriate to a country site than to the main residence street of Buffalo. The smeary tonality of the seam-faced granite would hardly have appealed to Richardson; yet it suits the rather barren treatment of the facades better than the rock-faced granite used on the Gratwick house.

It is difficult to say whether the project for the Hoyt Library in East Saginaw, Michigan, should be considered a late work of Richardson's or an early work of Shepley, Rutan and Coolidge. Had it been built, the commission would not have entered the office until after Richardson's death. But the competition drawings were prepared during the early months of 1886, and were, probably, at least seen by Richardson. In the series of library designs, this project is superior to that for the University of Vermont, but to none of the others. For it is cold, and less Richardsonian than the New London Library, designed several years later by Shepley, Rutan and Coolidge, or even than the library by Van Brunt and Howe, which was actually built in East Saginaw.

The Agassiz lighthouse project exists in a sketch which is very probably holograph. This, like the ice-house project mentioned and illustrated by Mrs. Van Rensselaer, and several other sketches, is of uncertain date and hardly sufficiently developed for one to judge of its quality. If such things had been built, they might belong with Richardson's great successes in the field of utilitarian design. As it was, the conceptions were destined to die with him.

Richardson's career had really come to an end rather before his life. As has been pointed out in the preceding chapters, an increasing proportion of his production as the decade advanced must be considered less than his. If his life and career had gone on, he would have continued as the nominal head of a plan factory, producing occasionally fine personal works. Only a few architects in America, all cranks, have known how to protect their artistic integrity. Richardson at the beginning of his career had justifiably accepted the prerogatives of his great individuality as an artist. He had broken the bonds of convention, set up his own style and looked neither to the left nor to the right. But, with recognition, his exuberant nature saw only an opportunity for more and more great work. He was unwilling to accept the necessary limitation of individuality, and to refuse all commissions above the number to which he could give the fullest creative attention.

It is not the fault of his staff that they were not of his calibre. Why should they have been? Very few architects ever are. They were not at all creative in the way he was: what they felt within themselves as a personal direction was only the ripple of a rising national fashion. As they were to some extent isolated in his office from the currents of the day, they had to work with his manner whether they liked it or not. But his manner was not a national nor even exactly a contemporary style. If they did not understand it, there was nowhere they could really learn about it. They looked vainly in books for what they thought was his way of doing things. He, himself, did not understand his style in the sense in which it is implicitly explained throughout this study. He was an artist and not a critic. What he did he *knew* was right. Sometimes he could have supported this assurance rationally, sometimes not.

286

But for himself he never needed articulate support. If he erred in one direction in a certain work, he soon righted the balance by a move in another when he designed the next. His work grew continuously from the Unity Church to the Field Store. What was right for him to do was always what he had not already done. With the best will in the world, what was right for his assistants had to be either what he had done or what others were doing.

On Richardson's death, Charles Rutan, who had been the engineer XIV-20 of the office for many years, John Shepley, who was the head of the drafting force, and Charles A. Coolidge, one of the most active younger men in the office, formed the firm of Shepley, Rutan and Coolidge to complete the work in hand. Wisely and fairly they did not continue to use Richardson's name. Thus although much of Richardson's prestige descended to them, they did not try to obtain commissions under false pretences. Rutan was not a designer and neither Shepley nor Coolidge was a personal disciple of Richardson in the sense that McKim and White had been. By the time they entered the office in the early eighties, the atmosphere there was no longer the same as in the seventies. Everyone in the office still had the advantage of seeing Richardson do his own preliminary designing. Everyone had the opportunity of working out Richardson's original studies under his supervision. But the office was to some extent subdivided into practical men like Rutan, designers like Shepley, supervisors of construction, and ordinary draftsmen.

But although Richardson's office had already become something like a modern American architectural office, of the type particularly developed by Burnham in the nineties, as long as Richardson lived an older tradition of communal work under the master's leadership continued. Much work came out that was only rubber-stamped with Richardson's approval, but the important commissions he still made his own as long as he lived. When he died the office lost more than an executive: it lost all possibility of personal and even of consistent creation. The executive became a general staff; and the commissions, which still came in almost as great numbers as in the last few years of

Richardson's life, were handled by committees. Some were more the work of Shepley; some more the work of Coolidge; some largely the product of other designers and draftsmen. But with Richardson gone, there was no one individual to maintain the old standard, nor anyone apparently with a sufficiently strong artistic personality to set a new one. The leadership of American architecture passed away from the firm.

For all of being Richardson's heirs, Shepley, Rutan and Coolidge hardly stand out among the innumerable architectural firms who imitated Richardson's style in the late eighties and early nineties with more or less success. Moreover, like all Eastern architects of prominence, they soon deserted even the Richardsonian formulas to follow the lead of McKim, Mead and White in the nineties. This they were neither the first nor the last to do. After Richardson's death their work became essentially anonymous and increasingly academic. Where it was imitative of Richardson's earlier work, it was sometimes of higher quality than the inferior workshop productions which issued from the office in the years just before his death. Much of their early work, such as the New London Library, has rather justly been accepted as Richardson's own. In some cases, such as the Lionberger Warehouse in St. Louis, a small-scale Marshall Field Store, or the Springfield railroad station, the assumption is further justified by really Richardsonian quality as well as passable application of the familiar formulas.

On the whole, however, the best work of Shepley, Rutan and Coolidge in the late eighties developed those tendencies in the work of the last years of Richardson's life for which Shepley or Coolidge must have been in part responsible in the first place. More symmetrical composition, less heavy mass, and avoidance of profuse Romanesque detail characterize these more personal productions. The Nickerson house is perhaps the best example. Some of their wooden houses are also excellent, although obviously not by Richardson himself.

The commercial buildings by Shepley, Rutan and Coolidge, for which there was so much demand in these years, grew more and more mechanical in design. Although the detail even down into the nineties is usually Romanesque, the cornices are heavy and projecting in the Renaissance manner. The attempt to adjust a masonry style to skeleton construction is far less skilful than in such Chicago work as Jenney's second Leiter Building. In really tall buildings, Shepley, Rutan and Coolidge succumbed to the temptations of mere facade design quite as much as their riavls in New York, who worked from the late eighties in a Renaissance idiom. Thus, although Shepley, Rutan and Coolidge were Richardson's successors, they were in no creative sense his artistic heirs.[9]

[9] A list of men working in the office at the time of Richardson's death is provided by the office time book. Most of these men must have continued, at least for a time, as the staff of Shepley, Rutan and Coolidge: G. L. Billings, G. F. Bosworth, H. C. Burdett, John Burrows, J. E. R. Carpenter, C. F. Crosby, A. H. Everett, A. H. Granger, J. G. Howard, F. H. Kendall, H. G. King, T. H. Randall, L. B. Riley, F. A. Russell, R. G. Schmidt, F. M. Wakefield.

CHAPTER FIFTEEN

1886-1936

RICHARDSON died at a crucial moment in the history of American architecture. Of most great artists it may be said that their life had a measurable effect on the general current. In Richardson's case it may also be said that his illness and death, by diminishing the force of his influence when it should have been most formative, all but cancelled the positive effect on American architecture of his entire previous activity. Except through Sullivan, Richardson's connection with the future was severed since the future was in birth in the very years when his career was ending. His immediate influence was otherwise almost meaningless.[1]

XV-1

Before any estimate of Richardson's real importance can be made, the general architectural situation in the mid-eighties must be reassessed. For it was more complicated and more subtle in its contrasts than is ordinarily realized. No simple dichotomy of "form versus function" explains American architecture in this period or, even, in the nineties.

The eighties saw the rise of a practical technique of using metal in architecture. Without further important innovations in principle, this technique was capable of producing buildings of even greater height than have yet been built. Within a generation the entire urban scene

XV-2

[1] A detailed study of the general "Richardsonian" school might lead to revision of this drastic dismissal. But, on the whole, it is obvious that the school was responsible for no fruitful development before its death in the early nineties except in the shingled domestic vernacular.

had been changed. Cities were no longer conglomerations of two- and three-storey houses, like London, out of which rose churches, and public buildings individualized by their massiveness and the complexity of their design.[2] To their inhabitants and to outside visitors, the new tall buildings of skeleton construction were naturally more conspicuous than any other sort of monuments. Every few years in New York and Chicago attention was focussed on a new skyscraper, not because it was the finest, but because it was the tallest. Such a dramatization of the quantitative in architecture naturally overshadowed any critical counter-current of judgement by qualitative criteria. But American skyscrapers, as time has proved, were not sociologically functional; and the "forms" recognized by contemporary criticism were rarely anything but garments borrowed from the past with little relation to any comprehension of abstract form. XV-3 XV-4

Richardson's career ran parallel with early experiments in the use of metal. His death coincided with its triumph. How little the use of metal impinged upon his architecture has been indicated in detail in earlier chapters. But the reasons may well be summarized. The early heyday of the use of castiron in America was in the sixties. Then the dome of the Washington Capitol rose, a conspicuous symbol of the absolute power of the Congress, borrowed from the age of Baroque absolutism. Beneath its white paint the dome was all of iron, as if to make more complete the symbolism of the form by a specific suggestion of the powers of which Congress was but the governing agent. XV-5

The same not altogether unconscious symbolism appears elsewhere. Broadway in New York, from the City Hall to Union Square, is still almost solidly lined with the commercial castiron facades of six or seven storeys which were, in all the Eastern and Northern cities, the most conspicuous expression of capitalist arrogance. But, by the early seventies, although the elevator had at last been introduced in a commercial XV-6

[2] The average height of the buildings in New York is, however, even today less than the average height of those in Paris. The areas still covered by low masonry buildings are very large compared to the more conspicuous districts filled with tall buildings of metal skeleton construction.

building making greater height practical, great fires in several cities were wiping out the castiron buildings in the congested downtown districts. Doubtless the width of Broadway protected the castiron facades there, for when one building burned the collapse of its neighbors was due to the heat and not to actual burning.

Thus, in the period when Richardson was forming and imposing his style, iron was distrusted for sound practical reasons. It was doubtless distrusted after 1873 for symbolic reasons as well. As we know well enough, during a depression the conspicuous forms of production of the preceding boom are assumed to be in part the cause of the decline. Thus, through the seventies, advances in the use of iron were made, not so much by architects as by technicians, who developed new methods of fireproofing and hybrid methods of construction with an alternation of masonry and metal supports.

In the seventies and early eighties, some of the other essential steps leading to the skyscraper were taken literally underground in experiments with foundations capable of supporting taller and heavier buildings on the soft Chicago soil. It is not surprising that Richardson, who was interested in the visual expression of construction rather than its engineering, and whose urban structures were rarely very large before the mid-eighties, should have taken no active interest in the technical experimentation that was going on. He continued to use iron in an inconspicuous way where it seemed absolutely necessary, but no more than was conventional in Paris in the sixties.[3]

His success with the Marshall Field Wholesale Store would undoubtedly, had he lived, have brought him more commissions for large commercial buildings. In these he would have had to come to some sort of terms with the new skyscraper construction. But he died too soon, and his career finished, as it began, within the period of reaction back to solid masonry construction after the early heyday of castiron in the sixties.

[3] It is of interest that when the Cincinnati Chamber of Commerce burned the catastrophe was the worse because of the failure of the iron suspension members by which the upper floors hung from the roof trusses over the great hall.

Thus, the only prominent model he offered for the skyscraper was almost the most massive and powerful expression of masonry construction which even he had ever built. It is not surprising that few beside Sullivan were able to apply its fundamental architectural lessons to metal skeleton construction. Indeed, even in Sullivan's case, the immediate effect of the Field Store was a reactionary one. The Auditorium Building—in which the influence is most marked—is distinctly less adventurous in construction and expression than his earlier commercial buildings of hybrid construction. His temporary Festival Opera House was likewise superior to the Auditorium itself in boldness of design. But the early work of Sullivan, although amazingly light and open, was of an almost incredible corruption of form, inspired by the bold vagaries of his master, Frank Furness. From Richardson Sullivan only XV-7 needed to learn how to handle scale and how to subordinate decoration to more important considerations of rhythm and proportion and coherence. Something of the massive monumentality of the masonry Field Store was carried over into the first of his great skyscrapers: the Wainwright Building in Saint Louis and the Schiller Building in Chicago, both of the early nineties. Such monumentality was not inappropriate for buildings which were, for a time at least, to dominate the architectural scene by their conspicuous isolation. The associated vertical treatment was equally justified by the way these buildings soared above their surroundings. But, when urban building rose to comparable heights throughout whole districts of the city, the conglomeration of apparently massive towers produced the chaotic and terrifying architectural scene so familiar today in the downtown heart of New York and Chicago. It is thus evident, as Hugh Morrison makes clear in his study of Sullivan,[4] that the doctrine "form follows function" was interpreted liberally by Sullivan. In his early skyscrapers he really achieved an abstract symbolic form far more than any direct expression of function.

Sullivan, of course, realized the limitations of his first vertical

[4] Which I was permitted to examine in manuscript before its publication by W. W. Norton, New York, 1935.

"form." By the end of the nineties his characteristic buildings of skeleton construction, the Gage Building and the Schlesinger-Mayer Building in Chicago, were of appropriate "form" to take their place among buildings of equal or greater height and were quite different from his early skyscrapers. They were horizontal in design, with wide windows and light terra cotta facing which was obviously not self-supporting. All trace of masonry monumentality had disappeared. Thus, by the time Sullivan reached his most mature work, the overt influence of Richardson had been dissolved. It has been suggested earlier that if Richardson had lived to build an early skyscraper it would have been more like Jenney's second Leiter Building. Except for somewhat ambiguous testimony of the Harrison Avenue Ames Building (which may be office work) there is little reason to believe that Richardson would have so far deserted his characteristic balance of proportions as to parallel the verticalism of Sullivan's first skyscraper style of the early nineties.

The most exciting development of the mid-eighties, and the one destined to change most drastically the direction of American architecture, was the technical one which produced the skyscraper. But there was an aesthetic change of almost equal significance which was more ubiquitous in its effects and which all but stifled the appropriate expression of steel skeleton construction except in Sullivan's work. This was the academic reaction of which the leaders were McKim, Mead and White. This academic reaction, like those of the sixteenth and the eighteenth centuries, had two sides. On the one hand, it represented a conscious desire for order and simplicity, which may be considered "Form"—with a majuscule. On the other, it sought order, if not simplicity, in a revival of traditional disciplines: in other words, the "forms" of the past.

Richardson's reaction against the chaos of the sixties began with the Brattle Square Church. Throughout his career he struggled perpetually within himself to control the undisciplined picturesqueness in which contemporary English and American architects were indulging. His key works of monumental architecture are progressively more restrained, both as regards order and simplicity, yet with little loss of imaginative power. The Field Store exceeds, indeed, the severity and regularity of most academic architecture of the past. On the other hand, it is also more emotional. Richardson by his training, and also by his temperament as he matured, was on the side of order. But the influence of his works on others was almost entirely on the side of disorder. In the eighties, and even into the nineties, his vernacular imitators continued to copy his most picturesque and confused works, like the North Easton Town Hall and the Newton Baptist Church. XV-9 Such a "Romanesque Revival" as there was turned more picturesque in the late eighties than it had been at its beginning in the seventies. A comparison of Earle's Springfield Cathedral, or Potter's project for the Brown University Library, with almost any example of the Richardsonian vernacular in the early nineties makes this only too evident.

What was true for the general Richardsonian school even into the nineties was equally true of his abler and more personal followers, McKim and White—at least in the seventies and the early eighties. Their picturesqueness, however, derived far more from the English Queen Anne of the sixties and early seventies than from Richard- XV-10 son. One or two rare early instances of a tendency toward order in McKim's work of the mid-seventies were mentioned in Chapter IX, but it is obvious that he did not then achieve a personal discipline at all comparable to Richardson's. In White's early work the only traces of restraint derive directly from Richardson.[5]

But the Queen Anne, like so many foreign movements, was leaving its American votaries behind. By the late seventies it had in England become increasingly what Americans would call a "Georgian Revival." At its best, however, it was still of a rather free and unarchaeological character, more comparable to Richardson's Romanesque. At what point McKim and White awoke to this, it is hard to say. For the change XV-11 in their work which took place in the mid-eighties, paralleling Norman

[5] It is significant that the large *Monograph of the Work of McKim, Mead and White,* New York, 1915, included few of the buildings mentioned in this book; nor does Charles Moore attempt to describe or even to list McKim's work of the early and mid-seventies: *op. cit. ante.*

Shaw's evolution into the "Monumental Queen Anne", was predominantly derived from other sources. Babb and Wells were most responsible.

George Fletcher Babb, who had been in charge of Russell Sturgis' office when McKim was there, was a man justly admired by the young New York architects around 1880. Having imbibed something of the German Romantic tradition which continued in Sturgis' work, he was a vigorous, if not whole-hearted, critic of excessive picturesque confusion. His masterpiece, built in 1885 with his partners Cook and Willard, is the De Vinne Press Building in Lafayette Street. It is more delicate than Richardson's commercial work and slightly more elaborate in composition. But it is in no way archaeological. Like Burnham and Root's magnificent First Regiment Armory in Chicago, it seems to have been inspired by the rationalistic designs of Durand under the First Empire. The houses of the next few years by Babb, Cook and Willard, although they sometimes have some eighteenth century detail, are XV-12 among the best in that conventional version of Richardson's shingled manner which proved his most acceptable legacy. Whatever may have been Babb's advice, it is evident that his example was not so very different from Richardson's.

The particular agent of McKim, Mead and White's drastic reform, XV-13 after the picturesque orgy of their early years, was Joseph M. Wells, a draftsman who had joined McKim and Mead a few months before White. In the spring of 1882 Henry Villard commissioned the group of houses on the east side of Madison Avenue between Fiftieth and Fifty-first Streets in New York. From Villard, himself, came the suggestion that they should be grouped around an open court. The plans were probably due to McKim and Mead; the designing of the exterior was at first in the hands of Stanford White, whose New York reputation had just been made by his picturesque design for the Tiffany XV-14 apartments on Seventy-second Street. White intended to use on the Villard houses, as on the Tiffany basement, Richardsonian rock-faced stone. Then White went on a trip to New Mexico lasting several months. The designing which had been in his hands was divided up

296

among the other draftsmen, Wells receiving the Villard commission. This he accepted only on condition that he might use smooth-faced stone and draw his inspiration from the Cancelleria Palace. He also desired to use light limestone rather than brownstone. But Villard insisted, very wisely as time has proved, that the soberer and then more conventional material should be retained. The Villard houses were executed between 1883 and 1885 with rich interior decoration by White in an increasingly Renaissance vein. They were at once accepted as establishing a fashion newer than Hunt's or Richardson's houses. Commissions began to come to the firm with the expectation that the designs would be consistently in some more or less similar Renaissance style.

This story is worth telling here in detail, as it makes plain the accidental way in which the firm of McKim, Mead and White came to produce the first building characteristic of the mature manner on which their fame is based. It is perhaps significant that the death of Wells in 1890 coincided with a distinct decline in the level of the work of the firm. It cannot have been entirely a joke when he refused, the previous year, to have his name added to that of the firm because he would not "sign his name to so much damned bad work." [6]

In the years immediately following the completion of the Villard houses, in other words, at exactly the time of Richardson's death, McKim, Mead and White developed a variety of academic types of design. These ranged from the symmetrical, and often ornate, late XV-15 eighteenth century Colonial of the H. A. C. Taylor house in Newport to the monumental severity of the Albertian Boston Public Library. In these same years of increasing restraint and discipline, they also came closest to Richardson's best late work in such things as the Narragansett Pier Casino, St. Peter's Church in Baltimore, and, even, in certain simple shingle houses like the William G. Low house in Bristol, Rhode Island. In these they stripped off their exotic Queen Anne detail,

[6] V. Baldwin, Charles C.: *Stanford White*. New York, 1931, p. 357 *et seq.;* and Moore, Charles: *The Life and Times of Charles Follen McKim*, Boston, 1929, pp. 47, 48. It is, perhaps, unjust to point out further that almost all the members of the office force of McKim, Mead and White who later made names for themselves in architecture were there before 1890.

and simplified the masses in a quite distinguished and original way. Yet, under Wells' leadership, they were also seeking in Letarouilly and other more modern documents of Renaissance architecture a wholly different type of composition and a more meretricious sort of ornament. The search for "Form" and for "forms" was thus most ambiguously coincident and the biographers of McKim and White have made little attempt to distinguish between them.

The Boston Public Library, which gave the younger firm as much publicity as Trinity had given Richardson, has already been mentioned in an earlier chapter. This monument gave McKim, Mead and White the same leadership in the profession and established in the same way a new fashion of design. Yet, paradoxically, the Boston Public Library, designed in 1887 and largely built in the next five years, is, with little question, the best and in all fundamentals the most Richardsonian of

XV-16 their works. The simplicity of the composition, based, like that of the Brattle Square Church, on French work of the mid-century;[7] the powerful expression of arcuated masonry design; the restraint in the use of borrowed detail; the bold use of inscriptions and isolated sculpture for decorative interest: all are quite worthy of Richardson's own achievement. The substitution of Renaissance for Romanesque forms and the use of smooth-cut, instead of rock-faced granite, hardly diminish the essential similarity. Sullivan also substituted smooth-faced masonry on the Walker Warehouse at this time and began to use detail considerably suaver than Richardson's. Richardson, or his office force, had used light smooth stone on the Warder house. Moreover, the Byzantine detail and French Renaissance forms so prominent on this house are, actually, less Richardsonian in feeling than the way the Italian precedent is modified to suit the granite of the Boston Public Library.

In considering what Richardson's work might have been like had he lived longer, the Boston Public Library is as suggestive as Jenney's

XV-17   [7] The relation to Henri Labrouste's Bibliothèque-Sainte-Geneviève is disputed. McKim claimed to have been inspired by the Colosseum. The resemblance to Alberti's work at Rimini is closest.

second Leiter Building. Richardson would never have accepted the rule of Letarouilly, which he had thrown off once and for all after he designed the Western Railway offices twenty years before his death. But he could just as appropriately have used the sparse Renaissance detail of the Library, so well adjusted in scale to the heavy masonry, as the dry Norman forms of the Pittsburgh courthouse or the slick Byzantine arabesques John Galen Howard detailed on his last masonry houses.

Had Richardson lived to build things compárable to the second Leiter Building and the Boston Public Library, the effect of the 1893 World's Fair in Chicago need not have been so catastrophic. With Richardson's accrued prestige, Burnham would undoubtedly have sought direction from him and not from the pompous Hunt and the brash McKim. The rising tide of order in design would not necessarily have led then into increasingly sterile imitation of Classical and Renaissance forms; and the East as well as Chicago might have had skyscrapers in the nineties which were not ludicrous in their archaeological garments.[8]

The significance of Richardson can now be made clearer. He was not the first modern architect: he was the last great traditional architect; a reformer and not an initiator. Dying when he did, his architecture remained entirely within the historic past of traditional masonry architecture, cut off almost entirely from the new cycle which extends from the mid-eighties into the twenties of the present century. His inspiration helped Sullivan for a time. Yet Sullivan might have found his way from his bold hybrid commercial architecture of the early eighties to the Schlesinger-Mayer building even without knowing the Field Store. In the end, McKim and White had learned from Richardson almost nothing. White himself, by his skilful pastiche of the Salamanca lantern which Richardson unwisely used on Trinity, pre-

[8] A careful study of Root's work and projects suggests that his death made little difference. (V. Monroe, Harriet: *John Wellborn Root*, Boston, 1896.) The Eastern architects were destined to set the new fashion and Atwood was a better Classical designer than Hunt or McKim and certainly very superior to Root at this sort of adaptation.

pared the way for the usual contemporary interpretation of Richardson as a precursor of archaeological revival. Wells, before his death, offered the tempting example of the gaudy Century Club in New York to replace the sounder if duller model of the Villard houses. McKim, in the nineties, founded his hopes for American architecture on an American Academy in Rome. In less than ten years after Richardson's death the Roman had replaced the Romanesque as the official American style.

To the only great American architect of the twentieth century, Frank Lloyd Wright, Richardson's work still seems to belong, not so much with the great architecture of the far past, as with the most sterile archaeological forces of the present. To save Richardson from such a misinterpretation and to make his work available for emulation today, it is important to realize clearly the ambiguity of its relation to the contemporary context. The qualities which make his architecture great are the qualities of all the great free architecture of the past, not imitated but profoundly recreated to serve the functions of the nineteenth century. This the vernacular imitators understood perhaps better in their way than more educated architects. The relatively more functional character of their work proved, however, no defense against the rising aesthetic desire for order. They never had, moreover, any real comprehension of his way of using materials;[9] even less did they understand his principles of composition.

The Richardsonian tradition, such as it was, has in fifty years entirely died out. The academic tradition of archaeological adaptation sponsored by McKim, Mead and White is now almost gone also. A new tradition of modern design is rising, equally academic perhaps, based on a European development of the innovations of Sullivan and Wright and their generation abroad. This "International Style" of Le Corbusier, Oud, Gropius and Miës van der Rohe can at least

XV-18

XV-19

[9] Except in shingled houses, which were an old national vernacular tradition, and even in such work, they understood Richardson only very partially as the frequent combination of shingles with clapboards and elaborate Colonial detail makes plain.

provide a modern vernacular superior to any that has existed in the last hundred years. The vernacular of the preceding generation in America was only a spurious improvement over that of Richardson's lifetime. But great architecture, while it rises highest when it is based on a sound vernacular, must also find kinship in the work of all the great creative geniuses of the past.

For more than a generation the work of Richardson has had almost no sound inspiration to offer except to architectural genius of equal distinction. But the problem of the aesthetic expression of fine materials is rising to attention again after the simplification of the late twenties, and ornament, but lately buried, is now in an embryonic state preceding rebirth. Richardson's work is relevant once more. Again and again these chapters have broken the silence with which this gestation has been respected, not because Richardson solved even for himself the problem of ornament, but because the discussion should no longer be avoided. Before we rush, in reaction against the standing ban on all applied decoration, into an ecstatic revival of the paranoiac XV-20 comestibles of Gaudì and Sullivan, the problem of ornament in modern times must be analyzed in detail. In this respect, although Richardson's construction was traditional, the time in which he lived was already modern. Architectural carving was no better than it has been since, and even the best that was available could be obtained only at considerable expense. Ornament was designed on paper by draftsmen, dependent on documents, and unfamiliar with the processes of execution.

Under these conditions, which still continue, ornament is impossible on vernacular building unless, as was still sometimes the case in Richardson's day, it is a sort of folk-art hobby of those who occupy the buildings. A revival of individual Gingerbread production hardly seems now more feasible than any other revival of folk art. But with an increase of leisure and a satisfactory provision for the practical necessities of modern living, it might flourish again. As Ruskin, the fascist, and Morris, the socialist, realized, the return of an economically stable society might release again the universal artistic talent evident in the Middle Ages and in the work of young children.

Academic architecture whether traditional or in the International Style, offers no hope for ornament, Academic design by definition means the following of existing rules and cannot develop creatively nor rise above the level of the work from which those rules derive. But free creative architecture, as in the past, may well be distinguished by the quality of its applied ornament quite as much as by originality of composition and by intense aesthetic expression of particular methods of construction and fine building materials. As the work of Richardson and that of the best modern architects alike makes plain, such applied ornament is hardly likely to enhance sound architecture in modern times unless it is the work of independent painters and sculptors. But we have today new resources, lately revealed as equivalent to independent art in their effect, which were not aesthetically available in Richardson's day. These resources lie particularly in the scientific document wrenched out of context, and the products of photography and comparable reproductive processes. Photo-sculpture of reality would be very different from the photo-sculpture of ornament of the past.

An air-map covering a wall, or groups of photographs of textures and microphotographs of what is invisible to the eye: these may become by dislocation not scientific documents but aesthetic realities. Used in architectural decoration, they are not unlike the fortuitous encounter of a sewing machine and an umbrella upon a dissecting table, to use the famous image of Lautréamont. But the dislocation need not be of such paranoiac intensity. The Swiss critics who found obscenity in the microphotographs in Le Corbusier's Swiss Pavilion at the Cité Universitaire were obviously better informed scientists than most observers would be.

Brown Derby roadside stands, and the less abstruse symbolism of those which imitate at enormous scale ice-cream freezers or milk bottles, are an instance of the vernacular acceptance of a comparable idea in America. The combination of strict functionalism and bold symbolism in the best roadside stands provides, perhaps, the most encouraging sign for the architecture of the mid-twentieth century. XV-22 Obviously, ice-cream boxes with silvered sundae dishes on top, filled with canvas strawberry ice cream and provided with ribbon windows for outside service, are incidental to our culture. But the very fact that those who condemn them as breaches of "taste" prefer anachronistic Colonial or Tudor filling stations is proof of their symptomatic actuality.

So much of a discursion from Richardson's architecture should serve to indicate how, in the mid-twentieth century, the study of the architecture of the past must differ from what has been conventional. The study of the work of an architect was once a device for facilitating imitation. Later the study of art became more disinterested, aiming at a scientific picture of the flow of history. This sort of scholarship was less concerned with individual achievements, or even with "styles", except as they took their place in that flow. Now the criticism of the work of the past may be frankly *interessé* again. We must accept that its direction is determined by some motivation in the present, and that it should seek to reveal both the essential quality of the art of the past and the particular relevance of different phases of that art at different moments in the present.

The history of modern architecture at the present moment is no longer very relevant. What we know as modern architecture has XV-23 reached completion and is applicable as an academic discipline. The story of Richardson's architecture, however, falls in a period when the context was not dissimilar to that of the present, but when the technical methods that have predetermined later architecture were still undeveloped. It can, therefore, be of the highest interest today.

Richardson's life, for all its success, was something of a tragedy. But the contemplation of a tragedy has greater spiritual value than the contemplation of any other history. The greatest heroes have all been tragic ones.

NOTES TO THE NEW EDITION

CHAPTER I

I-1. Since this brief sketch of American architectural developments in the years of Richardson's youth was written a quarter century ago I and others have amended the story in many particulars. See, for example, my article, "Art of the United States: Architecture," in *Encyclopedia of World Art*, I, cols. 246-77, pl. 74-95, New York, 1959, and various writings published since 1936 listed in the bibliography there (cols. 276-7).

In these Notes I have thought it chiefly necessary to correct what I now believe to be actual mis-statements. For the greater part the original text must stand as representing the opinions—and the tastes also—of a quarter century ago, with the addition of occasional ironic asides.

I-2. The books of Downing and his contemporaries are listed in my *American Architectural Books*, 3rd rev. ed., Minneapolis, 1946. A subtle analysis of Downing's principles and influence will be found in Vincent J. Scully's article, "Romantic Rationalism . . . and the 'Stick Style,' 1840-1871," *Art Bulletin*, XXXV (1953), 121-42.

I-3. All Saints', Margaret Street, was designed in 1849 not 1848, largely built over the years 1850-53, and consecrated in 1859. For discussion and illustrations of the Victorian Gothic in England and America, see my *Early Victorian Architecture in Britain*, 2 vols., New Haven, 1954, especially chapters III-V and XVII, and Chapters 10 and 11 in my *Architecture: 19th and 20th Centuries*, Harmondsworth, 1958.

I-4. These editions are listed in my *American Architectural Books*, 3rd rev. ed., Minneapolis, 1946.

I-5. The National Academy of Design must have been first designed by Wight several years earlier but the exact date is not certainly known.

I-6. See Note I-2. (In cross-references to other Notes, the Roman numeral indicates the chapter.)

I-7. See C. L. V. Meeks, "Romanesque before Richardson," *Art Bulletin*, XXXV (1953), 17-33.

I-8. The name of Latrobe should precede that of Bulfinch, who succeeded him as Architect of the Capitol in 1817.

I-9. Actually built in 1850-51. See my pamphlet, *The Crystal Palace*, Northampton, 1951.

I-10. The date should be 1852-54.

I-11. Bogardus was not the only American involved in the introduction of cast iron fronts. See Turpin C. Bannister, "Bogardus Revisited, Part One: The Iron Fronts," *Journal of the Society of Architectural Historians*, XV (1956), 12-22.

I-12. The elevator in the Haughwout Store in New York was installed at least as early. For commercial architecture in mid-century New York, see Winston Weisman, "Commercial Palaces of New York," *Journal of the Society of Architectural Historians*, XXXVI (1954), 285-302.

I-13. In the Deacon house of 1848. Later studies give more attention to New York and to Detlef Lienau's Shiff house there of 1849-50; see Ellen W. Kramer, "Detlef Lienau, an Architect of the Brown Decades," *Journal of the Society of Architectural Historians*, XIV (1955), 18-25. A more significant development began with the work of Renwick a decade later; see Rosalie Thorn McKenna, "James Renwick, Jr., and the Second Empire Style in the United States," *Magazine of Art*, XLIV (1951), 97-101.

The international story is outlined in more detail in Chapter 9 of my *Architecture: 19th and 20th Centuries*, Harmondsworth, 1958.

CHAPTER II

II-1. St. John's Chapel was *not* building at this time. George Hersey informs me that the design was accepted in 1869, the whole quadrangle being completed by 1873. See J. A. Miller, *The Episcopal Theological Seminary, 1867-1943*, Cambridge, [1943].

II-2. The mansard has been retained in the extensive renovation of Boylston Hall carried out by The Architects' Collaborative in 1959-60. Very likely it was not a later addition since mansards were already in current use in Germany by 1857 and by no means an absolute novelty in the United States. (See Note I-13.)

II-3. There were, of course, professional schools in Germany; but before the rise of the Bauhaus in the 1920's they seem rarely to have attracted American architectural students in the way that American painters were drawn to Dusseldorf in the mid-nineteenth century.

II-4. Chapter 8 in my *Architecture: 19th and 20th Centuries*, Harmondsworth, 1958, offers a fuller account, with illustrations, of the Paris in which Richardson lived and worked for five years during the Second Empire building boom.

II-5. The Opéra competition was held in 1861.

II-6. Actually the Empress Eugénie was opposed to the design, having wished her friend Viollet-le-Duc to win the competition. (See Note II-4.)

II-7. The design of the Place de l'Opéra dates from 1858 but the execution, though well under way by 1861, presumably extended over some years. (See Note II-4.)

II-8. The greater part of the new Louvre as we know it was complete by 1857. The terminal pavilions—de Flore and de Marsan—transformed 1860-7 by Lefuel, were restored by him 1871-76 having been badly damaged when the Tuileries was burned under the Commune.

II-9. Historically, priority goes to Renwick's Main Building at Vassar College, not to the Boston City Hall. (See Note I-13.)

II-10. See Note I-13.

II-11. Labrouste was appointed architect of the Bibliothèque Ste. Geneviève in 1838 and his original project for the new building dates from the following year Robin Middleton informs me.

II-12. Saulnier's better known Chocolat Menier factory at Noisiel-sur-Marne postdates Richardson's departure from France by five or six years.

II-13. It is unlikely that Richardson knew of the Docks although he must have been familiar with the Halles and perhaps with St. Eugéne. The designer of St. Eugéne was L.-A. Boileau although the nominal architect was L.-A. Lusson.

II-14. The LeVésinet church was built in 1863 by L.-A. Boileau's son L.-C. Boileau.

II-15. It is doubtful whether St. Augustin should be considered at all Romanesque. Although designed as early as 1860, the construction may not have been very far advanced when Richardson left Paris.

II-16. "Interior" not "exterior," of course.

II-17. The architect responsible for the design of these façades was Charles Rohault de Fleury; the round pavilions, however, were by Henri Blondel.

II-18. The Hotel Pereire and its twin, both by Alfred Armand, are in the Place Pereire and more *Louis XVI* than *Louis XIII* as regards the exterior treatment; the Hotel Fould was at 29-31 Rue de Berri. It was begun in 1856 John Jacobus informs me.

CHAPTER III

III-1. This is probably an exaggeration. There was a very considerable amount of Gothic church-building, but in the provinces rather than in Paris.

III-2. Eiffel's iron skeleton carrying the bronze "curtain-wall" of Bartholdi's Statue of Liberty is actually contemporary with Jenney's Home Insurance Building. Although Richardson employed Bartholdi for the frieze on the tower of his Brattle Square Church in the early 70's he was not involved in this rather special early example of "skyscraper construction".

III-3. Hunt was, in fact, very eclectic in the 60's and 70's, working more in the High Victorian Gothic and the domestic Stick Style than in the modes in which he had been trained in Paris.

III-4. This is an exaggeration as regards the early 60's however true it would have been in the 40's.

III-5. "Apparently" is the proper word, for Jane Morris was in fact deeply involved with D. G. Rossetti!

CHAPTER IV

IV-1. This is not true, although the work he did in 1870-71 at the Hotel Brunswick on Fifth Avenue at 26th Street, to an estimated cost of $50,000, was the only considerable commission, and even that was an alteration and enlargement of an existing structure. Very modest changes in the house of George E. Stone at 12 East 37th Street in 1868, to an estimate of $3,000, and more extensive alterations for the Century Association at 42 East 15th Street in 1869, to an estimate of $21,000, preceded the work at the Brunswick Hotel. Other very modest remodelling work followed for Charles F. Livermore at 225 Fifth Avenue ($10,000) in 1870-71; for H. B. Hyde on 40th Street between Fifth and Madison Avenues in

1871-72 ($700); for Francis M. Wild at 58 West 45th Street ($3,800) in 1874; for Joseph H. Choate at 50 West 47th Street ($4,000) and for All Souls' Church ($1,300) in 1875; and finally for the Century Association again ($800) in 1878.

I owe these details on Richardson's—or more accurately except for the last—the firm of Gambrill & Richardson's employment in New York to the researches of Ellen W. Kramer in the archives of the New York City Department of Buildings. Unhappily no one has turned up any visual evidence that might, at least in the cases of the Century Association and of the Brunswick Hotel, be of real interest. It is just possible, but unlikely, that certain extant but so far unidentified perspective sketches and elevations of New York house-tops at the Houghton Library (such as that shown in Figure 6 of the 1936 edition) may refer to some of the minor commissions of these years that are listed above.

IV-2. Vincent Scully has since supplied that vaguer name: Stick Style. (See Note I-2.)

IV-3. As is noted in the Preface to the New Edition the drawings are now on deposit in the Houghton Library at Harvard.

IV-4. Littell's middle name was "Trenchard"; "T. Penchard" is an error.

IV-5. Narthexes are not common on High Victorian Gothic churches in England. Richardson perhaps noted that on St. Andrew's, Camberwell. by E. Bassett Keeling illustrated in the *Illustrated London News*, XLVIII (April 7, 1866), 344, which the one at Unity Church somewhat resembles. There is no close similarity to the narthex of Keeling's St. George's, Camden Hill, in London, illustrated in the *Building News*, XI (1864), 563.

IV-6. Similar windows can be seen in the aisle of William Butterfield's St. Mathias', Stoke Newington, in the project illustrated in the *Ecclesiologist* in 1850. Richardson is more likely, however, to have borrowed them from some more nearly contemporary source.

IV-7. See Figure 4. The more complete perspective to which reference is made is in M. G. Van Rensselaer, *Henry Hobson Richardson and His Works*, New York and Boston, 1888, 48.

IV-8. This applies to the better-trained architects. Men of what Sir John Summerson has called the "Lower School," such as the already mentioned Keeling or Thomas (Victorian) Harris, had for a decade been at least as free in their treatment of mediaeval precedent as Richardson was here, and so had E. B. Lamb from a much earlier date.

IV-9. Although Grace Church is hardly more archaeological than Unity Church, the subtler proportions and more carefully organized asymmetrical composition, with the tower in a transeptal position, suggest that Richardson was now looking in the English professional magazines at the illustrations of work by more sophisticated, if less original, English architects of the period such as G. E. Street and William Burges. The bold scale of the tracery in the rose window recalls Burges, the composition rather Street; but the extreme roughness of the materials and the lack of moulded trim can hardly be matched in English work.

CHAPTER V

V-1. The actual prototype must surely have been the National Discount Offices in Cornhill in London, built by the Francis Brothers in 1857 and illustrated in the *Builder* for Jan. 2, 1858, 11; indeed, Richardson followed this model very, very closely although he reduced the elaboration of the ornament, doubtless (as suggested) because of difficulties of execution in granite.

V-2. It is surprisingly like Otto Wagner's work of the 80's in Vienna also.

V-3. See Note I-12.

V-4. Post, Gambrill's former partner, was the engineer; the architects were Arthur Gilman and Edward Kimball.

V-5. The project probably dates back to the 50's in any case.

V-6. The first commercial use of this device in England seems to have been on the Schwabe Warehouse at 46-54 Mosley Street in Manchester built by Edward Walters in 1845. From the mid-60's it was gradually replacing the more characteristic treatment of commercial façades with successive arcades, one to a storey, a *parti* that also notably influenced Richardson from the mid-70's. (See my article, "Victorian Monuments of Commerce," *Architectural Review*, CV [1949], 61-74.) For American examples (which Richardson is not likely to have known) see Winston Weisman, "Philadelphia Functionalism and Sullivan," *Journal of the Society of Architectural Historians*, XX (1961), 3-19.

V-7. One may now say that the Stimson house illustrated the Stick Style, but not very effectively except in the entrance gate.

V-8. "Eastlake," of course, in the inaccurate American sense; Charles L. Eastlake disowned with great vehemence such American furniture as was thus ornamented and named for him.

V-9. The external use of colored tiles goes back some twenty years in England. (See my *Early Victorian Architecture in Britain*, 2 vols., New Haven, 1954, 578-9.) Like other characteristic High Victorian Gothic decorative treatments this was most popular in America from the mid-60's after such external polychromy had begun to go out of fashion in England.

V-10. Such sash had begun to appear in England at least by 1850 and must certainly have been imitated in America from English models quite as much as the various types of sash that preceded these in common domestic use. (See my *Early Victorian Architecture in Britain*, 2 vols., New Haven, 1954, 481.)

V-11. It is now evident that these plans do indeed refer to a later projected house for Dorsheimer, presumably one to have been built, c. 1875, in Albany, where most houses had party walls rather than being free-standing as in Buffalo. (Dorsheimer was Lieutenant Governor of New York, 1874-78, and must have needed a residence in Albany at that time.) Since the discussion in the text applies entirely to these sketch plans, it will be well to comment here on the real Dorsheimer house of 1868 as well as on Richardson's own house of the same year at Arrochar, which has also been brought to light since 1936, and on another project for a house carrying the stamped date August 10, 1868.

When I was preparing an exhibition of Buffalo architecture some twenty years ago I found that the Dorsheimer house of 1868 was still standing in Delaware Avenue (Figure 10). Although no one who knew only Richardson's later work from Trinity on would be likely to guess that it was by him, the house nevertheless has real dignity, with excellent choice and use of materials, and yet shows a discreet acceptance of the common American standards of the post-Civil-War decade. There is little that is Parisian about it beyond the mansard roof that was by this time thoroughly acclimated in America, and nothing reflecting the English Victorian Gothic that had so strongly influenced his churches at Springfield and Medford designed in the preceding years since his return in 1865. Unfortunately the interior had been so pulled about that it is difficult to determine the original plan; it seems doubtful, however, that it had any original or interesting features.

Richardson's own house at 45 McClean Avenue, Arrochar, on Staten Island, also of 1868, was found and photographed some years ago by Wayne Andrews (Figure 9). Generally one expects to find the houses that architects build for themselves—Soane's in London, say, or the two Taliesins of Frank Lloyd Wright—especially revelatory of their personal aspirations. This would hardly seem to be true of Richardson's house which is less distinguished in almost every way than the Dorsheimer house. The mansard roofs are more-boldly massed here and the conventional American clapboarding of the walls rather timidly panelled with flat boards along the lines of the Stick Style. But the general effect is gauche and indeterminate, even less Parisian than the house in Buffalo yet no more influenced by the English High Victorian Gothic. Now that the exterior has been stuccoed the house is of even less visual interest.

A plan, traced by S. L. Catlin in 1951, indicates that the T-shaped front portion of the house was—and still is—divided into three reception rooms of nearly equal size opening into one another through relatively wide doorways, with the kitchen to the rear. The staircase is not a prominent feature since it opens off a small rear hallway, but the entrance hall to some extent forms the core of the plan. (See Note VI-4.)

The house project dated August 10, 1868, is rather more interesting than the Arrochar house, but less solid and severe than the Dorsheimer house (Figures 11 and 12). The semi-gambrel, semi-mansard roof is modelled more agreeably than the more conventional mansards of the executed houses and both inside and out the composition is looser and more flowing. Stick woodwork is fairly conspicuous on the exterior, although the porte-cochere was apparently to be of stone. The hall, though still fairly modest in size, is enlarged spatially by the main staircase rising in an ell. Comparison with the undated Codman house project (Figures 15, 16) reveals that Richardson's ideas of house-design, and especially of house-planning, advanced very rapidly in the next two or three years. At the same time this 1868 project is much superior in coherence of organization, and even in restraint of detailing, to the executed Crowninshield house in Boston of the following year.

V-12. Additional evidence for a late redesigning of the church at the time of building in 1872-73 is perhaps provided by the special character of the spire as executed. The undated sketch in M. G. Van Rensselaer, *Henry Hobson Richardson and his Works*, New York and Boston, 1888, [54], already shows a consistent use of round arches and a tall stone dormer breaking the nave roof, but the tower is capped with a rather conventional broach spire. The executed termination of the tower is quite different, and much more effective, with four square pyramidal spirelets at the corners of the octagonal spire. The spirelets are joined with the main spire just above the base in such a way that a single square pyramid rises a short distance from the square top of the shaft.

This arrangement seems almost certainly to have been derived either from Burges or from Street; just possibly from the former's stone spire on Christ the Consoler at Skelton, Yorkshire, built in 1871, which it most closely resembles—

and, indeed, improves upon in its simplicity and sturdy stoniness—but more probably from the slated spire of the latter's principal London church, St. James the Less, Westminster, of 1858-61. The latter had been illustrated in the English magazines; the former was certainly not illustrated before 1872. But it is just conceivable that McKim or some other traveller returned from England might have seen it, or the drawings for it, and described it to Richardson.

Since Street's spire at St. James's echoes French slated spires of the 12th century, it might seem simpler to suggest that Richardson also drew directly from a mediaeval source. There is no other evidence, however, of his borrowing a motif from old work on the Continent so early except for his use of Auvergnat polychromy on the apse of Trinity Church in the competition project of 1872. Moreover the placing of the tower, its squat proportions, and its stoniness—all so markedly "Richardsonian" already—hardly recall French mediaeval prototypes and do suggest Burges more than anyone else as the probable inspiration.

The likelihood of influence from Burges is increased by the fact that Richardson was, in 1871, borrowing the design of a tower from the English architect's project of 1866 for the London Law Courts to crown his Hampden County Courthouse (Figures 23, 24) and also by the close similarity of the final design of the towers of the administration building of the Buffalo State Hospital (Figures 21, 22) to another tower of that project.

The final form of the North Church seems to indicate a thorough redesigning in 1871 or early 1872, even though the plan may well have been established in 1868. Its place in the sequence of Richardson's work should be after, not before, the Brattle Square Church in Boston which was designed in 1870. It is notable in this connection that the Boston church shows very little High Victorian Gothic influence from either the "Higher" or the "Lower" school in England except for the very personal version of Butterfieldian polychromatic banding in the arches and the corner location of the tower.

V-13. Similar colonnettes flank the clerestorey windows inside G. E. Street's All Saints', Maidenhead, of 1854-57; and there are plenty of other English examples of the late 50's and early 60's.

CHAPTER VI

VI-1. One may presume that the sketch plan for a projected Worcester General Hospital (Figure 2), which gives even clearer evidence of what Richardson had learned in France about the planning of large institutions, dates from the years of his activity on the Worcester High School. In any case it would seem to precede the earliest plan for the Buffalo State Hospital and may be several years earlier still, perhaps the earliest of his large projects that has survived.

VI-2. This is exaggerated. The evidence of his own house of 1868 (Figure 9), of the house project of that year (Figure 11) and of the Codman project (Figure 15), which cannot be far off the date 1869-71 of the Worcester High School, indicates that he already took a lively interest in the asymmetrical massing of freestanding houses.

VI-3. See Note IV-1.

VI-4. Since this "living-hall" must certainly precede that in the Andrews house, designed in 1872, it becomes of real importance to determine the inspiration of this important feature of the later American Shingle Style which probably made its first appearance here. It might seem that the one in the Sherman house of 1874-75 (Figure 39) would have been based on those in the early houses of Norman Shaw since the exterior treatment there is so obviously Shavian Manorial, and by 1874 Shaw's plan of Hopedene had indeed been published in the *Building News* for May 8, 1874. But that was the very first such Shavian plan to be made available.

This problem has naturally been discussed by Scully at some length (*The Shingle Style,* New Haven, 1955, 5-9) with the plausible suggestion that the Codman living-hall derives either from Waterhouse's Hinderton, published by Robert Kerr in the second edition of *The English Gentleman's House* . . ., London, 1865, (Scully's Figure 3) or from other English examples illustrated in English magazines in the late 60's. Some historians have understandably sought for American prototypes, Ellen Kramer suggesting the wide central halls of the Southern plantation houses Richardson had known in his youth.

Without denying the probable convergence of other influences both American and foreign, I would at least like to call attention to the house Vaux & Withers designed for Nathan Reeve of Newburgh, N.Y., published as Design 22 in Calvert Vaux, *Villas and Cottages,* New York, 1857, of which later editions appeared in 1864, 1867, 1869, 1872, and 1874. The continued popularity of this book in the relevant years supports the suggestion that its contents may well have been known to Richardson. Moreover, Richardson probably had seen, at least by 1872 when he first worked in Hartford, Withers' very Waterhouse-like Goodwin house there which was built in 1871. (See Note VIII-2.)

VI-5. The "thin, chamfered half-timbering", so to call it, is of course characteristic of the Stick Style as defined by Scully (see Note I-2) and reflects no direct foreign influence at this date any more than does the semi-mansard type of roof so nearly identical to that in Figure 11.

VI-6. This is not quite true. Samuel Sloan's *Architectural Review and American Builder's Journal,* issued monthly from July, 1868, through June, 1869, at least deserves mention. The material in it was later reissued by Sloan in book form as *City homes, country houses and church architecture,* Philadelphia, 1871.

VI-7. The English commercial work referred to, and hence Richardson's Agawam Bank, is better called Round-arched High Victorian Gothic, a mode that seems to have been initiated by G. G. Scott in the new chancel of Camden Church, Camberwell, in 1853 with the direct approval of Ruskin. (See *Architecture: 19th and 20th Centuries,* Harmondsworth, 1958, 175-6.)

Something very like it was brought to America the following year by Jacob Wrey Mould when he designed All Souls' Church in New York. That is, however, rather more Byzantinoid, and also recalls mid-century German work in the *Rundbogenstil.* The word "corruption" here might better be replaced by the phrase "originality of un-archaeological detailing."

VI-8. This reference to Nesfield's work of the 60's confuses two quite different lodges: that of 1864 in Regent's Park, demolished in the blitz, "which revived in effect the Picturesque Cottage mode of half a century earlier" and pre-figured the "Shavian Manorial" of Shaw's Glen Andred of 1867 and later country houses, with the lodge at Kew Gardens of 1866, which is specifically "Queen Anne" and to which Note 6 at the foot of page 99 applies fairly well.

The first example of the Shavian Manorial to be illustrated, Shaw's Leyswood, was in the *Building News,* for March 31, 1871. Little work that may be plausibly called "Queen Anne" was published for a year or two; and the "Queen Anne" can hardly be said to have affected Richardson before 1878 when he designed Sever Hall which reflects English work of four or five years earlier. The relationship of the drawings of details of late mediaeval craftsmanship in the periodicals to either the Shavian Manorial or the "Queen Anne" is certainly tenuous though perhaps somewhat closer to the current work of Philip Webb with its consistent emphasis on quality of workmanship.

VI-9. The title of Nesfield's book is more properly *Specimens of Mediaeval Architecture . . . in France and Italy*; Burges's book was *Architectural Drawings*, London, 1870; and Shaw's of 1872 was the second edition of his *Architectural Sketches from the Continent*, London, 1858.

VI-10. The project dates from 1873 though construction was not begun until 1880. Richardson's contact with Hartford clients over the years 1872-78 make it probable that he knew the project. The Richardsonian quality of that portion of Burges's *chef d'oeuvre* which was built derives from the massive proportions and simple mediaevalizing detail, already evident in the project, as well as from the use of rockfaced brownstone walling, which Burges may very well not have foreseen.

VI-11. That is, to plan large complex edifices. English domestic planning was certainly in advance of French, and even still of American, at this early date in the 70's.

VI-12. Perhaps not by Shaw even at this point. While still a Royal Academy student he had begun as an academic planner in the early 50's and he returned to academic planning in the late 80's. As to Webb, the return to orderly and even symmetrical house-planning came earlier than with Shaw: at Trevor Hall (1868-70) and, more notably of course, at Smeaton Manor a decade later (1877-79).

VI-13. That Richardson's copy of Texier and Pullan is the Paris edition rather than the London one of the same year 1864 might, however, seem to provide evidence that Richardson had acquired it before returning to America.

VI-14. As Fernand de Dartein was French this was not a translation. The last plates did not appear until 1882.

VI-15. The copy of G. Rohault (not "Rohaut) de Fleury, *Monuments de Pise au moyen age*, at the Royal Institute of British Architects is dated 1866 not 1865.

VI-16. The Royal Institute of British Architects' copy of *Syrie Centrale* is in 2 vols., Paris, 1867; the dates given here are from Richardson's own copies of the two volumes of this work.

VI-17. This was a second edition or second issue of Jules Gailhabaud's work which had first appeared in 4 vols. of text and 1 of plates, Paris, 1858. The edition Richardson owned was in four not five volumes.

VI-18. The reference should be to T. H. King and G. J. Hill, *The Study-book of Mediaeval Architecture and Art*, 4 vols., London, 1858-68; but only the later volumes (III and IV) of 1868 were in Richardson's library.

VI-19. Not "Talberg" but Bruce J. Talbert, a highly original English designer of furniture and of chintzes who was almost a rival of Morris.

VI-20. There are four volumes of Sauvageot's work.

VI-21. The date of Shaw's work should, of course, be 1858 even though Richardson owned only the later (1872) edition.

VI-22. This was to underestimate the intrinsic vitality of the Stick Style, a vitality that continued (or was revived) in much of Maybeck's and Greene & Greene's domestic work in California of the years 1900-1910.

CHAPTER VII

VII-1. The loggia, however, might have been suggested by that of E. W. Godwin's Northampton Town Hall of 1861-64 of which Richardson could well have seen the illustration in the *Building News*, VII (1861) , [893]. He presumably knew of Godwin as Burges's collaborator on the Law Courts project of 1866. As with Burges, there is a certain kinship of scale and character in Richardson's and Godwin's work of these years that obscures, at the same time that it reinforces, the probability of direct influence.

VII-2. The phrase "had been commissioned in 1868 but was not executed" should read "commissioned but not executed."

VII-3. Martin's church is in Cambridge, not Boston.

VII-4. The interior space in fact is T-shaped not cruciform.

VII-5. If a Harvard education can be obtained in a single year! McKim was there only in 1866-67 when, to quote Scully, "he distinguished himself at right field for the baseball team."

VII-6. Actually, he had worked very briefly for Russell Sturgis before joining Richardson.

VII-7. "makes" not "make".

VII-8. The plan is certainly not as French as that for the Worcester General Hospital (Figure 2) which is therefore almost certainly rather earlier, as has already been suggested (Note VI-1).

VII-9. As has been noted, the improvement over the Worcester tower is without doubt due to emulation of the front corner tower in Burges's and Godwin's project of 1866 for the Law Courts, published in the *Builder* for May 4, 1867, 311, from which in this same year 1871 Richardson borrowed another corner tower for the Hampden County Courthouse (see p. 127, *infra,* where the date of publication in the *Builder* is given incorrectly as 1870), following his model on that occasion considerably more closely.

VII-10. Before its final disappearance from respectable English work in the late 60's polychromatic banding in Britain had generally become much chastened.

CHAPTER VIII

VIII-1. Another existing project in the Houghton Library for a Boston & Albany railroad station, with no indication of location, but presumably for either Boston or Albany—it would not fit the site in Springfield nor presumably in Worcester, and is too large for the intervening towns—also survives from this period, but might be of 1873 or even slightly later. There is something about the draftsmanship, however—in ink on tracing cloth—that suggests McKim; certainly it would not appear to have been drawn either by Richardson himself or by Stanford White, who joined the office in 1872 as McKim was beginning work on his own.

VIII-2. F. C. Withers, who as Calvert Vaux's partner shared responsibility — perhaps — for the introduction of the "living-hall" to America in the Reeve house. (See Note VI-4.) Richardson, working in Hartford on the Phoenix Insurance Building at least from its commissioning in March, 1872, would almost certainly have known this house, then the newest and the largest in the city.

I owe to Mrs. A. Everett Austin of Hartford, whose grandfather the Reverend Francis Goodwin, a clergyman deeply interested in architecture and well aware of current English developments, collaborated with Withers on the design of this house for his brother James, rather than to my own dimmer memory of the interior, the assurance that the Goodwin house included a generous living hall, with stairs rising in an ell around a square well and with a big fireplace. She tells me, indeed, that through her great aunt's lifetime the gentlemen sat around this fireplace after dinner when the ladies retired to the drawing room. This Goodwin living hall, rather than the published plans of Vaux & Wither's Reeve house or of Waterhouse's Hinderton, may well have been the immediate inspiration of the living hall in the Codman project.

VIII-3. The balcony is actually at the left not the right.

VIII-4. The type is Late Gothic and French, but the immediate models would seem to have been the dormers on the rear of Nesfield and Shaw's Cloverly Hall of 1865-68 with the carved friezes omitted. The perspective of this is about the most advanced illustration provided in C. L. Eastlake, *A History of the Gothic Revival*, London, 1872, opp. 340, a book it is hard to believe that Richardson did not see soon after its appearance.

VIII-5. "Stone" not "storey." This was done to permit dividing the very tall second storey into two lower ones.

VIII-6. The date of the designing, or redesigning, of the North Church has been discussed in Note V-12. More surely fixed in 1871, or at the latest early 1872, is a project (Figure 25) for a church in Columbus, Ohio, published in *The Architect* for October 5, 1872, almost certainly the earliest reference to Richardson's work outside his own country, and preceding by five years the references to Trinity Church in the same English magazine for April 28, 1877, 274, and October 20, 1877, 210-211.

I quote from an article of mine in the *Journal of the Society of Architectural Historians,* IX (1950), 25-6, some brief comments on this project: "Although this design is not intrinsically very important, such early recognition of Richardson's rising star abroad is of some interest. The left-hand tower, moreover, capped with a sharp Butterfieldian spire"—it resembles most closely that of Butterfield's church at Baldersby St. James, Yorkshire, of 1856—"has something of the quality of that of the Brattle Square Church in Boston . . . The date of this design would probably be late 1871 or early 1872, just before the competition drawings for Trinity were started and the draftsman McKim rather than White."

VIII-7. Indeed, quite a lot has been written about this building since J. Carson Webster presented the contemporary and later illustrations he had found of it at a meeting of the Society of Architectural Historians in Chicago on January 27, 1950, just twenty years after its destruction by fire in 1930. See his article, "Richardson's American Express Building," *Journal of the Society of Architectural Historians,* IX (1950), 21-4, which includes both the original 1872 project given here (Figure

29) as well as its appearance in 1884, as modified in execution by Peter B. Wight, and various interiors.

With that article was published one of mine, based on the visual material he had brought together, "Richardson's American Express Building: A Note" (*loc. cit*, 25-30). It seems unnecessary to repeat here the long analysis of the façade included in that article, but some summary statements may be quoted: ". . . the Express project shows no coherent assimilation of English commercial modes of design. By its relatively great height and its prominent pavilion roofs and dormers it actually achieves a greater monumentality than most English work. . . . Yet the general effect of the design is definitely within the range of English High Victorian work, both as regards the articulation of the wall-screen in a way that echoes the iron skeleton of the interior and in the particular devices used to model this stone screen back from the façade plane.

"In its openness this façade vies with, but hardly emulates, the effects achieved by the founders and builders of American castiron fronts. But instead of the patently *ersatz* plasticity of Renaissance orders in hollow metal supporting archivolts or entablatures of an equal hollowness, it substitutes a crude but vigorous plasticity in the taste of High Victorian 'realism'. Frank and masculine, without being brash and aggressive, it might well have opened a line of development in Richardson's work toward a formula more open and less ponderous than the line of his arcaded commercial buildings. Subjected to the simplification that so much improved his domestic manner after 1880, it might have led to things as fine as the Field Store and yet more directly expressive of the iron skeleton behind. Actually in Chicago something of this sort did eventually occur. Jenney & Mundie's"—this is formally incorrect as the partnership had not yet begun, though Mundie was already working for Jenney—"second Lester Building of 1890 represents, in hands less accomplished than Richardson's, what could come of the later technical development . . .".

The article concludes with some discussion of the possible influence of this early Chicago work of Richardson's on local commercial architects before 1886 when emulation of his Marshall Field Store began.

The six-storey Express Building was no skyscraper; as it did not at first have an elevator it was not even an "elevator building." The year that saw it built, however, 1873, marked the initiation of the skyscraper in New York, with the designing of Richard M. Hunt's Tribune Building and George B. Post's Western Union Building, their ten-storey height made potentially profitable by the introduction of elevators such as had first served an office building in the Equitable Building of Gilman, Kendall and Post completed the year before the American Express Building was designed. See Winston Weisman, "New York and the Problem of the First Skyscraper", *Journal of the Society of Architectural Historians*, XII (1953), 13-20.

VIII-8. McKim's firm was originally known as McKim, Mead & Bigelow; White was first employed by the firm and then invited to replace Bigelow as a partner during the course of 1879, a crucial year in the firm's history. Their first mature Shingle Style house, the Alden house at Lloyds Neck, L.I., of 1879-80 was probably designed by McKim and White in collaboration.

VIII-9. This is, of course, not true; his own house at Arrochar was four years earlier.

316

VIII-10. The living-hall here, and indeed the general "agglutinative" organization of the plan, is far more like Shaw's domestic planning, especially his Leyswood of 1868, than the hall and the plan of the Codman project. The reference to the Goodwin house in Hartford is interesting even though I evidently did not, in 1936, realize its possible significance. (See Note VI-4 and VIII-2.)

VIII-11. Hunt vastly enlarged the Wetmore house but he also retained much of an earlier structure dating from 1852. This affected the design of the exterior and the planning, as well as requiring the continued use of Fall River granite.

VIII-12. The porch supports are definitely of Stick Style character, and the Stick Style had made its most notable early appearance in Newport only in 1862 in Hunt's Griswold house.

VIII-13. See Vincent J. Scully, *The Shingle Style*, New Haven, 1955. The use of clapboards on the lower storey perhaps reflected Shaw's frequent use of brick below tile-hung upper storeys, especially if the clapboards were here painted red as was frequently done on later Shingle Style houses. This Richardson could have noted in the perspective of Shaw's Leyswood published by C. L. Eastlake in *A History of the Gothic Revival*, London, 1872, opp. 343, as well as in the *Building News*. (See Note VI-8.)

VIII-14. It would be better to say "Shavian Manorial" rather than "Queen Anne manor" since no "Queen Anne" influence appears on the exteriors of the houses and projects referred to here.

VIII-15. Doubtless Richardson's personal taste and his knowledge of 18th-century American work played a part in the selection of shingles for the upper walls; but the general character of the Andrews design, combined with Norman Shaw's sort of planning—however information concerning that may have reached Richardson—make it all but certain that there was Shavian influence here.

VIII-16. Actually McKim in this very year was initiating the Colonial Revival, up to a point at least, in the new room he added to the 18th-century Robinson house in Newport. More extensive work in the same vein followed at the Dennis house across the street in 1876, by which time the Centennial Exposition in Philadelphia was beginning to focus public interest on Colonial architecture. See Vincent J. Scully, *The Shingle Style*, New Haven, 1955, chapters 2 and 3.

VIII-17. Nor, for that matter, the American Express Building.

VIII-18. The apse and all its furniture has, since 1936, been entirely redone by Maginnis & Walsh. Without being at all plausibly Richardsonian, the result is yet preferable to the earlier work of Richardson's successors. In richness of materials and color it is not perhaps too unlike what he himself might have wished to provide had there been more funds available and a rector less Low Church than his good friend Phillips Brooks.

Figure 35, from an elevation dated 1874 preserved at the Houghton Library, shows the West front as it was originally carried to execution by 1877 with no porch.

VIII-19. Today, I believe, those at all interested understand better the qualities peculiar to Richardson's best work, and the proper adjective is generally used with more accuracy.

VIII-20. At Houghton Library now. The Spanish lantern that provided White's model is, of course, that of the *old* Cathedral of Salamanca.

VIII-21. The model for this roof must have been that in the choir of Burges's Cathedral of St. Finbar, Cork, published in the *Builder,* May 16, 1863. Such round-ceiled roofs over sturdy kingpost trusses were also proposed by the English architect in his ambitious projects for Brisbane Cathedral in Australia and for St. Mary's Episcopal Cathedral in Edinburgh, but it fell to Richardson to execute the only large and conspicuous example.

VIII-22. The watercolor design in my possession for the three Morris windows in the north transept—the decorative work that fills most of their area presumably by Morris, the figure panels by Burne-Jones—does not suggest that the windows themselves *should* be much inferior in quality of color to those of the period executed by the Morris firm for English churches and colleges even though the color is somewhat paler than in their best windows of the 60's. Doubtless it is the relatively dark interior of the Boston church and the contrast with the very deep and rich color of the LaFarge windows which makes them seem weak—but "smeary" is hardly just!

VIII-23. Better artificial lighting now makes it possible to appreciate the color treatment of the interior walls. It does not, of course, improve the effect of the windows, either LaFarge's or Morris's.

VIII-24. Of the buildings mentioned the Brunswick Hotel and the S. S. Pierce Building have gone, and the Cluny Apartments are about to be demolished. If anything, however, Trinity has profited by the arrival of several cleaner, flatter, and crisper new buildings in its neighborhood, inferior though most of these are intrinsically even to what they have superseded.

VIII-25. Almost precisely thirty years before, since the final design for Trinity in New York dates not from 1839, when it was commissioned, but from the early 40's, only two or three years before its completion in 1846, George Hersey informs me.

VIII-26. This was the second edition; the first is dated 1855. "Rohaut," of course, should read "Rohault."

VIII-27. Curiously enough the Royal Institute of British Architects library *Catalogue,* London, 1937, supplies the date 1882 for this.

VIII-28. *La Decoration arabe* (Extraits de *L'Art Arabe*) , Paris, 1885. Richardson did not have the original work of 1877.

VIII-29. The author of this work was not "Bandol" but Anatole de Baudot, Viollet-le-Duc's most important disciple, who was the architect in the 90's of the epoch-making *ciment-armé* church of St. Jean de Montmartre in Paris. The first volume, at least of two, appeared in 1867, and therefore may have been some time in Richardson's possession; but the probability is that he acquired the work in 1877 or later.

CHAPTER IX

IX-1. William Jordy has called to my attention that Richardson's name as editor appears in an editorial Note at the beginning of the first volume of what is more accurately entitled the *New York Sketch-Book of Architecture;* also, that Montgomery Schuyler later asserted that McKim really served as *de facto* editor. (See M. Schuyler, "Charles Follen McKim," *Architectural Record,* XXVI, Nov. 1909, 381.) This helps to explain the appearance of so much of Richardson's work and projects in the *New York Sketch-Book* and confirms that this periodical illustrates on the whole the tastes and interests of himself and his close associates. The earlier publication of his Columbus, Ohio, church project (Figure 25) in *The Architect,* a year before the *American Architectural Sketch-Book* began to appear, is worth recalling, however.

IX-2. Earle's Christ Church Cathedral is in Springfield.

IX-3. Vincent Scully has examined this material exhaustively, at least as regards domestic architecture, in the first four chapters of his *Shingle Style,* New Haven, 1955. He has also rather significantly related specifically architectural developments to the general cultural and social climate of the depression years of the mid-70's.

IX-4. "English Queen Anne in its first and still mediaeval form" would be more accurately called "Shavian Manorial". (See Chapter 12 in my *Architecture: 19th and 20th Centuries,* Harmondsworth, 1958, especially pp. 207-211.)

IX-5. "American Second Empire" would be a less pejorative expression than "General Grant."

IX-6. New Zealand Chambers was also published in the *Building News* in 1873.

IX-7. Collaboration between McKim and White began only in 1879.

IX-8. I seem to have been quite unaware, in 1936, that Hunt's Tribune Building, as the first skyscraper, was far more epoch-making than Cady's project.

IX-9. Read "Shavian Manorial" for "Queen Anne."

IX-10. For "Queen Anne," read "Shavian."

IX-11. The painted decoration in the panel in the gable (see Figure 36) was taken straight from a house of 1870 by Shaw at Harrow Weald later known as Grim's Dyke after its purchase by W. S. Gilbert. This was published in the *Building News* for September 6, 1872. By 1874 several of Shaw's characteristic country houses had been illustrated in the English magazines so that their influence on Richardson and White was generic rather than specific. But in this instance precise copying of a particular feature is evident and hence points to White as the responsible agent, quite as in the case of the contemporary borrowing of the Salamantine lantern for Trinity.

IX-12. Plans have since come to light; see Figure 39.

IX-13. The original library, as seen in Figure 39, must have been an interesting room, with its Shavian polygonal bay window occupying the entire east end. Via the similar dining room in the Glessner house in Chicago of 1885-87 (Figure 106) this feature influenced Frank Lloyd Wright's early planning—specifically the dining rooms of his Blossom, Winslow, and Husser houses of 1892, 1893, and 1899.

IX-14. These quarries may have been imported from England; they are certainly very like those used by Morris in his non-ecclesiastical work of the 60's.

IX-15. For "Queen Anne," read "Shavian Manorial."

IX-16. The location of Grim's Dyke is often given as Pinner rather than Harrow Weald.

IX-17. For "American Queen Anne vernacular," read "Shingle Style."

IX-18. With the generation after Richardson the models began to be what might be called "the real thing"; down to his death the models were almost always contemporary English, i.e., the Shavian Manorial and its variants.

IX-19. In my *Rhode Island Architecture*, Providence, 1939, considerable attention was given to the "cottages" of Newport; Scully in *The Architectural Heritage of Newport Rhode Island*, Cambridge, 1952, carried investigations of the "Newport story" in American domestic architecture of the second half of the 19th century very much further.

IX-20. The Matthews house was a very large and fairly characteristic late example of the Stick Style.

IX-21. The particular details noted are certainly of White's invention; but the design as a whole, even to the very style of draftsmanship, rather reflect's White's more careful and total emulation of the Shavian Manorial.

IX-22. Discussion of the Blake project should have preceded that of the Rush Cheney project, and possibly even that of the Sherman house. Published in 1875, it may well have been designed before the Sherman house, as the size and prominence of the piazzas especially suggest. Yet it is true that it looks forward more definitely to Richardson's Shingle Style houses, the first of which was the Bryant house of 1880 (Figures 60-63), than to the Sherman house and the Rush Cheney project which are both so Shavian.

IX-23. Reverting thus almost to the relative modesty of the hall in the house project of 1868 (Figure 12). The drawing is actually signed by White.

IX-24. For "Queen Anne," read "Shavian Manorial."

IX-25. My own and most other historians' estimate of White would not be so harsh today.

IX-26. In Portland, Connecticut.

IX-27. And much less extreme than on the American Express Building of three years earlier.

IX-28. It is much closer to being the culmination of the English arcaded commercial style of the 50's and 60's than of the American arcaded style using cast iron that began with the Sun Building in Baltimore of 1851 by R. G. Hatfield for which Bogardus provided the prefabricated elements. The closest parallel—certainly unknown to Richardson—would be a warehouse in Strait Street, Bristol, of unknown authorship and uncertain date, but presumably of the early 70's. However, in quality it is most closely rivalled by another Bristol warehouse, that at 104 Stokes Croft, built by E. W. Godwin in the early 60's. The cruder formula of the American Express Building, however, was closer to the main line of development of American commercial façade design. (See Note VIII-7.)

IX-29. The Parliament House and associated structures at Ottawa were designed in 1859 and built 1861-67 by Fuller & Jones and by Stent & Laver respectively, all of whom were English. Thomas Fuller and Augustus Laver were in partnership when they obtained the Albany commission.

IX-30. It is hard to see much resemblance to Walter's Capitol wings in this typically Second Empire project.

IX-31. And Dorsheimer was presumably considering building a house in Albany at this time to Richardson's design. (See Note V-11.)

IX-32. The prototype again was English, specifically a façade at 65 Cornhill in London by Edward I'Anson that had appeared in the *Builder* for March 11, 1871.

IX-33. "Queen Anne" should again read "Shavian." But the cut-brick detail does come closer to Shaw's very early Queen Anne work such as that on his Lowther Lodge in London of 1873.

CHAPTER X

X-1. 1879-80, rather than 1878, is the date of the Vanderbilt house. The style, of course, was *François Premier*, and very archaeological in detail though not in general composition.

X-2. "Shavian," not "Queen Anne," at least before 1878.

X-3. When bound in three volumes, the work of Palustre carries the dates 1879-85.

X-4. "Stephenson" should be J. J. Stevenson, one of the major protagonists of the English Queen Anne, whose Red House of 1872 in the Bayswater Road was the first to be so designated by its architect.

X-5. London, 1881.

X-6. F. Ongania, *Basilica di San Marco,* 14 vols., Venice, 1881-86.

X-7. "Stevenson's," not "Stephenson's."

X-8. The turn Webb had taken in building Morris's Red House in 1859-60. Stevenson's Red House was not so consistently red since the walling was of purplish-brown London stocks and the trim painted white or cream.

X-9. The cut-brick ornamental panels on Sever and on the Trinity Rectory are perhaps the finest decorative work for which Richardson was ever responsible. Developing from the rather turgid foliate carving on the fireplace in the North Easton library (and ultimately deriving from contemporary English cut-brick decorative panels by Stevenson and others), this ornament has bolder relief and a less mincing scale so that it parallels, without at all precisely imitating, the vigorous patterns of Morris's wallpapers and chintzes of the 70's and 80's.

X-10. Since this carved decoration must be almost precisely contemporaneous with the cut-brick panels of Sever and the Trinity Rectory it is interesting to note how much more sympathetic brick was to Richardson than the more conventional marble.

X-11. Although hardly comparable to A. H. Mackmurdo's now famous chair-back of this same year 1881, there is a truly proto-Art-Nouveau quality in the whirling linearity of this carved work, so different from the more plastic and static quality of the fine cut-brick reliefs of a year or two earlier. Sullivan, probably without knowledge of this work in Albany, came to something comparable, but considerably more original, in the ornament sketches that he made for the remodelling of McVicker's Theatre well before the 90's in 1884-85. L. C. Tiffany's very interesting Veterans' Room in the Seventh Regiment Armory in New York of 1880, with its stencilled interlaces and tightly curled ironwork, seems at this point rather less premonitory of the Art Nouveau, to which he was later to make the principal American contribution, than does Richardson's carved woodwork.

X-12. On the contrary, ornamental invention in America was never livelier than in these years of the very early 80's, and White's docile use of Renaissance models only began about 1884.

X-13. Despite all the scholarly interest of the last few years in the Art Nouveau and its origins, the American beginnings of a parallel—and only later perhaps partially contributory—development have not yet been adequately studied. Colonna, whose first name is more uncertain than that of Siegfried (not Samuel or Solomon) Bing, although originally a German, was with Tiffany in New York for some years after he left Ohio before he began to work for Bing in Paris at the Maison de l'Art Nouveau in the mid-90's. The beginnings of "Sullivan's characteristic ornament of the nineties" are now known to have preceded by some two years the Richardsonian influence that was first apparent in the Auditorium Building of 1886-89. (See Note X-11.) The whole issue, however, is rather peripheral to Richardson whose ornament did not have even a vaguely proto-Art-Nouveau character except for a year or two around 1880-81.

CHAPTER XI

XI-1. The pedestal of this statue, designed by St. Gaudens in collaboration with Stanford White, is, in the realm of figural relief, the most Art Noveau work ever produced by Americans. It is surprising that it has attracted so little attention.

XI-2. For "Queen Anne," read "Norman Shaw."

XI-3. For "Queen Anne," read "Shavian."

XI-4. Although very similar in character, the cut-brick panels are somewhat less happily scaled and disposed than on Sever Hall.

XI-5. The lower storey provided a year-round house for a caretaker; the upper storey served for winter house-parties when the main house was closed or for overflow.

XI-6. This statement rather confuses the chronology of the Shingle Style as established since by Vincent Scully: W. R. Emerson, as well as McKim, Mead & Bigelow, whose Alden house was mentioned in Note VIII-8, arrived at the mature Shingle Style in 1879, a year before Richardson. (See Note XI-11.) His and their best work of the sort followed in the next five years. The latest notable example was McKim, Mead & White's Low house in Bristol, R.I., of 1887, built a year after their first real Colonial Revival paradigm, the H. A. C. Taylor house in Newport.

XI-7. Early photographs have since come to light; see Figures 62 and 63.

XI-8. For 'Queen Anne," read "Shavian."

XI-9. Not exactly "rubble," nor yet consistently the rounded glacial builders of the Ames gate lodge; "rough stones," as used for the material of the chimneys, is perhaps the most accurate term.

XI-10. For "English Queen Anne," read "Shavian Manorial."

XI-11. In this connection a house built by Emerson at Mount Desert in 1879 might better have been cited (see Vincent Scully, *The Shingle Style*, New Haven, 1955, Fig. 46). Scully's discussion of the Bryant house (*loc. cit.*, 93), with his comments on the water-table above the stone base, are of considerable interest in this context.

XI-12. For "right," read "left."

XI-13. Maitland Armstrong also worked on the decorative setting here.

XI-14. For "Puddingstone," read "seamfaced granite."

XI-15. Jenney's designer was William Bryce Mundie, who shortly afterward became his partner.

CHAPTER XII

XII-1. For 1868, read c. 1875.

XII-2. Omit "effect."

XII-3. Actually, the flow of space is remarkable for the date, approaching as it does so closely a total unification of parlor and dining room, with intimate relationship also to the piazza that is sunk in the mass of the house.

XII-4. Lewis Mumford in *Architecture*, Chicago, 1926, was certainly the first in this century to call attention to the virtues of what Scully later christened the Shingle Style.

In the last few years there have been a few attempts, not altogether unsuccessful, to revive the Shingle Style; and shingled walls have reappeared not only in the San Francisco Bay Region but even in England.

XII-5. This perhaps suggests that Richardson's own design for the porch of Trinity Church (Figure 34) should be dated c. 1882. It would thus be related to his European travels of 1882 as the very archaeological project for Albany Cathedral certainly is. Not surprisingly, the porch as shown in the earlier project for Austin Hall—better dated 1882 than 1881 as it was in Figure 96 of the 1936 edition —is considerably closer to the French mediaeval model, yet also (as noted in the text) neither so over-scaled nor so ponderously plastic.

XII-6. This is too hard on Richardson's assistants. It must be assumed in the case of so important a commission as this that Richardson took full responsibility for the final design of details and for the supervision of the work in construction.

XII-7. Add "plain seamfaced granite" before "Fenway Bridge."

XII-8. The Kelmscott Chaucer is considerably later, having been produced in the 1890's, but the generic reference to Morris's earlier two-dimensional work is nonetheless relevant.

XII-9. It is amusing to recall that in an article on "Modern American Architecture" in the *British Architect* for January 5, 1883, 7, the first foreign article to mention any of Richardson's executed work other than Trinity, the buildings discussed—Ames Library, Ames Town Hall and Quincy Library—were attributed to Peabody & Stearns. This was corrected in the number for March 30, 1883, 154-5. Two years later the *Builder* for December 19, 1885, 858, published a group of plans and views of Austin Hall taken from *Monographs of American Architecture*, I, Boston, 1885. In the following year R. Phené Spiers, Beaux-Arts-trained like Richardson, commented very favorably on the Austin Hall views in the discussion that followed a paper on "Some American Methods" given by John B. Gass at the Royal Institute of British Architects that was published in the *R.I.B.A. Journal of Proceedings*, March 18, 1886, 179-88: . . . "a large amount of originality and peculiar refinement mixed with extreme breadth and boldness of treatment."

XII-10. Definitely Queen Anne, but not "monumental" Queen Anne in the present-day English usage of the qualifying adjective; "Monumental Queen Anne" is almost synonymous now with "Edwardian Baroque."

XII-11. The plan is in the direct line of descent from that of the Codman project. Here as generally in mature Shingle Style houses—of which, of course, this is one of the finest examples—the agglutinative plan, if probably English in origin, has been completely Americanized by the wide openings that provide almost as much spatial flow as in the Brown house and definitely prepare the way for Frank Lloyd Wright's "Prairie House" planning after 1900.

XII-12. The Channing house was demolished very shortly after the 1936 edition appeared.

XII-13. Seddon was hardly a major influence in America. G. F. Bodley is usually considered the prime English Late Victorian leader in this field, more than rivalling John L. Pearson in influence at home and abroad.

XII-14. Charles B. Atwood is reputed to have been the designer.

XII-15. See Wayne Andrews, *The Vanderbilt Legend,* New York, 1941, which has much to say about the Vanderbilts as patrons of architecture in the 70's, 80's and 90's.

XII-16. For "American Queen Anne," read "Americanized Shavian Manorial." The Shingle Style work of McKim, Mead & White mentioned in the next four paragraphs is, of course, considered in much more detail by Scully in *The Shingle Style,* New Haven, 1955, with many excellent illustrations.

XII 17. Actually the design was worked up by the architects from a sketch made by L. C. Tiffany, the son of the client. The principal interiors were certainly almost entirely the work of the younger Tiffany.

XII-18. Or, at least, few of the leading architects had yet come face to face with them. The whole question of the development of commercial design between the first skyscrapers of the early 70's in New York and the rise of the Chicago School in the 80's is being studied by Winston Weisman. He presented a paper on the subject at the Society of Architectural Historians meetings in Minneapolis in January, 1961, that will shortly be published. It is a story with which Richardson had little contact except for his American Express Building of 1872-73; the later influence of his Marshall Field Wholesale Store in Chicago of 1885-87, although potent, proved within a few years to have been quite tangential.

CHAPTER XIII

XIII-1. This is a slight exaggeration at this early date in the 80's.

XIII-2. This may well indicate that the early porch project for Austin Hall, so closely based on St.-Gilles, was designed before and not after he saw the original. (See Note XII-5.) The Trinity porch project is as close to St. Trophime as to St. Gilles, and may therefore be later

XIII-3. This is unjust to Guadet. Even though his more original executed work is always disappointing, the importance of his theories for the next generation—the first generation of modern architects—and even for the following one should be recognized. (See Reyner Banham, *Theory and Design in the First Machine Age,* London, 1960, especially Chapter I.)

XIII-4. For "Van de Velde," read "Horta." Voysey in England and Berlage in Holland might well have been mentioned here also.

XIII-5. The correct dates of the Rijksmuseum are 1877-85.

XIII-6. An early project—c. 1885—for the Palau Güell is curiously like Richardson's undated Boston & Albany railroad station project of the early 70's, just as Berlage's Beurs and his Diamond Workers' Building in Amsterdam, both of the late 90's, rather resemble various buildings by Richardson in brick such as Sever Hall and the New London Union Station. So far no explanation has been offered of these similarities other than that these younger men in Europe evidently passed through a phase of development parallel to early and middle Richardsonian, but a decade or two later than he did. The apparently Richardsonian character of their work almost certainly does not derive from study of any illustrations of his work published in Europe, for it was chiefly his more monumental work in stone that was known abroad. (See Note Bibl. 1, II.) That, however, did quite definitely influence Bruno Schmitz in Germany, who already knew some of the originals at first hand.

XIII-7. By 1882 there was a vital new movement in decoration in England led by Mackmurdo, but this was only just getting under way. On the Continent there were the engineering works of Eiffel. In neither case was Richardson likely to have been aware of the very latest developments.

XIII-8. This building, which is no longer standing, was at 515-521 Washington Street. Commissioned in April, 1882, it was built 1883-85 for F. L. Ames at a cost of $180,000, Rumery & Co. being the masons and the carpenters Creesy & Noyes. (See C. S. Damrell, *A Half Century of Boston's Building*, Boston, 1895, 54.) Photographs as well as drawings exist at the Houghton Library. The detail is rather *François Premier* and the general effect not at all Richardsonian. There were stores below and offices above.

XIII-9. Apparently this façade was not of brownstone but of granite, at least the rockfaced ashlar. The rather elaborately carved detail was presumably of light-coloured sandstone or limestone, not distinguishable in tone from the granite in old photographs.

XIII-10. The interior elevation is very Burges-like, recalling not only St. Finbar's in Cork but also his project for the Episcopal Cathedral in Edinburgh and his as yet unexecuted nave at St. Michael's, Brighton. The broad, very slightly pointed arches used throughout are also characteristic of Burges: Richardson's disenchantment with the English architect was evidently not total! The 12th-century Continental features throughout closely resemble the "Early French" sort of detailing used by many English High Victorian Gothic architects besides Burges from the late 50's to the early 70's. Thus there is some flavor of James Brooks's best work here, and even of his work of as late a date as this—although no echoes, curiously enough, of J. L. Pearson's current production. Gibson's project, faintly reflecting the work of Bodley, would probably have seemed more up-to-date by this time in England; that may have played some part in its selection.

XIII-11. "1833" should read "1883" of course. The research of James D. Van Trump on Richardson's works in Pittsburgh has provided considerable additional information. (See his article, "The Church beyond Fashion . . . ," *The Charette*, XXXVIII [April, 1958], 26-9.) The lot was acquired in 1882 and the drawings, commissioned in August, 1883, reached Pittsburgh early in 1884. In July more modest plans were requested and these were received in February, 1885. The contract was awarded in April of that year and the church dedicated March 7, 1886.

The parish house of 1887-88 was probably designed by Frank E. Alden and the altar and reredos of 1898 are by Lake & Greene. The building is now being recorded for the Historic American Buildings Survey.

An undated project for a church at Brighton by Burges, now preserved at the Victoria & Albert Museum, is extraordinarily like Emmanuel. It is not clear how Richardson could have known it; but, if he did not, the resemblance provides even more remarkable evidence of the parallelism between his approach to church design and that of Burges than does the Albany Cathedral project.

XIII-12. Drip-moulds had reappeared on the Kingston and Bedford Street Wholesale Store designed the previous year. They are minor evidence of a more archaeological approach to detailing in these years.

XIII-13. There may have been two Buffalo projects for the same trapezoidal site. Additional plans preserved at the Houghton Library make evident that the holograph sketch that Mrs. Van Rensselaer published (p. 83) was definitely for a library. I am not now able to trace the publication of the Y.M.C.A. project "in an English magazine."

XIII-14. An earlier courthouse having been destroyed by fire in the spring of 1882 the County Commissioners invited five architects to submit designs in competition by January 1, 1884. The invitation to Richardson, the last of the five to be approached, was dated February 28, 1883; his selection as architect came on January 31, 1884. Revised drawings were accepted on July 1 and the contract with Norcross Brothers followed on September 1, when construction actually started. As promised to Richardson, supervision continued under his successors Shepley, Rutan & Coolidge after his death in 1886, and the building was completed March 10, 1888, and dedicated September 24. The stairs at the main entrance were designed in 1912 by Alden & Harlow when Grant Street was lowered 12 feet; these were removed and the entrance extended downward by Stanley Roach when the street was widened in 1928. (See James D. Van Trump, "Romanesque Revival in Pittsburgh," *Journal of the Society of Architectural Historians*, XVI [1957], 22-9; and "Allegheny County Buildings, Pittsburgh, 1884-87," *Architectural Record*, CXXI [1957], 172.)

XIII-15. The jail was begun at the same time as the courthouse but, as required by the terms of the contract, it was finished in May, 1886, and occupied in September of that year. Additions that are remarkably faithful to the original design were made by F. J. Osterling in 1909, and some changes were made at the main entrance when Ross Street was lowered in 1912. (See William S. Huff, "Richardson's Jail," *Western Pennsylvania Historical Magazine*, 41 [1958], 41-59, and James D. Van Trump, "Of Footbridges and Preservation," *loc. cit.*, 43 [1960], 135-46.) The future of the jail is uncertain, but active efforts have so far preserved it from destruction.

XIII-16. In the Villard houses of 1883-85 in New York, which follow so closely Italian High Renaissance precedent.

XIII-17. But see Note XIII-9.

XIII-18. The narrow courses are undoubtedly bonded deep into the brickwork behind, while the wide courses must be relatively thin in section.

XIII-19. Not "John," but "George Foster."

XIII-20. For "quite without," read "not entirely."

XIII-21. The courthouse, but not the jail, was cleaned again in 1957.

XIII-22. It is worth noting that the tower of the Minneapolis City Hall, designed by Long & Kees in 1887 before the Allegheny County Buildings were entirely finished, is perhaps finer than the Pittsburgh original they followed so closely.

XIII-23. Figure 115 in the 1936 edition.

XIII-24. The description given in this paragraph applies to another church in Newton by H. L. Faxon as was immediately pointed out to me in 1936 by K. J. Conant. The church from the Richardson office follows very closely the early studies by C. A. Coolidge mentioned in the previous paragraph. As has been indicated, the result is hardly to be considered Richardson's own design and the church, although perhaps superior to Faxon's, does not deserve illustration.

CHAPTER XIV

XIV-1. See Note XIII-22.

XIV-2. Especially in *Monographs of American Architecture*, I, III, and V, dealing respectively with Austin Hall, the four buildings in North Easton, and Trinity. It is worth noting that illustrations of his buildings in brick and his Shingle Style houses were never, or hardly ever, published. The image most contemporaries acquired of the Richardsonian canon was therefore a rather narrow one, predominantly monumental, and with a higher content of specific Romanesque influence than was characteristic of his work as a whole.

XIV-3. It is very unlikely that the exterior of the Home Insurance Building was intended by Jenney to be at all Richardsonian, much less Romanesque. Designed in 1883 and completed in 1885, the year the Marshall Field Wholesale Store was begun, it could not have been influenced by that, nor was it influenced by the American Express Building as Dankmar Adler's Central Music Hall in Chicago of 1879 may have been. The brief Richardsonian episode in Chicago architecture began only in 1886, the year of Richardson's death, but it lasted long enough to have a definite if limited effect on the development of the young Frank Lloyd Wright in the late 80's which was not without its faint echoes even after 1900.

XIV-4. Richardson was less influenced by Japanese art than many of his generation in England and America, and not at all by Japanese architecture. Nor was it likely that he should be: E. S. Morse's *Japanese Homes and Their Surroundings,* the first American study of Japanese architecture, appeared, in an advance issue only, late in 1885; the first regular edition was Boston, 1886. The stencilled decoration in Richardson's late interiors is hardly different from Godwin's and Nesfield's *Japonisme* of the 60's and 70's.

XIV-5. For "tower," read "lower."

XIV-6. For "shaft," read "shift."

XIV-7. In connection with the building of the Adams house, see E. Schreyer, "Henry Adams and Henry Hobson Richardson," *Journal of the Society of Architectural Historians,* XII (1953), 7-12.

XIV-8. See Figure 102. The long thin Roman bricks, of the shape McKim, Mead & White had introduced in their Tiffany house of 1882-83 but not as yellowish in color, give a new flavor to the walls of the Hay house that is certainly not characteristically Richardsonian (*cf.* Figure 73) but by no means intrinsically inferior—Wright was to use such bricks well beyond 1900.

XIV-9. It must today be a moot point how far the influence of Richardson was a help to Sullivan. His work of the late 80's seems rather to have been an interruption in the lines of development that lead from such early buildings as the Rothschild Store of 1881 and the Troescher Building of 1884 to the Wainwright Building of 1890-91 and Carson, Pirie & Scott of 1899-1904.

XIV-10. Chicago has now become more conscious of its architectural heritage. Since 1960 many buildings, including Richardson's Glessner house, carry plaques indicating their status as historical monuments.

XIV-11. The interior partitions and probably the court walls were of brick, not of stone masonry like the exterior walls. For a rendering of the Field Store, which suggests smoother masonry, see Figure 97.

XIV-12. This is not true. The Ames Building in which the offices of Richardson's successors are still located at the corner of Court and Washington Streets was the "first" (and for that matter long the sole) skyscraper in Boston only because of its altitude. After it was built a local restriction to 125 feet made impossible the construction of other buildings of comparable or greater height, a rule broken only by the Custom House Tower of 1913-15 by Peabody & Stearns. As a Federal building, this was exempt from the local height restriction and thus, until the 1930's when that restriction was finally lifted, the only other early skyscraper.

XIV-13. Much study in the last twenty-five years, and more particularly the last decade, has modified my own and most historians' picture of the development of the skyscraper. While not incorporating the very latest contributions of Carl W. Condit in *American Building Art, The Nineteenth Century,* New York, 1960, Chapter II, and Winston Weisman in his article, "Philadelphia Functionalism and Sullivan," *Journal of the Society of Architectural Historians,* XX (1961) 3-19, the account I give in *Architecture: 19th and 20th Centuries,* Harmondsworth, 1958, Chapter 14, is sufficiently up-to-date to correct most of the errors of fact and emphasis in this paragraph. In the 1958 book see especially p. 242.

XIV-14. See Note XI-15.

XIV-15. The following quotation from a book by J. J. Glessner written for his children, although rather discursive, is sufficiently revelatory of Richardson's relations with his clients to be given here at some length. (Only two copies of this book were printed and I quote from it thanks to the kindness of George Mathey of the present Shepley, Bulfinch, Richardson & Abbott staff, a Glessner great-grandson, who possesses one of these copies).

"Let me explain why we built our house on this plan, and how we came to select this architect.

"Though I had heard much of Richardson, I didn't go to him first when seeking an architect, for Boston friends had told me that he would undertake only monumental buildings. In New York I saw Stanford White of McKim, Meade [*sic*] & White, and also Willie [William A.] Potter, and engaged the latter to make plans, with the distinct understanding that I might ask others to plan also and should be at liberty to take the one I liked best, paying for the others. When I got home I decided to consult Richardson anyhow, and wrote him what I had heard. His reply was: 'I'll plan anything a man wants, from a cathedral to a chicken coop. That's the way I make my living. I am going out to Cincinnati about the Chamber of Commerce, and then to Chicago about Field's wholesale store and will see you there.' I told Franklin MacVeagh of this and promptly called on Richardson at Grand Pacific Hotel, as did MacVeagh a few hours later. Then I wrote to Mr. Warder, and he engaged Richardson to plan his house in Washington.

Richardson asked me what I wanted in a house, and in trying to tell him I suggested that if he would come into my present house I could tell him in half an hour what it would take a day to do elsewhere. He was agreeable, and we got into a carriage at once and went home. On entering he said: 'I'll sit on the piano stool if you don't mind. I can't get up easily from one of these easy chairs.' He wanted to know what rooms on first and what on second floors, and then: 'How will you have them placed?' Oh, no, Mr. Richardson, that would be me planning the house. (Observe my grammar.) I want you to plan it. That's your job. If we don't like it we'll change it. He laughed and made note of the rooms.

"On the library mantel stood a small photograph of a building at Abingdon Abbey. 'Do you like that?' Yes. 'Well, give it to me: I'll make that the keynote of your house.' After his death his office young men sent it back to me with the blot of ink that had been dropped on it while using it for inspiration. Richardson and I drove down to see the lot; your mother couldn't go. He didn't get out of the carriage, but looked at the place attentively and in silence for some minutes, and then blurted out—'Have you courage to build the house without windows on the street front?' And promptly I said 'Yes,' knowing that I could tear up the plan if I didn't like it. Then he added, 'I wish I didn't have to go to dinner this evening. I'd give you the plan of your house in the morning.' He was to dine at Mr. Field's that night, and with us the next night, and go from our house to the train. While the last course of our dinner was being removed before dessert, he called for pencil and paper, saying: 'If you won't ask me how I get into it, I will draw the plan for your house.' First making a few marks to get an idea of scale, he rapidly drew the first floor plan, almost exactly as it was finally decided on. The dessert was strawberry shortcake, for which our cook was famous. He asked for a second piece, with the added remark: 'Mrs. Glessner, that's the best pie I ever put in my mouth.'

"Stanford White had given me a card to see a house he had just completed in 5th Avenue opposite Central Park for a New Yorker who had large timber interests in the South and who had used only his own woods in the house. There was no furniture in the rooms, and I was struck with the beauty of the eighteen-inch-wide base-boards and the lower rails of the doors exactly the same height. I wanted mine the same way. Richardson said 'No; each baseboard would have to be jointed and glued up; it would cost much more and be no better, and they couldn't be seen anyhow when curtains were hung and furniture in place.'

"I asked the probable cost of the house, but he couldn't tell, and to my suggestion that I should have to add perhaps twenty-five per cent for extras he said: 'Not at all; when I tell you the cost, that will be the whole of it.' And it was.

"When he showed his preliminary sketches the first time and we had expressed hearty approval, he said: 'That's for show, now we'll throw that away and go to work on your real house.'

"Some months later, when we saw the plans nearly completed one Sunday morning at his office, which was connected with his house at Brookline, your mother said she didn't like part of the second floor. 'Well, madam, you don't need to have it that way. What is it you don't like?': 'The servants' bedrooms haven't any closets.' There was one of those flat oval pencils such as carpenters sometimes use lying on the drawing table. He picked that up, drew a broad "I" over that beautiful drawing and, faster than I can write it, sketched in admirable closets for each room; and that was not changed.

"He was the most versatile, interesting, ready, capable and confident of artists; the most genial and agreeable of companions. Everybody was attracted to him at sight. He delighted in difficult problems: Among other things, he had a great desire to build a grain elevator in Chicago, and would have made it beautiful. Other architects didn't relish going into a competition with him—'he had such taking ways with the Committee.'

"Willie Potter, another charming man, came out from New York to explain his plan, and it was a good plan, too. While he was visiting in our house Richardson's plans came by express, but, of course, were not opened—not until after I had put Potter on the train for New York . . . When we looked at Richardson's plans that night our minds were made up.

"Richardson was an eccentric man. His assistants were devoted to him. The young men who took over his business after his death completed at their own cost every piece of work that was then in the office and turned over to Mrs. Richardson the entire commissions without any deductions whatever, and the amount was more than $85,000.00."

XIV-16. Just the same, there is some very ingenious detailing in the interior, especially the provision for radiant heating.

XIV-17. The Lionberger house was in Saint Louis. It has been demolished since 1936 Buford Pickens informs me. The MacVeagh house was already gone in 1936.

XIV-18. It is rather more probable that Richardson was influenced by English work of the 60's, which he must have seen in magazines, than that he knew the remarkable buildings of the 1850's by Stephen D. Button in Philadelphia—a city in which he never worked. Button's Swains' Building at Chestnut and Seventh Streets of 1852 subsumed the upper three storeys under rather narrow arches; his extant Leland Building is even more like the Harrison Avenue store as it is a storey higher. On the other hand, Sullivan, who had actually worked in Philadelphia in the early 70's, certainly knew the work of Button. (See in the Weisman article cited in Note XIV-13, figs. 22 and 24.)

XIV-19. English knowledge of Richardson and his work, such as it was, depended less on the actual presence near London of the Herkomer house than on the various obituaries and illustrated articles that followed his death. (See Note Bibl. 1, II) The most informative were the articles of John B. Gass, Alex. Graham, and Horace Townsend. The two latest, Townsend's of 1894 and one of Gass's of 1896, seem to mark the point at which interest in Richardson was strongest in England, as is perhaps evidenced by C. Harrison Townsend's somewhat Richardsonian Bishopsgate Institute, of 1893-94, and his Whitechapel Art Gallery, designed in 1895 and built 1897-99.

XIV-20. On April 27, 1886, the very day of his death, Richardson wrote this statement: "While I am unable to attend personally to the affairs of my office it is my wish that all my professional business shall be carried on by my assistants Messrs. Shepley, Coolidge and Rutan in all of whom I have full confidence. In case of any question as to the control of my affairs or as to the execution of my designs the final decision must rest with Mr. George F. Shepley whom I hereby appoint as my personal representative."

This statement was not in the office files but was given to Henry R. Shepley by his mother, George F. Shepley's wife and Richardson's daughter, in her 90th year and on his 70th birthday, together with an earlier letter of Richardson's dated March 21, 1886, in which he raised George F. Shepley's annual salary to $3,000. In that letter Richardson wrote: "This I assure you is a pleasure to me, as I feel that your assistance and my business both warrant me in doing so and I have felt it all the more since I realize, from your present trip, the great services you can render me in visiting my clients and watching my interests and work at a distance—saving me great discomfort and time and thereby allowing me to devote myself much more profitably to the work in the office. Until now I had never found one to whom I could heartily intrust this delicate and peculiar kind of work and I fully appreciate the relief."

I am most grateful to Mr. Shepley for permitting me to publish these documents. "John" in the text should, of course, read "George F."

CHAPTER XV

XV-1. Richardsonian influence reached Frank Lloyd Wright not only through Sullivan; he knew—and profited directly from his knowledge of—the Marshall Field Store and the Glessner house. (See my *In the Nature of Materials*, New York, 1942, Chapters I and II.)

XV-2. This statement is, of course, much too elliptical. What the 80's saw was the introduction, first by Jenney in the Home Insurance Building of 1883-85 somewhat tentatively, and then with more assurance in the court façades of Burnham & Root's Rookery Building of 1886 and in the street fronts of Holabird & Roche's Tacoma Building of 1887-89, of a method of supporting the cladding of the exterior walls—whether of stone, brick or terra cotta—on the metal skeleton. Also, as the decade proceeded, steel replaced more and more completely the long familiar cast iron and rolled iron as the material of which the elements of the skeleton were fabricated. In Chicago, furthermore, the development of spread foundations in this period was also of great importance to the eventual maturing of the skyscraper around 1890. (See Note XIV-13.)

XV-3. This is truer of New York than of Chicago, and most especially of the years 1900-32.

XV-4. Certainly a rather exaggerated statement; but who could be expected to foresee in 1936 the great revival of skyscraper building in New York that would begin a dozen or more years later and the increasing acceptance of the skyscraper outside of North America after World War II. It is ironic, moreover, to realize that the first considerable skyscraper outside this continent, the Ministry of Education in Rio de Janeiro, was being planned by Lúcio Costa and his associates in 1936.

XV-5. See Note XV-2.

XV-6. For "new," read "newest sort of."

XV-7. Although Sullivan was briefly employed by Furness it is hardly correct to call the latter his "master;" nor, for that matter, should one say he was "inspired," but rather merely "encouraged," by Furness's bold stylistic innovations—if, indeed, even that is not too definite a conclusion.

XV-8. In this connection, see my article, "Frank Lloyd Wright and the Academic Tradition," *Journal of the Warburg and Courtauld Institutes*, VII, 46-63.

XV-9. This, of course, refers to Faxon's, not to Richardson's, church, itself the work of an imitator. (See Note XIII-24.)

XV-10. For "English Queen Anne," read "Norman Shaw's work."

XV-11. The image here is almost certainly wrong; the change in direction evident in McKim, Mead & White's work in the mid-80's owed little to Shaw, and they certainly arrived at a consistent sort of academic revivalism well before he did. (See Note XV-8.)

XV-12. Their Cianferri-Atwater house of 1891 in New Haven is an excellent, if rather late, example of the Shingle Style which is in no way specifically Richardsonian.

XV-13. "Orgy" is far too strong a word, perhaps "indulgences" would be better.

XV-14. See Note XII-17.

XV-15. Omit "late."

XV-16. Add "larger" before "works."

XV-17. The inspiration from the Colosseum was evident in the arcaded design of the court as originally projected. The arches of the exterior follow those on the sides of the Tempio Malatestiano considerably more closely however.

XV-18. As a matter of fact Wright continued to have considerable respect for Richardson. His tributes, if always rather grudging, grew noticeably warmer in his later years.

XV-19. As usual, this fails to recognize the Shingle Style as an entity which was largely independent of Richardson despite the half dozen or more Shingle Style houses he himself built that are certainly among the finest.

XV-20. Was this a prophecy of certain developments, especially in this country, of the 1950's?

XV-21. The current interest in crude building materials might be considered more truly Richardsonian than the interest a quarter century ago in fine materials: *béton brut* seems closer to rockfaced ashlar in character than Miesian marble and travertine.

XV-22. Surrealism was still riding high in 1936. Will its current partial revival also affect our architectural ideals?

XV-23. Twenty-five years later the history of modern architecture has, however, become relevant again as the early twentieth century recedes into a past almost as remote as was Richardson's lifetime in 1936.

BIBLIOGRAPHY — NOTES

Bibl. 1. As is mentioned in the Preface to the New Edition, a large number of new references to articles and books are given in earlier Notes (I-1, I-2, I-3, I-4, I-7, I-9, I-11, I-12, I-13, V-6, VI-4, VI-6, VIII-4, VIII-6, VIII-7, VIII-13, IX-1, IX-19, XII-4, XII-9, XII-15, XIII-3, XIII-8, XIII-11, XIII-14, XIII-15, XIV-7, XIV-13, XIV-15, XV-1, XV-8). In addition to those, which need not be repeated here, further new bibliographical entries fall into three groups: publications listed under Richardson taken from my *American Architectural Books*, 3rd rev. ed., Minneapolis, 1946; English and German items that appeared between 1875 and 1900, all but one of them kindly supplied by Arnold Lewis; and a very few American articles, not referenced in other Notes, that have appeared since 1936. (See Note Bibl. 2.) Since it would be awkward to interpolate the items in the first two groups between the entries of the existing Bibliography, they may better be listed here in separate sequences.

I. Richardson Titles:

The Ames Memorial Building[s], North Easton, Mass.
> Boston, Ticknor & Company, 1886. 23 p.
> At head of cover title: Monographs of American Architecture, issued in connection with the American Architect and Building News, III.
> Boston, Ticknor & Company, n.d. 23 pl.
> It is not clear whether the undated issues of these monographs follow or precede the dated ones.

Austin Hall, Harvard Law School, Cambridge, Mass.
> Boston, James R. Osgood and Company, 1885. 18 pl.
> At head of cover title: Monographs of American Architecture [etc.], I.
> Boston, Ticknor & Company, 1886. 18 pl.
> Boston, Ticknor & Company, n.d. 18 pl.

The Billings Library the Gift to the University of Vermont of Frederick Billings.
> Boston. The Heliotype Printing Co., [188-?]. 11 pl. (2 col.) , cover title.
> Generally dated [1895] and listed under: University of Vermont. There is no apparent justification for so late a date.

Description of Drawings for the Proposed New County Buildings for Allegheny County, Penn.
> Boston, Printed for Private Circulation, 1884. 48 p., illus.

Trinity church, Boston.
> Boston, Ticknor & Company, 1888. 23 pl.
> At head of cover title: Monographs of American Architecture [etc.], V., "Gambrill and Richardson, Architects."

II. Foreign Books and Articles, 1875-1900:

"A Boston basilica" [Trinity Church], *Architect*, XVIII (April 28, 1877) , 274.

Perry, T. Sergeant, "Colour decoration in America" [Trinity Church], *Architect*, XVIII (Oct. 20, 1877), 210-11.

"Modern American architecture," *British Architect*, XIX (Jan. 5, 1883) .
> (Correction of the original attribution to Peabody & Stearns of the three buildings illustrated, the North Easton Library and Town Hall and the Quincy Library, *loc. cit.* [March 30, 1883], 154-5.)

"Austin Hall, Harvard Law Schools, Cambridge, Mass.," *Builder*, XLIX (Dec. 19, 1885), 858.

Gass, John B., "Some American Methods," *Royal Institute of British Architects, Journal of Proceedings,* II N. S. (March 18, 1886) , 179-88.

333

Gass, John B., "New York State Capitol, Albany," *Builder*, L (April 17, 1886), 574.

Hinckeldeyn, Karl, "Henry H. Richardson" [obituary], *Zentralblatt der Bauverwaltung*, VI (June 5, 1886), 221-2.

"The late H. H. Richardson" [obituary], *Architect*, XXXV (May 21, 1886), 306-7.

"The late H. H. Richardson of Brookline, Mass." [obituary], *Building News*, L (May 21, 1886), 817-18.

"Royal Institute of British Architects: Obituary," *Builder*, L (May 22, 1886), 740.

[Plate of Woburn Library], *Architect*, XXXV (June 25, 1886).

Graham, Alex., "Architecture in the United States," *Royal Institute of British Architects, Journal of Proceedings*, IV N.S. (March 8, 1888), 193-6.

"The late Mr. Richardson," *Royal Institute of British Architects, Journal of Proceedings*, IV N.S. (Feb. 9, 1888), 141-2.

Waterhouse, Alfred, "The President's address, Royal Institute of British Architects," *Builder*, LV (Nov. 10, 1888), 336-40.

Fergusson, James, and Kerr, Robert, *History of the Modern Styles of Architecture*, 3rd ed., London, 1891, 343-74.

Hinckeldeyn, Karl, "Henry Richardson and seine Bedeutung fur die amerikanische Architektur," *Deutsche Bauzeitung*, XXVI (Feb. 6, 1892), 64-6.

Townsend, Horace, "H. H. Richardson, Architect," *Magazine of Art*, 1894, 133-8.

Gmelin, Leopold, "Architektonisches aus Nordamerika," *Deutsche Bauzeitung*, XXVIII (Sept. 29, 1894), 481-3.

Gass, John B., "American Architecture and Architects, with Special Reference to the Works of the Late Richard Morris Hunt and Henry Hobson Richardson," *Journal of the Royal Institute of British Architects, III*, 3rd ed. (Feb. 6, 1896), 229-32.

Graef, Paul, and Hinckeldeyn, Karl, *Neubauten in Nordamerika*, Berlin, 1897.

Streiter, Richard, "Nordamerikanische Architektur," *Allgemeine Zeitung*, Nr. 125 (June 6, 1898), 4-7.

In connection with Richardson's foreign reputation, it is worth mentioning that Richardson was an Honorary Corresponding Member of the Royal Institute of British Architects at the time of his death *(Builder* obituary, May 22, 1886) and that Alfred Waterhouse at least implied (*R.I.B.A. Journal of Proceedings*, Feb 9, 1888) that had he lived longer he would probably have been nominated for the Royal Gold Medal.

The increase in interest in Richardson's work both in England and in Germany in the 90's, when his influence was rapidly waning at home, is notable and probably historically significant. It is unfortunate that Mr. Lewis's researches did not extend to the periodicals and other architectural publications of Holland and the Scandinavian countries where one might expect to find considerable interest in

Richardson's work in the 90's. Boberg in Sweden had actually worked for Sullivan in Chicago, and many historians have noted the resemblance of Berlage's Amsterdam Beurs to Richardson's Sever Hall and New London Station. See also the article by Robert Koch given in the next Note.

Bibl. 2.
    Pickens, Buford L., "H. H. Richardson and Basic Form Concepts in Modern Architecture," *Art Quarterly*, III (1940), 273-91.

    Bosworth, Welles, "I knew Richardson," *Journal of the American Institute of Architects*, XVI (1951), 115-27.

    Koch, Robert, "American Influence Abroad," *Journal of the Society of Architectural Historians*, XVIII (1959), 66-9.

BIBLIOGRAPHY

THE most useful items for the study of Richardson after Mrs. Van Rensselaer's life are the volumes of plates published by Ticknor and Company in the series *Monographs of American Architecture*. Volume I deals-with Austin Hall, III with the buildings at North Easton, and V with Trinity. Handsome descriptive monographs were issued on the Crane Library in Quincy and the Billings Library at Burlington by those institutions. A privately printed *Description*, 1884, gives Richardson's own account of his plans for the Allegheny County Buildings in Pittsburgh; and the *Consecration Services*, 1877, includes a description of Trinity Church by Richardson. Guide books to Trinity Church (Chester, 1888, Graff, 1924) exist as also for the New York State Capitol.

The following items arranged chronologically deal more generally with Richardson and his work. The list is, of course, not exhaustive. Magazine publication of individual buildings has usually been indicated in the footnotes of the main text.

Bibl. 1

May 1879. Van Brunt, Henry: The New Dispensation in Monumental Art. *Atlantic Monthly*.

May 1886. Editorial. *Inland Architect*, vol. VII, p. 57.
Wight, P. B.: H. H. Richardson. *Inland Architect*, vol. VII, pp. 59-61.

July 1886. Bloor, A. J.: H. H. Richardson. *Building* Budget.

1886. Olmsted, F. L.: H. H. Richardson. *American Architect*.

Aug. 1886. S., M. C.: H. H. Richardson. *Scientific American*, vol. II, p. 21.

Oct. 8, 1886. Letter from Brooklyn woman in Boston *Evening Transcript*.

Oct. 1888. Brooks, Phillips: Henry Hobson Richardson. *Harvard Monthly*, vol. III, pp. 1-7.

Nov. 1886. Van Brunt, Henry: Henry Hobson Richardson. *Atlantic Monthly*, vol. 58, p. 685.

1888. Van Rensselaer, Marianna Griswold (Mrs. Schuyler van R.): Henry Hobson Richardson. Boston, 1888.

1891. Schuyler, Montgomery: The Romanesque Revival in New York. *Architectural Record*, vol. I, pp. 7 ff.

1892. Schuyler, Montgomery: The Romanesque Revival in America. *Architectural Record*, vol. II, pp. 151 ff.

1892. Schuyler, Montgomery: *American Architecture*. New York. *passim*.

1892. Andrews, R. D.: The Broadest Use of Precedent. *Architectural Review*, vol. II, pp. 31 ff.

1893. Anon.: *Homes in City and Country*. New York.

1894. Flagg, Ernest: Influence of French School on Architecture in the United States. *Architectural Record*, vol. IV, pp. 211 ff.

1894. Hale, Edward: H. H. Richardson and His Work. *New England Magazine*, vol. II, N.S., p. 513.

1894. Townsend, Horace: H. H. Richardson, Architect. *Magazine of Art*, London, 1894, pp. 133-138.

1896. Wyatt, J. B. N.: Modern Romanesque Architecture. *Architectural Review*, vol. VI, p. 103, p. 127.

1899. Gardner, E. C.: Some Handicaps of Provincial Architecture. *Architectural Record*, vol. IX, pp. 405-423.

1901-2. Sturgis, Russell: H. H. Richardson, in *A Dictionary of Architecture and Building*.

1910. Vogel, F. R.: *Das Amerikanische Haus*. Berlin, 1910.

1913. Cortissoz, Royal: *Art and Common-sense*. New York, pp. 384-389.

1918. Kimball, Fiske and Edgell, G. H.: *A History of Architecture*. New York, pp. 552-553.

1924. Mumford, Lewis: *Sticks and Stones*. New York, 1924, pp. 100-106.

1926. Hamlin, T. F.: *The American Spirit in Architecture*. New Haven, 1926. Chapter XIII.

1927. Tallmadge, T. E.: *The Story of Architecture in America*. New York. Chapter VII.

1928. Kimball, Fiske: *American Architecture*. Indianapolis, pp. 125-126.

1929. LaFollette, Suzanne: *Art in America*. New York, pp. 253-259 *passim*.

1929. Hitchcock, Henry-Russell, jr.: *Modern Architecture*. New York. Chapter IX, *passim*.

1930. Cortissoz, Royal: *The Painter's Craft*. New York. (Chapter: "A Group of American Architects.")

1931. Mumford, Lewis: *The Brown Decades*. New York, pp. 114-133.

1934. Hitchcock, Henry-Russell, jr.: Henry Hobson Richardson, in *Art in America in Modern Times*, Barr, A. H., jr. and Cahill, Holger, ed. New York, pp. 63-64.

Bibl. 2

Richardson's daughter, Mrs. George Foster Shepley, suggests that anyone desiring more information on Richardson's life and character as distinguished from his work as an architect should examine the article written for the Saturday Evening Club, Homer Saint-Gaudens' life of his father, and La Farge's *Reminiscences*.

INDEX

343

THE M.I.T. PAPERBACK SERIES